More-Than-Human Histories of Latin America and the Caribbean

More-Than-Human Histories of Latin America and the Caribbean

Decentring the Human in Environmental History

Edited by
Diogo de Carvalho Cabral,
André Vasques Vital and
Margarita Gascón

UNIVERSITY
OF LONDON
PRESS

Available to purchase in print or download
for free at https://uolpress.co.uk

First published 2024 by
University of London Press
Senate House, Malet St
London WC1E 7HU

A CIP catalogue record for this book is available from The British Library.

ISBN 978-1-915249-50-0 (hardback)
ISBN 978-1-915249-51-7 (paperback)
ISBN 978-1-915249-53-1 (.epub)
ISBN 978-1-915249-52-4 (.pdf)
ISBN 978-1-915249-69-2 (.html)

DOI https://doi.org/10.14296/cmpd3083

Cover image: Ouragan aux Antilles. From 'Histoire philosophique et politique
des établissements et du commerce des européens dans les deux Indes', tome six.
Guillaume-Thomas Raynal (Genève: Jean-Leonard Pellet, 1780).

Cover designed for the University of London Press by Hayley Warnham.
Book design by Nigel French.
Text set by Westchester Publishing Service UK in Meta Serif Pro-Book,
designed by Erik Spiekermann.

Contents

List of illustrations

Figures

Maps

Tables

Graphs

Notes on contributors

Diogo de Carvalho Cabral is an assistant professor in environmental history and a member of the Trinity Centre for Environmental Humanities (TCEH) at Trinity College Dublin (Ireland). Before that, he was a British Academy-funded Newton International Fellow based at the Institute of Latin American Studies/School of Advanced Study, University of London (United Kingdom). His academic awards include the *Journal of Historical Geography* Best Paper Prize (2016) and an honourable mention in the Milton Santos Prize (2017). He is the author of *Na Presença da Floresta: Mata Atlântica e História Colonial* (Rio de Janeiro, 2014) and co-edited *Metamorfoses Florestais: Culturas, Ecologias e as Transformações Históricas da Mata Atlântica* (Curitiba, 2016) with Ana Bustamante. Sitting at the interface between history, geography, ecology and anthropology, his work addresses the historical dimensions of multispecies environmental change in modern Brazil.

Bruno Capilé is a professor in the master's programme in Integrated Management of Territory at the Universidade Vale do Rio Doce (GIT/Univale), Minas Gerais, Brazil. He is currently the coordinator of the Interdisciplinary Observatory of the Territory (OBIT). His research interests include urban environmental history, public history, history of science, territorial studies and nonhuman agency.

José Marcelo M. Ferreira Filho is a professor at the department of history at the Federal University of Pernambuco (UFPE). His areas of interest are environmental history and social history of labour. He is particularly interested in the multitrophic ecological interactions between humans, animals (especially insects) and plants, and is currently working on a research project about the environmental history of sugar in Northeast Brazil.

Margarita Gascón earned her master's and PhD from the University of Ottawa, Canada. She is a tenured researcher of the National Council for Scientific and Technological Research (CONICET) in Argentina and also teaches at undergraduate and graduate levels in Mendoza. Among her most recent publications are the Afterword to *De viejas y nuevas fronteras en América y Europa*, edited by Macarena Sánchez Pérez and Katherine Quinteros Rivera (Editorial Universidad Finis Terrae, Chile, 2022), the chapter 'Las múltiples identidades étnicas en la frontera colonial del último sur hispanoamericano', in *Critica de la Razón Indígena*, edited by Carlos Felimer del Valle Rojas and Alejandra Cebrelli (La Plata, Argentina,

Editorial Universidad Nacional de La Plata, 2023, 208–26), the chapter 'Hispanoamérica colonial/Colonial Hispanic America (19°-y 34°de latitud sur)' in the volume *Land Use* and the chapter 'Cambio climático en el sur de Hispanoamérica colonial/Climatic change in the south of colonial Hispanic America' in the volume from the series 'Climatic Change' Handbooks, *The Anthropocene as Multiple Crisis: Perspectives from Latin America* (CALAS, University of Bielefeld, Germany, 2024).

Magdalena Gil is an assistant professor at P. Universidad Católica de Chile School of Government and a researcher at CIGIDEN, the Research Center for Integrated Disaster Risk Management [ANID/FONDAP/1523A0009]. She received her PhD in sociology from Columbia University in 2016. Dr Gil specialises in disasters and their impacts on state and society. Her current research focuses on public policy and climate change adaptation. This research was partially funded by ANID/INICIACION/11220562.

Denise Maria Cavalcante Gomes is an associate professor at the department of anthropology, graduate programme in archaeology, National Museum, Federal University of Rio de Janeiro. She is a specialist in Amazonian archaeology, having conducted field research in the region of Santarém, Pará, for twenty years. She is a CNPq Productivity Fellow 2 with the project 'Theory and method in iconography of the Amerindian world'. Proponent of an interpretative model on the existence of an American aesthetics, based on the theory of the Amerindian perspectivism, she has supervised theses and dissertations on Amazonian, Andean and rock art iconography, which contribute to a comparative view on the subject.

Claudia Leal is a full professor at the department of history and geography at Universidad de los Andes, in Bogotá, Colombia, and holds a PhD in geography from the University of California at Berkeley. She is the author of *Landscapes of Freedom: Building a Postemancipation Society in the Rainforests of Western Colombia* (The University of Arizona Press, 2018) and has edited several books, among them *A Living Past: Environmental Histories of Modern Latin America* (Berghahn Books, 2018, with John Soluri and José Augusto Pádua). She is finishing a history of Colombian national parks and is also researching the history of animals.

Luisa Vidal de Oliveira holds a master's in visual languages and a master's in archaeology from the Federal University of Rio de Janeiro (Brazil). Her research is mainly directed at ceramic ritual objects, and deals with the encounter between ontology and visual language. She has worked since 2016 on the Konduri iconography collection that burned down in the

2018 Museu Nacional fire. She currently lives in Santiago de Chile con-
ducting her doctoral research on South-Central Andean archaeological
iconography.

Hannah Regis is an assistant professor of Caribbean literature at
Howard University. Her research interests include Caribbean poetics,
Caribbean literary and theoretical history, Caribbean spectrality, haunting,
counter-archival engagements, reparative writing, theories of embodiment
and cultural memory. She has published widely on Caribbean spectrality
in several scholarly journals including *Caribbean Quarterly*, *The American
Studies Journal* (AMSJ), *eTropic* and *The Journal of West Indian Literature*.
Her single-authored book, *A Caribbean Poetics of Spirit,* is published with
the University of the West Indies Press.

Lise Sedrez is an associate professor of environmental history at the
Universidade Federal do Rio de Janeiro, Brazil. Her work has been published in Italy, Colombia, Brazil and the USA. She is a research scholar for
the Conselho Nacional de Desenvolvimento Científico e Tecnológico –
CNPq and was a postdoctoral fellow at the Universidade Federal de Minas
Gerais and at the Rachel Carson Center, in Munich. Her research interests
include urban environmental history, global environmental governance
and history of disasters.

Olivia Arigho Stiles is an interdisciplinary researcher of Indigenous histories and the rural world in Bolivia. She completed her PhD in sociology
at the University of Essex, United Kingdom, in July 2022. Her research
examines the history of ecological thought within highland Indigenous
movements in Bolivia, 1920–90. She holds a BA in history from the
University of Oxford and an MA in Latin American studies from University
College London (UCL). She is currently a postdoctoral fellow in Indigenous
ecologies and environmental crisis at University College London. Her
work engages with decolonial theory, environmental history and the
Anthropocene in historical perspective.

María Dolores Ramírez Vega holds an MA and a PhD (history) from Colegio
de Michoacán, Mexico. In 2021 she completed her postgraduate studies
with a dissertation about droughts, locust plagues and agriculture crisis
in the viceroyalty of New Spain between 1765 and 1780. Currently, she is a
postdoctoral fellow at the Centre for Research and Higher Education in
Social Anthropology in Mexico DC. She holds a position as secretary in the
Seminar on History and Climate under the coordination of Dr Luis Alberto
Arrioga in the Colegio de Michoacán. She is also a member of the group

that Dr Armando Alberola Romá leads in the project entitled 'Catastrophe of climatic and natural origins, emergency management and political, scientific and religious discourses in the West Mediterranean and Hispanic America, eighteenth century'.

Luis Alberto Arrioja Díaz Viruell holds a PhD in History from El Colegio de México (2008). He is a member of the National System of Researchers, level 2. He has been working since 2009 as a full professor at El Colegio de Michoacán. He has published ten books and more than thirty articles in specialised academic journals on Indian towns, agrarian and economic structures, and political culture in Mexico in the eighteenth and nineteenth centuries. For the last ten years, his research projects have been about climate history and disaster in Central America and Mexico, between the eighteenth and twentieth centuries.

André Vasques Vital is an associate professor in environmental sciences at the Evangelical University of Goiás – UniEVANGELICA, Brazil. He is co-editor of *Águas no Brasil: Conflitos, Atores, e Práticas* (Editora Alameda, 2019) and has published articles in important international journals such as *Feminist Media Studies* and *ISLE: Interdisciplinary Studies in Literature and Environment*. He also co-edited the special issue 'Tropical Imaginaries and Climate Crisis: Embracing Relational Climate Discourses' (eTropic, 2021). His works propose a non-humanist historical perspective, mainly through fantasy and science fiction animations, where water and nonhuman animals are understood as active agents in the constitution of the past.

Introduction: Latin America and the Caribbean's more-than-human pasts

Diogo de Carvalho Cabral, André Vasques Vital
and Margarita Gascón

In early May 1901, the colonial authorities in Kingstown, capital of the island of St Vincent, then a British colony in the Lesser Antilles, were taken by surprise by requests from the Carib populations living on the flanks of Mount La Soufrière to be removed to the south of the island. They were afraid of the increasing frequency of small earthquakes in the area. Stories had been circulating about the volcano being on the verge of going off, which the colony's government treated as mere hearsay and superstition.[1] Mild tremors were common in the region, thus, for colonial authorities and the white population in general, there was nothing to worry about. (On the other hand, Afro-descendent workers in the sugar economy were very concerned about the Caribs' warnings.) This came amid a deep economic crisis. Most of the island's approximately 41,000 inhabitants lived in poverty, the sugar sector – by far the biggest employer – was in decline and land was concentrated in the hands of just five companies. Four years earlier, a massive hurricane swept through the island, leaving 225 people dead and nearly half the island's population homeless. The catastrophe had helped the colonial government put into practice an ambitious agricultural diversification plan that had not yet yielded results.[2]

Mild tremors continued to be felt throughout the first quarter of 1902 until, on 13 April, a very intense shake was felt in the village of Owia at the island's northern end. Towards the end of the month, the tremors became more frequent and severe; eighteen of them came to be felt in just twenty-four hours. Furthermore, alarming news arrived from other places in the Caribbean and surrounding areas. Tremors were known to be occurring in Martinique, a French colony less than 200 kilometres to the north.

1

Finally, on 23 April, Mount La Pelée became active, with its small eruptions fuelling debates about whether or not to evacuate the capital, St Pierre.[3] From the mainland, just over 3,000 kilometres to the west, came news of a strong and mysterious earthquake on 18 April, destroying towns and cities between Quetzaltenango and San Marcos, Guatemala, and claiming hundreds of lives.[4] Even so, authorities in St Vincent did not see any connection between these occurrences and the signs of La Soufrière activity, seeing the news only as a negative influence on the mood of the local population. Despite the authorities' scepticism, the Indigenous people of Morne Ronde had begun to prepare for a possible mass flight.

On the morning of 6 May, authorities in Kingstown began to be inundated with reports coming from various locations in the north of the island about the sounds of explosions, flashes in the sky, earthquakes and steam clouds, among other signs that the volcano had, indeed, awakened. The town of Chateaubelair, south of Morne Ronde, began to receive hundreds of Indigenous and black refugees fleeing an alleged eruption. At first, these people were ridiculed by the sceptical townspeople. By late afternoon, however, scepticism would give way to perplexity: the city dwellers could observe two large explosions accompanied by ash columns. Authorities in Kingstown only recognised La Soufrière's activity the following morning, when the explosions became more extreme, being felt even in the capital. Later that day, a colossal blast provoked widespread panic, and the boiling water overflowing from the rivers stopped many who tried to flee. The entire northern part of the island was hit by pyroclastic flows, causing 1,295 deaths, according to the official count.[5] The next day, it was La Pelée's turn to explode powerfully, destroying the burgeoning capital, St Pierre, leaving only two survivors among its 28,000 inhabitants.[6] In October, the Guatemalan volcano Santa María also exploded, ruining the coffee economy and killing over 5,000 people.[7] Maya-Mam communities like San Martín found protection in their traditional practice of combining resources from different altitudinal zones, taking refuge in the lowlands that were part of the village's territory.[8] These three eruption events (La Soufrière, La Pelée and Santa María) are among the strongest and deadliest in the twentieth century and may have induced the cooling of the Americas' climate in the following years.[9]

How should one interpret the Indigenous and Afro-descendant inhabitants' prescience of the eruption? Visiting St Vincent and Martinique a few weeks after the blasts under a Royal Geographical Society commission, the photographer Tempest Anderson and the geologist John Smith Flett could not decide whether it was ancestral knowledge arising from a long experience (the last eruption had occurred in 1811) or an intuition based on direct sensory contact.[10] There is no evidence to support the former.

Unlike earthquakes, storms, landslides and other environmental phenomena, volcanic eruptions did not elicit the development of any specific Carib lexicon. They were – and still are – too infrequent, occurring at intervals that hamper the creation of an intergenerational tradition.[11] Whatever its origins, the Caribs' premonitory ability suggests a different conception of and relationship to volcanoes – and everything else Europeans deemed 'natural', for that matter. In his study of hurricanes in the Greater Caribbean, Stuart Schwartz remarks how colonial-age Spaniards would generally despise (and fear) the Indigenous inhabitants' capacity to detect the signs of upcoming hurricanes. For pragmatic reasons, the colonisers learned with them, for example, that 'on the approach of a hurricane, the birds had certain uneasiness and flew away from the coast and toward the houses'.[12] Constructed in partnership with nonhumans, Caribbean and Latin American Indigenous cultures were based on what the political scientist Jane Bennett called 'enchantment', in reference to how humans are struck, crossed and shaken by the 'extraordinary that lives amid the familiar and the everyday'.[13] However, as Schwartz shows, the Europeans themselves retained much of this enchantment. It was firmly rooted in their popular cultures and conducive to a complex hybridisation with Indigenous ways of knowing. In this regard, it is suggestive that it was the Kingstowners – not the Caribs – who described the eruption 'as having a long, drawn-out, weird, unearthly character, recalling the roar of a wounded animal in intense pain'.[14]

This book draws inspiration from these 'animist' ways of looking at and relating to the nonhuman world to tell stories very different from those found in the historiography about Latin America and the Caribbean, including significant parts of the environmental historiography.[15] In this Introduction, we set the stage for the upcoming chapters by taking up three tasks. First, we discuss the pertinence of this book's spatial assumption, namely that Latin America and the Caribbean make up a geographical region with a discernible and shared socio-natural history. We argue that the regional character of Latin America is defensible as long as one maintains a radically relational perspective about it. Second, we review the literature to establish how past historians of the region have portrayed 'nature' and its influence on human trajectories. This reveals several attempts to engage with the notion of an agential nonhuman world in various theoretical hues. Finally, we examine the rationales informing the writing of the upcoming chapters, putting them in conversation with recent theoretical and methodological developments. Drawing on Philip Howell's typology of animal agency, we briefly discuss the approaches and findings of each chapter, pointing to intellectual genealogies and prospects for further research.

It might be illuminating to begin by remembering that Latin America and the Caribbean are supposed to be a *region*. According to classic geography, regions are defined by two interconnected conditions: they (1) differ from adjoining regions by (2) having a certain unique combination of features. Late nineteenth- and early twentieth-century geographers defined regions as assemblages of people and biophysical environments mutually adjusting over time. Paul Vidal de La Blache, one of the most important among these scholars, wrote that 'Every region is a domain where many dissimilar beings, artificially brought together, have subsequently adapted themselves to a common existence'.[16] Some Latin American geographers echoed this perspective, but almost always in studying specific countries. For example, describing the processes that shaped the colonial territory that would become Brazil, Milton Santos and Maria Laura Silveira observed that 'Men, plants and animals from three continents, under the empire of the Europeans, met and, in their obligatory coexistence, created a new geography in this part of the planet'.[17] Space intensifies relationships and transformations, imposing an inevitable conviviality that alters beings and things arriving from other parts. These mutual adaptations shape landscape patterns discernible cartographically, meaning regions have spatial boundaries.

Does Latin America and the Caribbean fit La Blache's definition? Is there any evidence that Latin America, as a loosely defined cluster of nation states, expresses a distinct amalgam of 'culture' and 'nature'? There have been some positive answers to these questions. For example, in 1950, palaeontologist George Simpson opened his article on the 'History of Latin American Fauna' by noting the awkwardness of using boundaries 'defined by human linguistics and culture' to delimit the historical study of non-human creatures spatially. 'The animals inhabiting this area', he remarked, 'can hardly have foreseen that the dominant languages of the twentieth century would here be Spanish and Portuguese or that the European cultural elements imported here would come mainly from Latin Europe'. However – and in this lies the real puzzle – there is, indeed, a clear distinction between the faunal assemblages north and south of Mexico, especially the northern part of the country, which functions as a sort of transitional zone. Current biogeographical regionalisations tend to corroborate this by having the northernmost inroads of the Neotropics reach no farther than southern Sonora. While '[e]xact correspondence of native fauna and imported culture would be a miracle', Simpson argued, the influence of environmental factors explains the spatial overlap, as both faunas and cultures would have been demarcated by climate.[18]

Simpson was certainly right to point out the substantial spatial overlap between Latin America and the Neotropics, one of the 'kingdoms' of tropical biogeography – the one found in the 'New World', as opposed to the 'Old World' one. Except for Patagonia and the Chilean Andes, the Neotropics encompass all of South America, extending northwards to include Central America and the Caribbean, most of Mexico, and the southern tip of Florida. Although the reasons are still hotly debated, it is now generally agreed that this region's biodiversity is much higher than that of Africa and Southeast Asia. To get an idea, compared to these other tropical regions taken together, the Neotropics have more species of vascular plants, butterflies, amphibians and snakes.[19] This astounding biological richness has been noted and praised since the visit of the earliest biogeographers, such as Alexander von Humboldt and Alfred Russell Wallace. In fact, it was instrumental in creating a regional identity, especially in the eyes of Europeans (and neo-Europeans). Most of these observers, especially those arriving after the collapse of the great Amerindian empires, conflated what was to become Latin America with 'nature', taken as the opposite of 'culture' and 'civilisation'. While it is evident that colonial politics played a major role in shaping this attitude, the complex ecological history accounting for the staggering Neotropical biodiversity also influenced how Europeans conceptualised Latin America. As we will see, this landscape-based identity – or at least certain versions of it – was eventually embraced by Latin Americans themselves, including influential intellectuals.

In any case, let us not leave any room for doubt: geography is *not* 'destiny'. To say that landscape diversity and dynamics played a role in shaping regional identities does not imply the defence of any biophysical determination of human social life. Instead, it means broadening the concept of history, seeing it as 'a maze of contingent series, which converge, coalesce, dissolve, and bifurcate on the basis of their constituent events and movements',[20] human and nonhuman, in different spatiotemporal scales. In this regard, it can't be stressed enough that the Neotropics are themselves historical. 'This static picture', wrote Simpson himself, 'is the result of a long and dynamic historical process' unfolding in geological time.[21] Prominent in this story is the 50-million-year-long isolation of South America since its tectonic breakup from Africa, which helps explain the uniqueness of the continent's life forms. This 'splendid isolation', as Simpson would call it in a later work,[22] began to end around 2.8 million years ago when combining geological and atmospheric events produced a permanent land bridge between South and Central America – the Isthmus of Panama.[23] This allowed for the dispersal of countless species, especially mammals, with the vast majority of successful migrants coming from the north rather than the other way around. Known as the 'Great American Biotic Interchange',[24] about 40 per cent of South America's extant mammal families stem from this asymmetric exchange.[25] Evidently, biophysical processes like these are ongoing and will continue to shape the Neotropics in the future. How will the region react to Anthropocenic climate change? Neotropical forests seem to have thrived – and even expanded – during past periods of global warming,[26] but the conditions now are different, especially considering wholesale human encroachment on habitats. Be that as it may, the Neotropics are far from the 'steady, unchanging geographic element'[27] that some early twentieth-century environmental determinists sought.

This historicity puts Simpson's hypothesis of nature–culture overlap in a tight spot. Will Latin American nations expand northward when the Neotropics do the same in the next few decades and centuries in the trail of global warming? This is, of course, very unlikely, especially if one assumes a strict biophysical form of causation. Deterministic claims about the past are equally puerile. The argument that English (or Northern European) colonisation was incompatible with Neotropical climatic conditions does not withstand the simplest empirical verifications. How could one explain, for example, that so many Caribbean islands – some of which, like Barbados, became key centres of sugar production – were taken by the English from the Spaniards from the early seventeenth century onwards? As Alfred Crosby argued in *Ecological Imperialism*, it is true that in long-term demographic terms, northern European colonisers were much more successful in areas ecologically similar to their homeland. Here one can, indeed, speak of climatic influences on cultural geography. But contrary to how thinkers like Montesquieu would have described it, this was not an impact of climate on culture via human physiology. Instead, the link was what Crosby famously called 'portmanteau biota', or the nonhuman companions Europeans brought in their ships, which needed suitable habitats. It was in the climatically temperate areas of the Americas, Oceania and Africa that Europeans managed to replace local Indigenous populations and their agricultural systems with their own people and domesticated plants and animals. Success in tropical areas was partial, according to Crosby, as the demand for labour had to be met with enslaved Africans, whom the Europeans often sought for mates – more often than not in nonconsensual ways – the same happening with Amerindians.[28] In any case, there is no physiological incompatibility between Europeans and the tropics, or even epidemiologically. For example, compared to adult Europeans travelling to the New World for the first time, genetically 'European' – or mixed-heritage – individuals born in America were more likely to be immune to yellow fever because they had probably contracted the disease in childhood.[29]

On the other hand, the case of differential immunity to yellow fever is a fine example of La Blache's concept of regions as melting pots. In his study of the role of yellow fever and malaria in the geopolitical history of the Caribbean, John McNeill nicely captured the concept – even without engaging directly with La Blache – by referring to the 'creole ecologies' created by European colonisation. McNeill described them as 'motley assemblage[s] of indigenous and invading species, jostling one another in unstable ecosystems'.[30] Indeed, Latin America has been commonly described in the historiography as resulting from encounters and mixings – both cultural and biological – of Amerindian, European and African populations and species.[31]

But while this is a common theme throughout the region, the specific collisions and combinations varied widely. Sometimes even regions of the same colony and empire, such as Rio de Janeiro and São Paulo, differed markedly in terms of social makeup due to different inputs of enslaved Africans. Furthermore, what Marshall Eakin called the 'powerful Iberoamerican tradition' – consisting of the spiritual conquest by the Catholic Church, the racial and cultural mixture of Iberian, Amerindian and African peoples, slavery, and profound social inequities – slowly gave way in many of the Caribbean islands as they were gradually transformed by their English, Dutch and French conquerors from the early seventeenth century on.[32] Thus, while the theme of the socioecological crucible lends some support to the thesis of Latin America as a region, other elements need to be considered.

To a large extent, the idea of Latin America – developing out of the notion of a 'Latin race'– emerged in the mid-nineteenth century in reaction to American imperialism. Unravelled by historian Michel Gobat, this is the story of the complex confluence of the rise of American overseas expansion (especially the 1856 William Walker episode in Nicaragua, with the US president Franklin Pierce eventually recognising the 'piratical' regime), the democratisation of electoral participation in several Latin American countries, the crushing of the 1848 revolutions in Europe and the sprawling ideologies of whiteness. Economic concerns linked to the plundering of natural resources and the destruction of native industry also informed the concept. For example, in 1862, the Bolivian journalist Benedicto Medinaceli published *Proyecto de Confederación de las Repúblicas Latino-Americanas*, in which he envisioned Latin America as an economic unit standing against the expansion of North Atlantic capitalism.[33] As in any process of regional identity construction, proud allusions to the landscape appeared early on. In his famous 1856 poem 'La Dos Américas', José María Torres Caicedo talked of a 'Beautiful continent' blessed by God, a 'Virgin who stands between two oceans lulled to sleep and shaded by the high Andes'.[34] This attachment to landscapes and the nonhuman world would live on in what might be called the 'Latin American canon', in which the 1891 essay 'Nuestra América' by the Cuban writer José Martí stands out. To demarcate the region, Martí used the Rio Bravo in the north and the Strait of Magellan in the south as 'horizontal' boundaries, while the Andes and their silver veins served as a 'vertical' boundary. More importantly, he praised the 'natural man' shaped by intimate contact with the land and who has the knowledge necessary for good government, which was 'nothing more than the balance of the country's natural elements'.[35]

Therefore, if regions are understood as what scientists call 'natural kinds' (that is, grouping of things that reflect the world as it is, without the interference of human interests and biases), then, clearly, Latin America is not one. However, if we accept the geographic precepts about the power of space to amalgamate and transform everything that it forces to coexist – including people's feelings – then it is possible to treat Latin America as a region. Evidently, this interweaving happens historically. 'Space' itself is not an empty receptacle but a mesh of bodies and their mutual constitutive relationships established over time. The Neotropics are as historical as European colonisation, economic underdevelopment and the very idea of Latin America. Even in its effort to include other forces and agencies – or perhaps precisely because of it – a non-anthropocentric environmental history must recognise the historical contingency of regional entanglements. At the same time, this does not mean that nonhumans and their doings are mere products of human representation, or that Latin America is a fanciful 'invention' of culture and politics. Latin America is a precarious and transitory assemblage of people, animals, plants, soils, water, microorganisms, air and ocean currents, among other elements, which came together in/from different places and timeframes and eventually adapted to each other but remain in tension, always ready to break free.

How has Latin American historiography approached the nonhuman world? For the analyst of the contemporary era, it is relatively easy to conclude that it exacerbated the anthropocentrism that has often characterised the historical discipline. This is explained by the strong influence of Marxism and nationalism, making Euro-American imperialism a central thread in most regional historical narratives. These are stories about how 'places privileged by nature have been cursed by history', as Eduardo Galeano put it in his classic *Open Veins of Latin America*, originally published in 1971. Echoing dependency theory and the 'resource curse' debate that had emerged in the 1950s and 1960s, one of the book's main themes is the 'wealth which nature bestows and imperialism appropriates'.[36] Reflecting the broader intellectual climate in the region's political and academic left, Galeano's account portrays 'nature' as a generous Mother Earth whose gifts attracted the covetous eyes and powerful claws of northern powers. In this guise, 'nature' – as opposed to 'history', conceived as the domain of human agency – acts only passively, that is, by being seized, spoiled and devastated.

To this day, most environmental historians *from* Latin America 'present nature as something "out there," something that people and the global economy destroy'.[37] For example, Stephania Gallini was one among many scholars to argue that the nineteenth-century material 'progress' in the region was based on the exploitation of natural resources, especially through primary exports.[38] But one should not exaggerate the association of this 'paradigm' with Latin American scholars, as it also informs recent works by foreign authors (or mixed-origin co-authorships). For example, John Soluri, Claudia Leal and José Augusto Pádua's *A Living Past: Environmental Histories of Modern Latin America* might be argued to frame 'nature' in this traditional way. The material phenomena analysed seem secondary in relation to human actions and intentions (whether of historical characters or of historians themselves), thus leaving the impression that it is nonhuman life that takes place in its irremediable immersion in human culture, politics and economy – not the other way around. Another example is David Pretel's paper on the Caste War, in which he argues the Maya Forest acted within the conflict, especially by offering marketable natural resources (timber, henequen, chicle) to the rebels. Moreover, Pretel eventually comes to the conclusion that, in the end, the forest was little affected by the outcome of those long years of struggle.[39]

Interestingly enough, however, nonhuman agency has always been difficult to ignore when a volcano eruption, a destructive earthquake or the consequences of extreme climate (to name a few but decisive events) were in command of human history. Take the example of the nineteenth-century Chilean historian Benjamin Vicuña Mackenna, who, in 1877, published *Ensayo histórico sobre el clima de Chile*. His aim was to prove that climate fluctuations had altered the country's routine since pre-Hispanic times, so at the centre of the story was the climate, indeed, but, in the end, he could not completely get rid of the anthropocentric perspective that prioritises human will above natural constraints. He confessed that he wanted to show to some of his contemporaries who were complaining about devastating floods and extreme weather that Chileans had always faced similar difficulties. Maybe the best pre-1980s debates stressing nonhuman agency come from some Peruvian archaeologists and historians. In 1972 John

Murra cemented the role of a vertical control of ecological niches to understand the reciprocity and complementarity displayed by Indigenous
societies.[40] In a way, Murra unearthed ideas dating back to the 1930s when
the geographer Carl Troll, following in the footsteps of his conational
Alexander von Humboldt, travelled the Andean areas of Ecuador, Peru
and Bolivia. Between 1926 and 1929 Troll's observations reinforced
Humboldt's ideas of an Andean 'vertical zonification'. Similarly, for the
archaeologist Augusto Cardich, originally trained as an agricultural
engineer, to understand most Andean communities one needed first to
understand the Andes' nature. The rule is quite simple. Food availability
depends on the thermic spectre of the Andean flora and fauna, making
environmental conditions such as altitude and water accessibility influence the exchanges among Indigenous communities living in different
environments.[41] But Peru has around eighty ecological zones, so when
Murra proposed his model, he sparked controversies. But even though
many historians soon found gross inadequacies when the model was
applied to southern and coastal Peruvian societies, the debate helped to
foreground nonhuman agencies.[42]

There were important discussions about the role of the nonhuman world
in the history of Brazil, too. The late nineteenth and early twentieth centuries was a particularly prolific period, with authors such as Charles
Darwin, Herbert Spencer and Henry Buckle exerting a strong influence
on Brazilian thought. For example, in his history of national literature,
Sylvio Romero referred to the climate as an 'agent' that – alongside other
forces – forged a new people from diverse ethnic elements (Europeans,
Amerindians and Africans). Acting more directly on literary expression,
the climate would have helped to provoke the 'sentimental effusion' of
Brazilian lyricism.[43] In the second and third quarters of the twentieth
century, there were several authors who approached nonhumans as agentic without slipping into environmental determinism. Foreshadowing
Braudel in many ways, in 1936, the anthropologist Gilberto Freyre developed an eco-regional approach to the human–nonhuman entanglements
shaped by sugar plantations in Northeast Brazil.[44] Cassiano Ricardo's
Marcha para Oeste was published in 1942, proposing an ambitious interpretation of Brazilian history from a frontier perspective à la Frederick J.
Turner (who is oddly not cited). Although an in-depth study of this two-
volume magnum opus remains to be done, environmental historians today
will find abundant food for thought, including some conceptual foreshad-
owings, such as the notions of 'grafted' landscapes (similar to Crosby's
idea of portmanteau biota) and 'production of spaces'. Even more importantly for us here, Ricardo explores human–environment hybridisations
with a rare analytical sensitivity that includes something like the strategic

anthropomorphism advocated by Jane Bennett.[45] Sérgio Buarque de Holanda was another brilliant analyst of colonial frontiers. With rare brilliance and erudition, Holanda examined frontiers as the sites where humans and nonhumans, Europeans and Amerindians, clashed and transformed one another, often in contexts of asymmetrical power.[46] Informed by his geoscience expertise, geographer Aziz Ab'Saber traced the influences of soils and landforms in human adaptation to regional environments.[47]

In the 1980s and 1990s, the writing of Latin American history profited from the long-lasting and highly influential scholarship of gifted historians such as Alfred Crosby, Elinor Melville and Warren Dean. Pioneering a path towards the complex historical research on the colonial and postcolonial Americas, these scholars taught us how to master a multilayer approach to the relations between humans and nonhumans in those early days of conquest and colonisation. Historical explanations were missing the point, as Crosby suggested, because 'the success of European imperialism has a biological, an ecological component'.[48] Following in his footsteps, Melville's *A Plague of Sheep* created a fresco of sixteenth-century Mezquital Valley, in Mexico. True, sheep changed the environment and consequently induced societal changes, but they did that as *domesticated* animals, thus as instruments of human will, rather than full-fledged agents. Yet her richly textured narrative does suggest here and there the existence of an independent natural world, one that has always managed to pursue autonomous development.[49] For South America, Dean was one of the first scholars to call attention to the importance of the 'ecological conditions of production' in the region's agricultural history. His *Brazil and the Struggle for Rubber: A Study in Environmental History* is an underacknowledged monograph-length pioneer in showing how nonhuman environmental dynamics – in this case, the emergence of fungal epidemics – shaped regional history.[50]

Only latent in that book is the unremitting outrage towards humanity's destructiveness that Dean was to fully reveal in his subsequent monograph, *With Broadax and Firebrand: The Destruction of the Brazilian Atlantic Forest*. In a sweeping judgement, he affirmed that 'The aggrandizement of our species has been based upon the destruction of forests that we are ill equipped to inhabit'.[51] In a previous short essay, he had espoused the same fatalistic view by arguing that environmental degradation is 'the most consequential of human activities'. But alongside his strong moral indignation with human short-sightedness, Dean entertained a more general perspective about the 'interaction with the environment' being 'the central issue in human history', rather than a 'side-effect of other, supposedly more decisive activities such as class struggle, capital accumulation, the spread of imperialism, the triumph of science and technology, or the subjection of women'.[52] Indeed, his two environmental history monographs contain some of the boldest nonhuman agency arguments put forward in Latin Americanist historiography up to the mid-1990s. In *With Broadax and Firebrand*, for instance, Dean claimed that the *Atta* leaf-cutting ants – locally known as *saúvas* – and their voracious harvesting of introduced crops had been one of the single most important factors in shaping the transfer of European and African agricultural systems to South America:

> if an effective means had existed, during Brazil's first 450 years to com-
> bat saúva, its agriculture, and consequently its history, would have
> been very different. That an insect can deflect human designs is an
> abhorrent idea, surely more abhorrent than the pest itself, because it
> questions the hegemony of our species.[53]

By the beginning of the present century, the extra-human world was already firmly established in Latin Americanist historical-environmental analysis as an array of beings, things and forces not only subdued and manipulated by humans but also imposing conditions on their 'making of history'. As Steve Marquardt wrote in a 2001 essay on the Panama disease's impacts on Central American banana economies, human–environment relations were not to be 'reduced to a simple, unidirectional narrative of corporate planters degrading the environment. Ecological changes were indeed shaped and accelerated by the replacement of species-diverse tropical rainforest with a genetically uniform crop, but the processes set in motion themselves affected the subsequent human history of the plantation'.[54] The first synthesis to appear in the field, Shawn W. Miller's *An Environmental History of Latin America*, shows how consolidated this view was later in that decade. Laying out his approach, Miller observed:

> The stage for the human drama, we suppose, is stocked with cul-
> ture's props but is barren of nature's scenery. Until recently, there
> have been few beasts, creeks, food crops, dirt clods, or raindrops in
> our histories. Yet nature is more than mere backdrop to the human
> drama, more than the resource that sustains it. Nature's troupe –
> vegetable, animal, and mineral – forms part of the production's cast,
> actors whose agency rivals that of the human players. [. . .] Humans
> will remain at center stage in our drama lest environmental history
> shade into natural history; however, the stories of nonhuman life
> and of the inanimate resources on which life depends will be given
> place in our plots. In addition to Indians, colonists, slaves, industri-
> alists, peasants, urbanites, and tourists, our cast will include soils,

smallpox, sugar, mercury, egrets, butterflies, guano, whales, hurricanes, and reefs.[55]

One can still contend – and this is betrayed by Miller's ultimate refusal to
decentre people – that nonhuman doings remain somewhat reactive to
human actions and designs. In order to redistribute historical agency, it is
necessary to envision negotiation, which always runs the risk of incom-
pleteness and imbalance; different actors leave different traces of their
entanglement with changing environments. Moreover, the reconstruction
of the past allows for multiple interpretations. An example is the volume
edited by Margarita Gascón, *Vientos, Terremotos, Tsunamis y Otras
Catástrofes Naturales: Historia y Casos Latinoamericanos*. The label itself
points out that 'natural disasters' (or 'catastrophes') are the result of a
human-centred mindset. Thus, it mirrors the classic ecological model that
sees humans as disturbing agents in ecosystems: the focus is on human
societies as socio-economic, political and cultural systems that are now
and then disrupted and challenged by 'natural' events. Methodologically,
these anomalous occurrences – anomalous only from a human perspective, rightly understood – function as breaking points that paradoxically
reveal the normal workings of human societies. 'The catastrophe served
as a magnifying glass', pointed out Gascón, 'because the emergency and
reconstruction make the behaviours, tendencies and tensions that had
been hidden by routine and daily life more noticeable'.[56] According to
Gascón, there has been a complex relationship between natural disasters
and the evolution of colonial societies in southern South America.[57]

The same is true for the colonial Caribbean basin, where hurricanes and
severe tropical storms are impossible to disregard. They came to symbol-
ise all that was unique and dangerous in the region.[58] Several works
explored the role of the tempestuous Caribbean climate in human historical developments. In 2001, Louis A. Pérez published *Winds of Change*, a
groundbreaking study about the role of the hurricanes of the 1840s in the
national formation of Cuba. Pérez's pioneering approach traced the influence of hurricanes, which he saw as factors 'shaping the options and
outcomes to which huge numbers of people were obliged to respond', in
the strategies of economic development, labour organisation and the construction of a national feeling of belonging.[59] Michael Burn showed a
significant relationship between Spanish shipwrecks and tree-growth sup-
pression, both parameters and proxies for past hurricane activity.[60]
Alexander Berland, Georgina Endfield and Sherry Johnson are among
those who have consistently researched the multiple impacts of extreme
weather beyond damages to urban infrastructure and rural production.[61]
More recently, drawing on Greg Bankoff's work on the Philippines, Stuart

Schwartz and Matthew Mulcahy suggested that hurricanes and other hazards were 'agents of culture formation' in the premodern Caribbean, as 'Architecture, religious practices, mentalities, and economic and political concerns all reflected to varying degrees the reality of living in a space subjected to routine [. . .] disasters'.[62]

In the last decade, a few works set out to centre nonhumans as historical agents. At least at the level of intentions, this is the case of Martha Few and Zeb Tortorici's 2013 edited volume *Centering Animals in Latin American History*. However, the mere inclusion of animals as topics – even if central ones – is no guarantee of a nonhuman-agential interpretation. As the editors themselves admit, 'the mere analytical and figurative presence of animals – their visibility – by no means automatically centers them'.[63] This problem plagues most of the volume's chapters, where agency is still understood in its modern anthropocentric sense. Martha Few's paper on locusts in colonial Guatemala is an honourable, though still partial, exception. She argues that locusts were not only shaped by human social processes, 'but also helped to shape them', which makes them important historical players: 'it is possible to show that locusts, by periodically joining to creating mass streamways and travelling hundreds of miles, have played a significant role in the history of colonial Guatemala'.[64] But however keen Few is to acknowledge the insects' place in shaping history, she still equates agency with symbolic intentionality – or, as she called it, 'sentience'.[65]

Several other works highlight the agency of insects in Latin American history. Locusts and ants are the nuisances most alluded to in the Caribbean historical records. According to entomologist Edward Wilson, the tropical fire ant *Solenopsis geminata* arrived in 1516 along with sugarcane, imported from the Canary Islands. The plague badly hit the fledgling Spanish settlements on Hispaniola. Matthey Mulcahy and Stuart Schwartz stressed the long-term consequence of the episodes in the 1760s and 1770s, when swarms of ants and other hymenopterans devastated sugar fields in Martinique, Grenada, Barbados and several other islands. Not surprisingly, combating insects became an important goal for planters and entomology emerged as a necessary science of empire. Luis Alberto Arrioja Diáz has shown how the droughts of the late colonial period created the environmental conditions for locusts to swarm and sweep through Guatemala voraciously, provoking all kinds of human responses – from prayers to administrative measures.[66] However, all these works stop short of exploring the subjective world of insects, thus portraying them as obstacles for human enterprises.[67] As Diogo de Carvalho Cabral has pointed out, such an obstacle is not 'a part of the historical pathway; it is something alien, radically different from those agents/characters whose march

supposedly "makes history"'.[68] This limits the breadth of historical interpretation, as animal agency can in fact be analysed in terms of sentience
or – more appropriately termed – perception and semiosis. In a more recent
paper, de Carvalho Cabral has urged historians to treat landscapes as multispecies negotiations, bringing to light the diverse meanings that each
kind of organism attaches to material features.[69]

Although many other works could be included, this review cannot be
exhaustive for reasons of space. In any case, it seems to us that the sam-
ple of historiography discussed here is representative of the major trends
and lines of interpretation. From the nineteenth to the mid-twentieth
century, there were many attempts to analyse 'nature' as an agent in history. Some departed from deterministic – or at least biologistic – premises,
while others sought to preserve human 'cultural' creativity. In the post-war
period, a strong anthropocentrism dominated the scene, with nature portrayed as a victim of human projects, especially hegemonic and foreign
economic projects. In the late twentieth century, some environmental
historians introduced new frameworks, mainly based on the notion of
'unintended (environmental) consequences'. More recently, an increasingly varied historiographical mosaic has emerged. On the one hand,
declensionist stories continue to be told, something absolutely understandable (and necessary) in a climate emergency context. On the other hand,
researchers have been experimenting with new approaches in intense
dialogue with other disciplines, such as climatology and anthropology.
To end this Introduction, we now turn to the present book's chapters, trying
to situate them in the context of contemporary theoretical and historiographical debates.

Here is not the place to review the extensive theoretical literature on the
notion of historical agency. Suffice it to point out that agency outside
the human domain has sometimes been acknowledged, even by historians with no connection to any environmental interpretation lens. For
example, in his 1993 *The Structures of History*, Christopher Lloyd observed
that 'All complex systems that are characterized by evolutionary or historical forces, such as ecosystems, insect and animal societies, and human
societies, have agents for change within them'.[70] Later on, economic and
military historians such as Bruce Campbell and Geoffrey Parker embraced
climate dynamics as prime causative factors.[71] Recently, there have been
several moves towards writing histories more radically attentive to nonhuman causation, even though the underlying theoretical affiliations, as
well as the labels chosen for these approaches, are diverse ('more-than-
human history', 'multispecies history', 'post-anthropocentric history' are
some of the existing labels).[72] In one way or another, all these approaches

agree with the foundational claim made long ago by environmental historians that humans produce history in coexistence with beings, forces and structures that they have not strictly created or controlled.[73] However, these newer frameworks tend to reject the nature–culture dichotomy, with important implications for how humans and their actions are described and interpreted. Rather than a priori subjects, people (and their inner 'mental' worlds) are more explicitly examined as emergent effects of broader material-semiotic relations that feedback into that mesh. As abstract as they seem, complex ideas and motivations – the bread and butter of traditional historiography – are claimed to be 'inseparable from our material bodies and environments'.[74]

In recent decades, the aspect of this material realm most thoroughly studied and theorised by historians and historical geographers has arguably been nonhuman animals. Despite some countering voices, the concept of animal agency is now widespread among animal historians.[75] Philip Howell developed a general classification of animal agency approaches which might be useful here. He identified three broad types: 'ascribed agencies', or accounts of how people in the past attributed certain powers to animals (which might be connected with the animals' very being); 'agonistic agencies', or histories that portray animals (individually or collectively) as actors in themselves, mostly by resisting or refracting human projects; and 'assembled agencies', or approaches that consider animals' agencies to emerge from specific meshes or networks of heterogeneous beings and things.[76] While embracing a broader spectrum of nonhuman beings and things, the approaches adopted in this book can be profitably linked to Howell's types.

Some chapters use what can be considered a version of Howell's 'agonistic agencies', one linked to a traditional theme of environmental history, namely 'unintended consequences'. Richard White was one of the first to articulate it, noting that 'Humans may *think* what they want; they cannot always *do* what they want, and not all they do turns out as planned'.[77] Indeed, operationalised through intense recourse to scientific findings, this approach has been at the heart of environmental history since the 1970s and 1980s – since Crosby's and Donald Worster's early work.[78] People's doings are 'bigger' than they imagine because they are intertwined with landscapes and ecosystems of enormous complexity – individual humans being 'ecosystems' themselves. At the same time, this can blur the boundaries between 'agonistic' and 'assembled' types of agency. Especially where the unanticipated consequence proves beneficial for human initiators (for example, exotic pathogens emptying American native lands for European settlers), one might see an '"embedding" or "distribution" of agency within heterogeneous assemblages'.[79] Conversely, when unforeseen outcomes work against human intentions, scholars tend to talk of 'resistance'. Like in Dean's arguments about fungi and ants, these beings' agencies arise mostly as inadvertent consequences of humans' interventions in 'natural' systems they understood only poorly. This resonates with a view of environmental history as 'a kind of cultural history that analyzes the capacity of our species, under differing circumstances, to understand and manage its relationship with its natural environment'.[80] Therefore, in a sense, it is more about human ignorance, inexperience and myopia than the autonomy, vibrancy and power of earthly things. Be that as it may, such an ecological indeterminacy – that is, the practical impossibility of knowing certain things in advance, such as the effects of biological transfers – can be seen as an expression of nonhuman agency.[81]

Labelling a nonhuman agency claim as 'agonistic' or 'assembled' is also a matter of narrative emphasis. For example, in his chapter 'Human–insect relations in Northeast Brazil's twentieth-century sugar industry', José Marcelo Marques Ferreira Filho focuses on insects' role in shaping sugar plantations. However, it is clear that insects acted in close association with viruses and the broader landscape (including, of course, human agriculture and the environmental transformations it brought about), among other intervening elements. As Ferreira Filho himself observes, 'The human social history of sugar is inseparable from its botanical history, which, in turn, is inseparable from the history of the insects that affect both people and plants'. Thus, Ferreira Filho repositions human history within the web of material life by exploring the role of insects in the sugar economy through the heavy use of scientific literature. It is interesting to observe that there is a temporal distinction establishing the status of these sources individually: he tends to use scientific findings 'from the past' – that is, from the same time of the events examined – as evidence, while those 'from the present' provide him with the overall explanatory models. As in many other studies – including in this book – there is an implicit progressivism that assumes that current scientific knowledge is more reliable and, therefore, extrapolatable to the past. Although bringing some epistemological impasses, it is necessary to recognise that this is the methodological model that initially boosted environmental history in the 1970s and 1980s. In this sense, Ferreira Filho's study descends from an already long lineage going back to Crosby and Woster, for whom, 'with the aid of modern science', environmental history aims 'to discover some fresh truths about ourselves and our past'.[82]

In turn, the chapter 'Water labour: urban metabolism, energy and rivers in nineteenth-century Rio de Janeiro, Brazil' by Bruno Capilé and Lise Sedrez leaves no room for doubt. The authors themselves emphasise their theoretical affiliation to a 'networked' conception of agency mostly inspired by Bruno Latour's work. Investigating the role of rivers in the urban history of Rio de Janeiro, Capilé and Sedrez pay particular attention to how those moving bodies of water entangled themselves with other producers of labour/energy, such as the pack animals that transported materials for plumbing works and the grasses they fed on. Reminiscent of Richard White's approach to studying the Columbia River in his classic *The Organic Machine*, Capilé and Sedrez follow the complex chains of energy transformation centred around the rivers flowing into (and out of) Brazil's nineteenth-century capital city. The richly textured image that emerges from this historical tracing is that of networks precariously assembling water, people, animals, plants, soils and the technosphere into urban life in the periphery of the capitalist world system. In this ontological metabolism, one can hardly distinguish 'nature' and 'culture', as entities become historically in their constant mingling and transgressing. More than just physical things, rivers become a 'starting point for undertaking the archaeology'[83] of messy socio-natural relations.

What about extreme environmental events like droughts and earthquakes? Can they also be framed as agents resisting human projects or else taking part in heterogenous agentic assemblages, such as Ferreira Filho's insects and Capilé and Sedrez's rivers? There seems to be an essential difference in scale here. Faced with climate dynamics (and here we are thinking specifically of the pre-modern period) and plate tectonics, humans found themselves entangled in telluric histories moved by forces that greatly supersede the scales of action available in the eighteenth and nineteenth centuries, even for the most powerful empires. As Pérez argued about Cuba's hurricanes, they 'loomed as forces of vast proportions, larger than human effort and negating the proposition of humans as the center and measure of all things'.[84] Here, the 'agonistic agents' are people, who often seem like tragic characters in a plot whose driving forces are far beyond their control. Nowhere is this more evident than in Margarita Gascón's chapter 'Under a weak sun at the southern rim of South America (1540–1650)'. Due to magnetic factors not yet fully understood, the radiation emitted by the sun fluctuates over time, affecting the earth's climate. Gascón shows how these oscillations – activated by cosmic processes 150 million kilometres away – combined with El Niño Southern Oscillation (ENSO) events and human developments such as warfare and agriculture during Chile and Argentina's Little Ice Age (LIA). Methodologically, her approach is to detect and narrate the complex embranglements of climatic anomalies in multiple human storylines by searching convergences – or at least inferable relations – between scientific findings and the events extractable from written records. Similar to accounts centred on nonhuman 'resistants', here one sees people often engulfed in emergent, not-fully-controllable dynamics that reframe their horizons of possibilities and fields for action.

To a large extent, Gascón's and other similar studies of how past peoples resisted or adapted – to use a more usual term – to nonhuman forces endowed with their own historicities descend from a parallel intellectual lineage that predates the emergence of environmental history in the US. Initiated by Lucien Febvre, Marc Bloch and others in the 1920s, the so-called *Annales* school sought, among other innovations, to incorporate then-recent conceptual developments in the field of geography to study collective human trajectories in their biophysical contexts.[85] This search led to an emphasis on the long duration of the human experience of environments, a perspective that Fernand Braudel took to its ultimate consequences in the 1940s. As part of his triad of temporal layers, Braudel theorised the nonhuman world as a 'geographical time' that, in its friction with 'social' and 'individual' temporalities, proved almost immobile. While acknowledging that 'everything changes, even the [. . .] elements of physical geography', the changes he included in his pathbreaking account of the Mediterranean were mostly cyclical, not directional. 'So the climate changes and does not change', he observed, as 'it varies in relation to norms which may after all vary themselves, but only to a very slight degree'.[86] In any case, Braudel's concept of 'geohistory' profoundly influenced the work of Emmanuel Le Roy Ladurie, a third-generation representative of the *Annales* tradition. He argued vehemently against the 'anthropocentrism' of explaining human epochal crises and processes by recourse to climatic cycles and vagaries, proposing instead the historical study of 'meteorological factors in themselves: temperature, rainfall, and then, where possible, wind and barometric pressure, sunshine and cloud'. In other words, he was interested in examining 'nature for its own sake', which, according to him, has its 'own special time'. Drawing an analogy with geography and its two subfields (human and physical), Ladurie advocated for a 'physical history, a history of natural conditions' written through historians' traditional archival methods. Written records should be 'critically examined and duly translated into quantitative terms'. Only after a solid baseline of climatic processes had been established would historians be able to move on to analyse their meaning for humans – the climate 'as it is for us', Ladurie wrote, 'as the ecology of man'.[87]

The weight of this intellectual heritage is particularly noticeable in Luis Alberto Arrioja Díaz and María Dolores Ramírez Vega's chapter 'Extreme weather in New Spain and Guatemala: the Great Drought (1768–73)'. Following Ladurie's methodological guidelines, the authors invest in quantification, compiling 162 drought events from various written sources.

First, they use this method, including a qualitative ranking of drought intensity, to analyse an extended period between the mid-seventeenth and early nineteenth centuries, showing significant correlations with the Maunder Minimum and the Maldá and Dalton Oscillations. Next, they shift their focus to a short period in the late LIA (1768–73) that witnessed complex entanglements of planetary-scale atmospheric phenomena and regional zoogeographical dynamics (locust plagues), among other factors. Here, Arrioja Díaz and Ramírez Vega shift to a qualitative-narrative approach – even though resorting to numbers now and then – to show how the climatic changes translated into societal dynamics. Reactions to the drought were of many types, from the most instinctive (and sometimes horrific), such as migration and cannibalism, to the most elaborate (and socially cruel), such as laws forcing the commoners to plant food under pain of banishment. Some measures against the drought ended up aggravating it, such as reclaiming marginal land for plantings, which often resulted in failed crops and less pasture for animals.

Like the sun and the clouds above our heads, the earth under our feet has its own way of being in time. Of course, that includes soil, the earth's topmost layer of degraded, friable rock and decomposed organic matter formed over millennia in which we grow most of our food. However, if we go further down, we find an even more uncanny historical reality comprising continent-sized blocks of integral rock brought together and moved around by turbulent lava currents below. Forming and dismantling over geological time, these blocks or 'tectonic plates' move at a speed of a few centimetres per year, but every now and then the rearrangements of the unstable edifice of rocks and their fissures at the border of two plates generate terrible accelerations up on the surface. Magdalena Gil's chapter discusses how these dynamics helped shape the history of Chile, one of the world's most earthquake-prone countries. Here, too, there is the tragic sense of humans struggling against a larger and more powerful reality. However, Gil's approach to earthquakes – reminiscent of Pérez's study of hurricanes in Cuba – makes room for cultural creativity that arises precisely from environmental fragility: the construction of state institutions. Among other competencies, the legitimacy of modern states is based on the management of a bounded territory. But rather than abstract geopolitical entities, territories are the nations' 'natural bodies' defined by ecological contents and dynamics that pose concrete challenges to human communities. Simply put, earthquakes – like volcanic eruptions, droughts and hurricanes – do not *happen in (or to)* a territory but *are themselves (intrinsic components of)* territories. Gil argues that Chilean public authorities learned this early on, which strongly shaped the country's institutional makeup since the political independence, especially

from the early twentieth century. From seismological agencies and building codes to a more general predisposition to intervene in civil society's
affairs, Gil shows how earthquakes embedded themselves in Chile's
sociopolitical (and cultural) fabric.

A different approach to nonhuman agency stems from a more 'intimate' stance, so to speak, towards how people ascribe powers and
capabilities to the world around them. This concerns what is now widely
referred to in the anthropological literature as 'ontology', or the study of
'reality' as constructed by semiotic selves (human and nonhuman).[88]
The first is Luisa Vidal de Oliveira and Denise Maria Cavalcante Gomes's
'Performative objects: Konduri iconography as a window to precolonial
Amazonian ontologies', which closely dialogues with so-called Amerindian
perspectivism. One of the most impactful theoretical perspectives in the
humanities today – including environmental history – this theory was
initially developed by ethnographers and anthropologists philosophi-
cally informed by Indigenous knowledge itself. Amerindian perspectivist
theorists promote nothing short of an ontological implosion. According to
Eduardo Viveiros de Castro, its first and main articulator, Amerindian
communities do not separate nature from culture, or material from
immaterial (spiritual) forms; for them, what exists is a multiplicity of cor-
poreal forms (multinatures) that see themselves as human, while other
spatial elements are also culturally elaborated and defined in metaphysical continuity.[89] In a radically interdisciplinary fashion, Oliveira and
Gomes combine Indigenous ethnology, archaeology and history to analyse Konduri ceramic artefacts from precolonial Amazonia. These are
interpreted as indices of relationships that connect the visible and the
invisible, the natural and the supernatural, with the artefacts themselves having agency. In other words, these are not representations but
performative figurations of complex entanglements in continuous transformation processes. Challenging 'representationist' classification
schemes, the artefacts demonstrate their ritual potential as a 'shamanic
technology', reflecting and fostering different nonhuman perspectives.

The other chapter addressing Howell's 'ascribed agencies' is Olivia
Arigho-Stiles's '"We are the air, the land, the pampas . . .": *campesino* politics and the other-than-human in highland Bolivia (1970–90)'. Using an
interdisciplinary framework (history, environmental sociology and multispecies studies) to analyse print and audio sources, Arigho-Stiles offers
a fascinating account of the influence of Katarismo on the *Confederación
Sindical Única de Trabajadores Campesinos de Bolivia* (Unified Syndical
Confederation of Peasant Workers of Bolivia – CSUTCB) in the historical
process that led to the formation of an other-than-human politics. Katarismo
emerged in Bolivia in the 1960s, combining ideas that reinforced Aymara

ethnic consciousness with theories of racial and class exploitation and renewing the struggle against colonial oppression by the Bolivian state. Arigho-Stiles shows how the ontologies of Indigenous peoples and Bolivian peasants were crucial to the emergence of nonhumans in the political arena. In helping to shape the CSUTCB's claims, the recognition of the agency of land itself constituted a critical dimension of the struggle against neoliberalism.

Both these chapters touch on one of the most challenging and contentious issues today in animal and more-than-human history: to what extent are human attributions of agency shaped by the nonhumans themselves? Howell contends that 'representation' and 'agency itself' are 'always inseparable'. Citing literary criticism scholars, he goes on to posit that 'animals have the power to enter the space of human consciousness [. . .] rather than their animality merely being colonised and constructed and coded by cultural forms'.[90] But, if this is so, how can one access the animals – or, more generally, nonhuman beings and things – 'themselves', that is, apart from their human representations? Perhaps this is neither possible nor desirable. Instead, it may be that we should look for humans and nonhumans in our sources not detached from one another but inextricably conjoined – something about which Oliveira and Gomes have important things to say. Based on Amerindian perspectivism, they address their artefactual sources as amalgams of human and nonhuman standpoints, not mere products of human representation. This is in line with recent framings of written sources as resulting from embodied encounters between humans and animals.[91] Arigho-Stiles, too, takes this cue by suggesting that the 1982 El Niño left its mark on the CSUTCB's debates. Thus, one could argue that the anti-neoliberal movement she studies is an assemblage of people and climatic events rather than a purely human construction.

Another way still to explore nonhuman agencies (some of which arguably of the 'ascribed' kind) is by drawing on the environmental humanities. This transversal and recently institutionalised field brings together ecocriticism, environmental psychology, environmental communication and environmental philosophy, among other disciplines and approaches. Despite the effort to create interdisciplinary dialogues, only a few works connect, for example, environmental history, ecocriticism and environmental communication. A possible way forward is to be open to experimentations based on the concepts and objectives common to all these disciplines, in addition to drawing more intensely on philosophy, especially the new materialisms/realisms and critical post-humanism.[92] In Latin America, these experiments are on the rise with the study of plays, TV series, comic books and, especially, literary works.[93] They have demonstrated the analytical centrality of imploding the nature–culture binary, emphasising the strength of nonhumans in inducing feelings and perceptions – thus 'co-producing' the artworks.

Hannah Regis's chapter 'Tongues in trees and sermons in stones: Jason Allen-Paisant's ecopoetics in thinking with trees' exemplifies this trend in Latin America. Analysing poet Jason Allen-Paisant's *Thinking with Trees*, Regis emphasises the agency, resilience and intersections between race, class and environment in the Caribbean space, where black bodies not only resist but proliferate in communion with the forest, despite all the colonialist violence throughout Jamaican history. Thus, bridging environmental history and ecocriticism, the study shows how Allen-Paisant's poetry rejects European anthropocentrism in favour of an empathetical relationship with nature and, by extension, with the human self that is also nature. On the other hand, 'Animating the waters, hydrating history: control and contingency in Latin American animations' by André Vasques Vital brings environmental communication and environmental history closer together through an analysis of the water ontologies in the environmental animations *Abuela Grillo* (2009), by Denis Chapon, and *Nimbus, o Caçador de Nuvens* (2016), by Marco Nick and Matheus Antunes. Vital shows that the animations highlight the active role of water in the constitution of historical reality, whether through indifferent cooperation, challenge or the disruption of human meanings, intentions and actions.

Taken together, these chapters provide a complex, nuanced picture of how encounters between humans and nonhumans historically shaped Latin America and the Caribbean. Whether prosaic earthly companions like water, forests and insects, or distant and magnanimous forces like the sun or tectonic plates, nonhuman beings and things acted on varied spatial and temporal scales to constrain and enable not only the actions but the very thinking of those who came to define themselves as Latin Americans. Contrary to first appearances, this does not mean any neglect of ethical considerations on the part of students of the past. It just means that the domain of ethics must be extended to include the moral obligations that arise from humans' vital dependence on other forms of existence. Therefore, this is not about giving up analysing human responsibilities in creating injustices and inequalities, but examining how these 'social constructions' include other entities – some of them sentient – and not only as objects of destruction and degradation. It is crucial to be attentive to how people *suffer* in their friction with the material world, that is, how they are born and grow, reproduce and die, idealise and realise in unavoidable transactions with the rest of the cosmic fabric. After all, as Maria Puig de la Bellacasa observed, 'How could we affect the worlds we want to change if we consider ourselves untouched by them?'[94] Most likely, it was their openness to being touched by the nonhuman world – their openness to the possibility that it overflows towards us humans in a way that communicates their ways of being – that enabled the Indigenous peoples of St Vincent to presage La Soufrière's eruption months before it happened.

Notes

1. Tempest Anderson & John Smith Flett, 'Preliminary report on the recent eruption of the Soufrière in St. Vincent, and of a visit to Mont Pelée, in Martinique', *Proceedings of the Royal Society of London* 70, nos. 423–45 (1902).

2. David M. Pyle, Jenni Barclay & Maria Teresa Armijos, 'The 1902–3 eruptions of the Soufrière, St Vincent: impacts, relief and response', *Journal of Volcanology and Geothermal Research* 356 (2018), 183–99.

3. Fanny Benitez, 'La catastrophe de la Montagne Pelée le 8 mai 1902 en Martinique: Saint-Pierre, une ville résiliente ou un exemple archétypal de bifurcation', *Physio-Géo* 14 (2019), 227–52.

4. Gustav Eisen, 'The earthquake and volcanic eruption in Guatemala in 1902', *Bulletin of the American Geographical Society* 35, no. 4 (1903), 325–52.

5. Pyle, Barclay & Armijos, 2018, 183–99.

6. Benitez, 2019, 227–52.

7. Hannah C. Berry, Katharine V. Cashman & Caroline A. Williams, 'Data on the 1902 Plinian eruption of Santa María volcano, Guatemala', *Data in Brief* 35 415, no. 5 (2021), 107–67.

8. Stefania Gallini, 'A Maya Mam agro-ecosystem in Guatemala's coffee revolution: Costa Cuca, 1830s–1880s'. In: Christian Brannstrom (ed.) *Territories, commodities and knowledges: Latin American environmental histories in the nineteenth and twentieth centuries.* London, Institute of Latin American Studies, 2004, 27.

9. Stephen Self, Michael R. Rampino & James J. Barbera, 'The possible effects of large 19th and 20th century volcanic eruptions on zonal and hemispheric surface temperatures', *Journal of Volcanology and Geothermal Research* 11, no. 1 (1981), 41–60; Stanley N. Williams & Stephen Self, 'The October 1902 plinian eruption of Santa Maria volcano, Guatemala', *Journal of Volcanology and Geothermal Research* 16, nos. 1–2 (1983), 33–56.

10. Anderson & Flett, 1902, 378.

11. Philip D. Morgan, 'The Caribbean environment to 1850'. In: Philip D. Morgan, John R. McNeill, Matthew Mulcahy & Stuart Schwartz (eds.) *Sea and land: an environmental history of the Caribbean.* Oxford, Oxford University Press, 2022, 37.

12. Stuart B. Schwartz, *Sea of storms: a history of hurricanes in the Greater Caribbean from Columbus to Katrina.* Princeton, NJ, and Oxford, Princeton University Press, 2015, 25.

13. Jane Bennett, *The enchantment of modern life: attachments, crossings, and ethics.* Princeton, NJ, Princeton University Press, 2001, 22.

14. Anderson & Flett, 1902, 401.

15. The initial idea for this book arose from the collaboration of the three editors within GEOPAM, a network of researchers studying the spatiotemporal construction of the Americas over an extended modern era (fifteenth to nineteenth centuries).

16. Paul Vidal de La Blache, *Principles of human geography*, transl. M.T. Bingham. London, Constable Publishers, 1926, 10.

17. Milton Santos & Maria Laura Silveira, *O Brasil: território e sociedade no início do século XXI*. São Paulo, Record, 2001, 32.

18. George Gaylord Simpson, 'History of Latin American fauna', *The American Scientist*, July 1950, 361–2.

19. Peter H. Raven, Roy E. Gereau, Peter B. Phillipson, Cyrille Chatelain, Clinton N. Jenkins & Carmen Ulloa Ulloa, 'The distribution of biodiversity richness in the tropics', *Science Advances* 6 (2020), eabc6228.

20. Theodore R. Schatzki, *The site of the social: a philosophical account of the constitution of social life and change*. University Park, Pennsylvania State University Press, 2002, 95.

21. Simpson, 1950, 362.

22. George G. Simpson, *Splendid isolation: the curious history of South American mammals*. New Haven, Yale University Press, 1980.

23. The Isthmus of Panama is the result of the plate tectonics, on the one hand (the contact between the Arc of Panama – a semi-emergent island chain – and the Sudamericana Plate) and of the climatic change on the other hand. It was a long period of time during which global glaciations lowered the sea level allowing the consolidation of the terrestrial bridge; Aaron O'Dea et al., 'Formation of the isthmus of Panama', *Science Advances* 2, no. 8 (2016), e1600883.

24. Francis G. Stehli & S. David Webb (eds.) *The great American biotic interchange: topics in geobiology*. New York, Plenum Press, 1985, 532.

25. Larry G. Marshall, S. David Webb, John Sepkoski & David M. Raup, 'Mammalian evolution and great American interchange', *Science* 215, 1351–7.

26. Carlos Jaramillo & Andrés Cárdenas, 'Global warming and neotropical rainforests: a historical perspective', *Annual Review of Earth and Planetary Sciences* 41, no. 1 (2013), 741–66.

27. Ellen C. Semple, 'The operation of geographic factors in history', *Bulletin of the American Geographical Society*, 41, no. 7 (1909), 422–39, p. 424.

28. Alfred W. Crosby, *Ecological imperialism: the biological expansion of Europe, 900–1900*. Cambridge, Cambridge University Press, 1986.

29. Sheldon Watts, 'Yellow fever immunities in West Africa and the Americas in the age of slavery and beyond: a reappraisal', *Journal of Social History* 34, no. 4 (2001), 955–67. But this is a contentious issue; see Kenneth F. Kiple, 'Response to Sheldon Watts, "Yellow fever immunities in West Africa and the Americas in the age of slavery and beyond: a reappraisal"', *Journal of Social History* 34, no. 4, (2001), 969–74.

30. By importing both *Aedes aegypti* mosquitoes and huge numbers of human hosts in the form of coerced labourers from African regions with endemic yellow fever, as well as replacing native vegetation with sugarcane monocultures and spreading cisterns and pottery fragments around (containers of clean, stagnant water which are ideal nursery grounds for mosquitoes), European colonialisation created optimum yellow fever landscapes; see John Robert McNeill, *Mosquito empires: ecology and war in the Greater Caribbean, 1620–1914*. New York, Cambridge University Press, 2010, 15–62.

31. See, for example, Serge Gruzinski, *El pensamiento mestizo: cultura Amerindia y civilización del renacimiento*, transl. E.F. González. Barcelona, Paidós, 2007; Shawn W. Miller, *An environmental history of Latin America*. New York, Cambridge University Press, 2007; Marshall C. Eakin, *The history of Latin America: collision of cultures*. New York, St Martin's Griffin, 2008; Philip D. Morgan, John R. McNeill, Matthew Mulcahy & Stuart B. Schwartz, *Sea and land: an environmental history of the Caribbean*. New York, Oxford University Press, 2022.

32. Marshall C. Eakin, 'Does Latin America have a common history?', *Vanderbilt E-Journal of Luso-Hispanic Studies* 1 (2004), 47–8.

33. Michel Gobat, 'The invention of Latin America: a transnational history of anti-imperialism, democracy, and race', *The American Historical Review* 118, no. 5 (2013), 1345–75; see also Germán A. de la Reza, 'Proyecto de Confederación latinoamericana de 1862. Un ignorado precursor boliviano de la teoría de la integración regional', *Revista Aportes Para La Integración Latinoamericana* 26, no. 42 (2020), 1–23.

34. José María Torres Caicedo, 'Las dos Américas'. In: Arturo Ardao (ed.) *Genesis de la idea y el nombre de America Latina*. Caracas, Centro de Estudios Latinoamericanos, 1980, 182, 184.

35. José Martí, 'Our America'. In: Aviva Chomsky, Barry Carr & Pamela Maria Smorkaloff (eds.) *The Cuba reader*. Durham, NC, and London, Duke University Press, 2003, 123–4; Georg M. Schwarzmann, 'Latin America as a bio-region: an ecocritical approach to José Martí's Nuestra América', *Ciberletras* 40 (2018), 69.

36. Eduardo Galeano, *Open veins of Latin America: five centuries of the pillage of a continent*, 25th anniversary ed., transl. Cedric Belfrage. New York, Monthly Review Press, 1997, 3, 267.

37. Mark Carey, 'Latin American environmental history: current trends, interdisciplinary insights, and future directions', *Environmental History* 14 (2009), 221–52, p. 230.

38. Stephanía Gallini, 'Historia, ambiente y política: el camino de la historia ambiental en América Latina', *Nómadas* 30 (2009), 92–102, p. 97.

39. David Pretel, 'The Maya forest and indigenous resistance during the Caste War', *Global Environment* 14 (2021), 120–45.

40. John Murra, *Formaciones económicas y políticas del mundo andino*. Lima, Instituto de Estudios Peruanos, 1975.

41. Augusto Cardich, 'El fenómeno de las fluctuaciones en los límites superiores del cultivo en los Andes: su importancia', *Relaciones de la Sociedad Argentina de Antropología* 14, no. 1 (1980), 7–31.

42. For an extensive overview see David Block & Monica Barnes, 'Bibliography of works by, in honor of, and about John Victor Murra', *Andean Past* 9 (2009), 48–63.

43. Sylvio Roméro, *Historia da literatura Brasileira*, vol. 1. Rio de Janeiro, H. Garnier, 1902, 49–50.

44. Gilberto Freyre, *Nordeste: aspectos da influência da cana sobre a vida e a paisagem do Nordeste do Brasil*, 7th edn. São Paulo, Global, 2004.

45. Ricardo Cassiano, *Marcha para oeste*, vols. 1–2. Rio de Janeiro, José Olympio, 1942; Jane Bennett, *Vibrant matter: a political ecology of things*. Durham, NC, and London, Duke University Press, 2010, 98–100.

46. Sérgio Buarque de Holanda, *Monções*. Rio de Janeiro, Casa do Estudante do Brasil, 1945; *Caminhos e fronteiras*, 3rd edn. São Paulo, Cia. das Letras, 1994.

47. Aziz Ab'Saber, 'Fundamentos geográficos da história brasileira'. In: Sérgio Buarque de Holanda (ed.) *História geral da civilização Brasileira*, vol.1, 17th edn. Rio de Janeiro, Bertrand Brasil, 2010, 65–82.

48. Crosby, 1986, 7.

49. Elinor G.K. Melville, *A plague of sheep: environmental consequences of the conquest of Mexico*. New York, Cambridge University Press, 1994.

50. Warren Dean, *Brazil and the struggle for rubber: a study in environmental history*. Cambridge, Cambridge University Press, 1987.

51. Warren Dean, *With broadax and firebrand: the destruction of the Brazilian Atlantic Forest*. Berkeley, University of California Press, 1995, 6.

52. Warren Dean, 'The tasks of Latin American environmental History'. In: Harold K. Steen & Richard P. Tucker (eds.) *Changing tropical forests: historical perspectives on today's challenges in Central and South America*. Durham, NC, Duke University Press, 1992, 12–13.

53. Dean, 1995, 108.

54. Steve Marquardt, '"Green havoc": Panama disease, environmental change, and labor process in the Central American banana industry', *American Historical Review* 106, no. 1 (2001), 50–1.

55. Shawn W. Miller, *An environmental history of Latin America*. Cambridge, Cambridge University Press, 2007, 2, 5.

56. Margarita Gascón (ed.) *Vientos, terremotos, tsunamis y otras catástrofes naturales: historia y casos Latinoamericanos*. Buenos Aires, Biblos, 2005, 10.

57. Margarita Gascón, 'The defense of the Spanish Empire and the agency of nature: Araucanía, Patagonia and Pampas during the seventeenth century', *Research Paper Series* 46 (2008).

58. Stuart B. Schwartz & Matthew Mulcahy, 'Natural disasters in the Caribbean to 1850'. In: Morgan et al., 2022, 187–252, p.188.

59. Louis A. Pérez, Jr., *Winds of change: hurricanes and the transformation of nineteenth-century Cuba*. Chapel Hill and London, The University of North Carolina Press, 2001, 10.

60. Michael Burn, 'On the interpretation of natural archives of Atlantic tropical cyclone activity', *Geophysical Research Letters* 48, no. 13 (2021), 11–18, p. 5; Michael Burn & Suzanne Palmer, 'Atlantic hurricane activity during the last millennium', *Scientific Report, Nature* 5, no. 12838, (2015), 1–11.

61. Alexander Berland & Georgina Endfield, 'Drought and disaster in a revolution-ary age: colonial Antigua during the American Independence War' (2018–preprint, http://livrepository.livelpoop.ac.uk); Sherry Johnson, 'Climate, community and commerce among Florida, Cuba, and the Atlantic World, 1784–1800', *The Florida Historical Quarterly* 60, no. 4 (1981), 455–82; Tristan Korten, 'The Bahamas and the Caribbean have withstood hurricanes for centuries', *Smithsonian Magazine* 17 (September 2019).

62. Schwartz & Mulcahy, 'Natural disasters in the Caribbean to 1850'. In: Morgan et al., 2022, 188.

63. Zeb Tortorici & Martha Few, 'Introduction: writing animal histories'. In: Martha Few & Zeb Tortorici (eds.) *Centering animals in Latin American History*. Durham, NC, and London, Duke University Press, 2013, 3. Similarly, Jason Hribal had observed a few years earlier that, 'to simply study the history of cows does not mean then that the historical subjects, suddenly and without much effort, become actors', Jason Hribal, 'Animals, agency, and class: writing the history of animals from below', *Human Ecology Forum* 14, no. 1 (2007), 101–12, p. 102.

64. Martha Few, 'Killing locusts in colonial Guatemala'. In: Few & Tortorici, 2013, 64.

65. Few, 2013, 69.

66. Luis Alberto Arrioja Díaz Viruell, *Bajo el Crepúsculo de los Insectos: Clima, plagas y trastornos sociales en el Reino de Guatemala (1768–1805)*. Zamora, El Colegio de Michoacan, 2019.

67. Matthew Mulcahy & Stuart Schwartz, 'Nature's battalions: insects as agricultural pests in the early modern Caribbean', *The William and Mary Quarterly* 75, no. 3 (2018), 433–64.

68. Diogo de Carvalho Cabral, 'Into the bowels of tropical earth: leaf-cutting ants and the colonial making of agrarian Brazil', *Journal of Historical Geography* 50, no. 4 (2015), 92–105, p. 105.

69. Diogo de Carvalho Cabral, 'Meaningful clearings: human-ant negotiated landscapes in nineteenth-century Brazil', *Environmental History* 26, no. 1 (2021), 55–78.

70. Christopher Lloyd, *The structures of history*. Oxford, Blackwell, 1993, 94.

71. Bruce M. S. Campbell, 'Nature as historical protagonist: environment and society in pre-industrial England', *The Economic History Review* 63, no. 2 (2010), 281–314; Geoffrey Parker, *Global crisis: war, climate change and catastrophe in the seventeenth century*. New Haven and London, Yale University Press, 2013.

72. Michael Ziser, *Environmental practice and early American literature*. Cambridge, Cambridge University Press, 2013; Diogo de Carvalho Cabral, *Na presença da floresta: Mata Atlântica e história colonial*. Rio de Janeiro, Garamond, 2014; Timothy J. LeCain, *The matter of history: how things create the past*. Cambridge, Cambridge University Press, 2017; Ewa Domanska, 'The eco-ecumene and multispecies history: the case of abandoned Protestant cemeteries in Poland'. In: Suzanne E. Pilar Birch (ed.) *Multispecies archaeology*. London, Routledge, 2018, 118–32; Emily O'Gorman & Andrea Gaynor, 'More-than-human histories', *Environmental History* 25, no. 4 (2020) 711–35; Emily O'Gorman, *Wetlands in a dry land: more-than-human histories of Australia's Murray-Darling Basin*. Seattle, University of Washington Press, 2021; Diogo de Carvalho Cabral, André Vasques Vital & Gabriel Lopes, 'Tales from the dirt: post-anthropocentric perspectives on Brazil's past', *Journal of Historical Geography* 78 (2022), 95–104. These are just the works more directly affiliated with historians' traditional approach to (written) sources, otherwise this list would have to include many others.

73. Donald Worster, 'Appendix: doing environmental history'. In: Donald Worster (ed.) *The ends of the Earth: perspectives on modern environmental history*. Cambridge, Cambridge University Press, 1988, 289–307.

74. Timothy J. LeCain, 'Deep culture: a very brief brief of the New Materialism', *Agricultural History* 96, nos. 1–2 (2022), 225–30, p. 225. To be sure, discussions of 'embodiment' in environmental history date back to the 1990s and 2000s; see, for example, Richard White, '"Are you an environmentalist or do you work for a living?": work and nature'. In: William Cronon (ed.) *Uncommon ground: rethinking the human place in nature*. New York, W. W. Norton, 1995, 171–85; Christopher Sellers, 'Thoreau's body: towards an embodied environmental history', *Environmental History* 4, no. 4 (1999), 486–514; Linda Nash, 'The agency of nature or the nature of agency', *Environmental History* 10, no. 1 (2005), 67–9.

75. For an opposing voice, see Joshua Specht, '"Animal history after its triumph": unexpected animals, evolutionary approaches, and the animal lens', *History Compass* 14, no. 7 (2016), 326–36.

76. Philip Howell, 'Animals, agency, and history'. In: Hilda Kean & Philip Howell (eds.) *The Routledge handbook of animal-human history*. London, Routledge, 2018, 197–221.

77. Richard White, 'American environmental history: the development of a new historical field', *Pacific Historical Review* 54, no. 3 (1985), 297–335, p. 335.

78. Crosby, *Ecological imperialism*; *The Columbian exchange: biological and cultural consequences of 1492*. Westport, CT, Greenwood Press, 1972; Donald Worster, *Dust bowl: the southern plains in the 1930s*. New York, Oxford University Press, 1979.

79. Howell, 2018, 207.

80. Dean, 1995, 6.

81. 'The interrelationships of any ecological system', Dean wrote, 'are much too complex to offer the hope of a deterministic explanation'; Dean, 1995, 61.

82. Donald Worster, 'Transformations of the Earth: toward an agroecological perspective in history', *Journal of American History* 76, no. 4 (1990), 1087–106, p. 1106.

83. Erik Swingedouw, 'The city as a hybrid: on nature, society and cyborg urbanization', *Capitalism Nature Socialism* 7, no. 2 (1996), 65–80, p. 74.

84. Pérez, 2001, 11.

85. Lucien Febvre & Lionel Bataillon, *A geographical introduction to history*, transl. E.G. Mountford and J.H. Paxton. London, Kegan Paul, 1925.

86. Fernand Braudel, *The Mediterranean and the Mediterranean world in the age of Philip II*, vol. 1, transl. S. Reynolds. London and New York, Harper & Row, 1972, 267, 269.

87. Emmanuel Le Roy Ladurie, *Times of feast, times of famine: a history of climate since the year 1000*, transl. Barbara Bray. Garden City, NY, Doubleday and Co., 1971, 7, 11, 16–8, 20, 22.

88. Eduardo Kohn, 'Anthropology of ontologies', *Annual Review of Anthropology* 44, no. 1 (2015), 311–27, p. 312.

89. Eduardo Viveiros de Castro, *Araweté: os deuses canibais*. Rio de Janeiro, Jorge Zahar Editor/Anpocs, 1986; A natureza em pessoa. Encontro Visões do Rio Babel – Conversas sobre o futuro da bacia do Rio Negro. Manaus, Instituto Socioambiental e Fundação Vitória Amazônica, 2007. Among environmental historians, Amerindian perspectivism has been used mainly in studies on the human relationships with animals and forests, as well as the ontological alternatives that, with the advent of the Anthropocene, emerge to thinking about nonhuman agency in general; see Regina Horta Duarte, 'História dos animais no Brasil: tradições culturais, historiografia e transformação', *Historia Ambiental Latinoamericana y Caribeña (HALAC) Revista de la Solcha* 9, no. 2 (2019), 16–44; Carlos Frederico Branco, Miguel Angelo Perondi & Joao Daniel D. Ramos, 'Fág e Nen: Araucária e Floresta no Coletivo Kaingang', *Historia Ambiental Latinoamericana y Caribeña (HALAC) Revista de la Solcha* 13, no. 1 (2023), 165–87; Nicolás Cuvi, 'Indigenous imprints and remnants in the Tropical Andes'. In: John Soluri, Claudia Leal & José Augusto Pádua (eds.) *A living past: environmental histories of modern Latin America*. New York: Berghahn Books, 2018, 67–90; André Felipe Silva & Gabriel Lopes, 'Entre horizontes e sedimentos: o impacto do Antropoceno na história a partir de Chakrabarty e seus interlocutores', *Historia Ambiental Latinoamericana y Caribeña (HALAC) Revista de la Solcha* 11, no. 2 (2021), 348–96.

90. Howell, 2018, 203–4.

91. Diogo de Carvalho Cabral & André Vasques Vital, 'Multispecies emergent textualities: writing and reading in ecologies of selves', *ISLE: Interdisciplinary Studies in Literature and Environment* 30, no. 3, (2023), 705–27.

92. Hannes Bergthaller, Rob Emmett, Adeline Johns-Putra, Agnes Kneitz, Susanna Lidström, Shane McCorristine, Isabel Pérez Ramos, Dana Phillips, Kate

Rigby & Libby Robin, 'Mapping common ground: ecocriticism, environmental history, and the environmental humanities', *Environmental Humanities* 5, no. 1 (2012), 261–76.

93. Thomas P. Waldemer, 'The great chain of being: ecocriticism in Abel Poss's "Daimon"', *Romance Notes* 44, no. 1 (2003), 51–9; Adrian Taylor Kane (ed.) *The natural world in Latin American literatures: ecocritical essays on twentieth century writings*. Jefferson, NC, McFarland, 2010; Elaine Savory, 'Toward a Caribbean ecopoetics: Derek Walcott's language of plants'. In: Elizabeth DeLoughrey & George B. Handley (eds.) *Postcolonial ecologies: literatures of the environment*. Oxford, Oxford University Press, 2011, 80–96; Supriya Nair, 'Caribbean ecopoetics: dwellings in the *Castle of My Skin, Palace of the Peacock* and *A House for Mr Biswas*'. In: Michael A.Bucknor & Alison Donnell (eds.) *The Routledge companion to Anglophone Caribbean literature*. London, Routledge, 2011; Camilo Jaramillo, 'Green hells: monstrous vegetations in twentieth-century representations of Amazonia'. In: Dawn Keetley & Angela Tenga (eds.) *Plant horror*. London, Palgrave Macmillan, 2016; André Vasques Vital & Sandro Dutra e Silva, 'Darkness in the seasonal Savannah: the Brazilian Cerrado in stories by Hugo De Carvalho Ramos', *E-Tropic: Electronic Journal of Studies in the Tropics* 21, no. 1 (2022), 239–58; Laura Cristina Fernández, Amadeo Gandolfo & Pablo Turnes, *Burning down the house: Latin American comics in the 21st century*. London, Routledge, 2023.

94. Maria Puig de la Bellacasa, 'Foreword'. In: Juan Francisco Salazar, Céline Granjou, Matthew Kearnes, Anna Krzywoszynska & Manuel Tironi (eds.) *Thinking with soils: material politics and social theory*. London, Bloomsbury, 2020, xiv.

References

Ab'Saber, Aziz, 'Fundamentos geográficos da história brasileira'. In: Sérgio Buarque de Holanda (ed.) *História geral da civilização Brasileira*, vol.1, 17th edn. Rio de Janeiro, Bertrand Brasil, 2010, 65–82.

Anderson, Tempest & John Smith Flett, 'Preliminary report on the recent eruption of the Soufrière in St. Vincent, and of a visit to Mont Pelée, in Martinique', *Proceedings of the Royal Society of London* 70, nos. 423–45 (1902).

Arrioja Díaz Viruell, Luis Alberto, *Bajo el Crepúsculo de los Insectos : Clima, plagas y trastornos sociales en el Reino de Guatemala (1768–1805)*. Zamora, El Colegio de Michoacan, 2019.

Benitez, Fanny, 'La catastrophe de la Montagne Pelée le 8 mai 1902 en Martinique : Saint-Pierre, une ville résiliente ou un exemple arché-typal de bifurcation', *Physio-Géo* 14 (2019), 227–52.

Bennett, Jane, *The enchantment of modern life: attachments, crossings, and ethics*. Princeton, NJ, Princeton University Press, 2001.

Bennett, Jane, *Vibrant matter: a political ecology of things*. Durham, NC, and London, Duke University Press, 2010.

Bergthaller, Hannes, Rob Emmett, Adeline Johns-Putra, Agnes Kneitz, Susanna Lidström, Shane McCorristine, Isabel Pérez Ramos, Dana Phillips, Kate Rigby & Libby Robin, 'Mapping common ground: ecocriticism, environmental history, and the environmental humanities', *Environmental Humanities* 5, no. 1 (2012), 261–76.

Berland, Alexander & Georgina Endfield, 'Drought and disaster in a revolutionary age: Colonial Antigua during the American Independence War', *Environment and History* 24 (2018), 209–35.

Berry, Hannah C., Katharine V. Cashman & Caroline A. Williams, 'Data on the 1902 Plinian eruption of Santa María volcano, Guatemala', *Data in Brief* 35, no. 5 (2021), 107–67.

Block, David & Monica Barnes, 'Bibliography of works by, in honor of, and about John Victor Murra', *Andean Past* 9 (2009), 48–63.

Branco, Carlos Frederico, Miguel Angelo Perondi & Joao Daniel D. Ramos, 'Fág e Nen: Araucária e Floresta no Coletivo Kaingang', *Historia Ambiental Latinoamericana y Caribeña (HALAC) Revista de la Solcha* 13, no. 1 (2023), 165–87.

Braudel, Fernand, *The Mediterranean and the Mediterranean world in the age of Philip II*, vol. 1, transl. S. Reynolds. London and New York, Harper & Row, 1972.

Buarque de Holanda, Sérgio, *Monções*. Rio de Janeiro, Casa do Estudante do Brasil, 1945 ; *Caminhos e fronteiras*, 3rd edn. São Paulo, Cia. das Letras, 1994.

Burn, Michael, 'On the interpretation of natural archives of Atlantic tropical cyclone activity', *Geophysical Research Letters* 48, no. 13 (2021), 11–18.

Burn, Michael & Suzanne Palmer, 'Atlantic hurricane activity during the last millennium', *Scientific Report, Nature* 5, no. 12838 (2015), 1–11.

Campbell, Bruce M. S., 'Nature as historical protagonist: environment and society in pre-industrial England', *The Economic History Review* 63, no. 2 (2010), 281–314.

Cardich, Augusto, 'El fenómeno de las fluctuaciones en los límites superiores del cultivo en los Andes: su importancia', *Relaciones de la Sociedad Argentina de Antropología* 14, no. 1 (1980), 7–31.

Carey, Mark, 'Latin American environmental history: current trends, interdisciplinary insights, and future directions', *Environmental History* 14 (2009), 221–52.

Cassiano, Ricardo, *Marcha para oeste*, vols. 1–2, Rio de Janeiro, José Olympio, 1942.

Crosby, Alfred W., *Ecological imperialism: the biological expansion of Europe, 900–1900.* Cambridge, Cambridge University Press, 1986.

Crosby, Alfred W., *Ecological imperialism; The Columbian exchange: biological and cultural consequences of 1492.* Westport, CT, Greenwood Press, 1972.

Cuvi, Nicolás. 'Indigenous imprints and remnants in the Tropical Andes'. In: John Soluri, Claudia Leal & José Augusto Pádua (eds.) *A living past: environmental histories of modern Latin America.* New York, Berghahn Books, 2018, 67–90.

Dean, Warren, *Brazil and the struggle for rubber: a study in environmental history.* Cambridge, Cambridge University Press, 1987.

Dean, Warren, *With broadax and firebrand: the destruction of the Brazilian Atlantic Forest.* Berkeley, University of California Press, 1995.

Dean, Warren, 'The tasks of Latin American environmental history'. In: Harold K. Steen & Richard P. Tucker (eds.) *Changing tropical forests: historical perspectives on today's challenges in Central and South America.* Durham, NC, Duke University Press, 1992, 5–15.

de Carvalho Cabral, Diogo de, 'Into the bowels of tropical earth: leaf-cutting ants and the colonial making of agrarian Brazil', *Journal of Historical Geography* 50, no. 4 (2015), 92–105.

de Carvalho Cabral, Diogo de, 'Meaningful clearings: human-ant negotiated landscapes in nineteenth-century Brazil', *Environmental History* 26, no. 1 (2021), 55–78.

de Carvalho Cabral, Diogo de, *Na presença da floresta: Mata Atlântica e história colonial.* Rio de Janeiro, Garamond, 2014.

de Carvalho Cabral, Diogo de & André Vasques Vital, 'Multispecies emergent textualities: writing and reading in ecologies of selves', *ISLE: Interdisciplinary Studies in Literature and Environment* 30, no. 3, (2023), 705–27.

de Carvalho Cabral, Diogo de, André Vasques Vital & Gabriel Lopes, 'Tales from the dirt: post-anthropocentric perspectives on Brazil's past', *Journal of Historical Geography* 78 (2022), 95–104.

De la Reza, Germán A., 'Proyecto de Confederación latinoamericana de 1862. Un ignorado precursor boliviano de la teoría de la integración regional', *Revista Aportes Para La Integración Latinoamericana* 26, no. 42 (2020), 1–23.

Domanska, Ewa, 'The eco-ecumene and multispecies history: the case of abandoned Protestant cemeteries in Poland'. In: Suzanne E. Pilar Birch (ed.) *Multispecies archaeology*. London, Routledge, 2018, 118–32.

Eakin, Marshall C., 'Does Latin America have a common history?', *Vanderbilt E-Journal of Luso-Hispanic Studies* 1 (2004), 47–8.

Eakin, Marshall C., *The history of Latin America: collision of cultures*. New York, St Martin's Griffin, 2008.

Eisen, Gustav, 'The earthquake and volcanic eruption in Guatemala in 1902', *Bulletin of the American Geographical Society* 35, no. 4 (1903), 325–52.

Febvre, Lucien & Lionel Bataillon, *A geographical introduction to history*, transl. E.G. Mountford and J.H. Paxton. London, Kegan Paul, 1925.

Fernández, Amadeo Gandolfo, Laura Cristina & Pablo Turnes, *Burning down the house: Latin American comics in the 21st century*. London, Routledge, 2023.

Freyre, Gilberto, *Nordeste: aspectos da influência da cana sobre a vida e a paisagem do Nordeste do Brasil*, 7th edn. São Paulo, Global, 2004.

Galeano, Eduardo, *Open veins of Latin America: five centuries of the pillage of a continent*, 25th anniversary edn., transl. Cedric Belfrage. New York, Monthly Review Press, 1997.

Gallini, Stefania, 'Historia, ambiente y política: el camino de la historia ambiental en América Latina', *Nómadas* 30 (2009), 92–102.

Gallini, Stefania, 'A Maya Mam agro-ecosystem in Guatemala's coffee revolution: Costa Cuca, 1830s–1880s'. In: Christian Brannstrom (ed.) *Territories, commodities and knowledges: Latin American environmental histories in the nineteenth and twentieth centuries*. London, Institute of Latin American Studies, 2004, 23–49.

Gascón, Margarita (ed.), 'The defense of the Spanish Empire and the agency of nature. Araucanía, Patagonia and Pampas during the seventeenth century', *Research Paper Series* 46 (2008).

Gascón, Margarita (ed.), *Vientos, terremotos, tsunamis y otras catástrofes naturales : historia y casos Latinoamericanos*. Buenos Aires, Biblos, 2005.

Gobat, Michel, 'The invention of Latin America: a transnational history of anti-imperialism, democracy, and race', *The American Historical Review* 118, no. 5 (2013), 1345–75.

Gruzinski, Serge, *El pensamiento mestizo: cultura Amerindia y civilización del renacimiento*, transl. E.F. González. Barcelona, Paidós, 2007.

Horta Duarte, Regina, 'História dos animais no Brasil : tradições culturais, historiografia e transformação', *Historia Ambiental Latinoamericana y Caribeña (HALAC) Revista de la Solcha* 9, no. 2 (2019), 16–44.

Howell, Philip, 'Animals, agency, and history'. In: Hilda Kean & Philip Howell (eds.) *The Routledge handbook of animal-human history*. London, Routledge, 2018, 197–221.

Hribal, Jason, 'Animals, agency, and class: writing the history of animals from below', *Human Ecology Forum* 14, no. 1 (2007), 101–12.

Jaramillo, Camilo, 'Green hells: monstrous vegetations in twentieth-century representations of Amazonia'. In: Dawn Keetley & Angela Tenga (eds.) *Plant horror*. London, Palgrave Macmillan, 2016, 91–109.

Jaramillo, Carlos & Andrés Cárdenas, 'Global warming and neotropical rainforests: a historical perspective', *Annual Review of Earth and Planetary Sciences* 41, no. 1 (2013), 741–66.

Johnson, Sherry, 'Climate, community and commerce among Florida, Cuba, and the Atlantic World, 1784–1800', *The Florida Historical Quarterly* 60, no. 4 (1981), 455–82.

Kane, Adrian Taylor (ed.) *The natural world in Latin American literatures: ecocritical essays on twentieth century writings*. Jefferson, NC, McFarland, 2010.

Kiple, Kenneth F., 'Response to Sheldon Watts, "Yellow fever immunities in West Africa and the Americas in the Age of Slavery and beyond: A reappraisal"', *Journal of Social History* 34, no. 4 (2001), 969–74.

Kohn, Eduardo, 'Anthropology of ontologies', *Annual Review of Anthropology* 44, no. 1 (2015), 311–27.

Korten, Tristan, 'The Bahamas and the Caribbean have withstood hurricanes for centuries', *Smithsonian Magazine* 17 (September 2019).

LeCain, Timothy J., 'Deep culture: A very brief of the New Materialism', *Agricultural History* 96, nos. 1–2 (2022), 225–30.

LeCain, Timothy J., *The matter of history: how things create the past*. Cambridge, Cambridge University Press, 2017.

Le Roy Ladurie, Emmanuel, *Times of feast, times of famine: a history of climate since the year 1000*, transl. Barbara Bray. Garden City, NY, Doubleday and Co., 1971.

Lloyd, Christopher, *The structures of history*. Oxford, Blackwell, 1993.

Marquardt, Steve, '"Green havoc": Panama disease, environmental change, and labor process in the Central American banana industry', *American Historical Review* 106, no. 1 (2001), 50–1.

Marshall, Larry G., S. David Webb, John Sepkoski & David M. Raup, 'Mammalian evolution and great American interchange', *Science* 215 (1982), 1351–7.

Martí, José, 'Our America'. In: Aviva Chomsky, Barry Carr & Pamela Maria Smorkaloff (eds.) *The Cuba reader*. Durham, NC, and London, Duke University Press, 2003.

McNeill, John Robert, *Mosquito empires: ecology and war in the Greater Caribbean, 1620–1914*. New York, Cambridge University Press, 2010.

Melville, Elinor G.K., *A plague of sheep: environmental consequences of the conquest of Mexico*. New York, Cambridge University Press, 1994.

Miller, Shawn W., *An environmental history of Latin America*. New York, Cambridge University Press, 2007.

Morgan, Philip D., 'The Caribbean environment to 1850'. In: Philip D. Morgan, John R. McNeill, Matthew Mulcahy & Stuart Schwartz (eds.) *Sea and land: an environmental history of the Caribbean*. Oxford, Oxford University Press, 2022, 19–129.

Morgan, Philip D., John R. McNeill, Matthew Mulcahy & Stuart B. Schwartz, *Sea and land: an environmental history of the Caribbean*. New York, Oxford University Press, 2022.

Mulcahy, Matthew & Stuart Schwartz, 'Nature's battalions: insects as agricultural pests in the early modern Caribbean', *The William and Mary Quarterly* 75, no. 3 (2018), 433–64.

Murra, John, *Formaciones económicas y políticas del mundo andino*. Lima, Instituto de Estudios Peruanos, 1975.

Nair, Supriya, 'Caribbean ecopoetics: dwellings in the *Castle of My Skin*, *Palace of the Peacock* and *A House for Mr Biswas*'. In: Michael A. Bucknor & Alison Donnell (eds.) *The Routledge companion to Anglophone Caribbean literature*. London, Routledge, 2011, 173–80.

Nash, Linda, 'The agency of nature or the nature of agency', *Environmental History* 10, no. 1 (2005), 67–9.

O'Dea, Aaron et al., 'Formation of the isthmus of Panama', *Science Advances* 2, no. 8 (2016), e1600883.

O'Gorman, Emily & Andrea Gaynor, 'More-than-human histories', *Environmental History* 25, no. 4 (2020), 711–35.

O'Gorman, Emily & Andrea Gaynor, *Wetlands in a dry land: more-than-human histories of Australia's Murray-Darling Basin*. Seattle, University of Washington Press, 2021.

Parker, Geoffrey, *Global crisis: war, climate change and catastrophe in the seventeenth century*. New Haven and London, Yale University Press, 2013.

Pérez, Jr., Louis A., *Winds of change: hurricanes and the transformation of nineteenth-century Cuba*. Chapel Hill and London, The University of North Carolina Press, 2001.

Pretel, David, 'The Maya forest and indigenous resistance during the Caste War', *Global Environment* 14 (2021), 120–45.

Puig de la Bellacasa, Maria, 'Foreword'. In: Juan Francisco Salazar, Céline Granjou, Matthew Kearnes, Anna Krzywoszynska & Manuel Tironi (eds.) *Thinking with soils: material politics and social theory*. London, Bloomsbury, 2020, xii–xv.

Pyle, David M., Jenni Barclay & Maria Teresa Armijos, 'The 1902–3 eruptions of the Soufrière, St Vincent: impacts, relief and response', *Journal of Volcanology and Geothermal Research* 356 (2018), 183–99.

Raven, Peter H., Roy E. Gereau, Peter B. Phillipson, Cyrille Chatelain, Clinton N. Jenkins & Carmen Ulloa Ulloa, 'The distribution of biodiversity richness in the tropics', *Science Advances* 6 (2020), https://doi.org/abc6228

Roméro, Sylvio, *Historia da literatura Brasileira*, vol. 1. Rio de Janeiro, H. Garnier, 1902.

Santos, Milton & Maria Laura Silveira, *O Brasil: território e sociedade no início do século XXI*. São Paulo, Record, 2001.

Savory, Elaine, 'Toward a Caribbean ecopoetics: Derek Walcott's language of plants'. In: Elizabeth DeLoughrey & George B. Handley (eds.) *Postcolonial ecologies: literatures of the environment*. Oxford, Oxford University Press, 2011, 80–96.

Schatzki, Theodore R., *The site of the social: a philosophical account of the constitution of social life and change*. University Park, Pennsylvania State University Press, 2002.

Schwartz, Stuart B., *Sea of storms: a history of hurricanes in the Greater Caribbean from Columbus to Katrina*. Princeton, NJ, and Oxford, Princeton University Press, 2015.

Schwartz, Stuart B. & Matthew Mulcahy, 'Natural disasters in the Caribbean to 1850'. In: Morgan et al., *Sea and land: an environmental history of the Caribbean*. New York, Oxford University Press, 2022, 187–252.

Schwarzmann, Georg M., 'Latin America as a bio-region: an ecocritical approach to José Martí's Nuestra América', *Ciberletras* 40 (2018), 64–75.

Self, Stephen, Michael R. Rampino & James J. Barbera, 'The possible effects of large 19th and 20th century volcanic eruptions on zonal and hemispheric surface temperatures', *Journal of Volcanology and Geothermal Research* 11, no. 1 (1981), 41–60.

Sellers, Christopher, 'Thoreau's body: towards an embodied environmental history', *Environmental History* 4, no. 4 (1999), 486–514.

Semple, Ellen C., 'The operation of geographic factors in history', *Bulletin of the American Geographical Society* 41, no. 7 (1909), 422–39.

Silva, André Felipe & Gabriel Lopes, 'Entre horizontes e sedimentos: o impacto do Antropoceno na história a partir de Chakrabarty e seus interlocutores', *Historia Ambiental Latinoamericana y Caribeña (HALAC) Revista de la Solcha* 11, no. 2 (2021), 348–96.

Simpson, George Gaylord, 'History of Latin American fauna', *The American Scientist*, July 1950, 361–2.

Simpson, George Gaylord, *Splendid isolation: the curious history of South American mammals*. New Haven, Yale University Press, 1980.

Specht, Joshua, '"Animal history after its triumph": unexpected animals, evolutionary approaches, and the animal lens', *History Compass* 14, no. 7 (2016), 326–36.

Stehli, Francis G. & S. David Webb (eds.) *The great American biotic interchange: topics in geobiology*. New York, Plenum Press, 1985.

Swingedouw, Erik, 'The city as a hybrid: on nature, society and cyborg urbanization', *Capitalism Nature Socialism* 7, no. 2 (1996), 65–80.

Torres Caicedo, José María, 'Las dos Américas'. In: Arturo Ardao (ed.) *Genesis de la idea y el nombre de America Latina*. Caracas, Centro de Estudios Latinoamericanos, 1980, 175–85.

Tortorici Zeb & Martha Few, 'Introduction: writing animal histories'. In: Martha Few & Zeb Tortorici (eds.) *Centering animals in Latin American history*. Durham, NC, and London, Duke University Press, 2013.

Vasques Vital, André & Sandro Dutra e Silva, 'Darkness in the seasonal Savannah: the Brazilian Cerrado in stories by Hugo De Carvalho Ramos', *E-Tropic: Electronic Journal of Studies in the Tropics* 21, no. 1 (2022), 239–58.

Vidal de La Blache, Paul, *Principles of human geography*, transl. M.T. Bingham. London, Constable Publishers, 1926.

Viveiros de Castro, Eduardo. *Araweté: os deuses canibais*. Rio de Janeiro, Jorge Zahar Editor/Anpocs, 1986.

Viveiros de Castro, Eduardo. A natureza em pessoa. Encontro Visões do Rio Babel – Conversas sobre o futuro da bacia do Rio Negro. Manaus, Instituto Socioambiental e Fundação Vitória Amazônica, 2007.

Waldemer, Thomas P., 'The great chain of being: ecocriticism in Abel Poss's "Daimon"', *Romance Notes* 44, no. 1 (2003), 51–9.

Watts, Sheldon, 'Yellow fever immunities in West Africa and the Americas in the age of slavery and beyond: a reappraisal', *Journal of Social History* 34, no. 4 (2001), 955–67.

White, Richard, 'American environmental history: the development of a new historical field', *Pacific Historical Review* 54, no. 3 (1985), 297–335.

White, Richard, '"Are you an environmentalist or do you work for a living?": work and nature'. In: William Cronon (ed.) *Uncommon ground: rethinking the human place in nature*. New York, W. W. Norton, 1995, 171–85.

Williams, Stanley N. & Stephen Self, 'The October 1902 plinian eruption of Santa Maria volcano, Guatemala', *Journal of Volcanology and Geothermal Research* 16, nos. 1–2 (1983), 33–56.

Worster, Donald, 'Appendix: doing environmental history'. In: Donald Worster (ed.) *The ends of the Earth: perspectives on modern environmental history*. Cambridge, Cambridge University Press, 1988, 289–307.

Worster, Donald, *Dust bowl: the southern plains in the 1930s*. New York, Oxford University Press, 1979.

Worster, Donald, 'Transformations of the Earth: toward an agroecological perspective in history', *Journal of American History* 76, no. 4 (1990), 1087–106.

Ziser, Michael, *Environmental practice and early American literature*. Cambridge, Cambridge University Press, 2013.

Chapter 1

Performative objects: Konduri iconography as a window into precolonial Amazonian ontologies

Luisa Vidal de Oliveira and Denise Maria Cavalcante Gomes
Translated by Diogo de Carvalho Cabral

This chapter deals with the figuration of nonhuman beings in precolonial Amazonia, based on the iconographic analysis of Konduri ceramic artefacts (1000–1500 A.D.). We interpret zooanthropomorphic images and non-recognisable beings through a theoretical approximation between archaeology and Amerindian ethnology. Ours is a relational approach that decentres humans and emphasises the entanglement of socio-cosmological relations between different collectives and the Amerindian world's characteristic transformability. The leading author analysed 188 ceramic fragments from the Konduri collection of the National Museum, which was constituted through excavations and donations from scientific expeditions to the regions of the Trombetas and Nhamundá rivers, in the Lower Amazon, during the nineteenth and early twentieth centuries. The co-author, in turn, analysed another collection belonging to the Integrated Museum of Óbidos (Pará) containing eighty-five fragments.

Konduri ceramics is notorious for its unique style of figuration and the intense use of incised and punctate elements, which are abundant on the artefacts' surface. Its analysis allows us to discuss bodily transformation in Amazonian anthropology, emphasising the ambivalence of figurations. The Konduri duality enhances our visual perception and leads to the multiplicity, to the plurality of images. Therefore, approaching the relationship between humans and nonhumans in Konduri ceramics allows us to reveal fragments of a complex universe of relationships between beings that are not easily defined as humans, animals or artefacts. We approach these relationships through the movements the images engender, some occurring only at the ocular level.

Initial research by Peter Paul Hilbert in the 1950s showed that Konduri pottery is distributed across the region of the Trombetas and Nhamundá rivers, in the Lower Amazon, up to the confluence of both with the Amazon River, in the state of Pará. However, there are also occurrences further west, in Parintins, on the border with the Brazilian state of Amazonas[1] (Map 1.1). Peter Paul Hilbert and Klaus Hilbert continued their archaeological research in the region of the Trombetas-Nhamundá rivers in the 1970s, dating Konduri ceramics between the eleventh and sixteenth centuries A.D., linked to the incised and punctate tradition.[2] Guapindaia examined several sites in the Porto Trombetas region to address social complexity, primarily through an analysis of the sophisticated ceramics found in large settlements. Finding no conclusive evidence to support her social complexity hypothesis, she offered instead a regional chronology and described the ceramics' technology and style.[3]

Jácome and Jaime Xamen Wai Wai established ethnoarchaeological correlations between Konduri ceramics and shamanism.[4] Thus, one observes a significant change in the theoretical underpinnings of archaeological research on the Konduri culture over the last few decades. Initially influenced by cultural-historical approaches linked in the 1990s and 2000s to neo-evolutionist hypotheses about the emergence of complex and politically centralised societies (somewhat discredited nowadays), researchers gradually turned to symbolism, shamanism and ontologies. They now ask questions about the founding institutions of Amazonian Indigenous societies, an approach that shows great potential for revealing past social forms when coupled with iconographic analysis.

Recent interpretations of Konduri iconography by Alves have focused on overlapping figures, emphasising iconicity and rejecting their association with the concept of double and relating ornithomorphic motifs and seated zooanthropomorphic beings with the representation of shamans.[5] Alves's argument derives from a representational approach. Visual elements challenging the ontological perception were relegated to the decorative scope, and plural images were understood as style, remaining invisible.

The Konduri images connect the visible and the invisible, challenging the notion of representation. Here we propose an interpretation of two of this style's most important visual themes, the superimposed figures and the zooanthropomorphic beings with head adornments, both wrapped in incised-punctate fillets. We argue that their figuration is performative,

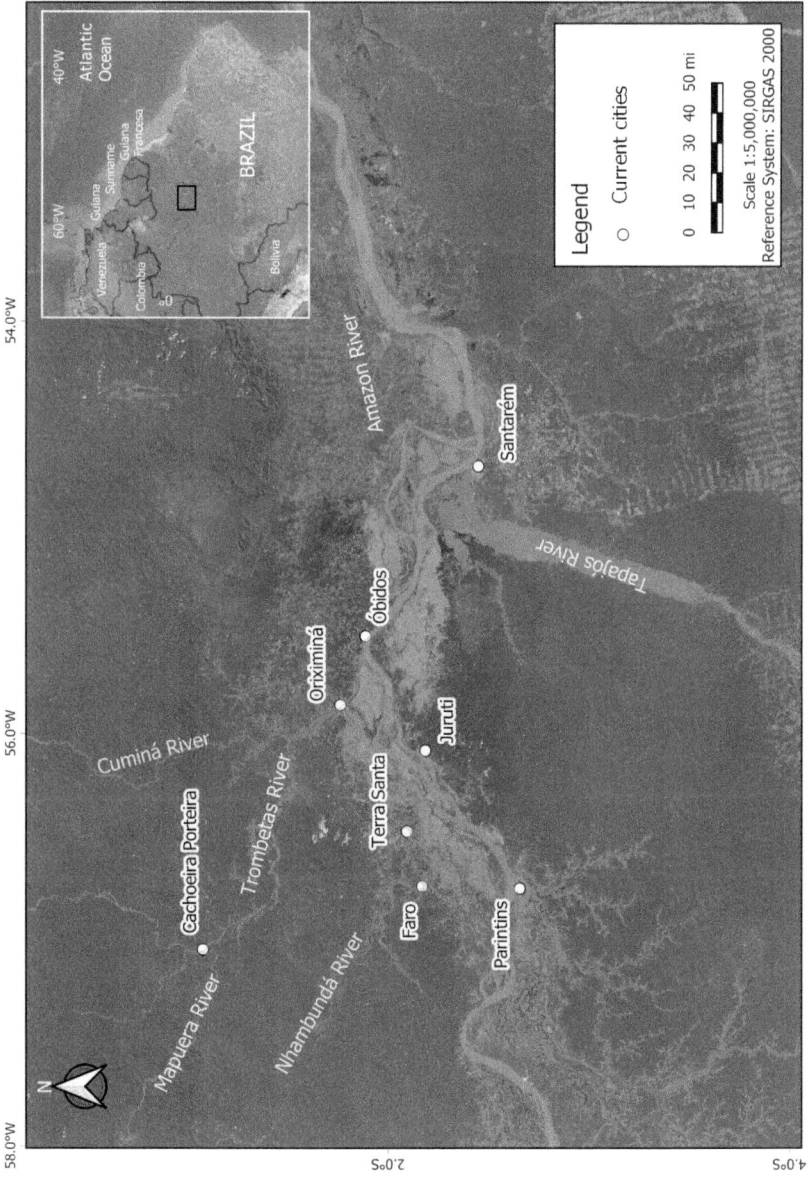

Map 1.1: Area of occurrence of Konduri pottery in the Lower Amazon, Brazil. Elaborated by João Paulo Lopes da Cunha.

that is, the images emerge from their relationship with the observer, either through the manipulation of objects or the acts of looking. Konduri iconography is interpreted from an animist/perspectivist approach, which considers the concept of multinaturalism and the idea of an anthropology beyond the human. Only through this lens do the artefacts reveal themselves as supernatural beings, and the suggested figures multiply in the context of shamanic practices.

Following recent trends in questioning the separation between nature and society, humans and nonhumans, signs and things – which link to the notion of the Anthropocene – we adopt a critical stance towards anthropocentrism.[6] Planet Earth emerges as an agent at the same time one and multiple, surpassing us human beings in all its dimensions. The challenges it poses require a relational approach considering all beings, their ontological differences and their territories as a geo-ontology.[7] This implies reshaping knowledge-production processes as forms of political-diplomatic translation in the scientific, political and aesthetic arenas to better understand the Indigenous past and face global and local challenges. Anthropology is invited to strategically reposition itself as a comparative methodology, translating concepts and modes of being also from nonhuman points of view.[8] Concerning understanding Indigenous material culture, the ontological turn problematises images from an animist point of view, seeking the relationships between humans, animals, spirits and artefacts, among other cosmological categories.[9]

The ethnological study of perception and other modes of figuration

To analyse the Konduri images, we departed from a naturalistic conception of the anthropomorphic and zoomorphic concepts, compatible with the nature–culture dichotomy, to arrive at their problematisation as a methodological equivocation.[10] Thus, the same categories – human, animal, artefact – that initially helped us to recognise patterns also showed us their insufficiency. Unlike animist ontologies, centred on human–animal relationships, in Konduri culture the artefacts play a central role. For example, headdresses emerge as distinctive features of supernatural zooanthropomorphic beings, revealing animacy and agency. Other ontological categories are expressed through dynamic visual strategies and focal alternation. These strategies point to the performative quality of ceramics and their images, which can only be seen from certain angles or points of view.[11] In other words, its ambiguous mode of figuration includes the observer, who becomes a participant in the performance. The tactile experience (the direct manipulation of objects) is fundamental in experiencing relational ontologies through materiality and sensoriality.[12] The formal and iconographic analysis allows approaching them in their relationship with shamanic knowledge in the Amazonian societies of the past.[13]

We analysed a group of fragments with common and well-discernible characteristics within the total of appendices, which are the different types of external features added to the object's main body, especially in the form of three-dimensional figures. The images present the visual theme of zooanthropomorphic beings with head ornaments (Figure 1.1) and superimposed figures. Originally called 'double face' by Hilbert, the superimposed figures comprise a larger zooanthropomorphic figure, with another smaller figure placed on top of its head (Figure 1.2). Generally, the smaller figure has a dotted fillet surrounding the composition, as long arms that embrace the more prominent figure, with the hands represented at their ends. It is important to emphasise the significant variability of this theme and the different plausible interpretations of elements such as the eyes, mouth, nose, wings and paws, which demonstrate the multivocal nature of Konduri compositions.

At first, the zoomorphic-anthropomorphic distinction helped us perceive differences and pointed to the formation of other possible categories and modes of figuration. This 'equivocated' methodology meets with the theoretical possibilities arising from the confluence of material studies,

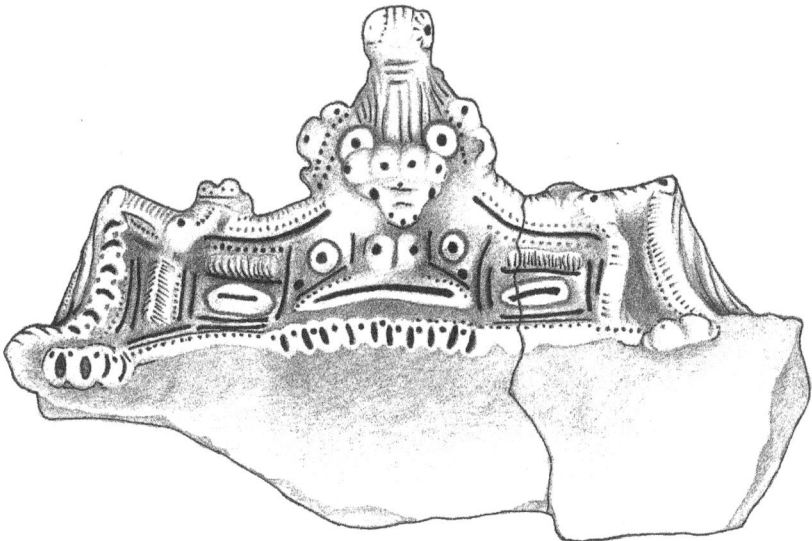

Figure 1.1: Fragment of the edge of a ceramic bowl. The figure bears a head adornment superimposed on a face with nonhuman morphological characteristics. Casa de Cultura de Oriximiná. Drawing by Luisa Vidal de Oliveira.

Figure 1.2: Fragment of the edge of a ceramic vessel with a chimerical representation of a zoomorphic being from which another figure emerges, as evidenced by an eye. Both are side-faced figures. Museu Integrado de Óbidos. Photograph by Denise Gomes.

Amazonian perspectivist anthropology and a renewed interest in figuration, preparing fertile ground for the archaeological study of precolonial iconographies.[14] Several authors have recognised the importance of questioning the modern Western concept of representation in the study of figuration. The anthropologists of art propose new methods and epistemologies that transform our way of seeing through animist/perspectivist visual technologies.[15]

The identification of a perspectivist iconography meets with Amazonian theories, centred on corporeity and the aesthetic production of artefacts and persons. The relationship between persons and things becomes more complex as ethnographies describe the ontological status of objects in Amazonian cosmologies.[16] In Amazonian mythologies, 'things, objects, artifacts, or at least some of these, are considered subjectivities that have a social life' that remains hidden and invisible to most people.[17] Their visibility is relational, created by the hands of artificers (especially shamans), in some cases capable of endowing them with a soul or controlling their agency. In some of these cosmologies, creating an ex-nihilo world gives way to transformations based on existing beings.[18] Amazonian peoples understand artefacts such as headdresses as compositions made from the reorganisation and rearrangement of body parts of different animals and materials – they are beings made out of other beings.[19]

Oliveira proposed that the headdresses depicted in Konduri ceramics were full of multiple interiorities, visible or only suggested, and that they should be interpreted as artefacts composed of parts of animal bodies that reveal the interiority of these beings, in certain circumstances. On the other hand, the emergence of small faces at the ends of the linear body of superimposed figures (hands, paws and joints) is an example that helps understand how headdresses oscillate between artefactual appearance and animated interiority.[20] This subjectivising mode of figuration reaffirms the idea of images whose interpretation requires a point of view that recognises the surrounding diversity of beings.[21]

These visual expressions characterise a way of knowing that is not anthropocentric but anthropomorphic, as the artefacts are also constituted as subjectivities with a social life, possessing a hidden human perspective.[22] They may present distinctions in the subjectivation regimes conferred by the shamans in the degrees of animation and agency. While some objects are inert, others are particularly powerful as they converse with humans and possess extraordinary powers, including the ability to self-transform. The manufacture of these objects is often seen as the materialisation of supernatural subjectivities, which give form to entities invisible to ordinary human perception.[23] The visual themes analysed here are directly related to the constructive dimension of Amerindian ontologies, which conceive of living beings as composite entities made from parts of other bodies, including artefacts. This composite character of forms is, in turn, related to the beings' capacity for transformation, hence the need to use adornments to keep them in their human-view shape.

Representational iconography tends to recognise the formal diversity of figures as the diversity of biological species. Thus, it categorises zooanthropomorphs and unidentified zoomorphs as difficult-to-define or fantastic beings. However, we can interpret these forms as beings of another type, valuing their shapes, traits and details as significant expressions of the diversity of spiritual or metaphysical beings. Thus, what naturalistic ontologies interpret as a biological diversity that continues to expand through identifying new species is, for perspectivist ontologies, a wide range of beings with fluid, invisible bodily forms living in other layers of the cosmos, below or above the world inhabited by humans and animals. These have different points of view and even pertain to different worlds, as expressed by Viveiros de Castro's concept of 'multinaturalism'.[24]

From a biosemiotic perspective, Eduardo Kohn proposes in *How Forests Think* that the diversity of life forms in the tropical forest is the relational result of countless interpretive layers in which human and nonhuman beings and/or collectives participate. His approach recognises the importance of thinking and seeing according to the perspectives of other beings with whom one lives. Thus, Indigenous thought and practice incorporate forms of semiotic engagement other than the symbolic. The interaction between these semiotic modes leads to ever more complex relationships, diversifying in the tangle of interpreted and interpretive forms in continuous transformation. Kohn describes how the Runakuna people insert themselves into these more-than-human circuits of signs, not only representing but also being represented (and imagining themselves being represented) by other beings. Thus, Kohn's semiotic materialism seeks to trace the origin of Amerindian perspectivism to what he calls the 'ecology of selves', that is, the concrete diversity of subjects (human and nonhuman) whose own forms of interpretations the Runakuna need to consider to live their lives:

> Perspectivism is certainly a historically contingent aesthetic orientation – an orientation that, pace Viveiros de Castro, we might, in this sense, describe as 'cultural' – but it is also an ecologically contingent amplificatory effect of the need to understand semiotic selves in a way that simultaneously recognises their continuity with us as well as their differences. It is a response to the challenges of getting by in an ecology of selves whose relational webs extend well beyond the human, and it emerges from everyday interactions with forest beings.[25]

Similarly, we interpret the diversity of Konduri figurations as the shamanic visual expression of a way of life that thought with the forest, interpreting how other beings saw the world and creating visibilities for others. Analysing their perspectives requires not only the methodological alternation between human and animal points of view, like in the hunter–prey formula, but also attending to relationships that include supernatural beings and artefacts, considering them as relational positions. The transformational element in the Konduri figurations reveals the practice of interpretive thinking and presents us with other ways of being synthesised in figures shaped through visual effects such as anatropy and reversibility.

In the case of Konduri ceramics, we can infer the referents of some images through formal similarities. But how to recognise beings in the tangle of figurative suggestions that seem to purposefully multiply before our eyes, welcoming and interpreting this multiplicity? We suggest that their identification is possible through attention to subtle elements, such as the orifices or simply the dots that – working at once as index and icon, texture and figure – reveal images that are only suggested. The richly dotted style is one of the most challenging expressions of Konduri ceramics. By paying attention to how the eyes and mouth are represented and the details that arise from a change in the focus of the observer's gaze, we can identify images of recognisable and unrecognisable beings and their relationships.

As revealed by Amazonian ethnographies, the relations between humans and animals, such as predator and prey, are considered potentially dangerous due to the otherness enacted by the Other's gaze. This encounter may imply an imagined bodily transformation involving participation, conviviality and food sharing, connecting inside and outside. The change of perspective generates instability in the body under transformation. Transformations can be visible or invisible, as these are changes in the relationships between people, each with their own visible world. In her ethnography of the Nambikwara (Mamaindê), Miller describes a healing session in which the shaman removes an internal ornament from the patient, making it visible. This shows that visibility/invisibility is not intrinsic to the object but emerges from the observer's visual capacity.[26] Thus, although fluid, images and forms persist as figurations through their resemblance to animals, humans and artefacts.[27]

The relationship between the figure and its visual referent is challenged, pointing to another referent. The connection between referent and image necessarily involves the presence of another that establishes a relationship with the visible images from a certain point of view. Severi proposes the concept of chimerical image as the condensation of two or more figures interpreted through a projection, thus enacting relationships between one or more beings and virtual figures in the same form or outline.[28] These two or more images correlate by expressing relationships between their respective visual referents, allowing one to see both (Figure 1.3). In the Konduri style, those images shown through anatropy – a term proposed by Rex González to describe images that can only be seen through a certain angle, highlighting the importance of the observer's positioning and/or moving the piece – stand out among the chimerical figures.[29] Another way of seeing is achieved through changing the focal attention, in which the gaze prioritises one figure over the other, thus figure–ground reversing.

This anatropic and reversible way of presenting the images is present in Konduri pottery through rotations of the artefacts in 45, 90 and 180 degrees, showing the bodily characteristics of different beings. Through the artefact's movements, guided by the figuration of the faces, these bodily states converge in a true dynamic labyrinth. Linked to Severi's

Figure 1.3: Fragment of the edge of a ceramic bowl. Zooanthropomorphs with head adornment, where the frontality and the alignment between the eyes, nose and mouth can be observed. Museu Nacional, UFRJ. Photograph by Luisa Vidal de Oliveira.

'chimerical image', we propose the term 'performative quality' for these characteristics of movement, visual attention and the positioning of a 'virtual' image. It is possible to identify several of these virtual chimeras in the composition of Konduri pottery motifs. These images are multivocal, endowed with a multiplicity that reveals itself in its fullness through movement and acts of looking. Depth and diversity are formed through excessive figuration, perceptible through existing details in the same image. These appear as additional images, suggested through indexes, acquiring iconic autonomy.

A perspectivist iconography: motifs, attributes, relevance and visual themes

Based on iconicity, traditional iconography has formal similarity as its primary form of analysis. Furthermore, it takes the image as a composition of elements. Motifs are the basic unit in the compositions, which may or may not have iconic relevance. On the other hand, attributes are supra-stylistic identifiers of a visual theme, which allow their association with particular referents, such as the specific characteristics of an animal (which may or may not be discrete). Finally, the filling motifs, widely documented by Boas for the iconography of the Northwest Coast of America, consist of elements that have no intrinsic meaning in the compositions.[30]

In the Konduri iconography, dots and incisions are used on the surface of the pieces to fill up spaces. They may or may not be relevant to iconographic analysis. The simple dots, forming a surface pattern, could easily be confused with filling motifs without greater relevance. However, our analysis shows that this same element is applied to represent the skin of different zoomorphs. Despite their filling function, such motifs are relevant for iconographic analysis. We suggest that they may indicate a bodily state of transformation. The vertical arrangement and the size of head decorations give the zooanthropomorphic figures a human-like appearance (Figure 1.4). The alignment between the eyes, mouth and nose in the configuration of the face and the diversity of head shapes also mark bodily differences.

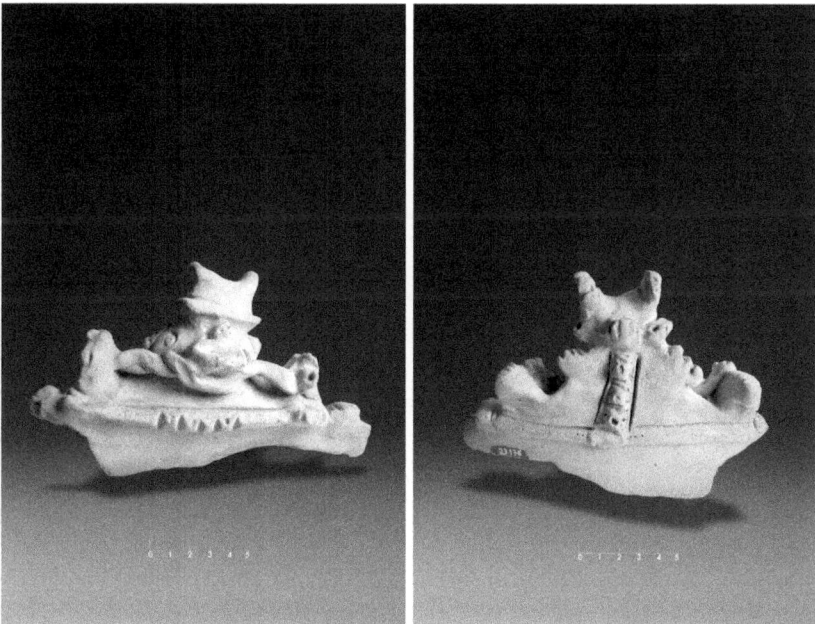

Figure 1.4: Fragment of the edge of a ceramic vessel with a zooanthropomorphic figure with head adornment, showing the neck-cover on its back. Museu Nacional/ UFRJ. Photograph by Luisa Vidal de Oliveira.

The human, animal and hybrid forms are expressed through human traits or attributes combined with those conventionally used for animal figuration. The anthropomorphism of these hybrid figures is expressed in aspects related to body posture: frontality, vertical positioning and the use of cephalic ornaments. The animal form, in turn, manifests itself in particular elements, details that promote a formal differentiation of the body, sometimes subtle and discreet, such as a beak, a tail or a paw, but sometimes highly conventional/abstract. These can be described as animist images due to the correlation between human attitude/positioning and animal body shape as expressions of interiority and exteriority, respectively, as argued by Descola.[31] Ingold approaches this correlation through the concept of clothing as an exchange of perspectives between species.[32] Related to zooanthropomorphism, animistic figures can reveal themselves through recurrent strategies.

Head decorations are attributes that confer a human quality on zooanthropomorphic motifs. As in Knight Jr.'s depiction, head adornments are sometimes presented as motifs, showing themselves discreetly, or even as attributes associated with the human relational position.[33] The analysis of head decorations shows that they are formed by applied dots, incisions and fillets, which vary significantly in shape: they can be made up of a row of dots or just a smooth, almost invisible line. This oscillation between relevance and non-relevance, alternately presenting and hiding figures, is characteristic of Konduri figuration and indicates its fluid quality of bodily/perspectival transformation. In his work on Teotihuacan (Mexico) art, one of the pioneering works of configurational analysis, G. Kubler, shows that headdresses can alternate between a figuration of central or secondary importance in relation to the main motif's composition, also alternating between adjectival and substantive functions.[34] The same happens in Konduri iconography. However, the head adornment gains figurative proportion in these figurations, showing the front part associated with face and hand motifs. This substantivation of the motif reveals the human interiority of Konduri images.

Visual themes are images composed of motifs, attributes and aspects that, expressing their variety in the analysed corpus, can be recognised by their patterns within a broad spectrum of compositions. There are differences in their conceptualisation. For Kubler, themes should be identified only through internal references to the style, while for Panofsky, themes are the elements interconnected to the reference narratives.[35] To allow greater methodological adaptability, Knight Jr. proposes the use of both concepts. He conceives of the visual theme as derived from configurational analysis internal to the corpus. He dubs 'reference themes' those themes identified in relation to their external reference.[36]

We opted for the concept of visual theme because there is no direct and literal relationship between the images analysed and textual, ethnographic or ethnohistorical references. Our references to ethnography are always made through a theoretical discussion based on Amerindian perspectivism, suggesting connections with ethnographic examples. Our analysis starts from the configurational elements internal to the Konduri figuration mode to arrive at the identification of icons.

Konduri visual strategies: alternation and anatropy

Our iconographic analysis showed the use of formal resources to configure chimerical images. The alternation between encompassing and encompassed figures makes it possible to see a face and another face within it, oscillating between a larger and smaller figure. Sometimes this is very subtle; for example, a face taking the place of the nose. In this way, one can focus on the smaller or larger figure, taking the smaller face as the nose of the larger one. This visual strategy might be associated with manipulating the ceramic object by slightly inclining it and alternating the visual focus.[37]

Thus, we suggest that Konduri figurations use an artifice similar to the visual strategy discussed by Lagrou through the notions of 'encompassing and encompassed' associated with the technique of figure and ground reversal.[38] It is the same visual dynamic that in Konduri ceramics makes the vision alternate between a larger and more prominent figure and a smaller one, shaped three-dimensionally. In addition, the sculpting of graphic elements on the surface transforms the body, pointing to the possibility of perceiving figures that only insinuate themselves in the relationship between the drawn surface and the volume. In this example, we find another visual technology, which allows one – through changing the gaze's focus and the observer's position in relation to the artefact – to recognise graphic elements that would not be visible from another perspective, also maintaining a subtle character of the figuration.

We argue that these complex and often indecipherable images are spiritual and changing beings. Lagrou discusses ways of figuring the invisible in Amazonian Indigenous arts. According to her, the figuration of the invisible produces a paradoxical presence, as the relationship between image and referent does not consist of an 'imitation of appearance'.[39] Americanist ethnologists have referred to invisible beings through the concept of the 'double', initially proposed by Vernant to identify the status of spirits, souls, images or ghosts in contrast to the living body.[40]

In the universe of Konduri iconography, full of different gazes and indecipherable shapes – and whose figuration of visible bodies has significant variability – invisible beings were materialised through ceramic technology. The images that emerge in the artefacts act on the observers. The images are indices of presences identified not only through the main theme but also through motifs that emphasise sense organs, connecting inside and outside, like eyes, mouths and noses.

There is a profusion of images that are intentionally visible from some points of view and invisible from others. This differential visibility constitutes a visual-figurational aspect of an animist/perspectivist ontology, highlighting the performance of ceramic artefacts in the context of shamanic technology. The motifs and figurative elements are affordances – or characteristics that emerge from the artefacts themselves, in the sense pointed out by Ingold after J.J. Gibson – which broadens our perception of these objects and their relationality.[41]

Through stippling, the figuration of the eyes is accentuated by its concentricity and intensity, which guides the gaze through visual empathy. But it also ceases to figurate those same eyes momentarily by sharing them with another figure. The motif we call an eye is also a temporal, ephemeral eye, as are the figurations that depend on the gaze to establish themselves. The variety of eyes can be classified in the following way: simple stippling, stippling with depth, stippling with one circular matrix, deep perforation, coffee bean (horizontal, vertical or inclined), subtle lines, stippling with more than two circular matrices; and even less recurrent variations such as the dotted protruding eyes, and the protruding eyes with dots and incisions.

The figuration of the nose is ambivalent. It represents noses and sometimes small heads. One recognises the characteristic incisions of the incised-dotted fillets applied to the noses of the zooanthropomorphic figures. These are not just noses but noses that transform themselves, showing something in common with the figures wearing headdresses, superimposed figures (double-faced), and incised-dotted fillet bands surrounding the pieces' outer perimeters (Figure 1.5). Morphologically, the nose can thus be represented through buttons, with two dots and a central incision, as well as two or three dots. These varieties are associated with the incised-dotted fillet, sometimes forming small faces. The ways of figuration of the mouth are related to the diversity of head shapes and face composition, as the proportion between the nose and the eye varies. Its main forms are the mouth configured between two points, the hourglass-shaped mouth, the mouth followed by protuberance, the bird's beak, the poured conical mouth, the mouth with a vertical notch and the mouth with dots. Beaks are easier to recognise, being associated with bird figures.

Figure 1.5: Fragment of the edge of a ceramic plate with a figure modelled with profuse dots suggesting a multiplicity of zoomorphic figures. Museu Integrado de Óbidos. Photograph by Denise Gomes.

The small heads that emerge from the nose sometimes also appear on other parts of the body. Its isolated figuration helps us perceive that it is a minimal face composition. But this also varies, indicating different visual references, which allows us to perceive the autonomy of its meaning, that is, its visual relevance and discrete quality. The theoretical position that interprets the profusion of dots as a decorative aspect does not capture the visual relevance of this motif. We recognise that when the motif occurs in isolation, one must always ask about its figurativeness, and when it appears associated with the face, it also carries this meaning. As a chimerical image, the possibility of this figuration remains latent and does not fade away – it adds to the resulting figure. We consider that the idea of a figurative nose is present even in those compositions enclosed in the figure of the nose as a potential figure. The potential figure then reveals itself through its supernatural interiority, which appears as a superimposed figure.

What makes the Konduri figurations even more complex is the incised-dotted fillet, which generally occupies the position of head adornment (or nape cover), discernible on the figure's front face and back. This fillet often discretely surrounds the entire figure and makes other figurations emerge. There are several identifiable compositions, but for the purposes of our argument, we point out just those related to the theme of superimposed figures and the theme of zoo anthropomorphic figurations bearing head adornment. Closer attention to the fillet allows the visualisation of small faces that appear on the central figures' elbows, shoulders, wings and endings, such as hands or paws, sometimes suggesting images of serpents.

An iconography of invisible beings

Our interpretation of Konduri iconography draws on Viveiros de Castro's reflections on the ontology of spirits in the Amazon, which cannot be classified as animals or humans but as 'disjunctive syntheses' of beings that defy any categorisation.[42] Discussing the Yanomami example through the narrative of Davi Kopenawa and Bruce Albert, the author explores the visuality or even the perceptual quality derived from the shamanic experience of Kopenawa, who describes the forest as full of reflections of crystals in which the xapiripë spirits dance. These spirits are tiny luminous beings seen as shining dust because of their infinity and dispersion, which inspire a broader discussion on cosmologies and shamanism in the Amazon.

According to Viveiros de Castro, there are common characteristics in the way of existence and manifestation of spirits in the Indigenous Amazon related to notions linked to the idea of an intensive virtual multiplicity. In the Yanomami example, Kopenawa refers to spirits, more than a class of distinct beings, as an image or vital principle, genuine interiority or essence of animals and other beings of the forest – immortal images of a primordial humanity. However, he points out that this notion also refers to human shamans, conceived as having the same nature as auxiliary spirits, suggesting a reverberation between the positions of shaman and spirit observed in different Amazonian cultures. These notions about generic and undifferentiated identities are present in Amazonian mythology, which often deals with speciation or the unstable emergence of different subjects, with humans and nonhumans finding themselves entangled.

Based on these notions – which seem to indicate empirical invisibility – the spirits are understood as non-representational images capable of assuming different forms. These beings are visible only to the shamans' eyes through hallucinogenic drugs and other manners of body sensitisation, such as masks, eye drops and sleep deprivation, contributing to a sort of 'deterritorialization of the gaze'.[43] Rather than sight, the perception of these spirits is linked to a luminous intensity, also observed in other Amazonian cultures. In this way, the invisibility of spirits for most people is related to their luminous visibility for shamans.

The Konduri iconography and its complex images suggest a connection with the arts arising from shamanic technologies as an expression of this universe of spirits. His intense and plural figurations, zoomorphic, anthropomorphic or hybrid in appearance, are neither human nor animal, indicating their belonging to a broad spectrum of images of invisible beings, evidenced by their transformational, performative, dynamic and fluid quality. As discussed, movement and fluidity are part of the perspectivist visual technologies described by Lagrou. They can also be interpreted with reference to virtual space, as proposed by both Lagrou and Séveri, in which the dynamic between abstractionism and figurativism momentarily blinds us – or opens our eyes to possible figurations. The profusion of images is the same formal strategy that makes the Konduri figure invisible (its invisibility/visibility device) – see Figure 1.6.

Figure 1.6: Fragment of the flange of a ceramic vessel showing heads with adornments and a figurative nose, outlined by an incised-dotted fillet whose ends form small heads. Museu Nacional/UFRJ. Photograph by Luisa Vidal de Oliveira.

Conclusion

Konduri ceramics present complex images linked to the Amazonian imaginary, which include a myriad of beings that, according to Indigenous ethnology, are only visible through specific perceptual states. Consequently, they are irreducible to a single typology. The artefacts analysed here are bearers of zooanthropomorphic figures, animals and unrecognisable beings, which share the same motifs and attributes. Subjective perception, attention and visual intensity are fundamental for their interpretation. Through an approximation from ethnological theory, we propose to observe the images challenged by equivocation, in a way critical to anthropocentrism and the representational paradigm that separates nature from culture and materiality from spirituality. In this sense, our iconographic analysis sought to understand visual effects, revealing the relationships between person and object, as well as intrinsically connected chimerical images.

This theoretical-methodological problematisation, arising from the visual agency of Konduri iconography, enables the recognition of different forms in a continuous flow of transformation. The identified motifs compose figurations with hybrid characteristics (humans and animals) connected in the same visual space, showing relationships between these diverse beings in a single composition. In this chapter, we explored two recurring themes in Konduri pottery. The first is zooanthropomorphic figures with head adornments. The second, designated as superimposed figures or 'double face', refers to a being with another face that is revealed above it.

We have argued that Konduri iconography presents performative figurations of natural, supernatural and artefactual beings in various relational states. These images include zooanthropomorphic figures and animals mingled with other animals whose gazes change the referents; the nose has the shape of a face, linear beings that populate the outer surface of the pottery, sometimes reappearing as (animated) head adornments of zoo-anthropomorphic beings, sometimes as figurative endings or as beings of superlative capacity, superimposed on others. Thus, Konduri pottery acts as a shamanic technology that highlights the potency of artefacts in ritual contexts in a way that assumes, imagines and investigates how other beings think and perceive. The transformations identified through our iconographic analysis – highlighting the motifs, their compositions and characteristics of specific themes – modify iconographic concepts and allow the recognition of nonhuman perspectives. In our interpretation, the highlighted categories establish a relationship with traditional iconography, while being aware of its shortcomings.

Over three decades, Amazonian archaeology sought to rescue social forms from the past, producing narratives that mirrored realities known in the Western world. This was an effort, often in vain, to value evidence of social hierarchies and political centralisation. An archaeology based on a transversal discussion with anthropology opens up other possibilities. Previously seen as a stylistic indicator, Konduri pottery is now understood as an active materiality whose artefacts were involved in shamanic ceremonies and indicate a way of thinking. The images refer to the plurality of modes of existence in the Amazon rainforest, where different forms of biological life interact, but also intangible, supernatural beings. This animated world that emerges in our analysis allows us to highlight sociocultural contexts and institutions from the past that have long-term historical continuity with contemporary Indigenous societies, whose survival has been threatened by a global crisis. One of Brazil's greatest challenges today is protecting the Amazonian biocultural heritage. At the same time, the country has in the forest itself the theoretical tools (ontological, metaphysical) to face the communicational crisis linked to the problem of human-nonhuman coexistence – which puts the forest itself at risk. By empirically evidencing the existence of beings other than humans and opening the way for recognising precolonial worldviews, archaeology – in conjunction with the study of visuality – contributes to decolonising our ways of thinking.

Notes

1. Peter Paul Hilbert, *A cerâmica arqueológica da região de Oriximiná*. Belém, Instituto de Antropologia e Etnologia do Pará, 1955.

2. Peter Paul Hilbert & Klaus Hilbert, 'Resultados preliminares da pesquisa arqueológica nos rios Nhamundá e Trombetas, Baixo Rio Amazonas', *Boletim do Museu Paraense Emílio Goeldi, Nova Série, Antropologia* 75 (1980), 1–11; Betty Meggers & Clifford Evans, 'An experimental formulation of horizon styles in tropical forest of South America'. In: Samuel Lothrop (ed.) *Essays in precolumbian art and archaeology*. Cambridge, MA, Harvard University Press, 1961, 372–88.

3. Vera Lúcia Calandrini Guapindaia, *Além da margem do rio – as ocupações Konduri e Pocó na região de Porto Trombetas, PA*, unpubl. PhD dissertation, University of São Paulo, 2008.

4. Camila Jácome & Jaime Xamen Wai Wai, 'A paisagem e as cerâmicas arqueológicas na bacia do Trombetas: uma discussão da arqueologia karaiwa e WaiWai', *Boletim Do Museu Paraense Emilio Goeldi. CiênciasHumanas* 15, no. 3 (2020), e20190140.

5. Marcony Lopes Alves, 'Revisitando os alter-egos: figuras sobrepostas na iconografia Konduri e sua relação com o xamanismo', *Boletim do Museu Paraense Emílio Goeldi. Ciências Humanas* 15, no. 3 (2020), e20190105.

6. Bruno Latour, *Reassembling the social: an introduction to actor-network-theory*. Oxford, Oxford University Press, 2007; 'Esperando a Gaia. Componer el mundo

común mediante las artes y la política', *Cuadernos de Otra parte. Revista de letras y artes* 26 (2012), 67–76.

7. Bruno Latour, 2019; Elizabeth A. Povinelli, *Geontologies: A requiem to late liberalism*. Durham, Duke University Press, 2016; Pierre Maniglier & Stephen Muecke, 'Art as fiction: can Latour's ontology of art be ratified by art lovers (an exercise in anthropological diplomacy)', *New Literary History* 47, nos. 2–3 (2016), 419–38.

8. Bruno Latour, *Investigação sobre os modos de existencia: uma antropología dos modernos*. São Paulo, Editora Vozes, 2019; Eduardo Viveiros de Castro, 'Perspectival anthropology and the method of controlled equivocation', *Tipití: Journal of the Society for Anthropology of Lowland South America* 2, no. 1 (2004), 3–22; 'Metaphysics as mythophysis. Or, why I have always been an anthropologist'. In: Pierre Charbonnier, Gilda Saldon & Peter Skafish (eds.) *Comparative metaphysics: ontology after anthropology*. London-New York, Rowman & Littlefield, 2016, 249–74.

9. Latour, 2007; Benjamin Alberti, 'Archaeology and ontologies of scale: the case of miniaturization in first millennium northwest Argentina'. In: Benjamin Alberti, Andrew Meirion Jones & Joshua Pollard, Jr. (eds.) *Archaeology after interpretation: returning materials to archaeological theory*. Walnut Creek, Left Coast Press, 2016, 43–58; Benjamin Alberti, Severian Fowles, Martin Holbraad & Christofer Witmore, 'Worlds otherwise: archaeology, anthropology and ontological difference', *Current Anthropology* 52, no. 6 (2011), 896–912; Benjamin Alberti & Yvonne Marshall, 'Animating archaeology: local theories and conceptually open-ended methodologies', *Cambridge Archaeological Journal* 19, no. 3 (2009), 344–357; Denise Maria Cavalcante Gomes, 'O perspectivismo ameríndio e idea de uma estética americana', *Boletim do Museu Paraense Emílio Goeldi. Ciências Humanas* 7, no. 1 (2012), 133–59; 'Politics and ritual in large villages in Santarém, Lower Amazon, Brazil', *Cambridge Archeological Journal* 27, no. 2 (2017), 275–93; 'Images of transformation in the Lower Amazon and the performativity of Santarém and Konduri pottery', *Journal of Social Archeology* 22, no. 1 (2022), 82–103; Philippe Descola, *Más allá de naturaleza y cultura*. Buenos Aires, Amorrortu, 2012; 'La fabrique des images', *Anthopologie et sociétés* 30, no. 3 (2006), 167–82; 'O avesso do visivel: ontología e iconologia', *Arte & Ensaios* 31 (2016), 127–37; 'La Fabrique des images. Exposition au Musée du Quai Branly (16 février 2010–11 juillet 2011)'; *La lettre du Collège de France* 28 (2010), 13; Tim Ingold, 'Totemism, animism and the depiction of animals'. In: Tim Ingold, *The perception of the environment*. London, Routledge, 2000, 125–45; Tamara Bray, 'An archeological perspective on the Andean concept of *Camaquen:* thinking through late Pre-Columbian ofrendas and huacas', *Cambridge Archaeological Journal* 19, no. 3 (2009), 357–66.

10. George Kubler, 'The iconography of the art of Teotihuacan', *Studies in Pre-Columbian Art and Archaeology* 4 (1967), 1–40; Vernon Knight, Jr., *Iconographic method in new world prehistory*. New York, Cambridge University Press, 2013; Viveiros de Castro, 2004, 2016.

11. Gomes, 2012.

12. Catherine Allen, Matias Lépori, Bill Sillar, Marisa Lazzari & Maria Florencia Becerra, 'Pensamientos de una etnógrafa acerca de la interpretación en la arqueología andina: comentado por Bill Sillar y Marisa Lazzari', *Mundo de Antes* 11 (2017), 13–68; Carlos Fausto, *Art effects: images, agency and ritual in Amazonia*. Lincoln, University of Nebraska Press, 2021; Denise Maria Cavalcante Gomes, 'Images of transformation in the Lower Amazon and the performativity of Santarém and Konduri pottery', *Journal of Social Archaeology* 22, no. 1 (2022), 82–103; Els Lagrou, 'Le graphisme sur les corps amérindiens. Des chimères abstraites?', *Gradhiva. Revue d'anthropologie et d'histoire des arts* 13 (2011), 68–93.

13. Bruno Latour, *Investigação sobre os modos de existência: uma antropologia dos modernos*. Rio de Janeiro, Editora Vozes, 2012; Pierre Maniglier, '¿Cuántos planetas Tierra? El giro geológico en antropología', *Avá* 29 (2016), 199–216.

14. Alfred Gell, *Art and agency: an anthropological theory*. Oxford, Clarendon Press, 1998; Amira Henare, Martin Holbraad & Sari Wastell, 'Introduction'. In: Amira Henare, Martin Holbraad & Sari Wastell (eds.) *Thinking through things: theorizing artefacts ethnographically*. London, Routledge, 2007, 1–37; Carlo Severi, *Le principe de la chimère. Une anthropologie de la mémoire*. Paris, Editions rue d'Ulme/Musée du Quai Branly, 2007; Gomes, 2012.

15. Tim Ingold, 2000; Descola, 2006, 13; 'O avesso do visível: ontologia e iconologia', *Arte & Ensaios* 31 (2016), 127–37; Lagrou, 2011; Allen, Lépori, Sillar, Lazzari & Becerra, 2017.

16. Lúcia Hussak Van Velthem, 'Artes indígenas: notas sobre a lógica dos corpos e dos artefatos', *Textos Escolhidos de Cultura e Arte Populares* 7, no. 1 (2010), 19–29; Anne Christine Tylor & Eduardo Viveiros de Castro, 'Un corps fait de regards'. In: Stephanie Breton (ed.) *Qu'est-ce qu un corp? Amazonie*. Paris, Musée du Quai Branly-Flamarion, 2006, 148–99; Els Lagrou, *Arte indígena no Brasil: agência, alteridade e relação*. Belo Horizonte, Com Arte, 2009; Lagrou, 2011.

17. Fernando Santos-Granero (ed.), *The occult life of things: native Amazonian theories of materiality and personhood*. Tucson, The University of Arizona Press, 2009.

18. Eduardo Viveiros de Castro, 'Exchanging perspectives: the transformation of objects into subjects in Amerindian ontologies', *Common Knowledge* 10, no. 3 (2004), 463–84.

19. Santos-Granero, 2016.

20. Luisa Vidal de Oliveira, 'Figuras zoo-antropomorficas e seus adornos corporais: ponteado, linha incisa e modelagem na cerâmica Konduri (1000–1500 A.D.)', *Revista de Arqueologia* 33, no. 1 (2020), 147–68.

21. Viveiros de Castro, 2016.

22. Viveiros de Castro, 2004.

23. Santos-Granero, 2016, 8.

24. Eduardo Viveiros de Castro, 'Perspectivismo e multinaturalismo na América Indígena'. In: Eduardo Viveiros de Casto, *A inconstância da alma selvagem*. São Paulo, Cosac Naify, 2002, 345–400.

25. Eduardo Kohn, *How forests think: toward an anthropology beyond the human*. Berkeley, University of California Press, 2013, 96.

26. Joana Miller, 'Things as persons: body ornaments and alterity among the Mamaindê (Nambikwara)'. In: Fernando Santos Granero (ed.) *The occult life of things: native Amazonian theories of materiality and personhood*. Tucson, The University of Arizona Press, 2009, 62.

27. Els Lagrou, *A fluidez da forma: arte, alteridade e agência em uma sociedade Amazônica (Kaxinawa, Acre)*. Rio de Janeiro, Topbooks, 2007.

28. Carlo Severi, *Le principe de la chimère. Une anthropologie de la mémoire*. Paris, Editions rue d'Ulme/musée du Quai Branly, 2007; 'L'espace chimérique. Perception et projection dans les actes de regard', *Gradhiva. Revue d'anthropologie et d'histoire des arts* 13 (2011), 8–47; 'O espaço quimérico. Percepção e projeção nos atos do olhar'. In: Carlo Severi & Els Lagrou (eds.) *Quimeras em diálogo: grafismo e figuração nas artes indígenas*. Rio de Janeiro, Editora 7 Letras, 2013, 25–66.

29. Alberto Rex González, *Arte, Estructura y arqueologia: análisis de figuras duales y anatropicas del N.O. Argentino*. Buenos Aires, La Marca Editorial, 1974; Mary Weismantel, 'Encounters with dragons: the stones of Chavin', *RES: Anthropology and Aesthetics* 65 (2015a), 37–53; 'Looking like an archeologist: Viveiros de Castro at Chavin de Huantar', *Journal of Social Archaeology* 15, no. 2 (2015b), 139–59.

30. Franz Boas, *Primitive art*. Mineola, Dover Publications, 1955; Vernon Knight, Jr., *Iconographic method in new world prehistory*. New York, Cambridge, 2013, 80.

31. Descola, 2006, 2012, 2016.

32. Ingold, 2000.

33. Knight, 2013.

34. Kubler, 1967.

35. Erwing Panofsky, *O significado das artes visuais*. São Paulo, Perspectiva, [1955] 2001.

36. Knight, 2013.

37. Gomes, 2022.

38. Els Lagrou, 'Perspectivismo, animismo y quimeras: una reflexión sobre el grafismo como técnica de alteración de la percepción', *Mundo Amazónico* 3 (2012), 54–78; 'Podem os grafismos ameríndios ser considerados quimeras abstratas? Uma reflexão sobre uma arte perspectivista'. In: Carlo Severi & Els Lagrou (eds.) *Quimeras em diálogo: grafismo y figuração na arte indígena*. Rio de Janeiro, Editora 7 Letras, 2013, 67–109; 'La figuración de lo invisible en Warburg y en las artes indígenas amazónicas'. In: Sanja Savkic & Hanna Baader (eds.) *Culturas visuales indígenas y las prácticas visuales en las Américas desde la antigüedad hasta el presente*. Berlin, Ibero-Amerikanische Institut Rreubischer Kulturbesitz/Gebr. Mann Verlag, 2019, 303–27; 'Learning to see in Western Amazonia', *Social Analysis* 63, no. 2 (2019), 24–44.

39. Lagrou, 2019.

40. Jean-Pierre Vernant, 'The birth of images'. In: Froma I. Zeitlin (ed.) *Mortals and immortals: collected essays*. Princeton, Princeton University Press, 1991, 165–85.

41. Ingold, 2000.

42. Eduardo Viveiros de Castro, 'A floresta de cristal: notas sobre a ontologia dos espíritos amazônicos', *Cadernos de Campo* 15, no. 14–15 (2006), 319–38.

43. Viveiros de Castro, 2006, 332.

References

Alberti, Benjamin, 'Archaeology and ontologies of scale: the case of miniaturization in first millennium northwest Argentina'. In: Benjamin Alberti, Andrew Meirion Jones & Joshua Pollard, Jr. (eds.) *Archaeology after interpretation: returning materials to archaeological theory.* Walnut Creek, Left Coast Press, 2016, 43–58.

Alberti, Benjamin, Severian Fowles, Martin Holbraad & Christofer Witmore, 'Worlds otherwise: archaeology, anthropology and ontological difference', *Current Anthropology* 52, no. 6 (2011), 896–912.

Alberti, Benjamin & Yvonne Marshall, 'Animating archaeology: local theories and conceptually open-ended methodologies', *Cambridge Archaeological Journal* 19, no. 3 (2009), 344–57.

Allen, Catherine, Matias Lépori, Bill Sillar, Marisa Lazzari & Maria Florencia Becerra, 'Pensamientos de una etnógrafa acerca de la interpretación en la arqueología andina: comentado por Bill Sillar y Marisa Lazzari', *Mundo de Antes* 11 (2017), 13–68.

Boas, Franz, *Primitive art*. Mineola, Dover Publications, 1955.

Bray, Tamara, 'An archeological perspective on the Andean concept of *Camaquen:* thinking through late Pre-Columbian ofrendas and huacas', *Cambridge Archeological Journal* 19, no. 3 (2009), 357–66.

Descola, Philippe, 'O avesso do visível: ontologia e iconologia', *Arte & Ensaios* 31 (2016), 127–37.

Descola, Philippe, 'La fabrique des images', *Anthopologie et sociétés* 30, no. 3 (2006), 167–82.

Descola, Philippe, 'La Fabrique des images. Exposition au Musée du Quai Branly (16 février 2010–11 juillet 2011)', *La lettre du Collège de France* 28 (2010).

Descola, Philippe, *Más allá de naturaleza y cultura*. Buenos Aires, Amorrortu, 2012.

Fausto, Carlos, *Art effects: images, agency and ritual in Amazonia*. Lincoln, University of Nebraska Press, 2021.

Gell, Alfred, *Art and agency: an anthropological theory*. Oxford, Clarendon Press, 1998.

Gomes, Denise Maria Cavalcante, 'Images of transformation in the Lower Amazon and the performativity of Santarém and Konduri pottery', *Journal of Social Archeology* 22, no. 1 (2022), 82–103.

Gomes, Denise Maria Cavalcante, 'O perspectivismo ameríndio e idea de uma estética americana', *Boletim do Museu Paraense Emílio Goeldi. Ciências Humanas* 7, no. 1 (2012), 133–59.

Gomes, Denise Maria Cavalcante, 'Politics and ritual in large villages in Santarém, Lower Amazon, Brazil', *Cambridge Archeological Journal* 27, no. 2 (2017), 275–93.

Guapindaia, Vera Lúcia Calandrini, *Além da margem do rio – as ocupações Konduri e Pocó na região de Porto Trombetas, PA*, unpubl. PhD dissertation, University of São Paulo, 2008.

Henare, Amira Martin Holbraad & Sari Wastell, 'Introduction'. In: Amira Henare, Martin Holbraad & Sari Wastell (eds.) *Thinking through things: theorizing artefacts ethnographically*. London, Routledge, 2007, 1–37.

Hilbert, Peter Paul, *A cerâmica arqueológica da região de Oriximiná*. Belém, Instituto de Antropologia e Etnologia do Pará, 1955.

Hilbert, Peter Paul & Klaus Hilbert, 'Resultados preliminares da pesquisa arqueológica nos rios Nhamundá e Trombetas, Baixo Rio Amazonas', *Boletim do Museu Paraense Emílio Goeldi, Nova Série, Antropologia* 75 (1980), 1–11.

Ingold, Tim, 'Totemism, animism and the depiction of animals'. In: Tim Ingold, *The perception of the environment*. London, Routledge, 2000, 125–45.

Jácome, Camila & Jaime Xamen Wai Wai, 'A paisagem e as cerâmicas arqueológicas na bacia do Trombetas: uma discussão da arqueologia karaiwa e WaiWai', *Boletim Do Museu Paraense Emílio Goeldi. CiênciasHumanas* 15, no. 3 (2020), e20190140.

Knight, Jr., Vernon, *Iconographic method in new world prehistory*. New York, Cambridge University Press, 2013.

Kohn, Eduardo, *How forests think: toward an anthropology beyond the human*. Berkeley, University of California Press, 2013.

Kubler, George, 'The iconography of the art of Teotihuacan', *Studies in Pre-Columbian Art and Archaeology* 4 (1967), 1–40.

Lagrou, Els, *Arte indígena no Brasil: agência, alteridade e relação*. Belo Horizonte, Com Arte, 2009.

Lagrou, Els, 'La figuración de lo invisible en Warburg y en las artes indígenas amazónicas'. In: Sanja Savkic & Hanna Baader (eds.) *Culturas visuales indígenas y las prácticas visuales en las Américas desde la antigüedad hasta el presente*. Berlin, Ibero-Amerikanische Institut Rreubischer Kulturbesitz/Gebr. Mann Verlag, 2019, 303–27.

Lagrou, Els, *A fluidez da forma: arte, alteridade e agência em uma sociedade Amazônica (Kaxinawa, Acre)*. Rio de Janeiro, Topbooks, 2007.

Lagrou, Els, 'Le graphisme sur les corps amérindiens. Des chimères abstraites?', *Gradhiva. Revue d'anthropologie et d'histoire des arts* 13 (2011), 68–93.

Lagrou, Els, 'Learning to see in Western Amazonia', *Social Analysis* 63, no. 2 (2019), 24–44.

Lagrou, Els, 'Perspectivismo, animismo y quimeras: una reflexión sobre el grafismo como técnica de alteración de la percepción', *Mundo Amazónico* 3 (2012), 54–78.

Lagrou, Els, 'Podem os grafismos ameríndios ser considerados quimeras abstratas? Uma reflexão sobre uma arte perspectivista'. In: Carlo Severi & Els Lagrou (eds.) *Quimeras em diálogo: grafismo y figuração na arte indígena.* Rio de Janeiro, Editora 7 Letras, 2013, 67–109.

Latour, Bruno, 'Esperando a Gaia. Componer el mundo común mediante las artes y la política', *Cuadernos de Otra parte. Revista de letras y artes* 26 (2012), 67–76.

Latour, Bruno, *Investigação sobre os modos de existencia: uma antropología dos modernos.* São Paulo, Editora Vozes, 2019.

Latour, Bruno, *Reassembling the social: an introduction to actor-network-theory.* Oxford, Oxford University Press, 2007.

Lopes Alves, Marcony, 'Revisitando os alter-egos: figuras sobrepostas na iconografia Konduri e sua relação com o xamanismo', *Boletim do Museu Paraense Emílio Goeldi. Ciências Humanas* 15, no. 3 (2020), e20190105.

Maniglier, Pierre & Stephen Muecke, 'Art as fiction: can Latour's ontology of art be ratified by art lovers (an exercise in anthropological diplomacy)', *New Literary History* 47, nos. 2–3 (2016), 419–38.

Maniglier, Pierre & Stephen Muecke, '¿Cuántos planetas Tierra? El giro geológico en antropología', *Avá* 29 (2016), 199–216.

Meggers, Betty & Clifford Evans, 'An experimental formulation of horizon styles in tropical forest of South America'. In: Samuel Lothrop (ed.) *Essays in precolumbian art and archaeology.* Cambridge, MA. Harvard University Press, 1961, 372–88.

Miller, Joana, 'Things as persons: body ornaments and alterity among the Mamaindê (Nambikwara)'. In: Fernando Santos Granero (ed.) *The occult life of things: native Amazonian theories of materiality and personhood.* Tucson, The University of Arizona Press, 2009, 60–80.

Oliveira, Luisa Vidal de, 'Figuras zoo-antropomorficas e seus adornos corporais: ponteado, linha incisa e modelagem na cerâmica Konduri (1000–1500 A.D.)', *Revista de Arqueologia* 33, no. 1 (2020), 147–68.

Panofsky, Erwing, *O significado das artes visuais.* São Paulo, Perspectiva, [1955] 2001.

Povinelli, Elizabeth A., *Geontologies: A requiem to late liberalism.* Durham, Duke University Press, 2016.

Rex González, Alberto, *Arte, Estructura y arqueología: análisis de figuras duales y anatropicas del N.O. Argentino.* Buenos Aires, La Marca Editorial, 1974.

Santos-Granero, Fernando (ed.), *The occult life of things: native Amazonian theories of materiality and personhood*. Tucson, The University of Arizona Press, 2009.

Severi, Carlo, 'L'espace chimérique. Perception et projection dans les actes de regard', *Gradhiva. Revue d'anthropologie et d'histoire des arts* 13 (2011), 8–47.

Severi, Carlo, 'O espaço quimérico. Percepção e projeção nos atos do olhar'. In: Carlo Severi & Els Lagrou (eds.) *Quimeras em diálogo: grafismo e figuração nas artes indígenas*. Rio de Janeiro, Editora 7 Letras, 2013, 25–66.

Severi, Carlo, *Le principe de la chimère. Une anthropologie de la mémoire*. Paris, Editions rue d'Ulme/Musée du Quai Branly, 2007.

Tylor, Anne Christine & Eduardo Viveiros de Castro, 'Um corps fait de regards'. In: Stephanie Breton (ed.) *Qu'est-ce qu'um corp? Amazonie*. Paris, Musée du Quai Branly-Flamarion, 2006, 148–99.

Van Velthem, Lúcia Hussak, 'Artes indígenas: notas sobre a lógica dos corpos e dos artefatos', *Textos Escolhidos de Cultura e Arte Populares* 7, no. 1 (2010), 19–29.

Vernant, Jean-Pierre, 'The birth of images'. In: Froma I. Zeitlin (ed.) *Mortals and immortals: collected essays*. Princeton, Princeton University Press, 1991, 165–85.

Viveiros de Castro, Eduardo, 'Exchanging perspectives: the transformation of objects into subjects in Amerindian ontologies', *Common Knowledge* 10, no. 3 (2004), 463–84.

Viveiros de Castro, Eduardo, 'A floresta de cristal: notas sobre a ontologia dos espíritos amazônicos', *Cadernos de Campo* 15, no. 14–15 (2006), 319–38.

Viveiros de Castro, Eduardo, 'Metaphysics as mythophysis. Or, why I have always been an anthropologist'. In: Pierre Charbonnier, Gilda Saldon & Peter Skafish (eds.) *Comparative metaphysics: ontology after anthropology*. London-New York, Rowman & Littlefield, 2016, 249–74.

Viveiros de Castro, Eduardo, 'Perspectival anthropology and the method of controlled equivocation', *Tipití: Journal of the Society for Anthropology of Lowland South America* 2, no. 1 (2004), 3–22.

Viveiros de Castro, Eduardo, 'Perspectivismo e multinaturalismo na América Indígena'. In: Eduardo Viveiros de Casto, *A inconstância da alma selvagem*. São Paulo, Cosac Naify, 2002, 345–400.

Weismantel, Mary, 'Encounters with dragons: the stones of Chavin', *RES: Anthropology and Aesthetics* 65 (2015a), 37–53.

Weismantel, Mary, 'Looking like an archeologist: Viveiros de Castro at Chavin de Huantar', *Journal of Social Archeology* 15, no. 2 (2015b), 139–59.

Chapter 2

Under a weak sun at the southern rim of South America (1540–1650)

Margarita Gascón

Historical documents and archival records contain traces of the sun's past cycles and activity because they interfere with earth's climate, ecosystems and societies.[1] Far from the human-agency controversy of the current global warming, in 1971, Emmanuel Le Roi Ladurie's book made the strong argument that humans have always recorded climate fluctuations and past solar activity (although indirectly) when considering the ups and downs of prices of foodstuff, frost dates, natural disasters such as a persistent drought or an increase in the frequency of floods, and disruptions in daily life due to plagues, famines and pandemics.[2] In the past, solar activity was registered in the records of agricultural yield, natural resources availability, environmental conditions, extreme weather and the overall wellbeing of animals and people.[3]

Within the broader field of environmental history, the climate in its relationship with the sun still lacks a multidisciplinary scholarship. Worse, the historical approach to climate has been accused of methodological problems like inappropriate data easily misinterpreted, large spatiotemporal scales, selection bias towards crisis and collapse, and societies mischaracterised as homogeneous entities.[4] These mishaps based on true examples are serious, but they also apply to many other historical themes. For example, is it proof of a 'bias towards crisis and collapse' that political history frequently focuses on revolutions, social unrest and warfare? By the same token, economic and social historians usually rely on documents produced by those affected by a legal or economic situation that impacted their livelihood. Would interpretations necessarily lead to a mischaracterisation of society 'as a homogeneous entity'? Each interpretation of the past, therefore, poses its own challenge.

Dealing with data based on the perception of varying weather and climate carries peculiar problems. In 2004, Jones and Mann argued that historical sources are impact-oriented and influenced by cultural factors, implying that they cannot be taken at face value. Both authors have based their scepticism on the often-misused pieces of evidence of the freezing of the River Thames as a proxy indicator of the Little Ice Age (LIA),[5] but for some historians, there is nothing implicitly wrong in the subjective factor of human reaction to weather abnormalities and climate-related hazards. On the contrary, it speaks volumes about the consequences of weather and climate on people as much as on environments without humans.[6] Difficulties with data interpretation, however, remain.[7] Events referred to in historical sources are proxy indicators that may relate neither to solar activity alone nor climate variability exclusively but to the interplay of multiple variables.[8] In need of insights into the complex relationship between climate, environment and society in regions and periods for which there are archival sources, Ljungqvist, Seim and Huhtamaa have advanced a model ranging from first-order effects of climate on biomass production to fourth-order cultural effects, with the latter interacting on all the preceding levels. In the first-order impact, the three authors place bio-physical effects, quantity and quality of primary products, including energy, built and natural environment, water availability and microorganisms. The second-order impact includes the influence of climate on livelihoods, economy and health; availability and prices of primary products, markets and transportation systems, epidemics and epizootics. The third-order impact involves social and demographic implications, demographic trends (mortality, fertility and migration), human well-being, subsistence crisis and social conflicts. These three interact with the fourth-order impact that comprises cultural responses, religious, scientific, artistic and societal rituals and reactions, crisis interpretation, cultural memory, learning process and adaptation.[9]

To help reconstruct the lesser-known paleoclimate of the southern hemisphere by using all the available sources of information, this chapter deals with the southern rim of South America as the LIA went on. The European invasion and the early decades of colonisation happened during the first half of this climatic period that lasted from the fourteenth century to the early nineteenth century.[10] By the mid-seventeenth century, the Maunder Minimum (MM) was the most recent grand minimum of solar activity, near its lowest levels in the past 8,000 years.[11] The LIA and the MM left traces in the historical sources and archival records,[12] although the tendency is to consider the MM indistinctively inside the LIA.[13]

We identify weather anomalies and environmental crises in the scattered documents produced in colonies in South America's southernmost areas. The majority of the chronicles are printed, such as the minutes of the town meetings of prominent settlers (*actas de cabildo*), which give insights into the ways of coping with the damages inflicted by heavy rains, river floods, snow in the Andes, disruptions in trading routes and plagues. Because several *actas* for the period of the LIA and the MM have vanished, the remaining ones only provide a patchy reconstruction instead of a continuous series. In the case of archival sources, they are of uneven value. Sources for the late sixteenth and early seventeenth centuries are abundant for Chile because of the war with the Araucanians. However, when the first settlers wrote about their experiences, sometimes it was several years after the fact and, not surprisingly, chronicles contain gaps and mistakes. Being aware of uncertainties, we include only events similar to those recorded for other parts of the planet or anomalies established by geo-chronological methods such as geomorphological, lacustrine, pollen and tree-ring analyses.[14] By so doing, we follow examples of how to use historical records to reconstruct paleo-climates.[15] Even with mishaps, valuable illustrations emerge, and the overall image contributes to understanding past solar activity from a more-than-human agency perspective.

The smoking gun of the LIA in southern South America

The LIA is a well-known climatic period whose impact was attested for much of Europe and the northern hemisphere, but proxy-climate records support the concept of a global scale and the claim for solar forcing of parts of the LIA climate.[16] The person who coined the term Little Ice Age to describe a glacial advance during the Holocene was the Dutch-born American geologist Francois Matthe in 1939. Later on, researchers started to note large regional variability in the timings of glacial advances, so the LIA became a more general term for global scales of cooler climate.[17] Common knowledge today establishes that cooling periods may be triggered by different agents such as solar activity, volcanic eruptions, alterations in the ocean currents, variations in earth's orbit, and even acute demographic changes.[18]

The latter agent is of interest to us. The demographic-change hypothesis considers that the conquest and colonisation of the Americas created the conditions for the onset of the LIA. This hypothesis connects the decrease in temperatures with the demographic collapse of natives that followed the introduction of pathogens by the Europeans. As Indigenous human organisms lacked proper immunisation, lethal diseases such as smallpox, measles and influenza decimated native populations quickly. War, hard-labour conditions, and social and cultural dislocation added to the devastating effects of the pandemics. The result was the massive death of Indians, from between 54 and 61 million in 1492 to just 6 million in 1650. The demographic collapse had environmental consequences, for vast areas of cleared and cultivated land were abandoned and soon reforested. The urban and agricultural retreat of more than 60 million hectares of the continent lowered the planet's temperature by capturing CO_2.[19] The plausibility of the thesis came under fire when Bonneuil and Fressoz calculated the carbon concentration in the atmosphere through proxy indicators. The final value went from around 279 to 272 parts per million (ppm) between the start of the sixteenth century and 1610, meaning that the demographic catastrophe was irrelevant to explain the LIA. In their own words, 'but if this low tide of atmospheric carbon is an ominous stratigraphic marker of one of the most terrible events in human history, the variation does not lie outside the general Holocene range of 260 to 284 ppm'.[20] Despite these figures, the discussion is not entirely over yet. Adding to the debate, two British geographers proposed that Indigenous demographic decline, Neotropical reforestation and shifting fire regimes allow us to set the starting date of the Anthropocene around the onset of the LIA and the European colonisation of the Americas.[21] There is little doubt that the Columbian exchange of people, domesticated plants and animals between Asia, Europe, America and Africa have all relentlessly transformed the biosphere since 1492, and in such an overwhelming way that there are enough tangible stratigraphic signatures to allow potential formal chrono-stratification too.[22]

In the southernmost portion of the Americas, changes in climate due to the reduced solar activity associated with the LIA, changes in different environments as the Europeans introduced domesticated species and lethal pathogens, and changes in most native societies and cultures all came together. Proxy indicators of the LIA are very much present in some sixteenth-century sources. One of them is the letter that the conqueror of Chile, Pedro de Valdivia (1497–1553), wrote to Gonzalo de Pizarro describing the supposedly pleasant and balmy Central Valley. He could not pass up the opportunity to mention that, according to the Indians, the weather was unusually colder and wetter.[23] Another eyewitness, Jerónimo de Vivar (1525?–1558), reported that the word *Chile* derived from *Anchachire*, meaning 'Great Cold' in the native language, although he stressed that Santiago was founded by mid-summer and in a valley with nice weather (12 January 1541). Even so, he reported continuous rains and a plague of voracious rats, frequently seen as a proxy indicator of climate fluctuation.[24] An outbreak of rodents relates to a favourable or otherwise change in the ecosystem for the breeding season or food availability. Thus too much or too little humidity may equally affect a rodent population and its behaviour.[25] Nonetheless, there are reasons to believe that, in the case of the event in Chile, this plague of rats was provoked by wetter conditions. Another indicator of the LIA in Chile comes from an earlier mission to conquer Chile. Diego de Almagro (1475–1538) travelled a pre-Columbian route in Argentina (the Inca route or *qhapac ñan*) that crosses the Andes through the pass of Comecaballos or Pircas Negras (both at 28°SL). It was not supposed to be the unbearable enterprise that it finally was. At 150 km northward of the Central Valley, a heavy snowstorm caught Almagro, already discouraged, unprepared for such unusual weather.[26]

Far from being isolated local events in Chile, that same year of 1536, heavy rains in Buenos Aires produced a flash flood that destroyed the first church and other buildings.[27] Similar continuous rains were recorded for Paraguay in 1539 when the *Adelantado* Domingo Martinez de Irala (1509–56) was unable to leave Asunción and control an Indian uprising due to overflowing rivers.[28] Farther north of Asunción, the pouring rains of 1539 flooded poorly drained flat lands, and the Spaniards who were recognising the area had to march for a month with water at waist level, drinking poor-quality water and barely eating a properly cooked meal.[29] In northern Patagonia, cold weather was predominant, with below-average temperatures.[30] Notwithstanding the difficulties, the first settlers in Santiago strongly believed in advancing colonisation southward. However, their optimism vanished at the end of 1598 when the natives in the Araucanía set the colonies ablaze, and all the Spaniards were either murdered or expelled northward of the Biobio River. The royal response to the rebellion was establishing a border in Concepción protected by a professional army. Afterwards, climate conditions associated with the LIA started to play an interesting role. Soldiers had only one summer month (January) to run a military campaign whose main goal was to destroy the planted fields and deprive the native rebels of agriculture. The rationale was that starvation would reduce warfare capacity and propel a truce.

It would eventually happen that way, but not because of human agency. As we will point out later, a more-than-human agency would create the conditions for peace in southern Chile. In the meantime, and adapting themselves very well to the challenge of the January expedition of the Spanish soldiers, the rebel Araucanians grew some maize (*Zea mays*) by the side of the few paths that the Spaniards would transit during a campaign. These plots, however, were a disguise, just to give the soldiers the illusion that they were destroying the next harvest. In truth, most of the croplands were inaccessible to the army, located in higher altitudes and far away from the paths, which made them impossible even to be seen. A report of 1621 to the king concluded that the Indians in Chile died of laughter, not starvation.[31]

In addition, since the earliest days of their interrelationship with the Europeans, the native diet expanded with growing plants with differential harvesting times. Wheat, for example, was a better fit than maize for a cooler weather. Indians also learned how to shepherd European cattle, mainly sheep (*Ovis aries*), and how to raise farm animals, which demonstrates a substantial output of adaptation to weather, environment and warfare at the same time. There are other examples of how environmental conditions became helpful in warfare. Rebels burned fields to deny pasture to the Spanish horses and forced soldiers into unknown and watery terrains where the Indians easily neutralised the effectiveness of both horses and guns. Likewise, increased rain – due to the LIA or otherwise – made navigable some rivers while others were impossible to cross. The Cautín River was navigable then (it is not today), and it was a safer and faster way of communication among tribes, in contrast with the muddy pedestrian paths that the Spanish soldiers were forced to take in case the rebels or a natural event made impassable an easier road. Indians also allowed large swamps to encroach on the surroundings of Purén and Lumaco since such environmental conditions gave their villages natural protection.[32]

Although lacking precise data, we may speculate that sustained cold weather helped spread or worsen respiratory diseases like influenza brought by the Spaniards. Between 1540 and 1650, at least fifteen outbreaks of undetermined epidemics referred to in the sources affected the tribes.[33] In general, the sources do not specify diseases, except in the case of a smallpox outbreak, perhaps because it was highly visible, often lethal, very contagious, and fast spreading. Between 1520 and 1530, the *variola virus* went from the Great Lakes in Canada to the Argentine pampas, killing in its wake half of the natives who became infected.[34] The so-called 'Spanish disease' terrified Araucanians to the point of revolts. An interesting episode occurred in 1611. Lentils were rejected violently because their appearance suggested to the Indians that they were the cause of smallpox, so when the governor Alonso de la Jaraquemada arrived in Chile with a load of olive oil, wine and varied seeds, and a bag containing lentils was accidentally ripped open, native onlookers spread the news. The governor planned to exterminate the Indians by spreading the horrific disease, so the rumour went, causing the violent insurgency of 1612.[35] *Variola virus* thrives in cold and dry winters.[36] Nonetheless, in the rainy 1619, while the Mapocho River in Santiago caused a flash flood, smallpox and chickenpox killed around 50,000 people.[37] Data accuracy is doubtful since this eyewitness wrote his account several years after the fact. However, the importance lies in a vivid memory that assigned a chronological synchronisation to a pandemic and a flood, the two most frequent and devastating disruptions of colonial life.

Regarding the impact of solar fluctuations on microorganisms and diseases, on account of Covid-19, Nasirpour et al. correlated solar activity and pandemics from 1750 to 2020. According to these authors, solar events not only impacted the atmosphere and led to storms, hurricanes and extreme winters but also influenced infectious disease outbreaks. Variations in the intensity of cosmic rays arriving on the earth, primarily due to sunspots, are related to changes in the sun's surface activity. The minimum sunspot number leads to an increase in cosmic ray flux reaching the earth and causing mutations of viruses. A magnetic field shields the earth against solar particles and cosmic rays, but the magnetic field cannot withstand certain elements during a maximum or a minimum sunspot. Three molecular mechanisms – point mutations, gene recombination and gene range – are responsible for the emerging pandemic virus strains; solar and cosmic rays may be a physical mutagen that causes point mutations that contribute to a pandemic.[38] The conclusion adds another interpretation to the spread of diseases in the Americas during the LIA.

On the Spanish side of the Araucanía, bad weather and severe storms were to blame for some military problems like the four-year delay in the reconstruction of the posts destroyed by the Indians during the uprising of 1553.[39] Persistent bad weather explains other disgraceful outcomes. According to a letter to the Crown in 1639, when an Araucanian chief was asked why he had not destroyed the small fort of Angol, he replied that nature alone would do it. His stealing of the horses was just for enjoyment since it made soldiers a bit more miserable when they had to go on foot to collect dry firewood. The chief was right. Angol was destroyed by the agency of nature and the will of desperate soldiers who needed an excuse to run away from duty. According to a report, not natives but soldiers set Angol on fire, not once but three times in a row.[40] Meanwhile, in the Central Valley, the *actas* of Santiago for 1559, 1567–8 and 1574 reported long rainy seasons. We associate some years with the wet cycle of El Niño Southern Oscillation (ENSO), whose effects from the coast of Ecuador to Chile are well known.[41] There was strong ENSO in 1559 and 1574, and a moderate one in 1567–8. The mega-ENSO of 1578–9 destroyed many native villages in Lambayeque, northern Peru, with storms that lasted '40 days'.[42] It seems that this same ENSO deteriorated environmental conditions in southern Chile. An account of 1580 depicted a 'biblical plague' with the horrific scene of rats eating babies in their cribs.[43]

In a broader regional context, sources from 1583 to 1605 for the Altiplano (a zone susceptible to ENSO) describe a cooler-than-usual period,[44] and we believe that the same applies to the Strait of Magellan. Harsh weather doomed Rey Felipe and Nombre de Jesús, the two settlements that Sarmiento de Gamboa had established in 1584 to control the entrance to the Pacific from the Atlantic. The two colonies were the royal response to the traumatising appearance of Francis Drake off the coast of Ecuador in 1579, where he plundered the heavily protected galleon *Nuestra Señora de la Concepción* (aka *El cagafuegos* or 'fireshitter'). To the surprise of the Spanish, Drake had crossed the Strait in seventeen days, half the time Hernando de Magallanes took. This may well be a proxy indicator of a favourable El Niño condition for navigators.[45] At any rate, the episode points to anomalous local conditions, as later on, Thomas Cavendish would navigate the same route in forty-nine days while John Hawkins did it in thirty-eight.[46] By January of 1587, Cavendish could save only a handful of survivors from Rey Felipe since most had already died of hypothermia, cold-related diseases and starvation. Understandably, Cavendish renamed the place as Port Famine.[47] The dramatic affair in the south paired with events in the north, where all 117 settlers in the Roanoke Island colony disappeared sometime between 1587 and 1590. There was a strong El Niño signal in 1590.[48] In Jamestown, founded in 1607, colonists wrote of bad weather, conflicts with Indians and famine to the point of cannibalism.[49] Once again, only 38 of 104 original settlers managed to survive during the first year.[50]

Meanwhile, Florida had 'nothing but rain all that time'.[51] The Paraná basin underwent the same situation,[52] and the Bolivian Altiplano experienced repeated freezes.[53] Consequently, natural resources to combat cool and wet weather became highly demanded. We cannot consider the following data a proper proxy indicator, but it sheds light on other situations associated with LIA's local effects. The need for firewood reached extremes in the treeless pampas, where the *cabildo* of Buenos Aires had to enforce protective measures to avoid unsustainable timber exploitation. Early in the seventeenth century, the *cabildo* fixed a quota and a fee to extract firewood from any ship arriving at the port. Likewise, cart owners had to provide their muleteers and workers with enough food and firewood before entering the city. Among other consequences of the lack of firewood was the poor quality of the buildings, as well-burnt bricks needed energy. Properties were of sun-dried mud and thatch or adobes, giving the impression of widespread poverty.[54]

According to Zeke Hausfather of the Breakthrough Institute (Oakland, California), worldwide, between 1615 and 1620, severe weather is a proxy indicator of the global LIA induced by a decrease in solar activity. In 1616 Japan experienced the coldest spring of the century. In 1620 an intense cold wave swept across Europe. And in a unique anomaly, the Bosporus froze, and people could walk across the ice between Europe and Asia.[55] Off the coast of Chile and Peru, storms battered for a longer period, extending the restrictive period for navigation imposed by the viceroy to avoid ship-wrecks. In central Chile and the lower Paraná basin, downpours provoked inundations and the loss of ploughed fields and grazing land. Advances of the Frías and Rio Manso glaciers in the Patagonian Andes indicate wet and cold years.[56] In the pre-Andean Uco Valley, 150 km southward of Mendoza, the increase in humidity in an otherwise desert environment induced changes that combined well with the new demographic condition of the beginning of the seventeenth century. The dense native population of pre-Columbian times had become irrelevant, probably as lethal diseases had already taken their toll.[57] Extensive tracks of land in the Upper Uco strip close to the mountains and with abundant rivers became easily avail-able for the Spaniards. They started grazing cattle brought in from the pampas, Cordoba and Paraguay. After crossing the Andes through the pass of Portillo de los Piuquenes and once in Santiago, most of the cattle pro-vided the tallow and hides exported to Upper Peru. Processed as jerked beef, this valuable commodity was shipped to the Peruvian coastal *haci-endas* to feed the slaves of the cotton plantations.[58]

Highly profitable, the tallow and hide trade involved civilians and the Jesuits in an extensive network. This was disrupted by El Niño when the Paraná River could not be crossed, the pampa plains were underwater, and snow storms kept the passes in the Andes closed. The best example of how El Niño cut each segment is the event of 1609–10. When in Chile, Captain Zavala was charged with purchasing horses in Paraguay. However, the high waters on the Paraná River foiled his efforts. He looked for horses around Córdoba, but herds had been reduced due to endless rains, lack of grasslands and recurring pestilence. Upon returning to Chile with a few horses, Zavala was informed that the pass across the Andes was still closed. At his arrival in Santiago, Zavala went to trial to no avail since bad weather – not him – was the culprit for the ruinous enterprise.[59] Besides, the Jesuit *Carta Annua* of 1610 attested to floods along the Parana River, and the *cabildo* of Santiago reported floods in the capital.[60] Similarly, the 1654 event – when the Jesuits completely lost the cattle sent from Uco to Santiago due to abnormal weather – was also recorded in Santa Fe.[61]

The coming of the Maunder Minimum

The 1640s was a decade of harvest failures in Spain. The year 1641 was the third coldest summer recorded over the past six centuries in the northern hemisphere, the second coldest winter in a century in New England, and the coldest winter ever recorded in Scandinavia. In the Iberian Peninsula, there was an increase in precipitation.[62] They were all proxy indicators of the MM. In 2014 Vaquero and Trigo proposed two phases of the MM based on data for the northern hemisphere. They pointed out a 'deep' phase from 1645 to 1700 and the 'extended' phase from 1618 to 1723.[63] Here we establish some correlations with events in southern Chile. Colder weather had dire consequences for the spread of infections, and in 1639 a pandemic raged among the Araucanians.[64] This time the disease combined with poor environmental conditions and the eruption of the Villarrica volcano in 1640. This eruption probably accelerated the 'deep' phase of MM. Earth System Sciences state that the temperature changes due to volcanic activity are one of the most striking features of LIA periods. It produces significant cooling events due to the emission of sulphur dioxide into the upper atmosphere, forming particulates that scatter incoming sunlight.[65] Proxy data of ENOS determine that it doubled after strong volcanic eruptions in the tropics.[66] Such a conjunction of agents was an eerie prelude to the developments preceding the most important interethnic event of the seventeenth century: the 1641 pact of Quillin.

The meeting in Quillin was celebrated in the long-standing Araucanian tradition of a *koyagtun*. During this annual ceremony, wars were declared, truces decided, marriages arranged and copious libations ingested. In the 1641 *koyagtun*, in Quillin, the natives asked the governor of Chile, Francisco López de Zúñiga, marquis of Baides, to join them, knowing in advance that a peace treaty would include sheep, goats and seeds of European grains among the 'gifts' natives would receive in exchange for peace. An eyewitness, the Jesuit Alonso de Ovalle, depicted the events in an account of a series of disasters common to volcanic activity in the mountains of middle latitudes.[67] The lava flows, gas emissions and hot water vapour melted the volcano's ice cap, causing mud avalanches that contaminated neighbouring water courses and the Villarrica Lake, killing fish and waterfowl, and polluting agricultural fields. Additional thunder and lightning activity, as well as earth tremors, lent a supernatural tone to the scene. In the sky, ashes spewed into the atmosphere, thickening a dust veil that reduced the already weak solar radiation and lowered temperatures. The natives believed mountains were home to spirits who expressed bad omens. More frightening still, this came amid rains that had already reduced agricultural yields, putting the natives on the brink of famine. An image from Ovalle's book shows a monstrous creature emerging from the underworld, high above in the clouds, with gas effluvia crowning the picture. Two armies are engaged in an allegoric fight below: on one side are the Spaniards under the command of Santiago *Matamoros* (the Spanish army's saint patron), and on the other, the Indians fleeing in disarray. According to Ovalle, this was God's way of helping the Spaniards to achieve the evangelisation of the Indians.[68]

The mid-seventeenth-century environmental situation in southern Chile has a proxy indicator of an international, imperial venue. The MM helps explain the Dutch's short presence in Valdivia. In 1643 an expedition under the command of Hendrik Brouwer headed for the island of Chiloé from what was at that time a Dutch possession in the northeast of Brazil. The mission was to find support from the rebellious Araucanians and start the Dutch colonisation of the southernmost area of the continent. The port of Valdivia would then be a stepping stone in the route to the Asian markets. This Dutch imperial dream ended up in a fiasco mostly due to a more-than-human agency. When in 1623, the Dutch forces established a bridgehead in northeast Brazil, Spanish authorities became aware that they intended to expand into outlying regions, most probably towards the Rio de la Plata. But instead, in 1643, the Dutch launched the expedition to Chile, just when natives would be of negligible help since they had little if any foodstuffs, blaming the shortage on several years of bad weather and earthquakes. After five months of hunger and a rainy winter, with Brouwer now dead of natural causes, the demoralised Dutch abandoned Valdivia and returned to Brazil, never returning to southern Chile.[69] Similar conditions were still prevailing in 1645 during the Spanish fortification of Valdivia. Complaints to Santiago were about food scarcity, lack of assistance from the natives and the never-ending storms.[70]

Conclusion

The two global fluctuations we have considered connect solar activity with the human developments in southern South America during the sixteenth and seventeenth centuries. The chapter has combined data from archival records with data produced by Earth System Sciences to attest to the impacts of the LIA, the MM and the ENOS in the southernmost portions of the Americas. Whenever possible, we contextualised local events in a broader frame of geohistorical developments. The aim was somehow to decentre humans from the account by stressing how climate change was a historical agent. Both the LIA and the MM were global fluctuations derived from the sun's activity interfering with our planet's climate. In Europe, the climax of the LIA was reached in the 1690s,[71] but we need more studies to clarify a chronology for the Americas. There are proxy indicators of extreme weather and disruptions in societies that can be associated with the effects of the LIA in southern South America. In the case of the MM, the impacts on the Araucanía are clear due to its associa-tion with the environmental consequences of the Villarrica eruption and a previous pandemic among the natives.[72]

Despite the difficulties and pitfalls when reconstructing past climate using historical documents, the sources used in this chapter attest to human reactions, and thus they are proxy indicators of climate variations. Earth System Sciences are researching for a better understanding of the relations between the sun and the climate on our planet, but since the dawn of time, historical documents illustrate that humans have always reacted to the sun. Cross-culturally, the sun tends to be the universal and most sacred of all natural things. Associated with light and warmth, weather and food production, as well as the general wellbeing of living organisms, the sun is a nonhuman agent that should be part of historical accounts and explanations.

Notes

1. Nils Stenseth, Atle Mysterud, Geir Ottersen, James Hurrell, Kung-Sig Chan & Mauricio Lima, 'Ecological effects of climate fluctuations', *Science* 297 (2002), 1292–6; Joanna Haigh, 'The sun and the earth's climate', *Living Reviews in Solar Physics* 4 (2007), 5–64; William Bruckman & Elio Ramos, 'El sol y el clima en la Tierra', *Revista Umbral* 1 (2017), 42–53.

2. Emmanuel Le Roi Ladurie, *Times of feast, times of famine: a history of climate since the year 1000*. New York, Doubleday, 1971.

3. There are several examples of the use of historical colonial sources to reconstruct the past Latin American climate; see Enrique Florescano, *Precios del maíz y crisis agrícolas. 1708–1810*. Mexico City, Colmex, 1969; Susan Swan, 'Drought and Mexico's struggle for independence', *Environmental Review: ER* 6, no. 1 (1982), 54–62; Virginia García Acosta, *Los precios del trigo en la historia colonial de México*. Mexico City, CIESAS-Casa Chata, 1988; Georgina Endfield, *Climate and society in colonial Mexico: a study in vulnerability*. Malden, MA, Blackwell, 2008; Bradley Skopyk, *Colonial cataclysms: climate, landscape, and memory in Mexico's Little Ice Age*. Tucson, AZ, University of Arizona Press, 2020. In 1983, the archeologist Gustavo Politis used archival records to understand colonial climate fluctuations and the possible impacts on inter-ethnic relations ('Climatic variations during historical times in Eastern Buenos Aires Pampas, Argentina', *Quaternary of South America and Antarctic Peninsula* 2 (1983), 133–61). Similarly, Margarita Gascón and César Caviedes have considered colonial sources for Argentina and Chile ('Clima y Sociedad en Argentina y Chile durante el periodo colonial', *Anuario Colombiano de Historia Social y de la Cultura* 39, no. 2 (2012), 159–85. For an environmental approach to climate and weather see Friederike Otto ('Attribution of weather and climate events', *Annual Review of Environment and Resources* 42 (2017), 627–46. Joao Lima Neto, 'Primeiras impressões dos cronistas e viajantes sobre o tempo e o clima no Brasil colonial'. *Biblio 3w: revista bibliográfica de geografía y ciencias sociales* 11 (2006), https://www.raco.cat/index.php/ Biblio3w/article/view/71890; Katherinne Mora Pacheco, *Entre sequías, heladas e inundaciones. Clima y sociedad en la Sabana de Bogotá, 1690–1870*. Bogotá, Universidad Nacional de Colombia, 2019. The recent book *Un pasado vivo. Dos siglos de historia ambiental latinoamericana* (Bogotá,

Fondo de Cultura Económica-Universidad de los Andes, 2019) edited by Claudia Leal, John Soluri and José Augusto Pádua does not include climate.

4. Dagomar Degroot, Kevin Anchukaitis, Martin Bauch, Jacob Burnham, Fred Carnegy, Jianxin Cui, Katryn de Luna, Piotr Guzowski, George Hambrecht, Heli Htamaa, Adam Izdebski, Katrin Kleeman, Emma Moesswilde, Naresh Neupane, Timothy Newfield, Quing Pei, Elena Xoplaki & Natale Zappia, 'Towards a rigorous understanding of societal responses to climate change', *Nature* 591 (2021), 539–50, p. 541.

5. Philip Jones & Michael Mann, 'Climate over past millennia', *Reviews of Geophysics* 42 (2004), RG2002.

6. The German cultural historian Wolfgang Behringer argues for a 'strong link between the Little Ice Age and witch persecutions in Europe' (*A cultural history of climate*. Cambridge, MA, Polity Press, 2010, 132). Nonetheless he does not imply a mechanical straightforward relation and, for example, he portrays a climate abnormality that once favoured the access to power of the Ming dynasty in China and a similar one in in 1643 that nevertheless created the deep social unrest that expelled the Ming from power (114). See also Behringer, 'Climate change and witch-hunting: the impact of the Little Ice Age on mentalities', *Climatic Change* 43 (1999), 335–51; Daniel Sandweiss & Alice Kelley, 'Archaeological contributions to climate change research: the archaeological record as a paleoclimatic and paleoenvironmental archive', *Annual Review of Anthropology* 41, no. 1 (2012), 371–91.

7. Hubert Lamb (1913–97) was a pioneer and influential historian with his classic *Climate, history and the modern world* (London, Taylor & Francis e-Library, [1982, London, Routledge], 2005, https://ens9004-infd.mendoza.edu.ar) whose detailed research opens the field of historical climatology but at the same time came under scrutiny about the reliability of the data provided by historical sources (see early criticisms in M. J. Ingram, D. Underhill & Tom M. Wigley, 'Historical climatology', *Nature* 276 (1978), 329–34).

8. A decade ago Stephania Gallini identified two problems; the geographical scale and the type of sources, see 'Problemas de método en la Historia Ambiental de América Latina', *Anuario IEHS* 19 (2004), 141–71, pp. 149–50.

9. Fredrik Ljungqvist, Andrea Seim & Heli Huhtamaa, 'Climate and society in European history', *WIREs Climate Change* 12, no. 2 (2021), 1–28.

10. Jean Grove, *The Little Ice Age*. London, Methuen, 1988; Michael Mann, Raymond Bradley & Malcolm Hughes, 'Global-scale temperature patterns and climate forcing over the past six centuries', *Nature* 39 (1998), 779–87; Mathew Owens, Mike Lockwood, Ed Hawkins, Ilya Usoskin, Gareth Jones, Luc Barnard, Andrew Schurer & John Fasullo, 'The Maunder Minimum and the Little Ice Age: an update from recent reconstructions and climate simulations', *Journal of Space Weather and Space Climate* 7, no. A33 (2017); Armando Alberola, *Los cambios climáticos. La PEH en España*. Madrid, Cátedra, 2014; Philip Blom, *El motín de la naturaleza. Historia de la Pequeña Edad de Hielo (1570–1700)*. Barcelona, Anagrama, 2019.

11. Judith Lean & David Rind, 'Evaluating sun-climate relationships since the Little Ice Age', *Journal of Atmospheric and Solar-Terrestrial Physics* 61 (1999), 25–36; Ilya Usoskin, 'A history of solar activity over millennia', *Living Reviews in Solar Physics* 14, no. 3 (2017); Hiroko Miyahara, Fuyuki Tokanai, Toru Moriya, Mirei Takeyama, Hirohisa Sakurai, Kazuho Horiuchi & Hideyuki Hotta, 'Gradual onset of the Maunder Minimum revealed by high-precision carbon-14 analyses', *Scientific Report* 11 (2021), 5482.

12. John Eddy, 'The Maunder Minimum. A reappraisal', *Science* 192 (1976), 1189–202; John Beckman & Terry Mahoney, 'The Maunder Minimum and climate change: have historical records aided current research?', *Library and Information Services in Astronomy* III (LISA III) 153 (1998), https://www.stsci.edu; Valerie Masson-Delmotte,

Michael Schulz, Ayako Abe-Ouchi, Jürg Beer, Andrey Ganopolski, Jesús González Rouco, Eystein Jansen, Kurt Lambeck, Jürg Luterbacher, Timothy Naish, Timothy Osborn, Bette Otto-Bliesner, Terence Quinn, Rengaswamy Ramesh, Maisa Rojas, Xue Mei Shao & Axel Timmermann, 'Information from paleoclimate archives', *Climate change 2013: the physical science basis. Contribution of working group I to the fifth assessment report of the Intergovernmental Panel on Climate Change*', Cambridge, Cambridge University Press, 383–464; Marc Oliva, 'The Little Ice Age, the climatic background of present-day warming in Europe', *Cuadernos de Investigación Geográfica* 44, no. 1 (2018), 7–13; Chantal Camenisch & Christian Rohr, 'When the weather turned bad: the research of climate impacts on society and economy during the Little Ice Age in Europe. An overview', *Cuadernos de Investigación Geográfica* 44, no. 1 (2018), 99–114.

13. Brian Fagan, *The Little Ice Age: how climate made history*. New York, Basic Books, 2002; Geoffrey Parker, *Global crisis: war, climate change and catastrophe in the seventeenth century*. London, Yale University Press, 2013; Dagomar Degroot, *The frigid golden age: climate change, the Little Ice Age, and the Dutch Republic, 1560–1720*. New York, Cambridge University Press, 2018.

14. Henry Diaz & Vera Markgraf, *El Niño. Historical and palaeoclimatic aspects of the southern oscillation*. London, Cambridge University Press, 1992; Ricardo Villalba, 'Fluctuaciones climáticas en latitudes medias de América del Sur en los últimos 1.000 años: sus relaciones con la oscilación del sur', *Revista Chilena de Historia Natural* 67 (1994), 453–61; Brian Fagan, *Floods, famines, and emperors: El Niño and the fate of civilizations*. New York, Basic Books, 1999; César Caviedes, *El Niño in history*. Gainesville, FL, University Presses of Florida, 2001.

15. Raymond Bradley & Philip Jones (eds.), *Climate since 1500 A.D.* London, Routledge, 1992, María R. Prieto & Ricardo García Herrera, 'Documentary sources from South America: potential for climate reconstruction', *Palaeogeography Palaeoclimatology Palaeoecology* 281 (2009), 196–209; Rudolf Brázdil, Andrea Kiss, Jürg Luterbacher, David Nash & Ladislava Reznicková, 'Documentary data and the study of past droughts: a global state of art', *Climate of the Past* 14 (2018), 1915–60; Teresa Bullón Mata, 'Little Ice Age, palaeofloods and human adaptation on the Jarama River (Tajo Basin, Central Spain) from documentary proxy data', *Cuadernos de Investigación Geográfica* 46, no. 2 (2020), 497–519.

16. Frank Chambers, Sally Brain, Dimtri Mauquoy, Julia McCarroll & Tim Daley, 'The Little Ice Age in the southern hemisphere in the context of the last 3000 years: peat-based proxy-climate data from Tierra del Fuego', *The Holocene* 24, no. 12 (2014), 1649–56.

17. Astrid Ogilvie & Trausti Jónsson, '"Little Ice Age" research: a perspective from Iceland'. *Climatic Change* 48, no. 1 (2001), 9–52.; John Matthews & Keith Briffa, 'The Little Ice Age: re-evaluation of an evolving concept', *Geografiska Annaler* 87 A(1) (2005), 17–36.

18. Stephen Self, Michael Rampino & James Barbera, 'The possible effects of large 19th and 20th century volcanic eruptions on zonal and hemispheric surface temperatures', *Journal of Volcanology and Geothermal Research* 11 (1981), 41–60; Gregory Zielinski, 'Climatic impact of volcanic eruptions: mini-review', *The Scientific World Journal* 2 (2002), 869–84; Thomas Cronin, *Paleoclimates: understanding climate change past and present*. New York, Columbia University Press, 2010; Gifford Miller, Geirsdóttir Áslaug, Yafang Zhong, Larsen Darren, Bette Otto-Bliesner, Marika Holland, David Bailey, Kurt Refsnider, Scott Lehman, John Southon, Anderson Chance, Helgi Björnsson & Thorvaldur Thordarson, 'Abrupt onset of the Little Ice Age triggered by volcanism and sustained by sea-ice/ocean feedbacks', *Geophysical Research Letters* 39 (2012), LO2708.

19. Robert Dull, Richard Nevle, William Woods, Dennis Bird, Shiri Avnery & William Denevan, 'The Columbian encounter and the Little Ice Age: abrupt land use

change, fire, and greenhouse forcing', *Annals of the Association of American Geographers* 100, no. 4 (2010), 755–71; Richard Nevle & Dennis Bird, 'Effects of syn-pandemic fire reduction and reforestation in the tropical Americas on atmospheric CO2 during European conquest', *Palaeogeography Palaeoclimatology Palaeoecology* 264, no. 1 (2008), 25–38; Richard Nevle, William Ruddiman & Robert Dull, 'Neotropical human–landscape interactions, fire, and atmospheric CO2 during European conquest', *The Holocene* 21, no. 5 (2011), 853–64; Matthew Liebmann, Joshua Farella, Christopher Roos, Adam Stack, Sarah Martini & Thomas Swetnam, 'Native American depopulation, reforestation, and fire regimes in the Southwest United States, 1492–1900', CEPNAS 113, no. 6 (2016), E696–E704; Alexander Koch, Chris Brierley, Mark Maslin & Simon Lewis, 'Earth system impacts of the European arrival and Great Dying in the Americas after 1492', *Quaternary Science Reviews* 207 (2019), 13–36.

20. Chistophe Bonneuil & Jean-Baptiste Fressoz, *The shock of the Anthropocene: the earth, history and us*. London-New York, Verso, 2016, p. 27.

21. Simon Lewis & Mark Maslin, 'Defining the Anthropocene', *Nature* 519 (2015), 171–80.

22. Yadvinder Malhi, 'The concept of the Anthropocene', *Annual Review of Environment and Resources* 42 (2017), 77–104.

23. 'Cartas de Pedro de Valdivia que tratan del descubrimiento y conquista de Chile', *Crónicas del Reino de Chile* – Pedro de Valdivia: Cartas; Alonso de Góngora Marmolejo: Historia de Chile desde su descubrimiento hasta el año de 1575'; Pedro Mariño de Lobera, 'Crónica del Reino de escrita por el capitán D. Pedro Mariño de Lobera, dirigida al Excelentísimo Sr. D. García Hurtado de Mendoza, Marqués de Cañete, Vicerrey y Capitán General de los Reinos del Perú y Chile, Reducido a Nuevo Método y Estilo por el Padre Bartolomé de Escobar de la Compañía de Jesús', *Crónicas del Reino de Chile*. Madrid, Maribel, 1960, 9–10.

24. Jerónimo de Vivar, *Crónica y relación copiosa y verdadera de los reinos de Chile*. Santiago, Chile, Fondo Histórico y Bibliográfico José Toribio Medina, [1558] 1966, Volume II, 37, 59.

25. Thomas Madsen & Richard Shine, 'Rainfall and rats: climatically-driven dynamics of a tropical rodent population', *Australian Journal of Ecology* 24, no. 1 (2009), 80–9.

26. Benjamín Vicuña Mackenna, *Ensayo histórico sobre el clima de Chile*. Valparaíso, Imprenta del Mercurio, 1877, 18–19.

27. Antonio Elio Brailovsky, 'Buenos Aires, ciudad inundable', *Lhawet* 1, no. 1 (2011), 15–23, p. 16.

28. *Historia del Paraguay*, vol. 2 has half-title, and v.3–6 added t.-p. 'Los jesuitas en el Rio de la Plata, 1586–1830'. First edition of the work published Paris [1756] 1910, www.archives.org.

29. Ulrico Schmidl, *Viaje al Río de la Plata*. Buenos Aires, Nuevo siglo, [1567] 1995, 3.

30. Villalba, 1994, 164.

31. Margarita Gascón, *Naturaleza e imperio: Araucanía, Patagonia, Pampas, 1598–1740*. Buenos Aires, Dunken, 2007, 45.

32. Jerónimo de Vivar was a soldier in the troops that first entered in southern Chile and described the Indian tactics of warfare with detail, see his *Crónica y relación copiosa y verdadera de los reinos de Chile*. Santiago, Chile, Fondo Histórico y Bibliográfico José Toribio Medina, [1558] 1966.

33. Alejandra Araya Espinosa, *Ociosos, vagabundos y malentretenidos en Chile colonial*. Santiago, Chile, Dibam, 1999, 29.

34. Alfred Crosby, *Ecological imperialism: the biological expansion of Europe, 900–1900*. New York, Cambridge University Press, 1999, 201–4.

35. Gerónimo de Quiroga, *Memorias de los sucesos de la Guerra de Chile*. Santiago, Chile, Andrés Bello, [1628–1704] 1979, 322.

36. Harald Frederiksen, Nemesio Torres Muñoz & Alfredo Jauregui Molina, 'Erradicación de la viruela', *Public Health Report* (1959), 207–15, p. 209.

37. Quiroga, 1979, 338.

38. Mohammad Nasirpour, Abbas Sharifi, Mohsen Ahmadi & Saeid Ghoushchi, 'Revealing the relationship between solar activity and COVID-19 and forecasting of possible future viruses using multi-step autoregression (MSAR)', *Environmental Science Pollution Research 28* (2021), 38074–84.

39. Eugene Korth, *Spanish policy in colonial Chile: the struggle for social justice, 1535–1700*. Stanford, CA, Stanford University Press, 1968, 41.

40. 'El marqués de Baides refiere largamente a su Majestad el Rey el estado de cosas de Chile y el que tienen las de guerra, que hoy está más viva que hasta aquí y más imposibilitado de contenerla por falta de hombres de guerra. Concepción, 19 de marzo de 1640', Biblioteca Nacional, Santiago, Chile, Sala Medina, Manuscritos, Volume 137, Document 2478.

41. William Quinn, Víctor Neal & Santiago Antunes de Mayolo, 'El Niño occurrences over four and a half centuries', *Journal of Geophysical Research* 92/C13(1992), 14449–61 (1987); with a reviewed in Quinn, 1992; Louis Ortlieb, 'Las mayores precipitaciones históricas en Chile central y la cronología de los eventos ENOS en los siglos XVI-XIX', *Revista Chilena de Historia Natural* 67 (1994), 463–85.

42. Lorenzo Huertas, *Ecología e historia. Probanzas de indios y españoles referentes a las catastróficas lluvias de 1578, en los corregimientos de Trujillo y Saña*. Chiclayo, Peru, Centro de Estudios Sociales Solidaridad, 1987, 44.

43. Mariño de Lobera, 1960, 520.

44. María Prieto, Roberto Herrera & Patricia Dussel, 'Clima y disponibilidad hídrica en el sur de Bolivia y NO de Argentina entre 1560 y 1720. Los documentos españoles como fuente de datos ambientales', *Bamberger Geographische Schriften Bd* 15 (1998), 35–56.

45. Caviedes, 2001, 70–1.

46. Juan Ladrillero, 'Relación del viaje al Estrecho de Magallanes', *Anuario Hidrográfico de la Marina de Chile*. Valparaíso: Instituto de Historia de la Marina de Chile, 1880, 423–525; Ricardo Padrón, 'América y el espacio transmagallánico, siglo XVI', *Magallania* 48 – especial 'El Viaje de Magallanes 1520–2020' (2020), 79–102.

47. Robert Southey, *English seamen: Howard, Clifford, Hawkins, Drake, Cavendish*. London, [1774–1843] 1897, 320–70, http://www.archive.org

48. Stuart Browning & Ian Goodwin, 'The Paleoclimate reanalysis project'. *Climate Past Discussion* 11 (2015), 4159–204.

49. Francisco Álvarez, *Noticia del establecimiento y población de las colonias inglesas en la América Septentrional*. Madrid, A. Fernández, 1778, 27.

50. Karen Kupperman, *The Jamestown Project*. Cambridge, MA, Harvard University Press, 2007, and 'The puzzle of the American climate in the early colonial period', *The American Historical Review* 87, no. 5 (1982), 1262–5; Frank Grizzard & Boyd Smith, *Jamestown colony: a political, social, and cultural history*. Santa Barbara, CA, ABD Clio, 2007.

51. Archives of the Indies, 54-5-16, f. 12; 54-5-9, f. 32.

52. María R. Prieto, 'Enso signals in South America: rains and floods in the Parana River region during colonial times', *Climatic Change* 83 (2007), 39–54.

53. Alain Gioda & María Prieto, 'Histoire de sécheresses andines: Potosi, El Niño et la Petite Age Glaciaire', *La Météorologie* 8 (1999), 33–42.

54. Gascón, 2007.

55. Parker, 2013, xxvii.

56. Jorge Rabassa, Aldo Brandani, José Boninsegna & Daniel Cobos, 'Cronología de la "Pequeña Edad del Hielo" en los glaciares Rio Manso y Castaño Overo, Cerro Tronador, Provincia de Rio Negro', 9no Congreso Geológico Argentino, Actas 3 (1984), 624–39; Ricardo Villalba, 'Tree-ring and glacial evidence for the medieval warm epoch and the Little Ice Age in southern South America', *Climatic Change* 26 (1994), 183–97; Mariano Masiokas, Andrés Rivera, Lydia Espizua, Ricardo Villalba, Silvia Delgado & Juan Carlos Aravena, 'Glacier fluctuations in extra-tropical South America during the last 1000 years', *Palaeogeography, Palaeoclimatology, Palaeoecology* 281 (2009), 242–6.

57. Margarita Gascón & María José Ots, 'Pulsos ocupacionales prehispánicos y coloniales en Uco – Xaurúa (Mendoza, Argentina). Conquista, enfermedad y adaptación', *Diálogo Andino. Revista de Historia, Geografía y Cultura Andina* 63 (2020), 67–77.

58. Gascón, 2007, 71–94.

59. 'Carta de Pedro Martínez de Zavala a Su Majestad el Rey, Tucumán, 24 marzo 1610', Biblioteca Nacional, Santiago, Chile, Sala Medina, Manuscritos, Volume 118, Document 2085.

60. Vicuña Mackenna, 1877, 18–19.

61. Actas del Cabildo de Santa Fe, Archivo General de la Provincia de Santa Fe, Rosario, Santa Fe, Argentina, http://www.webs.tecnodoc.com.ar

62. Mariano Barriendos, 'Climatic variations in the Iberian peninsula during the late Maunder Minimum (AD 1675–1715): an analysis of data from rogation ceremonies', *The Holocene* 7 (1997), 105–11.

63. José Vaquero & Ricardo Trigo, 'Redefining the limit dates of the Maunder Minimum', *New Astronomy* 34 (2014), 1–6.

64. 'Carta del Marqués de Baides a Su Majestad el Rey. Lima, 13 marzo 1639', Biblioteca Nacional, Santiago, Chile, Sala Medina, Manuscritos, Volume 136, Document 2467, f. 38.

65. Keith Briffa, Philip Jones, Fritz Schweingruber & Timothy Osborn, 'Influence of volcanic eruptions on Northern Hemisphere summer temperature over the past 600 years', *Nature* 393 (1998), 450–55.

66. Bert Rein, Andreas Lückge, Lutz Reinhardt, Frank Sirocko, Anja Wolf & Christian Dullo, 'El Niño variability off Peru during the last 20,000 years', *Paleoceanography and Paleoclimatology* 20, no. 4 (2005), PA4003, 15.

67. Alonso de Ovalle, *Histórica relación del Reyno de Chile y de las misiones que ejercita en él la Compañía de Jesús: A Nuestro Señor Jesucristo Dios y Hombre ya la Santísima Virgen y Madre Nuestra, Señora del Cielo y de la Tierra, a los Santos José, Joachin y Ana, sus padres y abuelos.* Rome, Imprenta de Francisco Cavallo, 1646.

68. Gascón, 2007, 33–7; *Relación Verdadera de las Pazes que Capituló con el araucano rebelado, el marqués de Baides, conde de Pedrosa, governador y capitán general del reyno de Chile, y presidente de la Real Audiencia / Sacada de sus informes y cartas y de los padres de la Compañía de Jesús, que aco[m]pañaron al real ejército en la jornada que hizo para este efecto el año pasado de 1641.* Madrid, Francisco Maroto, 1642, The John Carter Brown Library. Providence, RI. Book LCCN 43022438.

69. Hendrick Brouwer (1581–1643) *Journael ende historis verhael van der Reyse gedaen bij Costen de Straet Le Maire.* Amsterdam, Broer Jansz, 1646, 53–69, 53, 54,

69; for a general account, see Isidoro Vázquez de Acuña, *Las incursiones holandesas en Chiloé*. Santiago, Universidad de Santiago de Chile, 1992.

70. Francisco Enrich, *Historia de la Compañía de Jesús en Chile*. Barcelona, Roral, 1891, 497.

71. Jürg Luterbacher, Ralph Rickli, Elena Xoplaki, C. Tinguely, Christoph Beck, Christian Pfister & Heinz Wanner, 'The late Maunder Minimum (1675–1715): a key period for studying decadal scale climatic change in Europe', *Climatic Change* 49, no. 4 (2001), 441–62, p. 442.

72. Gascón, 'El Minimo de Maunder en el extremo sur de América. Algunos proxy indicators en fuentes del siglo XVII', *Proceedings* E-International Center for Earth Sciences – ICES 16–2021, Buenos Aires-Mendoza, Comisión Nacional de Energía Atómica y Universidad Nacional de Cuyo, 2022, 105–11, www.uncu.edu.ar/ICES

References

Alberola, Armando, *Los cambios climáticos. La PEH en España*. Madrid, Cátedra, 2014.

Araya Espinosa, Alejandra, *Ociosos, vagabundos y malentretenidos en Chile colonial*. Santiago, Chile, Dibam, 1999.

Barriendos, Mariano, 'Climatic variations in the Iberian peninsula during the late Maunder Minimum (AD 1675–1715): an analysis of data from rogation ceremonies', *The Holocene* 7 (1997), 105–11.

Beckman, John & Terry Mahoney, 'The Maunder Minimum and climate change: have historical records aided current research?' *Library and Information Services in Astronomy* III (LISA III) 153 (1998), Instituto de Astrofísica de Canarias, E-38200 La Laguna, Tenerife.

Behringer. Wolfgang, 'Climate change and witch-hunting: the impact of the Little Ice Age on mentalities', *Climatic Change* 43 (1999), 335–51.

Behringer. Wolfgang, *A cultural history of climate*. Cambridge, MA, Polity Press, 2010.

Blom, Philip, *El motín de la naturaleza. Historia de la Pequeña Edad de Hielo (1570–1700)*. Barcelona, Anagrama, 2019.

Bonneuil, Chistophe & Jean-Baptiste Fressoz, *The shock of the Anthropocene: the earth, history and us*. London-New York, Verso, 2016.

Bradley, Raymond & Philip Jones (eds.), *Climate since 1500 A.D.* London, Routledge, 1992.

Brailovsky, Antonio Elio, 'Buenos Aires, ciudad inundable', *Lhawet* 1, no. 1 (2011), 15–23.

Brázdil, Rudolf, Andrea Kiss, Jürg Luterbacher, David Nash & Ladislava Reznickóva, 'Documentary data and the study of past droughts: a global state of art', *Climate of the Past* 14 (2018), 1915–60.

Briffa, Keith, Philip Jones, Fritz Schweingruber & Timothy Osborn, 'Influence of volcanic eruptions on Northern Hemisphere summer temperature over the past 600 years', *Nature* 393 (1998), 450–5.

Browning, Stuart & Ian Goodwin, 'The Paleoclimate reanalysis project'. *Climate Past Discussion* 11 (2015), 4159–204.

Bruckman, William & Elio Ramos, 'El sol y el clima en la Tierra', *Revista Umbral* 1 (2017), 42–53.

Bullón Mata, Teresa,'Little Ice Age, palaeofloods and human adaptation on the Jarama River (Tajo Basin, Central Spain) from documentary proxy data', *Cuadernos de Investigación Geográfica* 46, no. 2 (2020), 497–519.

Camenisch, Chantal & Christian Rohr, 'When the weather turned bad: the research of climate impacts on society and economy during the Little Ice Age in Europe. An overview', *Cuadernos de Investigación Geográfica* 44, no. 1 (2018), 99–114.

Caviedes, César, *El Niño in history*. Gainesville, FL, University Presses of Florida, 2001.

Chambers, Frank, Sally Brain, Dimtri Mauquoy, Julia McCarroll & Tim Daley, 'The Little Ice Age in the southern hemisphere in the context of the last 3000 years: peat-based proxy-climate data from Tierra del Fuego', *The Holocene* 24, no. 12 (2014), 1649–56.

Cronin, Thomas, *Paleoclimates: understanding climate change past and present*. New York, Columbia University Press, 2010.

Crosby, Alfred, *Ecological imperialism: the biological expansion of Europe, 900–1900*. New York, Cambridge University Press, 1999.

Degroot, Dagomar, *The frigid golden age: climate change, the Little Ice Age, and the Dutch Republic, 1560–1720*. New York, Cambridge University Press, 2018.

Degroot, Dagomar, Kevin Anchukaitis, Martin Bauch, Jacob Burnham, Fred Carnegy, Jianxin Cui, Katryn de Luna, Piotr Guzowski, George Hambrecht, Heli Htamaa, Adam Izdebski, Katrin Kleeman, Emma Moesswilde, Naresh Neupane, Timothy Newfield, Quing Pei, Elena Xoplaki & Natale Zappia, 'Towards a rigorous understanding of societal responses to climate change', *Nature* 591 (2021), 539–50.

Diaz, Henry & Vera Markgraf, *El Niño: historical and palaeoclimatic aspects of the southern oscillation*. London, Cambridge University Press, 1992.

Dull, Robert, Richard Nevle, William Woods, Dennis Bird, Shiri Avnery & William Denevan, 'The Columbian encounter and the Little Ice Age: abrupt land use change, fire, and greenhouse forcing', *Annals of the Association of American Geographers* 100, no. 4 (2010), 755–71.

Eddy, John, 'The Maunder Minimum. A reappraisal', *Science* 192 (1976), 1189–202.

Endfield, Georgina, *Climate and society in colonial Mexico: a study in vulnerability*. Malden, MA, Blackwell, 2008.

Fagan, Brian, *Floods, famines, and emperors: El Niño and the fate of civilizations*. New York, Basic Books, 1999.

Fagan, Brian, *The Little Ice Age: how climate made history*. New York, Basic Books, 2002.

Florescano, Enrique, *Precios del maíz y crisis agrícolas. 1708–1810*. Mexico City, Colmex, 1969.

Frederiksen, Harald, Nemesio Torres Muñoz & Alfredo Jauregui Molina, 'Erradicación de la viruela', *Public Health Report* (1959), 207–15.

Gallini, Stephania, 'Problemas de método en la Historia Ambiental de América Latina', *Anuario IEHS* 19 (2004), 141–71.

García Acosta, Virginia, *Los precios del trigo en la historia colonial de México*. Mexico City, CIESAS-Casa Chata, 1988.

Gascón, Margarita, 'El Minimo de Maunder en el extremo sur de América. Algunos proxy indicators en fuentes del siglo XVII', *Proceedings* E-International Center for Earth Sciences – ICES 16–2021, Buenos Aires – Mendoza, Comisión Nacional de Energía Atómica y Universidad Nacional de Cuyo, 2022, 105–11.

Gascón, Margarita, *Naturaleza e imperio: Araucanía, Patagonia, Pampas, 1598–1740*. Buenos Aires, Dunken, 2007.

Gascón, Margarita and César Caviedes, 'Clima y Sociedad en Argentina y Chile durante el periodo colonial', *Anuario Colombiano de Historia Social y de la Cultura* 39, no. 2 (2012), 159–85.

Gascón, Margarita & María José Ots, 'Pulsos ocupacionales prehispánicos y coloniales en Uco - Xaurúa (Mendoza, Argentina). Conquista, enfermedad y adaptación', *Diálogo Andino. Revista de Historia, Geografía y Cultura Andina* 63 (2020), 67–77.

Gioda, Alain & María Prieto, 'Histoire de sécheresses andines: Potosi, El Niño et la Petite Age Glaciaire', *La Météorologie* 8 (1999), 33–42.

Grizzard, Frank & Boyd Smith, *Jamestown colony: a political, social, and cultural history*. Santa Barbara, CA, ABD Clio, 2007.

Grove, Jean, *The Little Ice Age*. London, Methuen, 1988.

Haigh, Joanna, 'The sun and the earth's climate', *Living Reviews in Solar Physics* 4 (2007), 5–64.

Huertas, Lorenzo, *Ecología e historia. Probanzas de indios y españoles referentes a las catastróficas lluvias de 1578, en los corregimientos de Trujillo y Saña*. Chiclayo, Peru, Centro de Estudios Sociales Solidaridad, 1987.

Ingram, M. J., D. Underhill & Tom M. Wigley, 'Historical climatology', *Nature* 276 (1978), 329–34.

Jones, Philip & Michael Mann, 'Climate over past millennia', *Reviews of Geophysics* 42 (2004), RG2002.

Koch, Alexander, Chris Brierley, Mark Maslin & Simon Lewis, 'Earth system impacts of the European arrival and Great Dying in the Americas after 1492', *Quaternary Science Reviews* 207 (2019), 13–36.

Korth, Eugene, *Spanish policy in colonial Chile: the struggle for social justice, 1535–1700*. Stanford, CA, Stanford University Press, 1968.

Kupperman, Karen, *The Jamestown Project*. Cambridge, MA, Harvard University Press, 2007.

Kupperman, Karen, 'The puzzle of the American climate in the early colonial period', *The American Historical Review* 87, no. 5 (1982), 1262–5.

Lamb, Hubert, *Climate, history and the modern world*. London, Taylor & Francis e-Library, [1982, London, Routledge], 2005.

Leal, Claudia, John Soluri and José Augusto Pádua, *Un pasado vivo. Dos siglos de historia ambiental latinoamericana*. Bogotá, Fondo de Cultura Económica-Universidad de los Andes, 2019.

Lean, Judith & David Rind, 'Evaluating sun-climate relationships since the Little Ice Age', *Journal of Atmospheric and Solar-Terrestrial Physics* 61 (1999), 25–36.

Le Roi Ladurie, Emmanuel, *Times of feast, times of famine: a history of climate since the year 1000*. New York, Doubleday, 1971.

Lewis, Simon & Mark Maslin,'Defining the Anthropocene', *Nature* 519 (2015), 171–80.

Liebmann, Matthew, Joshua Farella, Christopher Roos, Adam Stack, Sarah Martini & Thomas Swetnam, 'Native American depopulation, reforestation, and fire regimes in the Southwest United States, 1492–1900', CEPNAS 113, no. 6 (2016), E696–E704.

Lima Neto, Joao, 'Primeiras impressões dos cronistas e viajantes sobre o tempo e o clima no Brasil colonial'. *Biblio 3w: revista bibliográfica de geografía y ciencias sociales* 11 (2006), https://www.raco.cat/ index .php/ Biblio3w/article/view/71890

Ljungqvist, Fredrik, Andrea Seim & Heli Huhtamaa, 'Climate and society in European history', *WIREs Climate Change* 12, no. 2 (2021), 1–28.

Luterbacher, Jürg, Ralph Rickli, Elena Xoplaki, C. Tinguely, Christoph Beck, Christian Pfister & Heinz Wanner, 'The late Maunder Minimum (1675–1715): a key period for studying decadal scale climatic change in Europe', *Climatic Change* 49, no. 4 (2001), 441–62.

Madsen, Thomas & Richard Shine, 'Rainfall and rats: climatically-driven dynamics of a tropical rodent population', *Australian Journal of Ecology* 24, no. 1 (2009), 80–9.

Malhi, Yadvinder, 'The concept of the Anthropocene', *Annual Review of Environment and Resources* 42 (2017), 77–104.

Mann, Michael, Raymond Bradley & Malcolm Hughes, 'Global-scale temperature patterns and climate forcing over the past six centuries', *Nature* 39 (1998), 779–87.

Masiokas, Mariano, Andrés Rivera, Lydia Espizua, Ricardo Villalba, Silvia Delgado & Juan Carlos Aravena, 'Glacier fluctuations in extra-tropical South America during the last 1000 years', *Palaeogeography, Palaeoclimatology, Palaeoecology* 281 (2009), 242–6.

Masson-Delmotte,Valerie, Michael Schulz, Ayako Abe-Ouchi, Jürg Beer, Andrey Ganopolski, Jesús González Rouco, Eystein Jansen, Kurt Lambeck, Jürg Luterbacher, Timothy Naish, Timothy Osborn, Bette Otto-Bliesner, Terence Quinn, Rengaswamy Ramesh, Maisa Rojas, Xue Mei Shao & Axel Timmermann, 'Information from paleoclimate archives', *Climate change 2013: the physical science basis*.

Contribution of working group I to the fifth assessment report of the Intergovernmental Panel on Climate Change. Cambridge, Cambridge University Press, 383–464.

Matthews, John & Keith Briffa, 'The Little Ice Age: re-evaluation of an evolving concept', *Geografiska Annaler* 87 A(1) (2005), 17–36.

Miller, Gifford, Geirsdóttir Áslaug, Yafang Zhong, Larsen Darren, Bette Otto-Bliesner, Marika Holland, David Bailey, Kurt Refsnider, Scott Lehman, John Southon, Anderson Chance, Helgi Björnsson & Thorvaldur Thordarson, 'Abrupt onset of the Little Ice Age triggered by volcanism and sustained by sea-ice/ocean feedbacks', *Geophysical Research Letters* 39 (2012), L02708.

Miyahara, Hiroko, Fuyuki Tokanai, Toru Moriya, Mirei Takeyama, Hirohisa Sakurai, Kazuho Horiuchi & Hideyuki Hotta, 'Gradual onset of the Maunder Minimum revealed by high-precision carbon-14 analyses', *Scientific Report* 11 (2021), 5482.

Mora Pacheco, Katherinne, *Entre sequías, heladas e inundaciones. Clima y sociedad en la Sabana de Bogotá, 1690–1870.* Bogotá, Universidad Nacional de Colombia, 2019.

Nasirpour, Mohammad, Abbas Sharifi, Mohsen Ahmadi & Saeid Ghoushchi, 'Revealing the relationship between solar activity and COVID-19 and forecasting of possible future viruses using multi-step autoregression (MSAR)', *Environmental Science Pollution Research 28* (2021), 38074–84.

Nevle, Richard & Dennis Bird, 'Effects of syn-pandemic fire reduction and reforestation in the tropical Americas on atmospheric CO_2 during European conquest', *Palaeogeography Palaeoclimatology Palaeoecology* 264, no. 1 (2008), 25–38.

Nevle, Richard, William Ruddiman & Robert Dull, 'Neotropical human–landscape interactions, fire, and atmospheric CO_2 during European conquest', *The Holocene* 21, no. 5 (2011), 853–64.

Ogilvie, Astrid & Trausti Jónsson, '"Little Ice Age" research: a perspective from Iceland'. *Climatic Change* 48, no. 1 (2001), 9–52.

Oliva, Marc, 'The Little Ice Age, the climatic background of present-day warming in Europe', *Cuadernos de Investigación Geográfica* 44, no. 1 (2018), 7–13.

Ortlieb, Louis, 'Las mayores precipitaciones históricas en Chile central y la cronología de los eventos ENOS en los siglos XVI-XIX', *Revista Chilena de Historia Natural* 67 (1994), 463–85.

Otto, Friederike, 'Attribution of weather and climate events', *Annual Review of Environment and Resources* 42 (2017), 627–46.

Owens, Mathew, Mike Lockwood, Ed Hawkins, Ilya Usoskin, Gareth Jones, Luc Barnard, Andrew Schurer & John Fasullo, 'The Maunder

Minimum and the Little Ice Age: an update from recent reconstructions and climate simulations', *Journal of Space Weather and Space Climate* 7, no. A33 (2017).

Padrón, Ricardo, 'América y el espacio transmagallánico, siglo XVI', *Magallania* 48- especial 'El Viaje de Magallanes 1520–2020' (2020), 79–102.

Parker, Geoffrey, *Global crisis: war, climate change and catastrophe in the seventeenth century*. London, Yale University Press, 2013.

Politis, Gustavo, 'Climatic variations during historical times in Eastern Buenos Aires Pampas, Argentina', *Quaternary of South America and Antarctic Peninsula* 2 (1983), 133–61.

Prieto, María R., 'Enso signals in South America: rains and floods in the Parana River region during colonial times', *Climatic Change* 83 (2007), 39–54.

Prieto, María R. & Ricardo García Herrera, 'Documentary sources from South America: potential for climate reconstruction', *Palaeogeography Palaeoclimatology Palaeoecology* 281 (2009), 196–209.

Prieto, María R., Roberto Herrera & Patricia Dussel, 'Clima y disponibilidad hídrica en el sur de Bolivia y NO de Argentina entre 1560 y 1720. Los documentos españoles como fuente de datos ambientales', *Bamberger Geographische Schriften Bd* 15 (1998), 35–56.

Quinn, William, Víctor Neal & Santiago Antunes de Mayolo, 'El Niño occurrences over four and a half centuries', *Journal of Geophysical Research* 92/C13(1992), 14449–61 (1987); with a reviewed in Quinn, 1992.

Rabassa, Jorge, Aldo Brandani, José Boninsegna & Daniel Cobos, 'Cronología de la "Pequeña Edad del Hielo" en los glaciares Rio Manso y Castafio Overo, Cerro Tronador, Provincia de Rio Negro', 9no Congreso Geológico Argentino, Actas 3 (1984), 624–39.

Rein, Bert, Andreas Lückge, Lutz Reinhardt, Frank Sirocko, Anja Wolf & Christian Dullo, 'El Niño variability off Peru during the last 20,000 years', *Paleoceanography and Paleoclimatology* 20, no. 4 (2005), PA4003.

Sandweiss, Daniel & Alice Kelley, 'Archaeological contributions to climate change research: the archaeological record as a paleoclimatic and paleoenvironmental archive', *Annual Review of Anthropology* 41, no. 1 (2012), 371–91.

Schmidl, Ulrico, *Viaje al Río de la Plata*. Buenos Aires, Nuevo siglo, [1567] 1995.

Self, Stephen, Michael Rampino & James Barbera, 'The possible effects of large 19th and 20th century volcanic eruptions on zonal and hemispheric surface temperatures', *Journal of Volcanology and Geothermal Research* 11 (1981), 41–60.

Skopyk, Bradley, *Colonial cataclysms: climate, landscape, and memory in Mexico's Little Ice Age.* Tucson, AZ, University of Arizona Press, 2020.

Stenseth, Nils, Atle Mysterud, Geir Ottersen, James Hurrell, Kung-Sig Chan & Mauricio Lima, 'Ecological effects of climate fluctuations', *Science* 297 (2002), 1292–6.

Swan, Susan, 'Drought and Mexico's struggle for independence', *Environmental Review: ER* 6, no. 1 (1982), 54–62.

Usoskin, Ilya, 'A history of solar activity over millennia', *Living Reviews in Solar Physics* 14, no. 3 (2017), https://link.springer.com/article/10.1007/s41116-017-0006-9

Vaquero, José & Ricardo Trigo, 'Redefining the limit dates of the Maunder Minimum', *New Astronomy* 34 (2014), 1–6.

Vázquez de Acuña, Isidoro, *Las incursiones holandesas en Chiloé.* Santiago, Universidad de Santiago de Chile, 1992.

Villalba, Ricardo, 'Fluctuaciones climáticas en latitudes medias de América del Sur en los últimos 1.000 años: sus relaciones con la oscilación del sur', *Revista Chilena de Historia Natural* 67 (1994), 453–61.

Villalba, Ricardo, 'Tree-ring and glacial evidence for the medieval warm epoch and the Little Ice Age in southern South America', *Climatic Change* 26 (1994), 183–97.

Zielinski, Gregory, 'Climatic impact of volcanic eruptions: mini-review', *The Scientific World Journal* 2 (2002), 869–84.

Archival and primary sources

Actas del Cabildo de Santa Fe, Archivo General de la Provincia de Santa Fe, Rosario, Santa Fe, Argentina, http://www.webs.tecnodoc.com.ar

Álvarez, Francisco, *Noticia del establecimiento y población de las colonias inglesas en la América Septentrional.* Madrid, A. Fernández, 1778.

Archivo de Indias, Sevilla. España, 54-5-16; 54-5-9.

Biblioteca Nacional, Santiago, Chile, Sala Medina, Manuscritos, Volume 137, Document 2478: 'El marqués de Baides refiere largamente a su Majestad el Rey el estado de cosas de Chile y el que tienen las de guerra, que hoy está más viva que hasta aquí y más imposibilitado de contenerla por falta de hombres de guerra. Concepción, 19 de marzo de 1640'; Volume 118, Document 2085: 'Carta de Pedro Martínez de Zavala a Su Majestad el Rey, Tucumán, 24 marzo 1610'; Volume 136, Document 2467: 'Carta del Marqués de Baides a Su Majestad el Rey. Lima, 13 marzo 1639'.

Brouwer, Hendrick, *Journael ende historis verhael van der Reyse gedaen bij Costen de Straet Le Maire*. Amsterdam, Broer Jansz, 1646.

Crónicas del Reino de Chile, Madrid, Maribel, 1960, https://www.cervantesvirtual.com

Enrich, Francisco, *Historia de la Compañía de Jesús en Chile*. Barcelona, Roral, 1891.

Historia del Paraguay, vol. 2 has half-title, and v.3–6 added t.-p. 'Los jesuitas en el Rio de la Plata, 1586–1830'. First edition of the work published Paris [1756] 1910, www.archives.org

The John Carter Brown Library. Providence, RI. Book LCCN 43022438: *Relación Verdadera de las Pazes que Capituló con el araucano rebelado, el marqués de Baides, conde de Pedrosa, governador y capitán general del reyno de Chile, y presidente de la Real Audiencia / Sacada de sus informes y cartas y de los padres de la Compañía de Jesús, que aco[m]pañaron al real ejército en la jornada que hizo para este efecto el año pasado de 1641*. Madrid, Francisco Maroto, 1642.

Ladrillero, Juan, 'Relación del viaje al Estrecho de Magallanes', *Anuario Hidrográfico de la Marina de Chile*. Valparaíso: Instituto de Historia de la Marina de Chile, 1880, 423–525.

Ovalle, Alonso de, *Histórica relación del Reyno de Chile y de las misiones que ejercita en él la Compañía de Jesús: A Nuestro Señor Jesucristo Dios y Hombre ya la Santísima Virgen y Madre Nuestra, Señora del Cielo y de la Tierra, a los Santos José, Joachin y Ana, sus padres y abuelos*. Rome, Imprenta de Francisco Cavallo, 1646.

Quiroga, Gerónimo de, *Memorias de los sucesos de la Guerra de Chile*. Santiago, Chile, Andrés Bello, [1628–1704] 1979.

Southey, Robert, *English seamen: Howard, Clifford, Hawkins, Drake, Cavendish*. London, [1774–1843] 1897, 320–70, http://www.archive.org

Vicuña Mackenna, Benjamín, *Ensayo histórico sobre el clima de Chile*. Valparaíso, Imprenta del Mercurio, 1877.

Vivar, Jerónimo de, *Crónica y relación copiosa y verdadera de los reinos de Chile*. Santiago, Chile, Fondo Histórico y Bibliográfico José Toribio Medina, [1558] 1966.

Chapter 3

Extreme weather in New Spain and Guatemala: the Great Drought (1768–73)

Luis Alberto Arrioja Díaz Viruell
and María Dolores Ramírez Vega

Writing the history of the climate in the captaincy of Guatemala (current territories of Guatemala, El Salvador, Nicaragua and Costa Rica) and the viceroyalty of New Spain (current territories of Mexico and the southern United States), in the second half of the eighteenth century, involves addressing the final phase of the Little Ice Age (LIA) when atmospheric conditions underwent a series of alterations linked to a climatic chronology of great interest to the northern hemisphere. For this reason, it is necessary to focus on these topics and reflect on their scope in the agrarian world, where climatic conditions are crucial. This is so because a 'normal' year with stable temperatures, seasonal humidity and the absence of natural threats allowed people to get food supplies, including for cities and towns – meaning stable prices and security for homes.

The history of Guatemala and New Spain between 1760 and 1819 is entangled in meteorological episodes and extreme natural phenomena. Droughts were common, joining forces with volcanism, agricultural plagues and epidemic outbreaks, events that coincided with the *Maldá Oscillation* (1760–1800)[1] recorded for the Spanish Mediterranean. Some areas were more affected by such calamities than others. In seventeenth- and eighteenth-century Guatemala, recurrent droughts affected the Pacific Plains and the Central American Dry Corridor (CADC). On the other hand, excessive humidity occurred on the Atlantic Coast, while locust plagues struck in the Lowlands, the Central Depressions and the Pacific Plains.

They all generated food insecurity and upheavals in the agrarian economic and social structures.[2] This chapter examines one of the most severe climatic anomalies in the history of Guatemala and New Spain: the 1768–73 drought affecting different areas of both territories of the Hispanic monarchy. We study its characteristics, scope and limits, and the actions taken to deal with it, using documents stored in archives of Spain, Guatemala and Mexico.

The climate and its adverse effects

Both in Guatemala and New Spain between 1530 and 1819, we find hydro-meteorological events (frosts, torrential rains, droughts, snowfalls) and agricultural threats (plagues of locusts), especially in the periods 1665–1700, 1730–50 and 1760–1807. The period with the most frequent and damaging occurrences was between 1760 and 1810,[3] coinciding with the Maldá and Dalton oscillations (1790–1830).[4] It is known that ENSO (El Niño Southern Oscillation) is linked to climate behaviour and that, in its wet phase, it was reduced in different parts of the American continent between 1730 and 1850.[5] The low-humidity phase reached a higher frequency, especially in 1760–69, 1780–89 and 1800–09, when the most extreme episodes of ENSO were recorded in Central America. Álvaro Guevara, Caroline A. Williams, Erica J. Hendy, Pablo Imbach (for Guatemala) and Galindo (for Mexico) show the existence of this link between the seventeenth and twentieth centuries. However, their studies are limited to restricted areas such as San Cristobal de las Casas and Antigua Guatemala, Yucatan, Veracruz and Oaxaca (Map 3.1).[6]

Between 1750 and 1798, volcanic eruptions of magnitude 1–3 in Guatemala (Volcan de Fuego, 1750–51, 1799; Cerro Quemado and Tajumulco, 1765; Pacaya, 1757, 1775), San Salvador (Ilopango, 1765; Izalco, 1770, 1783, 1798; San Miguel, 1787) and Nicaragua (Momotombo, 1764; Masaya, 1772) also contributed to the emergence of droughts, agricultural plagues, epizootics and metabolic disruptions in the environment, since aerosols in the atmosphere altered solar luminosity and plant growth.[7] Guatemala and New Spain had different connections between climates and economies, but neither region was exempt from storms and water shortages, which caused hardships among the population, epizootics and health problems. In 1768, José Antonio de Alzate said that the 'slightest movement of the sky' – referring to droughts and frosts – was the cause of agricultural and livestock decline, hunger, disease and economic ruin in New Spain.[8] Found in New Spain and Guatemalan chronicles, stories and periodicals, this kind of statement warned that the climate was a changing phenomenon.

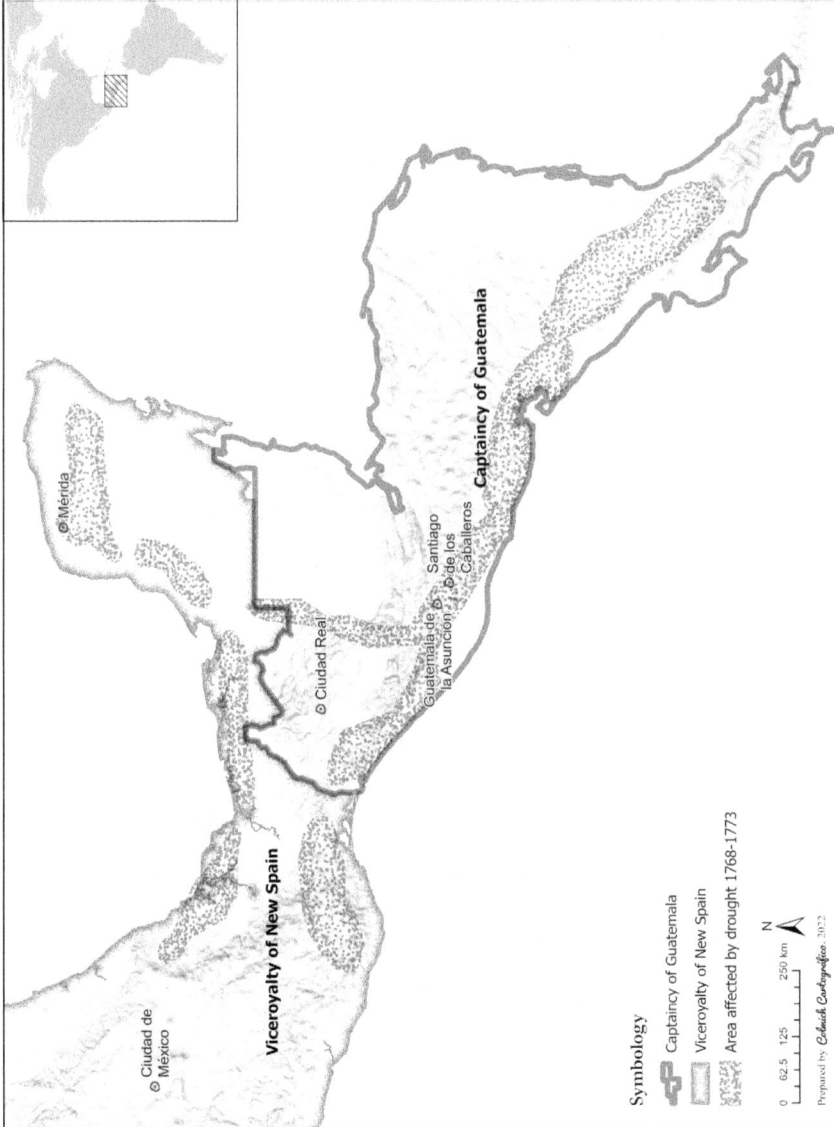

Map 3.1: The region affected by the great drought (1768–73). Elaborated by Marco Antonio Hernández Andrade.

Its most apparent manifestations were water scarcity during the farming season, frost and cold during harvest time, droughts and random storms, and the formation of agricultural pests with adverse effects on plants and other living beings.[9]

During the eighteenth century, the inhabitants of Guatemala and New Spain depended primarily on corn and beans to survive. Its pre-eminence stemmed from the ease with which it was cultivated in different latitudes, as read in a report from the province of Yucatan: 'Maize is the maintenance of the country, which is produced with very little work. This is reduced to opening a small hole with a stick and pouring in the grain, proceeding to sow the burning of the firewood or grass that the milpa grows'.[10] In Guatemala, Indigenous families allocated two ropes of land annually (i.e., 800 m²) to grow corn and beans and satisfy their needs, as well as generate certain reserves.[11] In New Spain, 'each Indian is more than supported with 4 bushels of corn each week which, reduced to loads made up of 12 each, comprise 17 loads and 4 bushels a year'.[12] However, in adverse weather conditions, crops failed, food problems emerged and diseases reached unprecedented proportions.

The 'mother of all evils'

Reconstructing the meteorological conditions in Guatemala and New Spain in the second half of the eighteenth century implies referring to the constant occurrence of low humidity or drought. Also called the 'silent elephant', the 'scourge of the poor' or the 'mother of all evils', it damaged the life cycle of numerous animal and plant species and directly influenced agricultural activities. For the people of the eighteenth century, there were more than six words to refer to this phenomenon: *sequía*, *seca*, *sequedad*, *secura*, *sed* and *sequeral*. It is striking that all these terms conjure up an image of the effects of low humidity on the physical environment and human beings. For example, Don Vicente Calvo y Julián's *Discurso Político, Rústico y Legal* defined drought as a long season in which 'the crops fail . . . without water and with hot air . . . and where the farmers cannot find wages . . .'.[13] Several treatises and memorials linked the droughts with their economic and social effects: 'the disease of animals and plants is caused by a great drought or a great heat that dries up the grass on which the animals take their sustenance and deprives plants of their nutrients . . . ; 'drought makes people fear the lack of bread . . . and it is known that the lack of bread is the sign of restlessness of miserable people . . .'; 'drought is a problem that affects, mainly, the fields, the jaws and the mouth . . .'.[14]

These notions about moisture scarcity bore a direct relationship with the agricultural cycle of the settlements. In Guatemala, people considered the *temporada de lluvias* (rainy season) or *humedad* (humidity) an ideal time for crops to grow and germinate, which was directly related to the *época invernal* or *inverno* (winter), which started in May and ended in October. In this regard, a note published in the *Gazeta de Guatemala* in 1802 pointed out that 'if, in the province of Verapaz, the winter continues to be favourable, the harvest will be very abundant . . .'. For its part, a testimonial from the province of León warned that 'there is some shortage of maise because although the plantings were copious, many were rendered useless by the waters and winter winds . . .'.[15] In contrast, the *temporada seca* (dry season) or *poco fecunda* (unfertile) was perceived as a time for people to till the land and prepare their crops and was linked to *verano* (summer): a cycle that began in November and ended in April. Regarding the latter, the *alcalde* of Quetzaltenango wrote in 1801 that in 'summer the rains are scarce . . . so the cobs cannot be of good or regular size . . . the only thing left to do is to cut those that are called *mulquito*, which because of their smallness they have endured the dry summer . . .'. Years later, the alcalde of Totonicapan recommended that all repairs to the Zacapulas bridge be carried out 'in the dry season, also known as summer, so that the work can be perfected . . . and take advantage of the fact that the river runs down almost without water . . .'.[16]

In New Spain, the agricultural cycle was subject to the rainy season between May and October, and a dry season from November to April. In this regard, Ignacio Galindo observes that the dry season could become an outright drought.[17] In Yucatan, during the rainy season – which in the Mayan language is known as *akyaabil* – there were intra-summer droughts or heat waves, which in the Mayan language is called *kinlan*, meaning 'great heat'.[18] Therefore, knowing these propitious times for rainfed agriculture, farmers began to prepare the land for sowing in April. However, the dry season occasionally lasted up to thirty days, which aroused fear among the population. It was well known that these lags could make the difference between a good or bad harvest and complete loss in the worst-case scenario. When the dry season prolonged in time and space, discussions about drought emerged among the population, leading to speeches, demonstrations and omens related to hunger, disease, famine and misfortune.

In this regard, the works by Álvaro Guevara, Caroline A. Williams, Erica J. Hendy and Pablo Imbach suggest that the bulk of the droughts that impacted the captaincy of Guatemala between the seventeenth and twentieth centuries have to do with the presence of ENSO and atmospheric oscillations. These studies have been formulated based on mathematical projections and historical observations. Although proposing novel inter-pretative horizons, these works address limited spaces, such as San Cristóbal de las Casas and Antigua Guatemala. Thus, it is necessary to broaden the scope of research, complementing the drought index with doc-uments deposited in civil and ecclesiastical archives of Guatemala, San Salvador, Honduras, Nicaragua and Costa Rica. For New Spain, Ignacio Galindo also uses quantitative variables and historical sources to demon-strate that droughts occurred during the ENSO seasons, as well as a lag and increase in torrential rains in regions with deficient rainfall. Specifically, for Yucatán, Veracruz and Oaxaca, he shows that the intra-summer droughts resulted from global climatic dynamics.[19]

To produce more accurate knowledge of the droughts in the captaincy of Guatemala and the viceroyalty of New Spain, we examined written sources for each of these regions. For Guatemala, we took up the Álvaro Guevara Index and the records made by Robert Claxton and other docu-mentary research. For New Spain, our primary source was the historical catalogue of agricultural disasters in Mexico by Virginia García Acosta, Manuel Pérez Zevallos and América Molina del Villar. This compilation of historical records provides a panoramic view of the climatic conditions in the different regions of that vast colonial territory. The preceding sources made it possible to form a database of drought episodes from 1640 to 1819. We established this timeframe based on the possibilities offered by docu-mentary records, as well as our interest in examining meteorological phenomena in one of the most troubled periods of the late LIA. Next, we systematised the quali-quantitative data according to temporal sequences and content categories. At the same time, we created an index to classify the intensity of each drought episode, taking climatic, agricultural, eco-nomic and religious factors, among others, into account. The index values are (1) episodes with dry conditions; (2) episodes with very dry conditions; (3) episodes with extremely dry conditions (Table 3.1).

Graph 3.1 shows fifty-two droughts in the captaincy of Guatemala. Not a single decade escaped their effects. One can also note an increase dur-ing the eighteenth century. There was a higher concentration of droughts in Guatemala in 1660–69, 1690–99, 1720–29, 1730–39, 1760–69, 1770–79 and 1780–89. Graph 3.2 shows 110 droughts in New Spain, most of them occurring in 1640–49, 1660–69, 1720–29, 1740–49, 1750–59, 1760–69, 1770–79, 1780–89, 1790–99 and 1800–09. Here we argue that these num-bers indicate not only a greater incidence of droughts but also a greater concern of the authorities to document their emergence and the damage generated in the environment and the economy.

Table 3.1: Classification index of droughts in the kingdom of Guatemala and viceroyalty of New Spain, 1640–1819[20]

Assigned values	Characteristics of the wet season	Descriptive elements
0	Normal conditions of humidity	-Rains in all provinces between May and October
		-Good harvests
		-Good reproductive cycles of animals
		-Stable grain prices
		-Increasing values in the auctions
1	Dry conditions	-Late arrival of the wet period
		-Rain scarcity
		-Lengthening of heat wave
		-Deficit crops
		-Death of some animals
2	Very dry conditions	-Absence of rain
		-Lost crops
		-Death of animals
		-Reduction of streams of water
		-Grain scarcity
		-Increase in food prices
		-Decreases in tithe auctions
		-Waivers for the collection of taxes
		-Rogations and novenas
3	Extremely dry conditions	-The records incorporated in this value are all of the above, plus:
		-References on migrations
		-Epidemic outbreaks
		-Deaths
		-Extraordinary prayers and processions to contain the problems of drought

These results suggest a correlation between the number of droughts and the global climatic effects of the Maunder Minimum (1645–1715) and the Maldá and Dalton Oscillations (1790–1830) in Guatemala in 1670–99 and 1780–89, and in New Spain in 1640–49, 1660–69 and 1760–1809. They also confirm that the eighteenth century began with low temperatures and a proliferation of droughts but, over time, attained a certain stability in its atmospheric conditions. Finally, our figures show that the last four decades of the eighteenth century were a period of cold, snowfall, heat, drought and storms, both in Guatemala and New Spain. From the early nineteenth

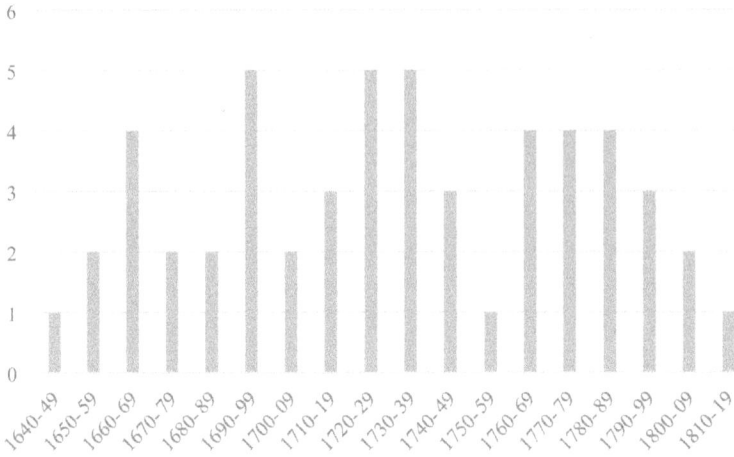

Graph 3.1: Droughts in the captaincy of Guatemala, 1640–1819

Source: Elaborated from Guevara-Murua et al., 2018, 175–91; Claxton, 1986, 139–63.

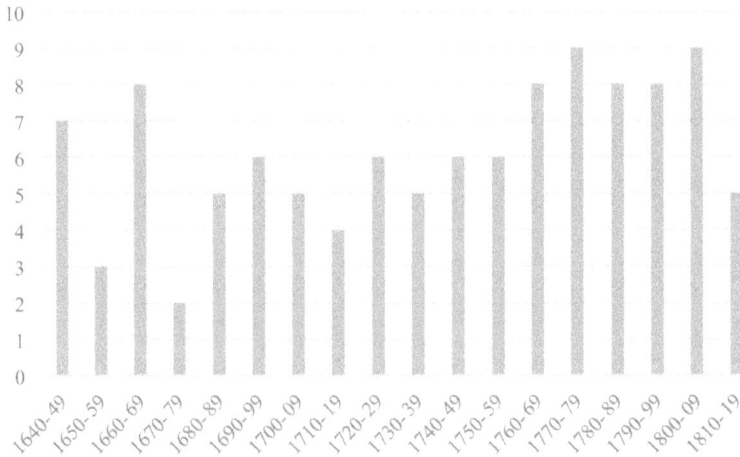

Graph 3.2: Droughts in the viceroyalty of New Spain, 1640–1819

Source: Elaborated from Florescano, 2000; García Acosta et al., 2003.

century, there was a reduction in drought occurrences, biological threats and atmospheric disturbances.

Graph 3.3 represents the 162 droughts (combining Guatemala and New Spain), classifying them according to intensity. It shows a similarity between the most severe occurrences in the two regions: in Guatemala, the decades of 1640–49, 1650–59, 1660–69, 1760–69 and 1790–99; and in New Spain, 1640–49, 1650–59, 1660–69, 1760–69, 1780–89, 1790–99 and 1800–09. Combined with the numbers in Graph 3.1, these results reveal that in Guatemala, between 1640 and 1659, there were three extremely catastrophic droughts. On the other hand, between 1710 and 1729, the eight episodes barely reached minimum values of affectation, such as crop deterioration, seed shortage or reduction of streams of water, on regional and local scales. A unique period was between 1760 and 1779, with fifteen very dry and extremely dry droughts. In New Spain, between 1640 and 1669, eighteen droughts were recorded, most of them intense, indicating that the Maunder pulsation was felt very intensely. In the eighteenth century, 1760–99 and 1800–09 stand out with forty-two droughts, most of them of high intensity. These latest droughts coincide temporally with those in the viceroyalties of Perú, Río de la Plata and New Granada and the territories of Louisiana and Florida, signs of an anomalous and uneven climate that caused significant food problems.[21]

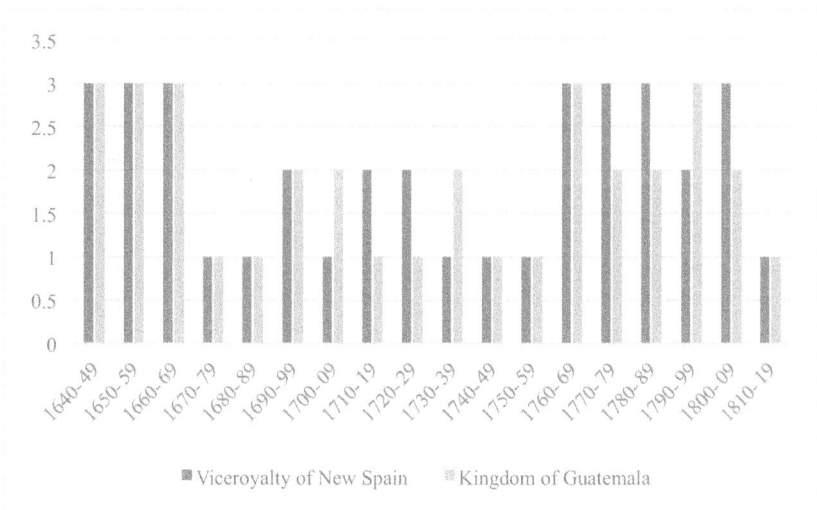

Graph 3.3: Index of droughts in the kingdom of Guatemala and the viceroyalty of New Spain, 1640–1819.

Source: Elaborated from Guevara-Murua et al., 2018, 175–91; Claxton, 1986, 139–63; Florescano, 2000; García Acosta et al., 2003.

Graph 3.3 shows that 27 per cent of the droughts were extremely dry, 33 per cent were very dry and 38 per cent had minimal effects. Often accompanied by biological hazards, the droughts of maximum intensity impacted agriculture and the regional economy of several provinces.[22] They disrupted the life cycle of plant and animal species – some of which were vital to containing soil erosion – triggering the emergence of insect pests, causing suffering to human groups from diseases due to changes in diet and immune system. To ponder the scope of these phenomena, we will now zoom in on the drought of 1768–73, one of the most severe of the eighteenth century.

Drought and crisis

Between 1768 and 1773, the captaincy of Guatemala experienced low levels of moisture in the eastern and central parts of Chiapas, the west and the highlands of Guatemala, as well as in the western portion of the province of San Salvador.[23] The first meteorological disturbances were felt between June and December 1768, with complaints from several towns in the Chiapas districts of Guardanía de Huitiupan, Zoques and Llanos about the lack of rainfall and excessive heat. At the same time, the authorities received reports of outbreaks of hunger, disease and human displacement in the mountains. The records of the *alcaldía mayor* of Ciudad Real and the death records of 1769 show the effects of 'great drought, poverty and disease' in the Cañada de Chilón. Some pueblos recorded the population shrinking: in Yajalón and Bachajón, around 30 and 46 per cent, respectively; in the Chol zone, 37 per cent in Petalcingo and 24 per cent in Tila.[24] Between 1769 and 1771, the alcaldías mayores of Tuxtla and Ciudad Real reported a reduction of about 4,401 taxpayers due to drought-related death or migration. In the Tuxtla alone, the numbers of dead and absent inhabitants amounted to 1,433 taxpayers, with the most affected pueblos being Tapalapa, Pantepeque, Coapilla, Copainala, Ocotepeque, Chicoazintepeque, Tuxtla, Chiapa, Zayula, Ystapanjoya and Sunuapa. Ciudad Real saw an increase of 2,965 taxpayers, the most affected pueblos being Acatepeque, Huistan, Ystacolcot, Totolapa, Acala, San Bartolomé, Socoltenango, Chiquimuzelo, Teopisca, Amatenango, Tumbala, Tila, Palenque, Petalcingo and Amatan.[25]

In New Spain, the southeastern region comprising Yucatán (provinces of Yucatán, Tabasco and Campeche), Veracruz and Oaxaca felt intense impacts of the great drought. Oaxaca (1766) and Yucatán (1767) were the first provinces to report scarce rains. In 1768, a 'considerable drought' in the district caused epizootics.[26] The milpas did not suffer from the phenomenon, as they had already matured; in fact, it was so copious that no one among the inhabitants had seen such successful harvests.[27] In Oaxaca, the reports on the common-use resources of the towns located in the Mixteca Baja and in the jurisdictions of Teposcolula, Coixtlahuaca, Yanhuitlán and Tetitepeque warn of the adverse effects of droughts and frosts.[28]

However, these events were just the prelude to a great calamity, as 1769 proved to be a catastrophic year for the governorate of Yucatán and Oaxaca. Heat waves – explained by some as 'a punishment of burning suns' – and locust plagues combined with drought to destroy spontaneous vegetation and crops. Between 1770 and 1773, there were episodes of drought in Yucatán (1770 and 1773), Oaxaca (1770 and 1771) and Veracruz (1770, 1771 and 1773).[29] The great drought of 1770 caused – along with the locusts – the ruin of crops, food shortage, migration, hunger, disease and death in Yucatan. In Oaxaca, most of the province suffered from drought, even in the central valleys, the most fertile lands in the region and the least likely to suffer from it. However, the jurisdictions of Teposcolula, Yanhuitlán, Juxtlahuaca and Nochixlán were the ones that suffered the most extreme impacts of the drought, as stated by some of the alcaldes mayores: 'in the last three years [1769, 1770 and 1771] one has experienced such a great dryness due to lack of rain that the crops have been completely lost'.[30] This forced some inhabitants to abandon their pueblos to not die of hunger. As far as Veracruz is concerned, however, the drought barely impacted the harvests.

The civil and religious authorities observed the lack of rain with great concern, as they were aware of its effects on agriculture, the tributes derived from it, and the general social behaviour. Following Enlightenment principles, civil officials and religious ministers took several measures to alert the population about the drought and provide means to alleviate it. In the captaincy of Guatemala, the bishop of Chiapas, Juan Manuel García de Vargas de Rivera, issued two *cordilleras* (letters) between 1769 and 1770: one intended to promote small-scale agriculture, meet the needs of the parishioners and mitigate food shortages, the other asked the parish priests to prepare population counts, record the havoc and seek mitigating measures.[31] Archbishop Pedro Cortés y Larraz insisted on attending parish emergencies and evaluating the drought's consequences in tithes. In places such as Santa Ana Malactán (Huehuetenango), as well as in the province of Sacatepequez, maize harvests were affected, cattle herds declined, and parishioners and inhabitants fled – some even went to Tabasco, in New Spain.[32]

The death records of various parishes in western and central Guatemala corroborate the drought's ravages during the 1768–70 period. In the town of Santiago Atitlan, district of Sololá, the sources show that for every 100 infants born in 1769, 83 died; meanwhile, the tax records reveal that of every 100 taxpayers, 25 died, and 10 were absent. To this must be added the death of ten widowers and five retired. One observed an equally harrowing panorama in San Cristóbal Totonicapan, district of Totonicapan, where records show that hunger and disease caused the death of 129 children, 72 taxpayers, 12 retired and two widowers in 1769. In San Cristóbal Palín, district of Escuintla, 1769 was a particularly chaotic year as it experienced a very high mortality rate: 94 children and 60 taxpayers. This situation was so anomalous that the Republic of Indians did not hesitate to contact the archbishop of Guatemala to request a deduction in tithes because of hunger, poverty and disease.[33] In 1770, the government of the captaincy requested reports from the alcaldes of Chiapas, Totonicapan, Suchitepeques, Chimaltenango, Sololá, Escuintla and Chiquimula, urging them to take steps against the hoarding of seeds, food shortage and inflation.[34] The meteorological conditions of 1770–71 were once again extremely dry and harmed the economy of the *mitra* and the Royal Appellate Court. The situation worsened and the drought-affected area was ever larger, being particularly intense in the provinces of Chiapas, Totonicapan, Quetzaltenango and Chiquimula; so much so that the 1769–71 triennium was referred to as the 'period of hunger, disease and remnant'.[35]

In the viceroyalty of New Spain, the droughts were also a matter of interest for civil and religious authorities. However, the New Spanish clergy was not as informed by enlightened principles as in the kingdom of Guatemala. As far as the sources show it, the intervention of New Spanish ecclesiastics was limited to the spiritual realm, that is, prayers, processions and novenas; and sometimes to charity.[36] On the other hand, the alcaldes and governors of Indian pueblos acted to restore order, encourage agriculture and sort the shortage of seeds by buying and storing grain, prohibiting the hoarding of grain by middlemen, promoting extemporaneous planting and punishing thieves. In Yucatan, Governor Antonio de Olivier stored 8,000 loads of maize – rationing its sale in the *alhóndiga* – requested agricultural reports, punished rustlers and thieves, and controlled food prices. Undoubtedly, the most effective measure – later emulated by the alcaldes of Tabasco and Campeche – was the obligation of extemporaneous planting imposed on Indians, creoles, mulattoes and mestizos, who were ordered to plant sixty mecates of milpas each, on pain of being accused of vagrancy and expelled from the province.[37] In January 1770, the alcalde of Teposcolula (Oaxaca) issued an edict establishing economic and physical punishments for those who 'extracted' seeds:

Due to the fact that the harvest last year and this year was very scarce, for which the price has increased every day and that the extraction of said seeds outside this jurisdiction, both by some neighbours and by foreigners, can be a cause that all the public of it suffer greater detriment, prejudice and total scarcity, I order that no person dares to extract or remove seeds of wheat and maise [. . .]. Prohibiting that they sell to the merchants under the penalties imposed on the offenders, being of Spanish quality, that of three times the value of what they sold or extracted. And to the mestizos, mulattoes and Indians, that of two months in prison and fifty whippings in the pillory that, inevitably, they will experience for the first time, and for the second time, the sentence doubled in one and the other.[38]

Although the severity of the drought was extensively recorded through these legal instruments, it was also documented in prayers, as well as documents about forced migration and food shortages. The prayers for rain were acts of public faith in which parishioners and religious and political authorities participated to implore divine help. From a spiritual point of view, 'turning to God in great need, invoking his help in the midst of tribulation, trusting in his omnipotence and begging him to look mercifully on our misfortunes is prescribed by religion, mandated by morality, and demanded by Christian character'.[39] For this reason, one finds masses, sermons, public processions and novenas dedicated to Our Lady of Socorro, in Guatemala, and to the Virgin Mary and that of Izamal, in New Spain.[40] These prayers intended to make the congregation aware of the divine character of droughts, finding their causes and amendments, requiring 'acknowledging sins, confessing crimes, asking for mercy and trusting in obtaining it. This is the end of prayers and sermons: turn to mercy and wait for the wrath of God to appease'.[41]

Population displacements were another consequence of the drought. In the short span of three years, pueblos in Chiapas and Guatemala experienced remarkable decreases in tax registrars. Between 1769 and 1772, San Juan Chamula, San Andrés Ixtacolcot, Santa María Tolotepeque, Santiago Huistan, San Miguel Pinula, San Andrés Yagaguita, San Francisco de Moyos, Chiquimula and Chicumuselo saw their populations decrease, either due to death or migration caused by hunger and misery. Unable to go after those who had left due to a lack of resources and, especially, food to support them if they returned, the Spanish and Indigenous authorities recognised that the situation stemmed from the 'great drought that has come from 1769 to today . . . and that has caused much hunger, disease and poverty . . . to the extent that the pueblos do not have utensils or beasts since they have sold all their necessities'.[42] In 1771, it was impossible to collect the tribute in the alcalde mayor of Chiquimula in 1770 and the province of Suchitepequez. In this context, civil and ecclesiastical authorities urged the people to restore agricultural work to mitigate the 'hunger that causes serious illnesses' and avoid migration, using common-use resources and feeding the sick.[43]

In the Guatemalan provinces, the aftermath of the drought also brought death, fear and hunger. In the 'Quadrant of the parish of the Holy Spirit of Quetzaltenango and its four annexes', in the years of 'hunger and disease', around 800 individuals – among 'infants, taxpayers and ladinos' – died without being able to cover burial expenses and the ringing of bells. Fear of drought drove the powerful men of Quetzaltenango to pay for masses to be sung to protect their properties from the threat. Ignacio de Urbina, for example, paid two pastures and ten pieces of farmland for twenty-three sung masses in favour of his haciendas (Porras and Tzalamcoch) between the months of September and December in 1770, 1771 and 1772.[44]

In New Spain, the drought also caused population displacement, health problems and death, as well as the collapse of agricultural, economic and social structures. In Yucatán, Campeche, Tabasco and Oaxaca, migration began in 1769, escalating to a massive exodus to pueblos, haciendas and other provinces the following year. Stopping these migrations and restoring order implied repatriation and encouraging agriculture with the support of the Church. In the governorate of Yucatán, vagrant and beggar Indians were assigned personal services in cities, fields and haciendas. However, sending the Indians back to their villages and reactivating agriculture was impossible as they were not always found or refused to return due to the lack of maize.[45]

Other evidence of the drought's severity was the news about food shortages and requests from towns to be exempt from paying taxes. The experience in the province of Chiapas in 1772 is very revealing. Despite the government's promotion of additional plantings and measures to regulate the seed trade, hunger and disease continued to take their toll. In some places, plantings were made in marginal, unsuitable land, which resulted in wasted seed. Moreover, the drought (indirectly) prevented the growth of grasses and herbs, which directly impacted some animal species. Several reports from Yajalón reveal that, given the scarcity of grains and stubble, the natives stopped 'maintaining their usual trade of raising pigs and chickens . . .'. Something similar happened in Ocosingo, Tumbala and Palenque, where justice officials reported that there were neither horseshoe nor farm beasts, as they had died due to lack of pasture or because the natives ate them to satisfy their hunger.[46]

This intense drought affected the interests of all social and economic sectors, including the most powerful. Several of the wealthiest men in the province of Chiapas suffered from the lack of humidity. For example, Manuel Esponda y Olaechea, captain of the second company of militias and commander of the arms of Chiapas, stressed that during 'the years of hunger . . . of 69, 70 and 71 . . .', his grandfather lost numerous crops and interests in the haciendas Nuestra Señora de la Candelaria and San Antonio, located in the district of Ixtacomitan, a situation for which 'the Tuxtla district was afflicted . . . and its wealth sacrificed to Christian charity, maintaining more than a thousand beggars daily, without which he expended in healing and assisting the sick. And he was charged with the subsistence and life of innumerable vassals who had inevitably perished . . .'.[47] The Church also experienced problems. The archbishopric of Guatemala detected a considerable reduction in tithes as the drought progressed. In the district of Suchitepequez, the tithe contractor reported the loss of 75 per cent of agricultural production. This situation directly affected the contract: while in 1768, it had been assessed at 1,900 pesos, in 1772, it did not exceed the expectations of collecting the minimum amount of 500 pesos in fruits and cattle. The ravages of the drought reached the point that several parish priests from the vicarage of Huehuetenango requested the archbishop of Guatemala that the alcaldes suspend for several years the repartimientos and deals they carried out in the Indian pueblos due to the misfortunes faced by the parishioners due to the 'dry conditions and diseases that have affected them in recent years . . .'.[48]

These testimonies show how officials, religious authorities and landowners coped with the drought's ravages. However, the most significant damages were felt in the Indian pueblos, with the loss of grain, lack of food supplies and epizootics, while the towns and cities demanded the provision of seeds, price reductions and punishments for the hoarders. To contain this social outcry, in 1770, Bishop García de Vargas requested the prosecution of landowners who withheld maize to make gains with inflated prices. He also encouraged parish priests and parishioners to denounce the haciendas and pueblos that hid their surpluses so one could distribute this food among those most in need. For its part, Guatemala's Audiencia asked the priests not to demand contributions and services from the pueblos, given their extreme poverty. According to the experience of 1769–70, 'a drought had left these miserable people unable to do the bare minimum because of the deplorable state in which the few that have remained find themselves, since they can barely look to maintain their lives, as they have absolutely nothing left . . . For which one asks in favour of the miserable Indians of this province, who always and today more than ever are worthy of greater compassion . . .'. In the curate of Zacapa, due to the 'deep scarcity', people suffered the drought's impact on their communal economy. They stopped delivering to the church a weekly *dieta* comprising four bushels of maize, two dozen chickens, two dozen eggs, a hundredweight of cocoa, a bunch of bananas, three bushels of beans, three loads of grass, two loads of firewood, twenty slabs of chocolate, thirty pitchers of water and two Indians millers.[49]

In New Spain, food shortages were no less severe. Not surprisingly, 1770 was labelled 'the year of hunger' – the worst of the eighteenth century,[50] as shown by evidence for Yucatan, Campeche and Tabasco. Curates such as Maxcanu (Camino Real), Octún (Beneficios), Temax (La Costa), Chemaco (Valladolid), Muna (Sierra) and Guadalupe (Mérida) experienced famine. The population was forced to consume all kinds of plants, roots and tree bark (some poisonous) that left them ill. The bodies of those deceased were left to putrefy in fields and mountains, where they were devoured by dogs and owls. Considered unclean by the Church, the meat of donkeys, horses, dogs and other animals were also eaten. But the most shocking was the practice of cannibalism, especially when infants and suckling children became food for their mothers. Some confessors were imprisoned. Many of the hungry, sick and needy arrived in the cities, begging for help in the churches. However, the number exceeded the capacities of the parish priests, who closed the doors, so most of the beggars expired without help. The corpses lay in the streets and were taken in carts to the ditches that served as cemeteries. This panorama explains why the number of dead men, women and children reached 70,000, a figure that contrasts with that of Mexico's Audiencia in 1774, which reported 23,830 (considering taxpayers only).[51]

In this context of famine, the countryside and the city saw their peace disturbed. In rural areas, the drought exacerbated banditry, cattle rustling, food theft and the destruction of maize fields in haciendas. In the city, vagrancy, begging and robbery from private homes prevailed, acts that demanded quick solutions from the authorities. To restore order, there were discussions about the penalties and punishments for 'criminals'. While some recommended issuing a single general proclamation, the typology of crimes made this proposal unfeasible, so various kinds of punishment were applied: whipping, public shaming, galleys or mines and, in the case of recidivism, hanging.[52]

Even the most privileged social groups – Crown officials, clerics, landowners, ranchers and *encomenderos* – felt the impact of the drought. The clergy stopped receiving the payment of parish perquisites as well as all kinds of emoluments, and the parish priests saw themselves deprived of the personal services performed by the natives. The ranchers – some of whom acted as royal officials or encomenderos – experienced economic ruin, as the province's total cattle herd was reduced from 150,000 to 200,000 in 1770 to 32,000 in 1773.[53] The same fate befell the encomenderos, whose income relied on Indigenous labour. In 1774, they were part of a delegation requesting the king's forgiveness of their fiscal obligations, arguing absolute poverty caused by the flight of their encomendados.[54] But without a doubt, the most impacted sector was made up primarily of Indians, but also some Spaniards, *castas*, mestizos and blacks. They were forced to put up goods such as land and even their clothes for sale to buy food; they tore down their humble homes to harness the wood as fuel; and, in the worst cases, they lost their lives.

Among the most striking evidence of the ravages wreaked by the drought are the tribute-exemption pleas of the pueblos of Guatemala and New Spain to the Crown. Demographic decline, disruption of crops and common-use areas, and the debts accumulated during the drought were all claimed as justification. In 1772, the Royal Audiencia of Guatemala informed the alcalde of Ciudad Real that, due to the 'sterility, lack of food and mortality that the Chiapas province' was experiencing, it was fair and reasonable to extend a pardon of 'two-thirds of tributes for the 36 towns of that Alcalde Mayor'.[55] In New Spain, Yucatán, Tabasco, Campeche, Oaxaca and Veracruz experienced a drastic decrease in tribute collection after 1769, and the pueblos appealed to the Royal Audience requesting extensions, deductions, or exemptions from paying their tributes. In the Yucatan governorate, tribute collection was a resounding failure, as no town or neighbourhood was able to fully cover their obligations between 1768 and 1774. There was no collection in 1770 whatsoever and, in 1771, barely 1,363 pesos 1 real were collected, despite the hiring of special collectors for the Indian escapees. In Campeche, 259 pesos 3 tomines were collected in 1770, and only 190 pesos 5 tomines in 1771. This was due to 'the few taxpayers that have been known to exist, after the famine and plague suffered, and many died and others who have gone to the mountains as refugees'.[56] In Tabasco, a debt of 3,575 pesos 12 reales 3 tomines was recorded in 1770, while in the alcalde mayor of Xalapa (Veracruz), 6,861 pesos 2-and-a-half tomines were forgiven between 1767 and 1771. In 1774, the disaster forced the Crown to forgive the tribute debt – corresponding to four years (1769–74) – amounting to almost 70,000 pesos. Even in these tragic circumstances and with the pardon approved, Diego de Lanz, an official royal accountant based in Campeche, demanded that the natives of the province pay 50,000 pesos.

These measures were unprecedented in the history of the Hispanic monarchy and can only be explained in the context of a severe environmental crisis. The effects of the drought of 1768–73 materialised through numerous physical, social and economic events resulting from the meteorological pulsations conjoined with the attitudes and actions of royal authorities, landowners and the pueblos to face the contingencies. Parallel to the drought, other natural phenomena fell on these spaces and contributed to the misfortune, such as the locust plague that wreaked havoc in the rural areas, deteriorating agroecosystems and triggering economic and social crises.

Conclusion

In this chapter, we have outlined a panoramic vision of the climatic conditions in the captaincy of Guatemala and the viceroyalty of New Spain throughout the eighteenth century, as well as in the shorter period between 1768 and 1773. Zooming in on this particular period allowed us to document and analyse one of the most adverse climatic anomalies ever occurring in the regions studied – more intense even than the one recorded in the 1780s. The great drought of 1768–73 resulted from complex atmospheric processes, including the drop in global temperatures and the cooling of air currents that were becoming less and less intense. We have shown that the drought unfolded in a particular geography, including the central and western highlands of Guatemala, the eastern and central portions of Chiapas and the western part of the province of San Salvador, while, in New Spain, the southeastern fringe was the most affected region – the provinces of Yucatán, Campeche, Tabasco, Veracruz and Oaxaca. The drought was characterised by specific temporalities and dynamics, as well as a particularly severe intensity, disrupting agricultural cycles and food production chains, accelerating soil erosion, and upsetting the interests of all social groups. The evidence indicates that the drought impacted the material base of the wealthy and the poor alike, even though the latter – most prominently the Indian pueblos and ladino settlements – bore the most devastating effects, such as food scarcity, desolation, disease, migration and death. Meanwhile, the towns and cities suffered the drought's ravages in the form of shortages, famine, begging, disease and social discontent.

If this chapter contributes anything, this is the attempt to document and analyse an atmospheric phenomenon that conditioned the life of various provinces of Guatemala and New Spain during the second half of the eighteenth century. The 1768–73 drought demands further research, especially in Central American archives, relying on the methods and techniques of historical climatology and the explanatory arguments from the field of history. Thus, a joint research horizon can be envisioned at the intersection between the social and the environmental sciences, a cooperation that will undoubtedly augment the possibilities of better understanding the historical processes connecting the natural world and human social groups and institutions. The droughts that occurred in the kingdom of Guatemala and the viceroyalty of New Spain during the second half of the eighteenth century reveal the complex relations between humans and climate. People's central task was to adapt and survive in the face of environmental transformations, with the climate displaying its physical complexities and imposing itself as a natural-historical element in the human world.

Notes

1. Climatic fluctuation recorded in the Mediterranean was 'a prolonged period of time in which climatic conditions are accentuated and acquire a simultaneous frequency in different types of phenomena not experienced in equal intensity in the last 500 years', see Mariano Barriendos & Carmen Llasat, 'El caso de la anomalía "Maldá" en la cuenca mediterránea occidental (1760–1800). Un ejemplo de fuerte variabilidad climática'. In: Armando Alberola Romá & Jorge Olcina Cantos (eds.) *Desastre natural, vida cotidiana y religiosidad popular en la España moderna y contemporánea*. Alicante, Universidad de Alicante, 2009, 253–86.

2. Murdo MacLeod, J., *Historia socio-económica de la América Central Española, 1520–1720*, second edition, Guatemala, Piedra Santa, 1990; Enrique Florescano (ed.), *Breve historia de las sequías en México*. Mexico, CONACULTA, 2000.

3. Robert H. Claxton & Alan D. Hecht, 'Climatic and human history in Europe and Latin America: an opportunity for comparative study', *Climatic Change* 1 (1978), 195–203; Robert H. Claxton, 'Weather-based hazards in Guatemala', *West Georgia College Studies in the Social Sciences* 25 (1986), 139–63; Christopher H. Lutz, *Santiago de Guatemala, 1541–1773 city, caste and colonial experience*. Norman, OK, University of Oklahoma, 1994, 243–50.

4. The Dalton Oscillation is the period of sunspot decline, the last cold period of the LIA, which is usually dated between 1790 and 1830; see Jürg Luterbacher & Gerard van der Scrier, 'Circulation dynamics and its influence on European and Mediterranean January-April climate over the past half millennium: results and insights from instrumental data, documentary evidence and coupled climate models', *Climate Change* 101, no. 1 (2010), 201–34.

5. Joëlle L. Gergis & Anthony M. Fowler, 'A history of ENSO events since A.D. 1525: implications for future climate change', *Climatic Change* 92 (2009), 343–87.

6. Ignacio Galindo, 'La oscilación del sur, El Niño: el caso de México'. In: Enrique Florescano (ed.) *Breve historia de las sequías en México*. Mexico, CONACULTA, 2000, 128–9. Appendix.

7. Richardson B. Gill & Jerome P. Keating, 'Volcanism and Mesoamerican archaeology', *Ancient Mesoamerica* 13, no. 1 (2002), 125–40; Bertrand Cédric, Jean-Pascal van Ypersele & André Berger, 'Volcanic and solar impacts on climate since 1700', *Climate Dynamics* 15 (1999), 355–67.

8. José Antonio de Alzate, *Gacetas de literatura de México*, volume IV, Puebla, Impresas en la oficina del Hospital de San Pedro, 1831, 30.

9. Domingo Juarros, Maury A. Bromsen, Alberto Parreño & Francisco de Beltranena, *Compendio de la historia de la ciudad de Guatemala*. Guatemala, Ignacio Beteta, 1808; Pedro Cortés y Larráz, *Descripción geográfico-moral de la Diócesis de*

Goathemala. Madrid, Corpus Hispanorum de Pace, Segunda serie, Consejo Superior de Investigaciones Científicas, [1700] 2001.

10. Informe sobre Campeche y Yucatán, 1766, Archivo del Museo Naval (hereafter AMN), Virreinato de México, Volume IV, Manuscript 570, Document 13, fs. 362f–362v.

11. Francisco de Solano, *Tierra y sociedad en el reino de Guatemala*. Ciudad de Guatemala, Universidad de San Carlos de Guatemala, 1977, 24–40.

12. Informe, 1766, f. 361v.

13. *Discurso político, rústico y legal sobre labores, ganados y plantíos en el cual se intentan persuadir los considerables beneficios que resultarán a esta Monarquía de la unión y concordia de aquellos tres hermanos donde conviene o disconviene su aumento y dilatación, las causas supuestas y verdaderas de su decadencia, los medios para lograr su restablecimiento y los abusos que lo detienen. Compuesto por el doctor don Vicente Calvo y Julián, noble de Aragón, abogado de los reales Consejos, presidente y fiscal de la Academia de Abogados de Zaragoza y opositor a prebendas doctorales*. Madrid, en la oficina de Antonio Marín, 1770, ff. 17, 68.

14. 'Veterinaria o albeiteria, (1782)', Hemeroteca Digital de la Biblioteca Nacional de España (hereafter HDBNE), *Correo literario de la Europa*, no. 53; Biblioteca Nacional de España (hereafter BNE), Fondo Biblioteca Digital Hispánica, *Memoria sobre la policía y régimen de los abastos de la ciudad de Santiago*, 1786, f. 44; *Manual para entender y hablar el castellano por el padre fray Francisco Guijarro*, 1796, f. 95.

15. 'Estado de las siembras y precios de granos, (1802)', Biblioteca Nettie Lee Benson (hereafter BNLB), Benson Latin American Collection, LAC-Z Rare Books, GZ 972.81 G258, *Gazeta de Guatemala*, no. 267.

16. Informe del alcalde mayor de Quetzaltenango sobre el estado de las cosechas, (1801), Archivo General de Centroamerica (hereafter AGCA), A1.11, leg. 2450, exp. 18878; Informe del alcalde mayor de Totonicapan sobre los daños en el puente de Zacapulas, (1807), AGCA, A1, leg, 5910, exp. 50545.

17. Galindo, 2000, 126.

18. Paola Peniche Moreno, *Tiempos aciagos. Las calamidades y el cambio social del siglo XVIII entre los mayas de Yucatán*. Mexico, CIESAS/Miguel Ángel Porrúa, 2010, 53.

19. Galindo, 2000, 128–9.

20. Elaboration by Luis Alberto Arrioja Díaz Viruell based on historical sources, Álvaro Guevara-Murua, Caroline A. Williams, Erica J. Hendy & Pablo Imbach, '300 years of hydrological records and societal responses to droughts floods on the Pacific Coast of Central America', *Climate of the Past* 14 (2018), 175–91, DOI:10.5194/cp-14-175-2018,2018; Robert H. Claxton, 'Weather-based hazards in Guatemala', *West Georgia College Studies in the Social Sciences* 25 (1986), 139–63; Virginia García Acosta, Juan Manuel Pérez Zevallos & América Molina del Villar, *Desastres agrícolas en México. Catálogo histórico: Épocas prehispánica y colonial (958–1822)*, Volume I, Mexico DF, CIESAS, 2003; *Compendio de la historia de Guatemala*, Volume I, Ciudad de Guatemala, Imprenta de Ignacio Beteta, 1808; Pedro Cortés y Larráz, *Descripción geográfico-moral de la Diócesis de Goathemala*. San Salvador, El Salvador, Consejo Nacional para la Cultura y las Artes, 2000.

21. *Papeles de la Luisiana*, Vol. III, BNE, Fondo Biblioteca Digital Hispánica, Manuscripts, 19248, ff. 113–17, 130–33.

22. Florescano, 2000, 28–31.

23. See the balance sheet and drought analysis in Guevara-Murua et al., 2018, 175–91.

24. Relación de pueblos en la provincia de Chiapas, 1769, AGCA, A3, leg. 300, exp. 4058-5; Libro de defunciones de Santiago Apostol Yajalón, 1720–1818, Family Search, Mexico, Chiapas, Registros parroquiales y diocesanos, 1557–1978; Libro de

defunciones de San Jerónimo Bachajón, 1768–1823, Family Search, Mexico, Chiapas, Registros parroquiales y diocesanos, 1557–1978; Libro de defunciones de Tila, 1747–1796, Family Search, Mexico, Chiapas, Registros parroquiales y diocesanos, 1557–1978; Libro de defunciones de Petalcingo, 1741–1808, Family Search, Mexico, Chiapas, Registros parroquiales y diocesanos, 1557–1978.

25. Tadashi Obara-Saeki & Juan Pedro Viqueira Alban, *El arte de contar tributarios, 1560–1821*. Mexico City, El Colegio de México, 2017, 496–504, 584–98.

26. Carta de Pedro de Urriola, 27 de Diciembre de 1768, Archivo General de Indias (hereafter AGI), Mexico 3054.

27. Carta de Cristóbal de Zayas sobre la carestía en Yucatán, 11 de agosto de 1767, AGI, Mexico, 3054.

28. Libro de cuentas de los bienes de comunidad del pueblo de Santa María Tataltepec, 1721–82, Archivo Histórico del Poder Judicial de Oaxaca (hereafter AHPJO), Teposcolula, Civil, leg. 23, exp. 18, Libro de cuentas de cargo y descargo de San Miguel Adeque, 1762–83, AHPJO, Teposcolula, Civil, leg. 38, exp. 9.

29. Deuda de pesos a favor de Cristóbal de San Andrés Sinastla, 1770, AHPJO, Teposcolula, Civil, Deuda de pesos, leg. 37, exp. 23, fs. 1–7; Libro de cuentas de cargo y descargo de San Miguel Adeque, 1771, AHPJO, Teposcolula, Civil, leg. 38, exp. 9; Carta de Pedro Gorrindo sobre siembra de tabaco y escasez de maíz, 26 de abril de 1770, Archivo General de la Nación (hereafter AGN), Alcaldes mayores, volume 1, exp. 265, fs. 380–82.

30. Relación de méritos de Jacinto Pérez de Arroyo, alcalde mayor de Juxtlahuaca, 1771, AGN, Alcaldes mayores, volume 13, exp. 20, fs. 199f, 238v; Carta del cabildo de Antequera para el virrey Croix sobre la escasez de semillas en la alhóndiga por la falta de lluvias, 1769, AGN, Indiferente virreinal, caja 6151, exp. 61.

31. Los nativos de Yajalon piden providencias para la destrucción de las plagas de langosta, 1769–70, AGCA, A1.22.8, leg. 1, exp. 10; Cordillera para que los curas animen a los feligreses a fomentar sus sementeras, 1770–71, Archivo Histórico Diocesano de San Cristóbal (hereafter AHDSC), Fondo diocesano, carpeta 3690, exp. 9; Informe de Marcos Novelo sobre el hambre y peste que sufre Palenque, 1770–71, AHDSC, Fondo diocesano, carpeta 1678, exp. 1.

32. Pedro Cortés y Larráz, *Descripción geográfico-moral de la diócesis de Goathemala*. Madrid, Corpus Hispanorum de Pace. Segunda Serie. Consejo Superior de Investigaciones Científicas, [1770] 2001, 367–8, 371, 409–10; Archivo Histórico de Arzobispado de Guatemala (hereafter AHAG), Archivo Parroquial de Nuestra Señora de Candelaria, Libro de la cofradía de Nuestra Señora del Carmen de la Ermita, f. 12.

33. Libro de defunciones de San Cristóbal Palín, (1743–1846), Family Search, Guatemala, Registros parroquiales y diocesanos (1581–1977), Escuintla, Palín, Defunciones, 1743–1846. Una experiencia muy semejante ocurrió en los pueblos de Jilotepeque, San Antonio de Padua, Momostenango y Sololá; Libro de defunciones de San Martín Jilotepeque, (1681–1776), Family Search, Guatemala, Registros parroquiales y diocesanos (1581–1977), Chimaltenango, Jilotepeque, San Martín Obispo, Defunciones, 1681–1776.

34. Informe sobre la situación que se vive en los pueblos de Chiapa, 1770–71, AHDSC, Fondo diocesano, carpeta 3965, exp. 31.

35. Informe del cura de Copainala sobre los decesos causados entre 1769–71, Family Search, San Cristóbal de las Casas, Cofradías y Cordilleras, 1702–71, leg. 2. One mecate was the equivalent to 400 square metres.

36. Solicitud de exención de tributos por esterilidad de los tiempos en la Mixteca Baja, 1780, AGN, Tributos, volume 48, exp. 4.

37. Informe de Antonio de Oliver sobre el estado de la provincia de Yucatán y las medidas para reactivar la agricultura (1773), AGI, Mexico 3018.

38. Bando de Joseph Mariano Cárdenas, alcalde mayor de Teposcolula, 1771, AHPJO, Teposcolula, Civil, leg. 38, exp. 7. f. 1.

39. Armando Alberola Romá, 'La cultura de la supervivencia: carencias y excesos hídricos en la Huerta de Alicante (siglos XV-XVIII)'. In: Carles Sanchis-Ibor, Guillermo Palau Salvador, Ignasi Mangue Alféres & Luis Pablo Martínez Sanmartin (eds.) *Proceedings irrigation, society, landscape: international conference tribute to Thomas V. Glick.* Valencia, Universitat Politécnica de Valencia, 2014, 362–76.

40. Testimonio sobre la falta de tributarios en la provincia de Yucatán, 1774, AGI, Mexico, 3057.

41. *Novena de la Gloriosa Virgen y Mártir Santa Irene.* Ciudad de Guatemala, Imprenta de Joaquín de Arévalo, 1772.

42. Informes sobre la situación de los pueblos de Chiapas, 1772, AGCA, AI.Io, 648.42; Solicitud de la Real Audiencia de Guatemala para que el obispo de Chiapas no visite a su diócesis, 1770, Family Search, San Cristóbal de las Casas, Cofradías y cordilleras, 1702–71, leg. 2.

43. Informe del alcalde mayor de Chiquimula sobre colecta de tributos, 1769, AGCA, A3, leg. 2843, s/e; Cuaderno de circulares giradas por el ayuntamiento de la ciudad de Guatemala sobre el exterminio de la plaga de langosta, 1771, AGCA, A1.2, leg. 2820, exp. 24984; Comunicación del cura de Jutiapa a los pueblos de su vicaria, 1769, AHAG, Diocesano, Secretaria de gobierno, Providencias, no. 103.

44. Libro del cuadrante del gasto y recibo de este curato del Espíritu Santo de Quetzaltenango y sus cuatro anexos, 1770–84, AGCA, A4.21. The Ladino Indians were an Indigenous sector that learned to speak, read and write in Spanish; some of them were cultural intermediaries and political negotiators. See Yanna Yannakakis, *El arte de estar en medio. Intermediarios indígenas, identidad india y régimen local en la Oaxaca Colonial,* Mexico, El Colegio de Michoacán, 2012.

45. Autos sobre suspensión de cobro de tributos en pueblos de Teposcolula, 1772, AGN, Tributos, volume 52, exp. 14.

46. Informe de la situación de los pueblos de Ocosingo y Tumbala, 1771–72, AHDSC, Fondo diocesano, carpeta 3695, exp. 31.

47. Composición de los señores Esponda por capitales piadosos, 1806, AHDSC, Fondo diocesano, carpeta 3339 expediente 3; Expediente sobre el embargo de una hacienda en Ixtacomitan, 1774, Family Search, Chiapas, San Cristóbal de las Casas, Cofradías y cordilleras, 1743–1812, leg. 1.

48. Misivas de varios curas de la vicaría de Huehuetenango, 1771, AHAG, Diocesano, Secretaria de gobierno, curatos Huehuetenango, exp. 116, s/f.

49. Cordillera del obispo García de Vargas sobre los problemas que se enfrentan en la diócesis, 1770, AHDSC, Fondo diocesano, carpeta 3965, exp. 3; Solicitud de la Real Audiencia de Guatemala para que el obispo de Chiapas no realice la visita a su diócesis, 1770, Family Search, San Cristóbal de las Casas, Cofradías y cordilleras, 1702–71, leg. 2; Misivas de varios curas de la vicaría de Huehuetenango, 1771, AHAG, Diocesano, Secretaria de gobierno, Vicaria de Zacapa, s/e.

50. Peniche Moreno, 2010, 171.

51. Testimonio de los autos de la falta de tributarios en Yucatán, 1770, AGI, Mexico, 3057; Informe del Ayuntamiento de Mérida sobre la mortandad de tributarios a causa de la langosta, 1774, AGI, Mexico, 3057.

52. Documentos pertenecientes al expediente de escasez de granos en Yucatán, 1770, AGN, Indiferente virreinal, caja 5989, exp. 16.

53. Informe del Ayuntamiento sobre la provincia de Yucatán, 1770, AGI, Mexico, 3018; Respuesta del Ayuntamiento de Mérida al Consejo de Indias sobre el estado de la provincia, 1774, Biblioteca del Museo Nacional de Antropología e Historia (hereafter BMNAH), Archivo de Microfilm, 'Antonio Pompa y Pompa', Yucatán, rollo 2, s/f.

54. Informe de Antonio de Oliver sobre el estado de la provincia de Yucatán y las medidas para reactivar la agricultura, (1775), AGI, Mexico, 3057.

55. Sobre el perdón de tributos en los pueblos de Ciudad Real, 1772–74, AGCA, A1.10, leg. 62, exp. 648.

56. Cuentas de las Cajas Reales de Tabasco y Mérida, 1769–75, AGI, Mexico, 3120, s/f.; Corte de la Caja Real de Tabasco, 1770, AGN, Alcaldes mayores, vol. 1, exp. 152; Pueblos exentos del pago de tributo en la alcaldía mayor de Xalapa, 1776, BMNAH, Serie Córdova, rollo 10, s/f; Carta de Juan Josef Zarabia, teniente oficial mayor de la Real Audiencia al Consejo de Indias, 19 de agosto de 1777, AGI, Mexico, 2103, s/f.

References

Alberola Romá, Armando, 'La cultura de la supervivencia: carencias y excesos hídricos en la Huerta de Alicante (siglos XV-XVIII)'. In: Carles Sanchis-Ibor, Guillermo Palau Salvador, Ignasi Mangue Alféres & Luis Pablo Martínez Sanmartin (eds.) *Proceedings irrigation, society, landscape: international conference tribute to Thomas V. Glick*. Valencia, Universitat Politécnica de Valencia, 2014, 362–76.

Barriendos, Mariano & Carmen Llasat, 'El caso de la anomalía "Maldá" en la cuenca mediterránea occidental (1760–1800). Un ejemplo de fuerte variabilidad climática'. In: Armando Alberola Romá & Jorge Olcina Cantos (eds.) *Desastre natural, vida cotidiana y religiosidad popular en la España moderna y contemporánea*. Alicante, Universidad de Alicante, 2009, 253–86.

Cédric, Bertrand Jean-Pascal van Ypersele & André Berger, 'Volcanic and solar impacts on climate since 1700', *Climate Dynamics* 15 (1999), 355–67.

Claxton, Robert H. & Alan D. Hecht, 'Climatic and human history in Europe and Latin America: an opportunity for comparative study', *Climatic Change* 1 (1978), 195–203.

Claxton, Robert H. & Alan D. Hecht, 'Weather-based hazards in Guatemala', *West Georgia College Studies in the Social Sciences* 25 (1986), 139–63.

Florescano, Enrique (ed.), *Breve historia de las sequías en México*. Mexico, CONACULTA, 2000.

Galindo, Ignacio, 'La oscilación del sur, El Niño: el caso de México'. In: Enrique Florescano (ed.) *Breve historia de las sequías en México*. Mexico, CONACULTA, 2000, 128–9.

García Acosta, Virginia, Juan Manuel Pérez Zevallos & América Molina del Villar, *Desastres agrícolas en México. Catálogo histórico: Épocas prehispánica y colonial (958–1822)*, Volume I, Mexico City, CIESAS, 2003.

Gergis, Joëlle L. & Anthony M. Fowler, 'A history of ENSO events since A.D. 1525: implications for future climate change', *Climatic Change* 92 (2009), 343–87.

Gill, Richardson B. & Jerome P. Keating, 'Volcanism and Mesoamerican archaeology', *Ancient Mesoamerica* 13, no. 1 (2002), 125–40.

Guevara-Murua, Álvaro, Caroline A. Williams, Erica J. Hendy & Pablo Imbach, '300 years of hydrological records and societal responses to droughts floods on the Pacific Coast of Central America', *Climate of the Past* 14 (2018), 175–91.

Luterbacher, Jürg & Gerard van der Scrier, 'Circulation dynamics and its influence on European and Mediterranean January-April climate over the past half millennium: results and insights from instrumental data, documentary evidence and coupled climate models', *Climate Change* 101, no. 1 (2010), 201–34.

Lutz, Christopher H., *Santiago de Guatemala, 1541–1773 city, caste and colonial experience*. Norman, OK, University of Oklahoma, 1994.

MacLeod, Murdo J., *Historia socio-económica de la América Central Española, 1520–1720*, second edition, Guatemala, Piedra Santa, 1990.

Obara-Saeki, Tadashi & Juan Pedro Viqueira Alban, *El arte de contar tributarios, 1560–1821*. Mexico City, El Colegio de México, 2017.

Peniche Moreno, Paola, *Tiempos aciagos. Las calamidades y el cambio social del siglo XVIII entre los mayas de Yucatán*. Mexico, CIESAS/ Miguel Ángel Porrúa, 2010.

Solano, Francisco de. *Tierra y sociedad en el reino de Guatemala*. Ciudad de Guatemala, Universidad de San Carlos de Guatemala, 1977.

Yannakakis, Yanna, *El arte de estar en medio. Intermediarios indígenas, identidad india y régimen local en la Oaxaca Colonial*. Mexico, El Colegio de Michoacán, 2012.

Archival and primary sources

Alzate, José Antonio de, *Gacetas de literatura de México*, volume IV, Puebla, Impresas en la oficina del Hospital de San Pedro, 1831.

Archivo General de Centroamérica, A1.11, leg. 2450, exp. 18878, Informe del alcalde mayor de Quetzaltenango sobre el estado de las cosechas (1801); leg, 5910, exp. 50545, A3, leg. 300, exp. 4058-5, Informe del alcalde mayor de Totonicapan sobre los daños en el puente de Zacapulas, (1807); Relación de pueblos en la provincia de Chiapas, 1769; Libro de defunciones de Santiago Apostol Yajalón, 1720–1818, Family Search, Mexico, Chiapas, Registros parroquiales y diocesanos, 1557–1978; Libro de defunciones de San Jerónimo Bachajón, 1768–1823, Family Search, Mexico, Chiapas, Registros parroquiales y diocesanos, 1557–1978; Libro de defunciones de Tila, 1747–1796, Family Search, Mexico, Chiapas, Registros parroquiales y diocesanos, 1557–1978; Libro de defunciones de Petalcingo, 1741–1808, Family Search, Mexico, Chiapas, Registros parroquiales y diocesanos, 1557–1978; A1.22.8, leg. 1, exp. 10, Los nativos de Yajalon piden providencias para la destrucción de las plagas de langosta, 1769–70; Cordillera para que los curas animen a los feligreses a fomentar sus sementeras, 1770–71; Libro de defunciones de San Cristóbal Palín, (1743–1846), Family Search, Guatemala, Registros parroquiales y diocesanos (1581–1977), Escuintla, Palín, Defunciones, 1743–1846;

Libro de defunciones de San Martín Jilotepeque (1681–1776), Family
Search, Guatemala, Registros parroquiales y diocesanos (1581–1977),
Chimaltenango, Jilotepeque, San Martín Obispo, Defunciones,
1681–1776; Informe del cura de Copainala sobre los decesos causados
entre 1769–71, Family Search, San Cristóbal de las Casas, Cofradías y
Cordilleras, 1702–71, leg. 2; Informes sobre la situación de los pueblos
de Chiapas, 1772, AGCA, AI.Io, 648.42; Family Search, San Cristóbal
de las Casas, leg. 2, Cofradías y cordilleras, 1702–71; A3, leg. 2843,
Solicitud de la Real Audiencia de Guatemala para que el obispo de
Chiapas no visite a su diócesis, 1770; Informe del alcalde mayor de
Chiquimula sobre colecta de tributos, 1769; A1.2, leg. 2820, exp.
24984, Cuaderno de circulares giradas por el ayuntamiento de la
ciudad de Guatemala sobre el exterminio de la plaga de langosta,
1771; Diocesano, Secretaria de gobierno, Providencias, no. 103,
Comunicación del cura de Jutiapa a los pueblos de su vicaria, 1769;
A4.21, Libro del cuadrante del gasto y recibo de este curato del
Espíritu Santo de Quetzaltenango y sus cuatro anexos, 1770–84;
Family Search, Chiapas, San Cristóbal de las Casas, Cofradías y
cordilleras, 1743–1812, leg. 1, Expediente sobre el embargo de una
hacienda en Ixtacomitan, 1774; A1.10, leg. 62, exp. 648, Sobre el
perdón de tributos en los pueblos de Ciudad Real, 1772–74.
Archivo General de Indias, Mexico 3054, Carta de Pedro de Urriola, 27 de
Diciembre de 1768; Mexico, 3054, Carta de Cristóbal de Zayas sobre la
carestía en Yucatán, 11 de agosto de 1767; Mexico 3018, Informe de
Antonio de Oliver sobre el estado de la provincia de Yucatán y las
medidas para reactivar la agricultura (1773); Mexico, 3057, Testimonio
sobre la falta de tributarios en la provincia de Yucatán, 1774;
Testimonio de los autos de la falta de tributarios en Yucatán, 1770;
Mexico, 3057, Informe del Ayuntamiento de Mérida sobre la mortan-
dad de tributarios a causa de la langosta; Mexico, 3018, Informe del
Ayuntamiento sobre la provincia de Yucatán, 1770; Mexico, 3057,
Informe de Antonio de Oliver sobre el estado de la provincia de
Yucatán y las medidas para reactivar la agricultura (1775); Mexico,
3120, Cuentas de las Cajas Reales de Tabasco y Mérida, 1769–75;
Mexico, 2103, Carta de Juan Josef Zarabia, teniente oficial mayor de la
Real Audiencia al Consejo de Indias, 19 de agosto de 1777.
Archivo General de la Nación, Alcaldes mayores, volume 13, exp. 20,
Relación de méritos de Jacinto Pérez de Arroyo, alcalde mayor de
Juxtlahuaca, 1771; Indiferente virreinal, caja 6151, exp. 61, Carta del
cabildo de Antequera para el virrey Croix sobre la escasez de semillas
en la alhóndiga por la falta de lluvias, 1769; Alcaldes mayores,
volume 1, exp. 265, Carta de Pedro Gorrindo sobre siembra de tabaco

y escasez de maíz, 26 de abril de 1770; volume 48, exp. 4, Solicitud de exención de tributos por esterilidad de los tiempos en la Mixteca Baja, 1780; Tributos, volume 52, exp. 14, Autos sobre suspensión de cobro de tributos en pueblos de Teposcolula, 1772; Indiferente virreinal, caja 5989, exp. 16, Documentos pertenecientes al expediente de escasez de granos en Yucatán, 1770; Alcaldes mayores, vol. 1, exp. 152, Corte de la Caja Real de Tabasco, 1770.

Archivo Histórico de Arzobispado de Guatemala, Archivo Parroquial de Nuestra Señora de Candelaria, Libro de la cofradía de Nuestra Señora del Carmen de la Ermita; Diocesano, Secretaria de gobierno, curatos Huehuetenango, exp. 116, s/f, Misivas de varios curas de la vicaría de Huehuetenango, 1771; Diocesano, Secretaria de gobierno, Vicaria de Zacapa, s/e, Misivas de varios curas de la vicaría de Huehuetenango, 1771.

Archivo Histórico Diocesano de San Cristóbal, Fondo diocesano, carpeta 3690, exp. 9, Informe de Marcos Novelo sobre el hambre y peste que sufre Palenque, 1770–71; carpeta 3965, exp. 31, Informe sobre la situación que se vive en los pueblos de Chiapa, 1770–71; carpeta 3339, expediente 3, Composición de los señores Esponda por capitales piadosos, 1806; carpeta 3965, exp. 3, Cordillera del obispo García de Vargas sobre los problemas que se enfrentan en la diócesis, 1770; Solicitud de la Real Audiencia de Guatemala para que el obispo de Chiapas no realice la visita a su diócesis, 1770, Family Search, San Cristóbal de las Casas, Cofradías y cordilleras, 1702–71, leg. 2.

Archivo Histórico del Poder Judicial de Oaxaca, Libro de cuentas de los bienes de comunidad del pueblo de Santa María Tataltepec, 1721–82; Teposcolula, Civil, leg. 38, exp. 9; leg. 23, exp. 18, Libro de cuentas de cargo y descargo de San Miguel Adeque, 1762–83; leg. 37, exp. 23, Deuda de pesos, Deuda de pesos a favor de Cristóbal de San Andrés Sinastla, 1770; leg. 38, exp. 9, Libro de cuentas de cargo y descargo de San Miguel Adeque, 1771; Teposcolula, Civil, leg. 38, exp. 7, Bando de Joseph Mariano Cárdenas, alcalde mayor de Teposcolula, 1771.

Archivo del Museo Naval, Virreinato de México, Volume IV, Manuscript 570, Document 13, Informe sobre Campeche y Yucatán, 1766.

Biblioteca Nacional de España, Fondo Biblioteca Digital Hispánica, *Papeles de la Luisiana*, Vol. III, Manuscripts, 19248, ff. 113–17, 130–33; *Memoria sobre la policía y régimen de los abastos de la ciudad de Santiago*, 1786, f. 44; *Manual para entender y hablar el castellano por el padre fray Francisco Guijarro*, 1796, f. 95.

Biblioteca Nacional del Museo de Antropología e Historia, Archivo de Microfilm, 'Antonio Pompa y Pompa', Yucatán, rollo 2, Respuesta del Ayuntamiento de Mérida al Consejo de Indias sobre el estado de la provincia, 1774; Serie Córdova, rollo 10, s/f, Carta de Juan Josef Zarabia, teniente oficial mayor de la Real Audiencia, 19 de agosto de 1777; Serie, Córdova, rollo 10, s/f., Pueblos exentos del pago de tributo en la alcaldía mayor de Xalapa, 1776.

Biblioteca Nettie Benson, Benson Latin American Collection, LAC-Z Rare Books, GZ 972.81 G258, *Gazeta de Guatemala*, no. 267, Estado de las siembras y precios de granos, 1802.

Cortés y Larráz, Pedro, *Descripción geográfico-moral de la diócesis de Goathemala*. Madrid, Corpus Hispanorum de Pace. Segunda Serie. Consejo Superior de Investigaciones Científicas, [1770] 2001.

Discurso político, rústico y legal sobre labores, ganados y plantíos en el cual se intentan persuadir los considerables beneficios que resultarán a esta Monarquía de la unión y concordia de aquellos tres hermanos donde conviene o disconviene su aumento y dilatación, las causas supuestas y verdaderas de su decadencia, los medios para lograr su restablecimiento y los abusos que lo detienen. Compuesto por el doctor don Vicente Calvo y Julián, noble de Aragón, abogado de los reales Consejos, presidente y fiscal de la Academia de Abogados de Zaragoza y opositor a prebendas doctorales. Madrid, en la oficina de Antonio Marín, 1770.

Hemeroteca Digital de la Biblioteca Nacional de España, *Correo literario de la Europa,* no. 53, 'Veterinaria o albeiteria, (1782)'.

Juarros, Domingo, Maury A. Bromsen, Alberto Parreño & Francisco de Beltranena, *Compendio de la historia de la ciudad de Guatemala*. Guatemala, Ignacio Beteta, 1808.

Novena de la Gloriosa Virgen y Mártir Santa Irene. Ciudad de Guatemala, Imprenta de Joaquín de Arévalo, 1772.

Chapter 4

Water labour: urban metabolism, energy and rivers in nineteenth-century Rio de Janeiro, Brazil

Bruno Capilé and Lise Fernanda Sedrez
Translated by Diogo de Carvalho Cabral

From a natural sciences perspective, work is the transfer of energy for the displacement of bodies. As rivers flow, they move bodies and carry vital energy to cities and human societies. Not unlike humans, rivers take advantage of external and internal elements, such as the solar energy needed to transform water into steam or the winds to transport them to fall as rain on mountains and hills. In the humanities, 'labour' implies a relational perspective between people and their environment, a connection that transforms both in their historical materiality. For Friedrich Engels, labour is an essential condition for human life, and culture has a critical role in the evolution of our species through labour.[1] Marx famously wrote that labour is 'a process by which man, through his own actions, mediates, regulates and controls the metabolism between himself and nature'.[2]

Rio de Janeiro lies just north of the Tropic of Capricorn, a tropical city port on the Atlantic Ocean. While Europeans founded the city in the sixteenth century, the area had a much longer history of Indigenous occupation, which benefited from the rich waters of Guanabara Bay. In nineteenth-century Rio de Janeiro, the labour of rivers intertwined with that of humans to shape the urban spaces of exchange and production in Brazil's imperial capital. A transformed world resulted from the indissociable labours of humans and rivers. Rio de Janeiro's urban metabolism relied on material and energy fluxes from adjacent river basins to the city.

As the population increased and changes in the social and technological dynamics took place, more rivers were transformed and incorporated into Rio de Janeiro's fluvial-urban system. By understanding how this intermingling occurred, we shed light on the workings of urban river systems as critical components of urban nature and as dynamic agents of city-building.

Most of Rio's rivers spring in the mountains and hills near the city. Rivers flow down the valleys, and in their path, they move rocks, sandbanks and sediments, as well as anthropogenic objects, such as boats, mills and garbage. Their work is not uniform along the way. Fluvial work generates different environments throughout the basin, which we categorise as upper, middle and lower course. By the early nineteenth century, rivers were essential parts of the city, and their channels defined the different ways their labour was incorporated into the city. In the upper reaches, the waters streamed through dense rainforests. In the minds of city dwellers, forests were mostly suppliers of wood and fuel, but they were also seen as part of a complex water system of rivers and rains. In other words, forests, rivers and rains were a single entity – mysterious, useful and sometimes dangerous. The river and human labour merged in the hills to ensure water supplies for the downtown social metabolism through reservoirs and waterways. In the middle course of rivers, the forests were mostly gone by the nineteenth century, replaced by sugarcane plantations, cattle pastures and subsistence agriculture – all activities that relied heavily on river labour. With the growth of the urban centre and the emergence of transportation challenges, old rural estates were refitted into a mosaic of suburban opulent houses and manors. The diverse topography of the rivers' middle course included rocky riverbanks sought by washerwomen, alluvial soils from floodplains, and sufficient water flow to power textile industries' wheel turbines and push forward industrial and domestic sewage. Finally, at the lower courses, the fine sediments favoured mangrove forests over other tree species common to the hills. Humans landfilled and dredged out the mangrove swamps and harnessed the rivers' labour to expand the imperial capital.

Thus, humans forever connected the rivers to the fate of the city, ironically called Rio (River) de Janeiro.[3] This chapter analyses how the work produced by rivers was appropriated in different but interconnected ways in Rio de Janeiro's upper, middle and lower course rivers. We use the rivers' trajectory to deliberately blur the city's limits. Although urban residents only saw the lower course of rivers in front of their houses, they drank water and built their homes with wood from the upper course, while their horses and mules grazed at banks in the middle course. Rivers brought the energy of the surrounding ecosystems to Rio's intra-urban space.

To end this introduction, a few words about the concepts of metabolism and agency. Within the scope of materialism, Marx reiterates that humans are natural beings endowed with bodies, sensitive and connected with all the nonhuman materiality that surrounds us. In need of this materiality outside their bodies, humans come to conceptualise their interactions with rivers, plants, animals, wind, sun and other things. Analogously to the example evoked by Marx on the relationship between the sun and the plant, it can be argued that rivers are objects for humans, just as the other way around, as people express the rivers' life-awakening power.[4] In *Estranged Labour* (1844), Marx makes it clear that human survival and work would not be possible without external materiality. This means that nature is in our bodies, exchanging matter and energy continuously with the rest of the universe.[5] The same applies to objects derived from human labour, such as cities and their relationships with rivers.

The metabolic connection between city and rivers, or between humans and nature, is labour – an interaction between people's physical and mental capacities and other human and nonhuman actors. This result produces elements in new metabolic processes mobilising new agents.[6] For example, we can think of the loading of sediments along the river. This work creates new fluvial landscapes that allow the extraction of sand for civil construction in the middle course and clay sediments, in the lower course. As a result of the river's agency, the landscape enabled new human metabolic processes. In this eternal becoming of processes that generate other processes, it makes sense to think of the agency of rivers shaping landscapes and how these became the material basis of new developments. Just like people, rivers act in relational contexts. Rivers constrain, enable and influence their surroundings and the agencies of non-river actors.[7] There is a constant risk of anthropomorphising actants when using frequently used words for human behaviour. Therefore, when we say that rivers allow or resist, what we have in mind is a contextual agency that manifests itself in a 'networked' way.[8] Anthropogenic action and river agency influence and affect each other. Before urbanisation, the waters of Rio de Janeiro's rivers followed their own free courses, and later, with the onset of constant urban metamorphosis, the work of these waters became strongly associated with humans.

Carrying energy and matter into the city

Despite its grandiose fluvial name, Rio de Janeiro city was not named after a river. Instead, a number of small streams, medium-sized rivers and even some large ones feed into Guanabara Bay, forming its watershed. The bay itself is a sunken estuary. So, we do not focus on any single river but on this ensemble of rivers, streams and creeks that shaped Rio de Janeiro's waterscape. Eugene Odum claimed that delimiting ecosystems makes more sense if we consider water basins, as the flow of water adds to the cycle of solar energy in a myriad of open biological systems. Likewise, we interpret the city as an open system and consider its influence and transforming power on its surroundings. The city casts a large shadow beyond its constructed structures (buildings, walls, human-made markers). But if the city is bigger than itself, it is through the rivers that the city grows both ecosystemically and socially.[9]

We propose thus a two-tier perspective: on the one hand, we discuss the fluxes of social transformation from a historiographic viewpoint; on the other hand, we incorporate both metabolic and ecosystemic analyses for the material and energetic fluxes into that account. As we look at the rivers' flow, we consider in this section the elements that *entered* the urban system through the rivers in the nineteenth century. The agency of the rivers was thus responsible for transporting energy, water, sediments and other materials into the city. At the same time, the protagonism of the rivers was tributary to their relations to other elements in their surroundings, such as the local topography, the retention of sediments by roots (trees or other plants), and even human labour. We argue that the interrelations of these agents – rivers, topography, plants and humans – were responsible for inputting materials essential to urban life.

In the environment, the geography of energy strongly connects to the geography of work. That is, rivers' work occurs unequally, as it depends on the energetic and material influences of the local topography. How rivers established connections with their environs depended on their material reality, whether waterfalls, floodplains, water courses or estuaries. Likewise, human labour establishes relationships with the same material reality when using or changing a river. Let's consider again our three categories: upper, middle and lower course rivers. The work by which nineteenth-century Rio de Janeiro's residents could divert part of the Carioca upper course river to the city's fountains was possible due to the environmental conditions resulting from the joint work of the rivers flowing downhill, the sun and the winds, as much as to the infrastructure of river pipelines. The fusion of human labour with the work of the fluvial environment was necessary to direct the waters to the fountains that supplied the city. It could hardly occur in the middle and lower course of rivers, obstructed by sediment deposition and often tainted by water contamination.[10]

Several water basins drained into Rio de Janeiro city. Rio's inhabitants were well aware of their dependence on the river's flow for fresh water.

Tellingly, these inhabitants became known as *Cariocas*, named after one of the first rivers they exploited for drinking water in the colonial period. The Tijuca massif influenced the distribution of fresh water and the city's expansion. Despite the existence of the Carioca River, the history of Rio de Janeiro was marked by successive water scarcity situations due mostly to inadequate water supply policies in the face of accelerated population growth. The Carioca could not supply enough fresh water. This made it necessary to invest in infrastructure and technical training of public engineers who had to learn how to manage the river for water supply. Before the 1860s, Rio de Janeiro's water policies were improvised, often unconnected to larger planning and frequently flawed, with rare studies on water regimes. The initial public works on the rivers Carioca (1750) and Maracanã (1817) could not harness the rivers' work, resulting in precarious water distribution and a massive presence of leaves and sediments. The 1860s marked a political watershed (pun intended) for Brazil's imperial government regarding the infrastructure projects in the capital. The imperial administration created important institutions with their technical staff strongly dominated by engineers – first within the Ministry of the Empire and then within the Ministry of Agriculture, Commerce and Public Works (henceforth Ministry of Agriculture). As civil engineering developed and the federal administration professionalised urban services, these new technical staff formed scientific commissions to research the rivers and their characteristics to inform public policies.[11]

Understanding the dynamics of the fluvial work was essential to carry out structural modifications and increase the city's water use efficiency. In the 1860s and 1870s, public investment in the water commissions for dozens of rivers and streams closest to the city simplified and reduced their characteristics to four types of variables: daily water flow, elevation of the water catchment outlet, capacity of the water tanks, and the condition of the forests near the water springs. A few years before the 1860s water commissions, the imperial government was concerned mainly with river flow and elevation of the water catchment outlet. Sound knowledge about the flow of the rivers enabled greater control over their work, improving the quality and quantity of water supply.

Water was just one of the substances that rivers carried from the upper course environment into the city. Sediments were also important. Due to their upper course's altitude and topographical gradient, the rivers could carry larger sediments and small stones. As fluvial energy dissipated along the river's course, its capacity to carry sediments diminished. Rivers in the middle course transported smaller and smaller particles and transformed their environments by depositing sediments of different sizes. As the water descended and lost energy, the heavier elements rushed to the bottom, and the rivers' labour could only carry the smaller ones. Thus, the river's labour defined the kind of sediment that remained in different terrains and which kind of biotic community emerged: in the lower river course, the small deposits composed the mud of Rio's mangrove forest, while in the upper course, only the heavier sediments remained, providing good soil for dense forests.

Humans often used these materials distributed by the rivers locally. However, they frequently added their own labour to the rivers', and carried the sediments to the city as raw material for constructing buildings, roads and draining systems, among other purposes. Tons of stones, sand and clay taken from the fluvial systems in the upper course reached Rio de Janeiro loaded on the back of working mules. These animals – and their work – were an essential part of the metabolic transformation of the city, as we will discuss later. The mules acted both locally and across the different levels of the river systems by transporting people and materials through the mountains of Rio. Animal traction was just one of the many forms in which combined labour of the biotic and non-biotic communities contributed to the shaping of Rio de Janeiro city.

The repairs to the water supply system that flowed into the Carioca Aqueduct in 1861 exemplify the importance of this complex combination of human, animal and fluvial energy. The Department of Public Works, a government agency subordinated to the Ministry of Agriculture, estimated this project would require the consumption of 1000 m³ of stones, 5000 m³ of sand and lime, and 400 m³ of clay for landfilling. In the same year, reforms of the water tanks in the Tijuca mountain, part of the Maracanã River's tributaries, demanded 2000 m³ of stone and lime. Thirteen years later, in 1874, paving with water-bound macadam a few access roads to the Tijuca massif (which rises from Gávea, Jardim Botânico and Andarahy, now Tijuca) used 2970 m³ of rocks and small stones. The estimated weight of these rocks and stones was around 5,000 tons. In the area's steep slopes, mules and donkeys seldom carried more than 100 kg, and therefore an estimate of 50,000 trips in the year 1874 were necessary only to bring these stones to roads – or about 130 trips a day. The fact that the work site was close to the area where the materials were extracted certainly reduced the work of these animals in constructing the roadways and railroads which climbed up the mountains. Nevertheless, the imperial government depended heavily on the energy produced by the mules and counted, among its 'staff', hundreds of these animals who took advantage of the upper course's fluvial environment to feed on the grass near the riverbanks and to quench their thirst in the springs.[12]

The presence of mules in the forested hills and mountains meant a drastic transformation due to the trampling of the soil. Soil compaction reduced the forest's regenerative capacity and added to deforestation, which had been dramatic since the early nineteenth century, with the first coffee plantations established in the valleys shaped by fluvial work. Deforestation in Rio de Janeiro's mountains had two main causes: slash-and-burn cultivation and logging. In the case of coffee cultivation, it was common practice to use fire indiscriminately to eliminate the dense forest and clear space for coffee. Ironically, coffee seedlings developed poorly when exposed directly to the sun, and therefore the areas most sought (and mostly burned) by the coffee planters were the shaded environments in the river valleys. A survey indicated that there were over 250,000 coffee trees scattered in nine locations of the Tijuca massif. The number may seem modest when we take into account the full extension of the massif (around 3,300 hectares), but we still know little about the human uses of the valleys.[13]

Logging, however, was intended to supply the metabolic demand of fuelwood and timber within the city and its immediate hinterland. Most of the wood was burned into charcoal still in the mountains and then easily transported by mule or/and by boat to feed the furnaces in the city. The data collected by Warren Dean for the year 1882 show that there were many furnaces in the city, including 173 bakeries, 33 coffee roasters, 36 sugar refineries, 60 ironworks and foundries, 66 felt-hat manufacturers, 11 potteries, 5 cardboard and paper factories, 5 glass and porcelain factories, and 22 boiler manufacturers. The 1850 census indicates that over 27,000 houses had one oven each, and the 1872 census reveals that this figure reached over 30,000 by then. In addition to the daily fuel consumption for cooking, cloth dyeing and other activities, each domestic space would have burned tons of firewood just in their construction. Even brick houses consumed huge amounts of firewood. Indeed, Dean argues that brick houses were wood houses. He estimated that a small house used around 30,000 bricks (63 m³), for which it would have been necessary to burn 18 tons of firewood.[14]

Despite the difficulties for historians to develop good estimates of forest loss in the nineteenth century, we know that urban society felt deforestation acutely. Forest clearing deeply damaged the symbiotic relationship between tree roots and soil microorganisms. Soil disintegration and erosion caused by the rain and the rivers hindered water circulation in the riverbeds. The consequent siltation in the plains transformed the fluvial environment in the medium and lower courses. Swamps expanded, therefore, due to deforestation in the upper courses. Physicians and other professionals trained in social medicine saw the swamps as unhealthy areas threatening the urban social body. And they were ready to fight the swamps with all the might of modern science.[15] The urban elite interpreted the outpouring of mud and sand in the city centre as an unwanted environment that needed modernisation.

Probably one of the most remarkable reforestation projects worldwide in the nineteenth century, the reforestation of the Tijuca mountain officially began in 1861 under the initiative of the Ministry of Agriculture. The area was considered critical for maintaining Rio's water supply and thus was purchased by the imperial government from private owners, mostly coffee planters. By 1889, when the imperial regime fell due to a republican coup d'état, more than 100,000 seedlings of over 100 species had been planted. In line with the rhetoric of exuberant nature pervading Brazilian culture –as can be noted, for example, in the national anthem lyrics – the reforestation project privileged native species. Between 1861 and 1889, native species (and otherwise) circulated through scientific institutions and reached the reforestation site, which became a sort of forest laboratory. The imperial government claimed several objectives for this initiative, and the most recurrent in the documents were the hopes for a healthier climate, the need to supply the city with water, a steady source of wood for urban building, and the beautification of the mountains. In the end, the mixture of scientific ideas with the classist and racist culture of the Carioca elite turned the enterprise into a project of exclusion, as we will see ahead.[16]

From a metabolic perspective, the change in forest dynamics severely affected rivers and their flows. The quality and quantity of water were directly related to deforestation and reforestation. Here, humans and other animals, as well as plants and rivers, worked together to transform the biophysical environment. Just like energy and matter, information entered and was metabolised by the urban ecosystem.[17] Fluvial systems store information in their topography and ecological relations, but they also experience structural modifications based on information generated by humans (scientific ideas, sanitary customs, urban irregularities). The information circulating within Rio's human society, such as ideas of forestry, race, class and private property, affected the river water regimes as much as the quantity of precipitation or the steepness of slopes.

The weight of European ideas was massive in nineteenth-century Brazil. Physicians trained at the Medical School of Rio de Janeiro, from its foundation in 1832 to the late 1860s, were strongly influenced by French social medicine. The Medical School's first generation of professors had graduated in Paris or at least at the Academia-Médico Cirúrgica de Rio de Janeiro (1813), whose faculty had also trained in France. It was not unrelated that Paris's urban transformation in the early nineteenth century became a blueprint to be tested in the Brazilian imperial capital, including the health rationale implicit in the new urban planning models. Very influential in

Rio, these medical professionals championed the neo-Hypocratic theory of miasmas to discern which environments benefited human health and which did not. The new social medicine interpreted and imagined an ideal healthy urban environment, pointing to several places supposedly unfit for human health. This rationale legitimised state policies within and beyond the city, including ones that removed traditional or poor communities from certain areas while making others unaffordable.[18]

Transformations within the river/urban system

Rio de Janeiro grew attached to Guanabara Bay. By the turn of the nineteenth century, the city was no longer a timid European entrepôt. Rio's inhabitants had drained mangrove swamps or landfilled large extensions of the bay since the foundation of Rio in the sixteenth century. The rivers draining to the bay near the harbour had also been incorporated into the workings of the city. However, in the early nineteenth century, the heavy influx of new migrants gave a new impulse to the old practices and techniques. In fact, by the mid-nineteenth century, it was no longer just a matter of scale. The way Rio's inhabitants saw the small rivers permeating the urban tissue had changed. An almost seamless tapestry of ditches, creeks, canals and streams ran from the hinterland to Guanabara Bay, a tapestry punctuated by houses, factories and buildings. Rivers and the city were joined in a complex spreading biosystem responsible for many urban services.[19]

The nineteenth century witnessed several changes in Rio's river-city system. Some of them were material, and others not. While the colonial government had actively drained lagoons, dredged swamps and sought to manage water supply, the reach of the modern city was more extensive and qualitatively different. The modern city-river biosystem did require active planning, large public works and regular maintenance, and this was the first significant change. No longer a task for a small group of residents in a neighbourhood, or an impromptu project by colonial authorities, ditches had to be dug and kept clean. In many instances, rivers and creeks were channelled and forced underground, while in other cases, they were domesticated into straight lines by concrete walls, destroying the meandering trajectory that characterised their lower curse. As Rio de Janeiro was the country's capital, the federal government invested a fair amount of its budget into local public works and hoped to tame the rivers that often overflowed during the rainy season. Thus, the modern city-river metabolism claimed more energy through public investments (for example, public funding and hired or enslaved labour). It was also a political metabolism.

The second prominent change was aesthetical in character. The rectification of rivers followed a geometrised urban design highly appreciated by Rio's boosters. But the rivers resisted such geometrisation. Likewise, the people using these rivers persisted in their traditional practices, though maybe not in the same places. For instance, in 1822, the British visitor Maria Graham thus described the Carioca River: 'At the entrance to the valley, a little green plain stretches itself on either hand, through which the rivulet runs over its stony bed, and affords a tempting spot to groups of washerwomen of all hues, though the greater number are black'.[20] The work of the river and the washerwomen merged at the local riverine topography, with a configuration of stream water, rocks and the sun that was useful for those people. Other travellers observed them 'standing in the stream and beating their clothes upon the boulders of rock' to clean them. And later they 'purified in the stream and bleached [the clothes] in the sun'.[21] This scene could no longer be seen in the modern city of the early twentieth century. The Carioca River was then surrounded by large *villas* forming an upscale neighbourhood, and black women with red scarves doing laundry were no longer welcome. But the city still needed the work of washerwomen, so they moved their business to other, less visible, streams and creeks. So, modernity reached certain rivers but not others. Segregated as it was, the urban fabric allowed the coexistence of transformed rivers and rivers that retained much of their traditional appearance and uses.

The third significant change concerned the cultural perception of the urban rivers. As the maintenance of modernised rivers demanded more investments, and as they changed the city's outlook – more or less visible, more decorated or more disguised, with drained areas or harnessed in a factory – the urban rivers of Rio de Janeiro also became cultural laboratories of the hygienist scientific culture. Were they the solution for or the source of the dreaded urban epidemics? What did the transformed rivers say about the moral character of Rio de Janeiro's inhabitants? Were there good and bad urban rivers? Were some healthy and others miasmatic?

These changes shaped the metabolism of urban rivers. The state's intervention, the coexistence of tradition and modernity, and the new cultural perception of urban rivers forged a segregated city that was shaped by the work realised by the rivers and on the rivers. Certain activities, such as the washing described by Maria Graham, would take place in specific sites – such as slum houses near small rivers, where washerwomen took out their laundry – or in rivers far from the city centre. Other activities, such as textile manufacturing, were located on high-priced urban lots with good access to water (used for powering the mills). But these lots were not so valuable that they would compete for space with upscale houses and public buildings. Still others, such as burning fuelwood harvested at the river's upper course, took place across the entire city as urban dwellers cooked, built houses and used river energy in their daily lives.[22]

Thus, the metabolic processes within the city accelerated over the nineteenth century. By the early twentieth century, the city used more energy, consumed more raw materials and produced more effluents than a hundred years earlier. It was an order-of-magnitude change. More importantly, however, the agents that operated these changes were quite diverse. They mixed their labour in planned and unplanned operations – and the rivers were both actors and space in which these actions occurred.

Therefore, we can identify human action in cleaning ditches, dredging rivers, and general public works such as landfilling, draining and bridge building; they all used energy and transformed urban rivers. Humans also planted edible cress on the riverbanks for human consumption and grass for their mules and horses and used river water to discharge garbage and animal remains. Also, having remained a slave society until 1888, Rio's inhabitants forced other humans to work in the rivers. These were mostly demeaning and unhealthy jobs, such as transporting and eliminating human waste, which those enslaved people known as *tigres* executed during the early hours of the day.

Human labour could also combine with animal labour – like the mules and the equines that transported materials from the rivers and trampled the river margins while grazing. These animals depended on the energy available in the *capinzais* (grass pastures) planted in the floodplains of the main rivers, especially on the city's outskirts. Advertisements for the sale and rental of farms mentioned capinzais to raise the price. Between the 1830s and 1880s, it was common for these ads to mention how many animals could be fed, describing the size and quality of the grasses. The rivers had a wider floodplain for grass planting in the urban periphery. The largest capinzais were located in the floodplains of rivers in the northern suburbs, such as the Joana, Maracanã and others.[23]

Suburban agriculture spread along the banks and designed new river paths to irrigate plants such as *agrião* (watercress). Agrião (*Nasturtium officinale*) is a plant that grows easily in small streams with gentle running water. More common in the northern suburbs, landlords near rivers had ditches dug to divert the water to where the crop would be planted. In the Catumby Valley, closer to the city centre, suburban farmers were so successful in this crop that the region became known as *Zona do Agrião* (Watercress Zone). After intense conflicts arising from the diversion of waters, the cultivation of watercress was prohibited in 1878.[24]

In fact, rivers and their human uses had been the target of municipal regulation for decades. However, efforts to tame and maintain the rivers intensified with the growth of the symbolic capital of physicians and their quest for urban health in the 1870s. In 1875, the Central Board of Public Hygiene organised the General Commission for Health. All sanitary activities carried out by the Commission focused on rivers and other bodies of water: cleaning and conservation of rivers, ditches and mangroves, back-filling swamps, and general urban cleaning. Thus, river metabolism converged more intensely with the interests of local elites. The river conservation and cleaning service began through a contract with Júlio Richard, and at the end of the nineteenth century, it became a municipal service. In the first year, the service focused on 15 km of rivers and ditches, including the Carioca, the Trapicheiros, the Joana, the Comprido, the Papa Couve, the Berquó, and a couple of ditches. As early as 1881, 464 kilometres of rivers and ditches were included in Júlio Richard's cleaning service. The waste that had to be dealt with ranged from sediments comprising sand and mud, small plants such as bushes and banana trees, to utensils and furniture such as mattresses and beds. In addition, the Comprido, Papa Couve, Berquó and Trapicheiros rivers were widened in the 1870s.[25]

These metabolic processes also included nonhuman agents – often in the opposite direction of what humans would plan. Thus, plants absorbed solar energy and flourished in the nutrient-rich river waters. This accelerated ecological succession, clogging riverbeds and forcing humans to regular and expensive dredging. The rivers themselves showed that they could not be tamed easily. Their ecological dynamics challenged the efficiency of the public works that sought to turn them into obedient organic machines. Frequent rainstorms, high tides and siltation helped the rivers overflow their artificial concrete beds, with flooding becoming a constant nightmare for Rio de Janeiro's public administration.

Effluents, waste and products leave the river/urban system

As we have seen, energy and material inputs were harnessed and transformed by the work of different agents in nineteenth-century Rio de Janeiro – humans, plants, animals and rivers. From these metabolisms, the city excreted things that influenced its surrounding areas – the rural hinterland, the beaches and the oceans. Some elements left never to return. This was the case, for instance, of commercial exports such as coffee or sugarcane, which were loaded in the large ships in the port of Rio de Janeiro and entered the international capitalist market. However, some outputs immediately returned to the urban territory due to local characteristics such as topography, winds and tides. Such was the unfortunate case of urban sewage, for which the federal administration sought a solution for decades.

In 1864 the Rio de Janeiro City Improvements Company was created, mostly with British capital. It obtained a concession from the imperial government to collect and treat domestic sewage for over 12,000 houses in the city. The administration had high expectations for a solution to its sanitary crisis. Rio had more than 200,000 residents by then, and enslaved African and Afro-descendent people discharged the sewage. At night, these workers gathered human waste from homes, shops and public buildings in wood barrels and dumped them on the beaches. They also relied on the tide's work to do the 'sanitary service' of cleaning the beaches. This system of sewage disposal – occasionally carried out by freedmen – survived until the end of the imperial period but began to decline with the implantation of the City Improvements Company's sanitation system.[26]

The City Improvements Company implanted a sewage separations system which was quite modern for the period. According to the engineers of the Ministry of Agriculture, the success of this system depended on a reliable and abundant supply of water to push the urban waste. However, in the secondary collectors, errors in the original construction and failure to consider the steep slopes caused frequent interruptions in water and sewage flows. The uneven terrain of the city provoked cracks and fissures in the thin-walled pipes that had little pressure due to the low volume of water. The consequence was 'that puddles of stagnant shit appeared everywhere'.[27] After a series of complaints from the population, two imperial commissions were established to inspect, monitor the works and indicate sites needing repairs. Even after completing the repairs in 1867, the system depended heavily on the river waters. When the water was not enough, the complaints persisted. The report of the Ministry of Agriculture of 1868 said: 'Some homeowners have [issued lawsuits] against the exhalations, that in the lateral entrances for the flushing tanks, ventilators, etc., are released, and they molest the residents of the neighbourhoods'.[28]

Legitimised by constant public complaints, state-employed engineers exercised some control over the City Improvements Company. Thanks to the advantageous concession contract, this levelled up the unequal relationship between the company and the city. Engineers and the company agreed they had to solve the problems of obstructions and lack of water for the proper functioning of the sewage system. The obstructions always worsened after heavy rains because sand and dirt ended up in the sewage tubes. Constant work to unblock them was necessary. The Company did 177 such works in 1869, 219 in 1870, 192 in 1871 and 197 in 1872 – a total of 785 cleanups in 4 years. José Pereira Rego, a member of the Central Board for Hygiene, suggested several solutions, including the following: to increase the supply of water and the slope in specific points for suitable sewage disposal; to lay subsidiary pipes on sound, solid terrain to avoid depressions caused by irregular landfills, often poorly done; to disinfect regularly the reservoirs; and to raise the level of the streets or to bury the pipes deeper in the soil to prevent them from breaking with the weight and vibration of the vehicles.[29] In 1874, the exhalation issue was almost solved, mostly due to fewer obstructions, good precipitation levels (1568 mm), and the inclusion of ventilator openings. Ten years after the City Improvements Company installed the first sewer plumbings, the situation appeared stabilised and satisfactory – at least for the city's high-end areas. Physicians and engineers emerged from the crisis as the champions for the modern city and valued members of the public administration.[30]

The city's sanitary metabolism became more efficient in the 1880s when an adequate daily water supply became available. In the nobler neighbourhoods of the suburbs, the system had good water intake from the reservoirs. Modernising the sanitary complex required new technologies, such as installing coal filters in the 351 ventilators and 52 lateral entrances and the replacement of the flushing tanks. The new flushing tanks enabled the release of water discharges from the rivers into the system. The City Improvements staff cleaned them, and the intermittent siphons regularly released water to avoid malodorous exhalations.[31] Again, river energy, human labour and technology enabled the urban metabolism to eject undesirable effluents.

Between the 1860s and 1870s, effluents were released into Guanabara Bay after the filtering out of solid material and dumped by barges and ships – and later by hydraulic steam pumps. The solid material was compacted, and a small part was directed to Rio's agricultural green belt. The larger share, however, ended up on the Island of Sapucaia, in Guanabara Bay. Sapucaia received both garbage and solid residues of human waste, functioning as a sanitary landfill from 1865 to 1949. In the 1880s, an engineer employed by the City Improvements Company developed a technology to reorient the urban metabolism's material flows towards recycling. Using calcination techniques to treat the solid waste, the final substance would become 'a kind of mortar, at first very fluid, but which by exposure to air and the sun hardens'.[32] After experiments, he claimed to have successfully turned the waste into cement through a simple and inexpensive method. By incineration, the material lost all its water and organic matter, showing high concentrations of lime and alumina, 'almost in the same proportions as these substances enter the Portland cement'.[33] By the end of the 1880s, the City Improvements Company used two kilns to produce cement via this technique. There is no evidence of the energy required, but we can deduce that this increased the demand for the fuelwood and charcoal obtained in the upper river courses.

However, in a clear breach of its contract, the company often discharged the sewage directly into Guanabara Bay without proper treatment. The waters turned brown in several sensitive areas, and the fishermen in the bay recognised them as the 'Aguas da City' (the Company's waters). Antonio Augusto Monteiro de Barros, the engineer who supervised the City Improvements Company on behalf of the imperial administration, reported 433 illegal discharges between 1883 and 1886. The fines were significant for each episode, but the discharges became less and less frequent over the years: 222 cases in 1883, 135 in 1884, 47 in 1885 and only 29 in 1886.

In 1889, at the end of the imperial era, Rio de Janeiro's sewage extended over 253,710 metres. It had expanded more than 30,000 metres in 1885 towards Riachuelo, Vila Isabel and Andarahy Grande, areas inhabited by a population much less privileged than the ones the system first had served. But it was a thirsty system. In 1887, it consumed over 3000 m³ of water daily for the flushing tanks, urinals and latrines.[34]

The need for more rivers

The imperial government transformed the river environments surrounding the city to ensure a specific regime of urban metabolism. The engineers interpreted the water bodies through a new technical language capable of modifying those realities. However, the city and its metabolic demand did not stop growing. To the rural population of Africans and Afro-descendants freed in 1888 – with the legislative abolition of slavery – was added a mass of European immigrants. The city's population was over 270,000, rising to half a million in 1890 and over 800,000 in 1900. It became necessary to capture and modify new rivers for the city's functioning.[35] Until the 1870s, water diverted from the rivers springing in the Tijuca massif (up to 10 kilometres away from the city) could supply 36 million litres per day, although the supply system captured just over 20 million (of which 13 were lost upon distribution). In this decade, new river commissions sought solutions to the distribution problems and to capture more distant rivers. These reports led to the collection of the Ouro, São Pedro and Santo Antônio rivers in the Tinguá mountains, just over 50 kilometres north of the city.

The works began in 1876 and ended in 1881, collecting and distributing 40 million litres daily through 53 kilometres of pipeline. The channelling of these rivers had some impasses, mainly due to local landowners who refused to cede their lots, which resulted in judicial expropriations and minor adjustments in the channel's path. Two large reservoirs were built in Serra do Tinguá – one to collect water from the São Pedro River and the other from the Ouro and Santo Antônio Rivers – and several smaller ones across the city. Although the collection of nearby rivers was well advanced, a severe drought compromised the supply of the imperial capital, imposing an intermittent distribution and requiring a water transport service through the new railroad built to support the rivers' channelling.[36] With the end of the contract, the railway began to be used to transport passengers and goods. Thus, the search for water eventually benefited the flow of people and objects.

Despite a substantial increase in the water supply to the city, its operation slowed substantially during drought events. Engineers measured the flows of rivers in the Tinguá Mountains from 1882. They collected data in rainy and dry seasons for a more realistic estimate of water resources. Environmental control required knowledge in an efficient and reductionist technical-scientific language.[37] Added to the then-recent collection of the d'Ouro and other rivers, the estimates of river flows in the Tinguá mountain suggested the supply of up to 60 million litres of water daily – the minimum amount for the functioning of the city, according to the engineers – in times of extreme drought. In other words, even with the new intake, the city still suffered from water shortages in years of moderate drought. The following year, the expropriation of land close to water collection sites began in the Serra Velha, Cantagalo, Brava and Macuco waterfalls and the São Pedro river headwaters in the Tinguá mountains.[38]

At the beginning of 1889, after a drought and a severe yellow fever epidemic, several proposals for the collection of rivers emerged amid political unrest in the imperial capital. The winning bid was the most daring (and least expensive): it proposed to have three rivers diverted through temporary gutters for more than 60 kilometres in just six days. Emperor Dom Pedro II was one of the few who believed in the incredible proposal, assisting with two trains to transport materials and personnel. On 24 March 1889, after the promised six days, 14 million litres per day had been collected for the city's supply.[39]

Months later, the imperial regime was replaced by a republican military government. The same urban elites retained control over the fluvial metabolism based on medical theories and civil engineering practices. The modernisation of Rio de Janeiro transformed the riverscapes into supposedly healthier environments, materialising the dream of a tropical capital city comparable to Paris and its great reforms of 1902 to 1906. The electricity demand of the growing industrial park and public transport (trams) also required the modification of riverscapes increasingly far from the city. That was the case with the construction of the Fontes Hydroelectric Power Plant, 80 kilometres from the city. It was inaugurated in 1908 to supply 24

MW of electricity generated from damming 180 million cubic metres of water. Rio de Janeiro's thirst increased exponentially throughout the twentieth century, affecting ever-distant river ecosystems.[40]

Conclusion

Urban metabolism relies on rivers carrying matter and energy through the urban territory. From a relational perspective, we have shown that the work of the rivers shaped the horizon of possibilities for historical developments in Rio de Janeiro. The increase in energy and water demand led to the optimisation of resources to reduce the inefficiency of collection and distribution. This required the urban technical staff to search for larger, ever-distant rivers, which brought to the front the prestige of engineers and doctors in the eyes of the municipal authorities.

Throughout the nineteenth century, the urban appropriation of the rivers' work occurred in myriad ways. The local topographical complexity enabled diverse riverscapes, including their use by different human social groups across rivers' upper, middle and lower courses. As the capital of the Brazilian Empire, Rio received varied migratory inflows, which shaped a diverse urban population as to attitudes to and uses of the work of the rivers. Being profoundly marked by class, race and gender, these social relations were also expressed in the river landscapes. Examples of this were the ban on bathing in waterfalls for enslaved Africans and Afro-Brazilians, and the restriction of the washerwomen's work.

The entry of water into the urban ecosystem occurred both through unmodified channels and a technosphere comprising aqueducts, gutters and other devices for the collection and distribution of water. Here, the work of the rivers facilitated, through gravitational energy, the supply of water through fountains spread through the city. The labour of people and other animals constructed and maintained the water technosphere, including forest restoration, a pioneering initiative in the nineteenth century. Therefore, the rivers worked in situ, shaping the complex relationship between forests, springs and humans, but also from afar, providing water and energy for the city.

Upon entering the river-city system, river work allowed for different activities in the suburbs of Rio de Janeiro, and water bodies were domesticated through channels, ditches and reservoirs. The transformation of riverscapes conformed to diverse interests, such as those of suburban farmers, with their use of floodplains, banks and ditches; textile manufacturers, who designed water systems for running mills and cooling them, as well as expelling the effluents; and doctors and engineers.

According to the sanitary mentality of the latter, nothing could stand still, especially water. In this way, the rivers and their works were intensely modified by draining flooded areas with stagnant water, dredging silted areas and constricting riverbanks by straightening channels in the more densely built-up areas. But the rivers resisted these domestication attempts, refusing to become fully compliant organic machines. At the exit of the rivers-city system, the rivers performed their most sordid work: pushing out organic waste and industrial efflux. The local topography did not facilitate this work, resulting in serious problems. The system for collecting and directing domestic sewage was redesigned, requiring greater consumption of river water.

The reliance on rivers' work for the city's ever-expanding functioning resulted in the search for larger and more distant rivers. The demand for water and energy led to systematic efforts by municipal engineers, who mapped the rivers of greatest interest for urban metabolism. In 1870, the rivers captured by the city were up to 11 kilometres away. In the first decade of the twentieth century, this distance increased to 80 kilometres. At this moment, a paradigmatic transformation in technology enabled the conversion of river work into electrical energy, which started to be directed to the urban territory to perform new works. By transforming local riverscapes and appropriating the rivers' work for electricity generation, the capitalist system connected Rio de Janeiro much more intensely to the river network of the hinterland. This process foreshadowed later developments covering the entire country, as hydroelectricity would become predominant in the Brazilian energy matrix throughout the twentieth century.

Notes

1. Friedrich Engels, *The part played by labour in the transition from ape to man.* Paris, Foreign Languages Press, 1975.

2. Karl Marx, *Capital: a critique of political economy*, vol. I. London, Penguin Random House, 1976, 284. Since then, other scholars, notably Hannah Arendt in her *The human condition* (Chicago, University of Chicago Press, 1998) have explored the distinction between labour and work. It is not the purpose of this text to engage in this debate. We propose, however, that as rivers do have historical, non-intentional agency, they realise both labour and work, as they on the one hand move energy and on the other hand transform the world; Justin Williams, 'Theorizing the non-human through spatial and environmental thought'. In: Teena Gabrielson, Cheryl Hall, John M. Meyer & David Schlosberg (eds.) *The Oxford handbook of environmental political theory*. Oxford, Oxford University Press, Oxford Handbooks online, 2016.

3. River (Rio) was the Portuguese word used for large bodies of water in the sixteenth century, when the Europeans first reached Guanabara Bay. Often considered a misnomer for the bay, it was nevertheless the appropriate word.

4. The sun is the object of the plant – an indispensable object to it, confirming its life – just as the plant is an object of the sun, being an expression of the life-awakening power of the sun, of the sun's objective essential power; Karl Marx, 'Critique of Hegel's philosophy in general'. In: *Economic and Philosophic Manuscripts of 1844*. Moscow, Progress Publishers, 1959, available at https://marxists.org.

5. Karl Marx, 'Estranged labour'. In: *Economic and philosophic manuscripts of 1844*. Moscow, Progress publishers, 1959, available at https://marxists.org; John Bellamy Foster, 'Marx's theory of metabolic rift: classical foundations for environmental sociology', *American Journal of Sociology* 105, no. 2, (1999), 366–405.

6. Erik Swyngedouw, 'Circulations and metabolisms: (hybrid) natures and (cyborg) cities', *Science as culture* 15, no. 2 (2006), 105–21.

7. Bruno Latour, *Reassembling the social: an introduction to actor-network-theory*. Oxford, Oxford University Press, 2005; André Vasques Vital, 'Water spells: new materialist theoretical insights from animated fantasy and science fiction', *Historia Ambiental Latinoamericana y Caribeña (HALAC)* 12, no. 1 (2022), 246–69.

8. Christopher Pearson, 'Beyond "resistance": rethinking nonhuman agency for a "more-than-human" world', *European Review of History* 22, no. 5 (2015), 709–25.

9. Eugine P. Odum, *Ecology: a bridge between science and society*. Sunderland, MA, Sinauer Associates Incorporated, 1997.

10. Richard White, *The organic machine: the remaking of the Columbia River*. New York, Hill and Wang, 1995.

11. Jorun Poettering, 'Paradise for whom? Conservatism and progress in the perception of Rio de Janeiro's drinking-water supply, sixteenth to nineteenth centuries', *Journal of Latin American Studies* 50, no. 3 (2018), 703–27; Alida C. Metcalf, Sean Morey Smith & S. Wright Kennedy, '"A mere gutter!": The Carioca Aqueduct and water delivery in mid-nineteenth-century Rio de Janeiro', *Urban History* 49, no. 1 (2022), 61–78; Diogo de Carvalho Cabral, 'Águas passadas: socie-dade e natureza no Rio de Janeiro oitocentista', *Raega-O Espaço Geográfico em Análise* 23 (2011), 159–90.

12. Bruno Capilé, 'Os muitos rios do Rio de Janeiro: transformações e interações entre dinâmicas sociais e sistemas fluviais na cidade do Rio de Janeiro (1850–1889)', Doctoral dissertation, Graduate Program on Social History (PPGHIS), Rio de Janeiro, Universidad Federal do Rio de Janeiro, 2018.

13. Mauricio de Almeida Abreu (ed.), *Natureza e sociedade no Rio de Janeiro*. Rio de Janeiro, Secretaria Municipal de Cultura, Turismo e Esportes, Departamento Geral de Documentação e Informação Cultural, Divisão de Editoração, 1992.

14. Warren Dean, *With broadax and firebrand: the destruction of the Brazilian Atlantic Forest*. Berkeley, University of California Press, 1995.

15. Dean, 1995; Abreu, 1992.

16. Claudia Heynemann, *Floresta da Tijuca: natureza e civilização no Rio de Janeiro, século XIX* (vol. 38). Prefeitura Da Cidade Do Rio de Janeiro Secretaria, 1995; Alexandro Solórzano, Gabriel Paes da Silva Sales & Rafael da Silva Nunes, 'O legado humano na paisagem do Parque Nacional da Tijuca: uso, ocupação e introdução de espécies exóticas', *Fronteiras: Journal of Social, Technological and Environmental Science* 7, no. 2 (2018), 43–57; de Carvalho Cabral, 2011.

17. Ramón Margalef, *Perspectivas de la teoria ecológica*. Barcelona, Blume, 1978.

18. Jaime Larry Benchimol, *Pereira Passos: um Haussmann tropical*. Rio de Janeiro, Prefeitura da Cidade do Rio de Janeiro, 1990; Richard Sennet, *Flesh and stone: the body and the city in western civilization*. 1st edn. New York, W.W. Norton, 1994;

Sidney Chalhoub, *Cidade febril: cortiços e epidemias na Corte imperial*. São Paulo, Cia. das Letras, 1996; Inês Andrade, 'Notes on the therapeutic values of historic gardens in neoclassical hospitals in Rio de Janeiro (1830–1900)', *Gardens and Landscapes of Portugal* 5, no. 1 (2018), 4–21.

19. Maurício de A. Abreu, *Evolução urbana do Rio de Janeiro*. 4th edn. Rio de Janeiro, Instituto Municipal de Urbanismo Pereira Passos, 2006.

20. Maria Graham, *Journal of a voyage to Brazil and residence there, during part of the years 1821, 1822, 1823*. London, Printed for Longman, Hurst, Rees, Orme, Brown, and Green, and J. Murray, 1824, 161.

21. Daniel Parish Kidder & James Cooler Fletcher, *Brazil and the Brazilians: portrayed in historical perspective and different sketches*. Philadelphia, Deacon & Peterson, 1857, 120.

22. Abreu, 1992.

23. Capilé, 2018.

24. Bruno Capilé, 'Os idealizadores da socionatureza urbana e a transformação da paisagem fluvial carioca'. In: Alexander Costa e Luisa Schneider (eds.) *Rios urbanos: diferentes abordagens sobre as águas nas cidades*. Curitiba, CRV, 2022, 19–37.

25. J. A. C. Oliveira, *Livro de registros dos trabalhos executados pela Comissão Geral de Salubridade, para o combate à febre amarela*. Rio de Janeiro, 18/02/1875–22/01/1876. Biblioteca Nacional, Manuscritos, 14,04,001.

26. Teresa Meade, '"Civilizing" Rio: reform and resistance in a Brazilian city, 1889–1930'. University Park, PA, Penn State University Press, 1997.

27. Diario do Rio de Janeiro. *Noticiário: companhia de esgotos*. Front page, issue 197, 18 July 1864.

28. J. A. F. Leão, *Relatório do Ministério da Agricultura, do Comércio e das Obras Públicas do ano de 1868*. Ministerial Report: Agricultura, 102, 1869.

29. Jose Pereira Rego, *Relatório apresentado à Academia Imperial de Medicina*. Ministerial Report: Agricultura, 1873.

30. Meade, 1997; Chalhoub, 1996.

31. J. A. Saraiva, *Relatório do Ministério da Agricultura, do Comércio e das Obras Públicas do ano de 1881*. Ministerial Report: Agricultura, 1882.

32. A. J. Oliveira, *Relatório do Engenheiro fiscal da Rio de Janeiro City Improvements Company Limited*. Ministerial Report: Agricultura, 1882, 5

33. Oliveira, 1882, 6.

34. R. A. Silva, *Relatório do Ministério da Agricultura, Comércio e das Obras Públicas para o ano de 1887*. Ministerial Report: Agricultura, 1888, 82.

35. Benchimol, 1990.

36. A. A. M. Penna, *Relatório do Ministério da Agricultura, Comércio, Obras Públicas para o ano de 1883*. Rio de Janeiro: Typographia nacional, 1884.

37. Upon reflecting on the role of technical-scientific knowledge in urban societies, Milton Santos emphasised the 'technicisation' of landscapes. For Santos, information is infused into things, being the primary vector of territorial transformation. After the Second World War, this profound environmental interference, limited initially to large cities, expanded to rural and protected areas; see Milton Santos, *A natureza do espaço. Técnica e tempo. Razão e emoção*. São Paulo, HUCITEC, 1996; see also James Scott, *Seeing like a state: how certain schemes to improve the human condition have failed*. New Haven-London, Yale University Press, 1998.

38. José de Santa Ritta, *A água do Rio: do Carioca ao Guandu: a história do abastecimento de água da cidade do Rio de Janeiro*. Rio de Janeiro, Synergia/ LIGHT/ Centro Cultural da SEAERJ, 2009.

39. Lise Sedrez & Bruno Capilé, 'Os modernos rios cariocas'. In: Lorelai Kury, Bruno Capilé, Lise Sedrez & Marcelo Motta, *Os rios do Rio*. Rio de Janeiro, Andrea Jakobsson Studio, 2021, 72–129.

40. Elisa Müller, 'O padrão tecnológico da Light'. In: Eulália Maria Lahmeyer Lobo & Maria Bárbara Levy (eds.) *Estudos sobre a Rio Light: relatório de pesquisa*. Rio de Janeiro, Instituto Light / Centro de Memória da Eletricidade no Brasil, 2008, 533–64.

References

Abreu, Maurício de A., *Evolução urbana do Rio de Janeiro*. 4th edn. Rio de Janeiro, Instituto Municipal de Urbanismo Pereira Passos, 2006.

Almeida Abreu, Mauricio de (ed.), *Natureza e sociedade no Rio de Janeiro*. Rio de Janeiro, Secretaria Municipal de Cultura, Turismo e Esportes, Departamento Geral de Documentação e Informação Cultural, Divisão de Editoração, 1992.

Andrade, Inês, 'Notes on the therapeutic values of historic gardens in neoclassical hospitals in Rio de Janeiro (1830–1900)', *Gardens and Landscapes of Portugal* 5, no. 1 (2018), 4–21.

Arendt, Hannah. *The human condition*. Chicago: University of Chicago Press, 1998.

Benchimol, Jaime Larry, *Pereira Passos: um Haussmann tropical*. Rio de Janeiro, Prefeitura da Cidade do Rio de Janeiro, 1990.

Capilé, Bruno, 'Os idealizadores da socionatureza urbana e a transformação da paisagem fluvial carioca'. In: Alexander Costa e Luisa Schneider (eds.) *Rios urbanos: diferentes abordagens sobre as águas nas cidades*. Curitiba, CRV, 2022, 19–37.

Capilé, Bruno, 'Os muitos rios do Rio de Janeiro: transformações e interações entre dinâmicas sociais e sistemas fluviais na cidade do Rio de Janeiro (1850–1889)', Doctoral dissertation, Graduate Program on Social History (PPGHIS), Rio de Janeiro, Universidad Federal do Rio de Janeiro, 2018.

Chalhoub, Sidney, *Cidade febril: cortiços e epidemias na Corte imperial*. São Paulo, Cia. das Letras, 1996.

Dean, Warren, *With broadax and firebrand: the destruction of the Brazilian Atlantic Forest*. Berkeley, University of California Press, 1995.

de Carvalho Cabral, Diogo, 'Águas passadas: sociedade e natureza no Rio de Janeiro oitocentista', *Raega-O Espaço Geográfico em Análise* 23 (2011), 159–90.

Engels, Friedrich, *The part played by labour in the transition from ape to man*. Paris, Foreign Languages Press, 1975.

Foster, John Bellamy, 'Marx's theory of metabolic rift: classical foundations for environmental sociology', *American Journal of Sociology* 105, no. 2 (1999), 366–405.

Heynemann, Claudia, *Floresta da Tijuca: natureza e civilização no Rio de Janeiro, século XIX* (vol. 38). Prefeitura Da Cidade Do Rio de Janeiro Secretaria, 1995.

Latour, Bruno, *Reassembling the social: an introduction to actor-network-theory*. Oxford, Oxford University Press, 2005.

Margalef, Ramón, *Perspectivas de la teoria ecológica*. Barcelona, Blume, 1978.

Marx, Karl, *Capital: a critique of political economy*, vol. I. London, Penguin Random House, 1976.

Marx, Karl, 'Critique of Hegel's philosophy in general'. In: *Economic and philosophic manuscripts of 1844*. Moscow, Progress Publishers, 1959.

Marx, Karl, 'Estranged labour'. In: *Economic and philosophic manuscripts of 1844*. Moscow, Progress publishers, 1959.

Meade, Teresa, '"Civilizing" Rio: reform and resistance in a Brazilian city, 1889–1930'. University Park, PA, Penn State University Press, 1997.

Metcalf, Alida C., Sean Morey Smith & S. Wright Kennedy, '"A mere gutter!": The Carioca Aqueduct and water delivery in mid-nineteenth-century Rio de Janeiro', *Urban History* 49, no. 1 (2022), 61–78.

Müller, Elisa. 'O padrão tecnológico da Light'. In: Eulália Maria Lahmeyer Lobo & Maria Bárbara Levy (eds.) *Estudos sobre a Rio Light: relatório de pesquisa*. Rio de Janeiro, Instituto Light / Centro de Memória da Eletricidade no Brasil, 2008, 533–64.

Odum, Eugine P., *Ecology: a bridge between science and society*. Sunderland, MA, Sinauer Associates Incorporated, 1997.

Pearson, Christopher, 'Beyond "resistance": rethinking nonhuman agency for a "more-than-human" world', *European Review of History* 22, no. 5 (2015), 709–25.

Poettering, Jorun, 'Paradise for whom? Conservatism and progress in the perception of Rio de Janeiro's drinking-water supply, sixteenth to nineteenth centuries', *Journal of Latin American Studies* 50, no. 3 (2018), 703–27.

Santa Ritta, José de, *A água do Rio: do Carioca ao Guandu: a história do abastecimento de água da cidade do Rio de Janeiro*. Rio de Janeiro, Synergia/ LIGHT/ Centro Cultural da SEAERJ, 2009.

Santos, Milton, *A natureza do espaço. Técnica e tempo. Razão e emoção*. São Paulo, HUCITEC, 1996.

Scott, James, *Seeing like a state: how certain schemes to improve the human condition have failed*. New Haven-London, Yale University Press, 1998.

Sedrez, Lise & Bruno Capilé, 'Os modernos rios cariocas'. In: Lorelai Kury, Bruno Capilé, Lise Sedrez & Marcelo Motta, *Os rios do Rio*. Rio de Janeiro, Andrea Jakobsson Studio, 2021, 72–129.

Sennet, Richard, *Flesh and stone: the body and the city in western civilization*. 1st edn. New York, W.W. Norton, 1994.

Solórzano, Alexandre Gabriel Paes da Silva Sales & Rafael da Silva Nunes, 'O legado humano na paisagem do Parque Nacional da Tijuca: uso, ocupação e introdução de espécies exóticas', *Fronteiras: Journal of Social, Technological and Environmental Science* 7, no. 2 (2018), 43–57.

Swyngedouw, Erik, 'Circulations and metabolisms:(hybrid) natures and (cyborg) cities', *Science as Culture* 15, no. 2 (2006), 105–21.

Vasques Vital, André, 'Water spells: new materialist theoretical insights from animated fantasy and science fiction', *Historia Ambiental Latinoamericana y Caribeña (HALAC)* 12, no. 1 (2022), 246–69.

White, Richard, *The organic machine: the remaking of the Columbia River*. New York, Hill and Wang, 1995.

Williams, Justin, 'Theorizing the non-human through spatial and environmental thought'. In: Teena Gabrielson, Cheryl Hall, John M. Meyer & David Schlosberg (eds.) *The Oxford handbook of environmental political theory*. Oxford, Oxford University Press, Oxford Handbooks online, 2016.

Archival and primary sources

Diario do Rio de Janeiro. *Noticiário: companhia de esgotos*. Front page, issue 197, 18 July 1864.

Graham, Maria, *Journal of a voyage to Brazil and residence there, during part of the years 1821, 1822, 1823*. London, Printed for Longman, Hurst, Rees, Orme, Brown, and Green, and J. Murray, 1824.

Leão, J. A. F., *Relatório do Ministério da Agricultura, do Comércio e das Obras Públicas do ano de 1868*. Ministerial Report: Agricultura, 102, 1869.

Oliveira, J. A. C., *Livro de registros dos trabalhos executados pela Comissão Geral de Salubridade, para o combate à febre amarela*. Rio de Janeiro, 18/02/1875–22/01/1876. Biblioteca Nacional, Manuscritos, 14,04,001.

Oliveira, J. A. C., *Relatório do Engenheiro fiscal da Rio de Janeiro City Improvements Company Limited*. Ministerial Report: Agricultura, 1882.

Parish Kidder, Daniel & James Cooler Fletcher, *Brazil and the Brazilians: portrayed in historical perspective and different sketches*. Philadelphia, Deacon & Peterson, 1857.

Penna, A. A. M., *Relatório do Ministério da Agricultura, Comércio, Obras Públicas para o ano de 1883*. Rio de Janeiro: Typographia nacional, 1884.

Pereira Rego, Jose, *Relatório apresentado à Academia Imperial de Medicina*. Ministerial Report: Agricultura, 1873.

Saraiva, J. A., *Relatório do Ministério da Agricultura, do Comércio e das Obras Públicas do ano de 1881*. Ministerial Report: Agricultura, 1882.

Silva, R. A., *Relatório do Ministério da Agricultura, Comércio e das Obras Públicas para o ano de 1887*. Ministerial Report: Agricultura, 1888.

Chapter 5

Forjadores de la nación: rethinking the role of earthquakes in Chilean history

Magdalena Gil

> The less apocalyptic geologists think of Chile not as a country of dry land but a ledge of the Andes in an ocean of mist and believe that the entire national territory, with its saltpetre meadows and its tender women, is doomed to disappear in a future cataclysm. [. . .] However, even with, or perhaps because of, this underlying uncertainty, Chileans have achieved a degree of natural civilisation, a political maturity, and a culture that constitute their best exceptionality.
>
> Gabriel García Márquez[1]

Most of the time, there is nothing safer than being 'on the ground', the earth being our natural domain as a species.[2] We call people 'grounded' when we think they are stable, level-headed and reliable. An idea is 'grounded in theory' when it has solid theoretical foundations. Yet, in seismic countries, the ground every now and then reminds us that earth is not the stable, inert background against which human action unfolds. When a violent earthquake disturbs your daily life, rattling and shaking, making it difficult to maintain your balance, and suddenly plunges everything into darkness, when you can hear the loud rumbling of the ground along with your children's scared voices, and your home suddenly feels fragile, like a potential death trap. In these moments, the liveliness of nature becomes manifest, reminding us of the relentless uncertainty in our relationship with our planet.

The 'modern dream' – as sociologist Jens Zinn has called it – imagines that the continuous growth of knowledge and rationalisation will make the world fully calculable and controllable.[3] But Max Weber already warned us that 'mastering all things by calculation is the modern's worldview but not our experienced reality'.[4] Even in a highly rationalised society, humans will continue to experience the constraints of nature. Earthquakes present one of the greatest examples of this. Thanks to scientific developments, we can estimate the probability of a certain earthquake occurring in a certain area within a certain number of years, but we cannot predict the exact date, time, location or magnitude of any event. We know that some earthquakes trigger tsunamis, landslides or even volcano eruptions, but the dynamics explaining these interactions and their possible outcomes are out of our control. In consequence, earthquakes remain one of the most destructive events world-wide, accounting for more than half of casualties and one-third of economic losses related to natural hazards in the period 2002–21.[5]

On the other hand, earthquakes have constituted one of modernity's greatest promoters. The Lisbon earthquake of 1755, in particular, has been regarded as the founder of modern thought.[6] Scientific conceptions of the phenomenon were developed across Europe in an attempt to stop blaming God for the state of the world. The Portuguese state was then forced to act in order to avoid a greater disaster. Since then, earthquakes have pushed seismic societies to 'take responsibility for the world in which one is thrown'.[7] As a response, earthquake-prone countries have aimed to organise the social and physical world in relation to earthquakes. Unfortunately, we lack comprehensive accounts of how this relationship has impacted the political, economic or social history of most of these countries.[8] In this chapter I explore the case of Chile, one of the most earthquake-prone countries on earth.[9]

Since 1900, more than one hundred destructive events (magnitude greater than 7 Ms) have been recorded in its territory, thirteen of them considered major (Ms > 8) earthquakes (see Figure 5.1).[10] These include the Valdivia earthquake-tsunami of 1960 which constitutes the largest earthquake ever recorded in human history (9.5 M_w). But despite this prominence of earthquakes, Chilean history has seldom been told taking earthquakes as a relevant political or economic actor. Their importance has become overshadowed by institutional stories that privilege the intentions and judgment of (mostly male) humans. On the contrary, my approach looks to highlight earthquakes' agentic contribution to Chilean history: shaping culture, cities, policy and, particularly, the state. I focus in particular on earthquakes' role in pushing an agenda of state-building onto human actors that were not always in line with this project.

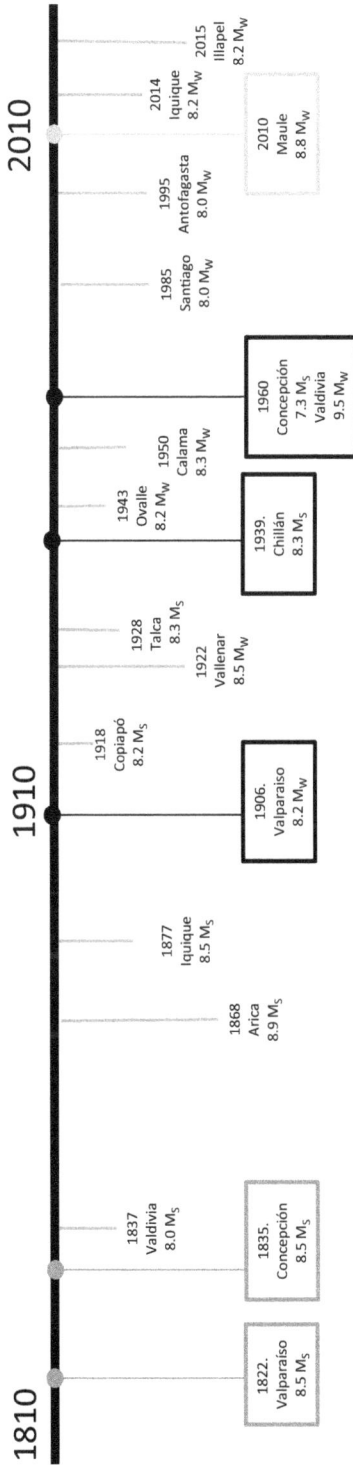

Figure 5.1: Timeline of notable Chilean earthquakes (1810–2020) (magnitudes according to the Chilean Seismological Centre – http://www.csn.uchile.cl).

By doing so, I don't aim to give earthquakes human-like historical power, but to provide further evidence that human agency – however we define it – 'cannot be separated from the environments in which that agency emerges'.[11]

This approach departs from current trends in disaster studies claiming that disasters are social *rather than* physical occurrences.[12] Instead, I suggest that just as earthquakes cannot be understood separately from the vulnerabilities and capacities of the societies in which they occur, the social experience of earthquakes cannot be considered independently from the physical aspects of them. This is why environmental sociology offers a better framework for the work I am presenting here. The field departs from the traditional sociological insistence that social facts can only be explained by other social facts, sustaining that the environment is relevant for understanding the social.[13] Increasingly, this includes elements of the natural environment (from rivers to germs) and the constructed physical environment (from electricity to bridges). This is not to say that environmental sociologists do not accept that nature is socially (co-)constructed, but we admit that there is a materiality to human life, and to social life, that must be incorporated to fully understand social organisation and cultural practices.[14] For the study of disasters, this means that a purely social understanding of events is inadequate since disasters always depend on social and physical (non-social) elements.[15] It also allows us to understand that the real issue is not whether earthquakes are *either* a physical *or* a social occasion but that this distinction is unsuitable for comprehending the issue's complexity: disasters are all-encompassing occurrences. As anthropologists Suzanna Hoffman and Anthony Oliver-Smith have masterfully concluded, disasters 'spring from the nexus where environment, society and technology come together – the point where place, people, and human construction of both the material and nonmaterial meet'.[16] The designation of an occurrence as a disaster indicates that the meeting has been judged particularly forceful.[17]

This also means rethinking the nature-society divide, recognising the inseparability of humans and nonhuman entities and forces, and even accepting the possibility of agentic contributions. While it is true that earthquakes and other nonhuman forces lack 'consciousness, intention, and judgment',[18] as William H. Sewell required of actors, it is also true that they are capable of producing social effects that are irreducible to the purposive energies of humans.[19] Recognising this does not mean slipping into environmental determinism, but adopting a more-than-human approach to society that focuses on the connections between humans and their environments. Historical work is particularly suitable for conveying this connectedness since the co-evolution of nature and society is a process better perceived over time.[20]

In this chapter, I aim to contribute to this more-than-human-history focusing on earthquakes' relationship with Chilean society, and particularly the modern state. I start in 1810, after Chile's independence, and cover more than two hundred years of history. Since there is clearly not enough space in this chapter to detail every earthquake, I focus on describing the dynamics of the most forceful encounters. While doing so, I aim to rescue earthquakes from the relative irrelevance that Chilean political history has given them, highlighting instead their important contribution to our institutional past and present.

Earthquakes in (traditional) Chilean history

It has become commonplace among scholars of Chile to mention the country's 'crazy geography' marked by earthquakes, volcanos and tsunamis.[21] But only cultural historians have shown serious interest, focusing on exploring Chileans' 'telluric character'. Historian Rolando Mellafe coined the term in the 1980s, when tracing the genealogy of Chile's mentality, claiming it is marked by 'ill-fated occurrences' (*acontecer infausto*) that create a disastrous identity 'by nature'.[22] Mellafe's view was influenced by psychoanalysis; he believed that a country's 'mentality' is defined by the traumas that its people have experienced throughout history. In the case of Chile, earthquakes and other types of natural hazards clearly stand out among these experiences (he counted). Mellafe's view has certainly been very influential in Chilean cultural history and beyond, but very few works explored this relationship analytically. On the contrary, literary works abound. In 1939, for example, poet Gabriela Mistral linked earthquakes with Chileans' fierce character and a certain 'stoicism' in the face of adversity.[23] Albert Camus's memoirs, on the other hand, record that during his 1949 visit, he was told that Chile's instability was due to a 'psychology of uncertainty' produced by earthquakes.[24] Author Gabriel García Márquez, in the quote that opens this chapter, points out another interpretation, claiming that earthquakes have helped Chileans achieve certain progress. These references allow us to grasp earthquakes' importance in shaping Chilean identity, but they do not offer a clear answer to the political or economic consequences of this telluric character.[25]

In recent years, however, some works on cultural history have aimed to explore this issue in more detail. Mauricio Onetto's work, for example, shows that a catastrophic narrative about *chileanness* was established by

European settlers early on, right after they experienced their first major earthquake, in 1647. The event helped Spaniards to connect different unfortunate stories about the Chilean territory into an official narrative of extreme difficulties and extreme heroism.[26] The disaster, he claims, is also an opportunity to praise the beauty and richness of the land, presenting Chilean geological hazards as the price to pay for these advantages.[27] For Onetto, these narratives about Chile's telluric destiny have not always been productive for Chilean society since the idea that Chile is a 'fateful land' may lead to conformism and lack of action. Another notable work is Bárbara Silva and Alfredo Riquelme's book *Identidad Terremoteada: Comunidad y Territorio en el Chile de 1960*. In it, the authors explore the issue of a shaken identity, starting by asserting that territories are crucial for the configuration of national identities everywhere.[28] Still, it seems that certain aspects of the natural environment are more suitable for constructing collective identities because they are relatable to most or all people in a community. This would explain that, even though *chileanness* has been narrated differently by different groups, its telluric quality is a shared and historically permanent experience. Importantly, it is a social construction that not only links *chileanness* with the territory, but actually assumes the ground is not inert, or dull. Also, it is an idea that has helped bridge Chileans and their territory, nature and culture, as coevolving. As the authors state, Chileans share not only the experience of earthquakes, but they have established a certain relationship with them, or even a 'symbiosis'. Mellafe himself describes the telluric character of Chileans in similar terms when he claimed that it 'is not a simple love for the land, nor a simple affinity with nature; it is a constant and unconscious dialogue of the psyche with nature'.[29]

For much of Chilean history, this relationship has been defined by antagonism. Earthquakes are portrayed as the villain, a force that often paralyses Chileans' ability to project expectations into the future. This antagonism, however, has also constituted a 'driver for reassembling and (re) building physical and social spaces'.[30] Folk artist Patricio Manns was the first to explore this ambiguity in his 1972 essay *Los Terremotos Chilenos*. Manns's work, remarkably progressive in its social view of disasters, aimed to educate Chileans on the risk of earthquakes. In the first volume, he refers to these events as the 'bad guy of the movie', retelling great events and highlining the pains and sorrows that they bring. In his second volume, however, the 'true goodness' (*verdadera bondad*) of earthquakes is revealed. When we look closely into these events – claims Manns – we realise that earthquakes are also teachers of life, imparting wisdom and life lessons for those who care to learn.[31] Whether Chileans have learned or not from these events is a matter of certain debate. On one side, Chile is clearly one of the countries better prepared to face these events worldwide. However tragic, experts agree that the number of casualties and damage of the latest great event, the 2010 Maule earthquake and tsunami (known as 27F), was surprisingly low for such a big event.[32] On the other side, historical analysis also shows that several lessons have been hard to grasp, especially in terms of urban planning, emergency protocols and human behaviour. Also, it is not at all clear that the lessons learned from earthquakes have been applied to the management of newer hazards, such as firestorms.

Still, I will argue here that the challenge of dealing with earthquakes has had an enormous impact on Chilean society that cannot be reduced to culture. Nineteenth-century historians such as Benjamín Vicuña Mackenna, Miguel Amunátegui and Diego Barros Arana understood this and included several earthquakes in their works. Barros Arana, in particular, presented detailed accounts of several events, linking them to the political, economic and social developments of the period and considering earthquakes as important nation-builders (*forjadores de la nación*, as described by Mauricio Onetto). This insight, however, was mostly lost in the following century, even though Chile suffered some of the most catastrophic earthquakes in world history. Modern historiography repeated the cliché of Chile's fateful destiny but failed to include earthquakes in their accounts of Chile's actual institutional path. Collier and Sater's renowned *A History of Chile*, for example, claims that earthquakes have 'probably left a mark on the Chilean mindset', at the same time blaming them for the delayed appearance of 'anything more than the simplest architecture'.[33] But in their review of almost 200 years of Chilean political history they don't explore any of these events. The great 1960 cataclysm is mentioned, but only in passing when discussing a decline in President Alessandri's political support. The same happens with other seminal historical books of Chilean economic and political history – such as Sofía Correa et al., *Historia del Siglo XX Chileno* and Patricio Meller's *Un Siglo de Economía Política Chilena* – that sometimes mention earthquakes as context but fail to reflect on their agentic contribution.[34]

Unfortunately, earthquakes have not been a salient topic in Chilean environmental history either. Although relevant and innovative in discussing nature/society assemblages, most environmental history in Chile is devoted to other phenomena.[35] Apart from cultural history, the two sub-disciplines that have incorporated earthquakes into their analysis are social and urban history.[36] In social history, the notable work of Joshua Savala on the 1906 Valparaíso earthquake allows for a better understanding of the different interpretations the disaster enhanced. In the case of urban history, one of the most interesting works is Samuel Martland's exploration of the 1906 earthquake, showing that it not only defined Valparaíso's city plan but it also strengthened Chile's central state to the detriment of city politics.[37] These works allow us to grasp the crucial role that Chileans' relationship with earthquakes has played in their history. Still, several aspects remain hidden, specifically the impact that threats and physical destruction have had on the economic and political organisation of the country.

My work aims to fill this gap, showing that earthquakes have been crucial partners for state-building, pushing an agenda of increased rationalisation and demanding social organisation for disaster risk reduction.[38] Earthquakes have forced institutions to develop new capacities and expand their authority, to the point that we cannot truly understand the Chilean state without considering its relationship with earthquakes.

In the next sections, I will expand on each of these assertions relying heavily on my own research and the primary sources I have collected through the years. Nonetheless, I also built upon the work of the cultural, social and urban historians who have contributed to highlighting earthquakes' active role in Chilean history.

Not God but earthquakes (1810–1906)

Certainly, earthquakes played an important role in the cultural and social organisation of Chile before 1810, the year of the country's declaration of independence. But it is the Chilean state who will eventually establish a relationship with the phenomena, transforming itself in the process. The first major earthquake in the Republic of Chile occurred in 1822, a few days after Supreme Director Bernardo O'Higgins had enacted the country's initial constitution. Independence from Spain had been declared in 1810, but war and political discontent continued in the southern regions. By 19 November, O'Higgins was in Valparaíso – Chile's main port – when a 8.5 Ms earthquake surprised him in his sleep. Valparaíso, epicentre of the event, was almost completely destroyed by shaking, a tsunami and subsequent fires. The catastrophe left O'Higgins hurt and unreachable for a few days, discontent became buoyant as people blamed the director's agnosticism for the earthquake.

Still, we can safely say that this earthquake marks Chile's first modern disaster. Religious fervour did not relent, but the earthquake allowed Chilean intellectuals to defy the Catholic Church's long-held 'symbolic monopoly of nature' by discussing the natural origins of the phenomena.[39] From the notion of an 'underground tempest' caused by the inflammation of hydrogen to a collapse of the internal caves of the earth, the discussion about the causes of the movement consumed Chilean intellectuals for months.[40] As we learn from Neiman's work on the Lisbon earthquake, understanding earthquakes and other phenomena as a product of natural forces is not only relevant for secularisation, it also changes the relationship society establishes with these hazards, and the expectations attributed to society. If disasters are understood as acts of God, damage and losses cannot be prevented by human action (with the possible exception of pious living). On the contrary, if earthquakes are understood as natural – albeit extreme – phenomena, society is called to action.

By Chileans' next encounter with a great earthquake, in 1835, this change of paradigm was much more advanced. Religious notions were mostly absent in the public sphere while natural, proto-scientific hypotheses looked to comprehend the phenomenon.[41] One of the main topics was their recurrence, with several people arguing that big earthquakes happened every fifty years.[42] Believed to have been magnitude 8.5 Ms, the quake and tsunami destroyed central-southern Chile (Figure 5.2).

British naturalist Charles Darwin, who arrived by ship in Concepción on the day after, found no words to describe the ruin of the city. Impressed by the wide destruction, he concluded that 'earthquakes alone are sufficient

Figure 5.2: *Concepción after the Ruin.* Drawing by John Clements, a passenger on the *Beagle.*

Note: Published in Robert Fitzroy and Charles Darwin's 'Narrative of the surveying voyages of his Majesty's ships Adventure and Beagle between the years 1826 and 1836 describing their examination of the southern shores of south America and the Beagle's circumnavigation of the globe' (London, Henry Colburn, 1839)

to destroy the prosperity of any country [. . .] Government being unable to collect the taxes, and failing to maintain its authority, the hand of violence and rapine would remain uncontrolled'.[43] He stayed in the city for only three days and was not able to see that this prediction turned out to be deeply mistaken. Far from collapsing, the government quickly restored order and organised public offices in the main square, financing the reconstruction of public buildings and forcibly relocating some towns.[44] A committee of scientists was created in order to analyse the ground in the area, concluding that the sandiness of the land explained its proneness to movement and establishing that 33 per cent of brick buildings, 71 per cent of *adobe* and 95 per cent of stone-built constructions were destroyed.[45] This knowledge allowed Chileans to consider new strategies to face earthquakes in the future.

As Chileans embraced natural views on earthquakes, they not only felt driven to develop earthquake science but also changed how they perceived responsibility for any loss or damage. As a 'concerned citizen' wrote in a letter to newspaper *El Mercurio* in 1829, if disasters are not a divine mandate, then we need to ask, 'What is the *Cabildo* doing about earthquakes?'[46] This question is important because a state's ability to protect the population from physical harm, to preserve its borders, tame violence and maintain internal peace are all crucial for its legitimacy. Of course, this perspective focuses on violence as a tool of political action and domination from human actors, but the definition also underlines that, if nonstate violence and physical harm are not repressed, the state is jeopardising the legitimacy of its rule. What happens, then, when earthquakes defy this promise of protection? The Chilean state understood this challenge early on, looking to comprehend earthquakes and – at the same time – resisting their overbearing hold on Chilean society.

After the 1835 earthquake came a period of relative 'seismic peace', meaning that no catastrophic earthquake happened in Central-Southern Chile, where economic and political power have historically resided. But earth did not stay calm, a series of relevant quakes were felt in the period 1847–59, and again in the period 1869–80.[47] These events allowed Chileans to continue discussing earthquakes' causes, even if no clear answer to the actual nature of the phenomenon was achieved. Seismology was not yet a well-developed science. Globally, there was a good understanding of how earthquake waves travel through the earth but not as to how they are generated.[48] Even after seismology officially became a sub-field of geology, in 1895, European scientists could not agree if it should address what happens on the surface during an earthquake. In Chile, this was not a relevant issue. As Venezuelan intellectual Andrés Bello said in the opening speech of the University of Chile, in 1842, Chile needed highly trained engineers and not only scientists devoted to the natural world.[49] The creation of the university allowed studies such as Paulino del Barrio's *Memoria sobre los temblores de Tierra* (1855) that tried to gather data and offer explanations about the phenomena, and Miguel Amunátegui's *Terremoto del 13 de Mayo de 1647* that constitutes the first historical approximation to a Chilean earthquake.[50] There is not enough space here to describe these works, but I want to emphasise that increased proto-scientific knowledge about earthquakes is crucial for understanding how Chile's relationship with earthquakes was established in the next century. As mentioned in the introduction to this chapter, scientific knowledge and perceived control over nature are profoundly intertwined in modernity. This means that increased rationalisation around the earthquake challenge will be tied to an expansion of society's efforts to control its impacts.

The earthquake's agenda (1906–2010)

By the beginning of the twentieth century, the Church and landed elites had lost some of their power, and emerging middle and working classes were starting to take shape in Chile.[51] The political arena was eager for social change, with many actors pushing for a growing, more subsidiary state. As I will show next, among these actors will be the earthquakes of 1906, 1939 and 1960. The declining role of religious explanations for disasters will reverberate in the state, which will be seen not only as an effective source of relief to victims but also as a protector from earthquakes' harm. This will lead to important institutional developments that would not have existed when they did, and as they did, if not for earthquakes.

The first of such events was the 'sad night' of 16 August 1906. No one alive could remember such a large shock. According to a local newspaper, 'the shakings were so strong that many people thought the earth was going to open itself in deep and long strips'.[52] Chile was significantly more populated (the 1907 Census counted 3,249,279 residents, three times more people than in 1835), urbanised (although 51 per cent of Chileans still lived in *Haciendas*) and economically more diverse than in 1835 (with robust mining and incipient industry), and therefore the damage caused by the 8.2 M_w quake was supreme. The affected region covered 2,620 kilometres from Tacna (on Peruvian territory) to Ancud (in southern Chile). But Valparaíso suffered the most; the earthquake and tsunami destroyed the port, and the subsequent fires consumed what was left of the city plain. There seemed to be no building standing and all vital services – sanitation, electricity, telegraphic lines and trolleys – were broken. In the rest of central Chile, the situation was similar, if less severe.

News of the destruction of Valparaíso arrived in Santiago two days later. Sadly, 3,886 bodies had been counted in the city, and chaos was reported to be pervasive.[53] Newly elected President Pedro Montt and his ministers travelled to Valparaíso to join the *Intendente* in organising the distribution of resources, removal of corpses and the demolition of buildings with risk of collapse. By 1906 Chile was a semi-parliamentary republic, and the central government had little to say in local politics, it was the municipality's responsibility to organise urban spaces and even collect taxes.[54] For decades, *laissez-faire* defined Chilean political economy. But this position is very difficult to maintain in the context of broad-spread destruction. As Samuel Martland has described, the 1906 earthquake defied this long-held governance. Not only did the central state lead the immediate rehabilitation of city functions, but it also directed Valparaíso's reconstruction plan, the first grand-scale experiment in urban development in Chile and Latin America.[55] The earthquake also pushed other agendas. Due to destruction, the rest of the country needed to rebuild roads, railways, telegraphic lines and other relevant infrastructure. To help organise this work, an Office of Bridges and Roads was created in the Ministry of Public Works. The 1906 earthquake also changed the geography of the labour market in Chile, which justified the creation of the Bureau of Workers' Statistics.[56] Finally, the 1906 earthquake is remarkable because it pushed the creation of Chile's first Seismological Service.

As head of the *Partido Nacional*, supported by businessmen, President Montt did not completely fit with the traditional landowner elite who thought he had been 'cruelly assaulted by a dangerous obsession for investing state money in all kinds of public works'.[57] Except for Valparaíso's port, reconstruction was the responsibility of each citizen, they argued.[58] But for the government, reconstruction and recovery were crucial for ensuring the sustainability of the Chilean state. The mechanism is similar to what has been described by sociologist Charles Tilly and the *bellicists* for the case of western Europe and the effects of war, in which threats, extraction and bureaucracies interact to shape state-building.[59] In this case, the enemy is not a foreign power but a natural phenomenon: earthquakes. By 1906, there were very few issues that the Chilean state considered its own responsibility beyond internal security and trade. But earthquakes were quickly becoming a major public concern, precisely because they challenged the continuity of such activities. The earthquake, then, forced the state to care about several issues in public policy that were being overlooked, and pushed to develop new capacities in areas such as infrastructure planning and seismology, effectively moving the standard for acceptable state intervention for years to come.

The creation of the Chilean Seismological Centre (*Centro Sismológico Nacional*, CSN) is especially relevant in this regard. Discussions about the nature of the quake were once again heated, with different theories trying to become the dominant paradigm to interpret earthquakes. Moreover, a navy officer claimed to have predicted the quake using *Solectrics*, a method based on the position of the stars in relation to earth. This led to a series of new announcements in the days after the event, creating anxiety and concern among the population and authorities.[60] To face this situation, the government created a Scientific Commission for the Study of the Earthquake that was, nonetheless, unsuccessful in delivering clear answers.[61] This experience, together with the increasing interest of the state in providing security and 'pursuing human welfare', led to the creation of the seismo-logical centre in 1908, the first of its kind in Latin America. Its first director was French scientist Fernand de Montessus de Ballore, who was hired as a 'state seismologist'. He installed one of the best seismological networks at the time, created a *Bulletin* and sought to help Chileans to advance in the 'art of building in seismic countries'.[62] The *Bulletin* published arti-cles accordingly and, in 1909, Montessus started to teach a class on earthquake-resistant construction at the University of Chile. Since then, Chilean strategy to deal with earthquakes will focus on the expansion of science and the search for seismic-resilient buildings. This will soon materialise in a building code that will significantly expand the state's involvement in a formerly private activity.

Even if most people today consider building codes as necessary for earth-quake resilience, they are a rather extreme form of state power. Regulations restrict people's liberty to choose where and how to build new houses or infrastructure, potentially making it much more expensive. This is why, across the world, these regulations have been met with opposition and fraud. In Chile, building codes constitute the cornerstone of risk manage-ment and they have advanced almost exclusively thanks to earthquakes.[63] Discussion about imposing norms in construction started around the 1906 event, but it was after another significant earthquake that a commission was formed to address the issue. The Talca earthquake of 1928 was small compared to that of 1906 and the one to come in 1939, but it led to the enact-ment of the first national construction and urban planning law. From 1929 onwards, Chileans in cities larger than 20,000 residents needed a permit to build any house or building.[64] A pioneer regulation, it also institutionalised seismic design, defining nine types of buildings depending on materials, foundations, design, acceptable loads, wind resistance and other character-istics. The regulation was very restricted on the use of *adobe*, the traditional material in Chilean houses, favouring the use of reinforced concrete.[65]

With this new regulation and institutions in place Chileans were better prepared, but earthquakes will not relent. An even more catastrophic earthquake hit central Chile on a hot summer night of 1939. Most Chilean earthquakes are interplate events, occurring at the boundary between two tectonic plates. But the Chillán earthquake emerged from the interior of a tectonic plate (intraplate), which made the shaking unusually abrupt and strong for a magnitude of 7.8–8.3 Ms (depending on the source). No one understood this difference at the time. By 1939 geologists were discussing the merits of the continental drift theory, a matter that would not be solved until 1967.[66] Still, newspapers in Chile did their best to incorporate scientific language to report the event, claiming that 'the seismic movement of last night had the status of an earthquake'.[67] The shock buried at least eight cities and twelve towns, making this event the most fatal disaster in Chilean history: about 8,000 casualties.[68]

Infrastructure was also heavily damaged, electricity was shut down in several regions, railroads were useless and roads were damaged. The building code, however, proved its worth. Reports after the event point out that the new buildings were more resistant: less than 20 per cent of the new constructions suffered irreparable damage, compared to 67 per cent of adobe construction (Figure 5.3). The state report concluded that: 'the law of constructions has proved its efficiency when faced with the earthquake, therefore it must be incremented', describing a series of reforms to be made, and a new version of the code was presented in 1949. The classical, most traditional way Chilean houses had been built for centuries was disappearing under the state's regulatory power. Old houses could still exist, but earthquakes were doing their part in leaving only a few upstanding. Still, the success of the code led to the population accepting new restrictions more willingly. As a newspaper at the time explained: 'The earthquake has acted as a tinkle of magic that, after shaking us brutally and by surprise, has prompted an awareness of the efficacy of edicts, decrees and laws of all kinds, whose weight we usually accept only reluctantly'.[69]

The earthquake also pushed the Chilean state to focus, once more, on organising recovery. And this time, the state had an even more impressive response. Two new agencies were created in the context of reconstruction: the Reconstruction and Assistantship Corporation (CRA), in charge of providing housing, and the Production Development Corporation (CORFO) in charge of economic recovery and development. The first agency will eventually become the Ministry of Housing, while the second one – CORFO – is today a crucial governmental organisation whose aim is to promote economic growth. Certainly, recently elected president

Figure 5.3: Chillán after the 1939 earthquake. Colección Archivo Fotográfico. Museo Histórico Nacional.

Pedro Aguirre Cerda was known for his strong views on the role of the state in society, promising to completely change Chile's economic policies during his campaign. A left-wing politician, governing with the Popular Front (*Frente Popular*), Aguirre Cerda represented the dreams and hopes of non-elite Chileans. Before the earthquake, however, he faced a hostile Congress, critiques of the legitimacy of his hard-won election and internal conflict in his own coalition. Consequently, he mostly failed to complete his ambitious presidential programme. But CORFO and the CRA were embedded in the reconstruction-development bill, together with a full tax reform, aiming to collect the 2.5 billion *pesos* needed to fund the plan.[70] The development corporation was opposed by several political and economic actors, who did not want the state to actively interfere on economic activity. CORFO, however, will succeed after the earthquake pushed conservative senators in the most affected areas to support a bill that promised reconstruction.

There are several other institutional legacies of this earthquake. The CRA, responsible for the assistance of victims in the areas directly affected by the earthquake, gave the state the power to act directly in the territory, providing houses for families. The corporation was meant to be momentary, but it never actually dissolved. After a series of smaller earthquakes, it would become institutionalised in the autonomous and permanent Housing Corporation (CORVI). Reconstruction also brought an extensive programme of roads and the development of the first and most ambitious state-led electrification plan in Latin America.[71] Finally, the tax reform – initially defined as temporary – also ended up becoming permanent; some taxes were scaled down in the 1970s, but the original sunset clauses were four or six years. This provides new evidence of the 'displacement effect' that political scientists have described for institutions created in the context of war.[72] As earthquakes increasingly became a formidable opponent to Chile's development, they triggered new efforts to increase state revenue, along with the development of new bureaucracies and administrative bodies to manage such revenue and implement the policies required for reconstruction and recovery.

By 1960, when the greatest earthquake ever recorded happened outshore Valdivia, southern Chile, the Chilean state faced its greatest test. The disaster began on 21 May, when a 7.3 M_w earthquake hit the city of Concepción. But the worst was yet to come when a second quake – magnitude 9.5 M_w – hit the area of Valdivia the next day. Because of the double epicentre, the amount of Chilean territory affected expanded over 186,000 square kilometres, containing about 65 per cent of agricultural land and six of Chile's most important cities: Concepción, Chillán, Talca, Valdivia, Puerto Montt and Temuco.[73] The tsunami devastated every port and coastal town south of Concepción, including Chiloé Island, and around 2,000 lives were lost.[74] What was left of Valdivia had to be evacuated because landslides blocked San Pedro River, the outlet of Lake Riñihue. CORFO took the responsibility to evacuate the lake, in a dangerous enterprise that was, nonetheless, successful.

Unsurprisingly, the earthquake left the Chilean state in a shaky position, and in dire need of funds for reconstruction. President Jorge Alesandri was very different from Aguirre Cerda, having won the election with the support of the ruling economic class. He was officially an independent and his cabinet was conformed mostly by 'apolitical' technocrats, but he was basically a conservative who had promised to shrink the Chilean state. After two years in office he had established a stabilisation programme meant to control inflation, balance the state budget and reduce taxes. But the earthquake had other plans. The event renewed the need for coordinated efforts for development, leaving the state with no choice but to increase its capacities. As a way to circumvent the Right's opposition to state expansion, the government created an office in charge of disaster recovery at the Ministry of Economy, changing its name to the Ministry of Economy, Development and Reconstruction. CORFO had gained a reputation as the technical advisor of the state in several issues, and following this line it established a Committee of Economic Planning and Reconstruction (*Comité de Programación Económica y Reconstrucción*, COPERE) to organise economic recovery. CORFO even developed a ten-year development programme arguing that 'we cannot limit ourselves in repairing the damage without giving due attention to economic recovery at the highest levels'.[75] Even though the government's plan relied heavily on loans from the United States, the government was also forced to push for a tax reform that spurred several hikes, including income and inheritance. Finally, the need to improve long-distance communication was clear after the quake and the whole system, heavily damaged, was modernised with the creation of Chile's National Telecommunications Office (ENTEL).

The urgency created by the disastrous events in 1960 was reinforced by another earthquake in 1965, which was the most serious to affect central Chile since 1906. After this, a National Plan for Emergencies was designed, in line with a 'Law of Quakes and Catastrophes' that allowed for special attributions to different institutions in the case of disasters. It also institutionalised the concept of *damnificado* ('damnified', a person affected by a natural disaster), among other things. Soon after, the state also created the Hydrographic and Oceanographic Service (SHOA), in order to be better prepared for tsunamis, which were now considered the major source of destruction. In the 1970s, after another minor earthquake in the area of La Ligua, the National Emergencies Office (ONEMI) was created. This office, however, was a rebranding of the Emergencies Office (OEMI) created after the 1965 earthquake inside the Minister of the Interior. Regulations to build seismic-resilient buildings were making earthquakes seem controllable, effectively changing their villain-like nature in the eyes of Chileans. Even if the 1960 earthquake was the strongest ever recorded, a year after, a newspaper at the time claimed that building codes and construction technologies allow Chile to say to the earth: 'it is true that you hit hard, but I have learned to be ready'.[76]

Conclusions: Chile's 200-year earthquake

Chile was preparing to celebrate 200 years of independence when, on the night of 27 February 2010, an 8.8 M_w earthquake woke up locals once more, forcing them to face a lively earth. It was an earthquake 500 times more powerful than the 7.0 M_w Haiti earthquake a month prior.[77] It also triggered a tsunami that heavily damaged several coastal towns, cities and the port in Talcahuano, and several landslides. According to official records,

520 people were killed, 25 missing, and more than 220,000 families lost their homes. Importantly, about a third of the fatalities were due to the tsunami.[78] This was particularly traumatic for Chilean society. Due to important institutional failings at SHOA and ONEMI, the system was unable to articulate an early warning for the tsunami hazard.[79] The social impact of the earthquake was amplified by this institutional failure. Still, the performance of infrastructure during the quake was impressive, and it is clear that the enforcement of seismic codes played a major role in the relatively low amount of damage and casualties.[80] This is due not only to the existence of such codes, but the networks of knowledge around them and the strength of institutions to enforce them. And the same can be said for other institutional capacities that managed reconstruction and recovery in record time: CORFO working to boost economic recovery; the Economic and Social Stabilization Fund to finance reconstruction; the Ministry of Housing; and the Ministry of Economy. As I have shown, these are all institutional legacies from past encounters, reflecting the effect that living with earthquakes had not only in the Chilean mindset, but also in the Chilean state. These legacies are the product of earthquakes pushing an agenda of increased social organisation. While it is true that earthquakes have been mobilised to push human political objectives, the cases show that a government's alignment with the earthquake's agenda is not a necessary condition for the earthquake to impose certain needs and demand intervention. As many scholars have argued before me, vulnerability and capacities are historically produced, which means that the aftermath of the 2010 earthquake had been in the making for 200 years or so[81].

The Chilean state still has a lot to learn in terms of disaster management and the 2010 earthquake provided a new opportunity to do so. Several new institutional capacities were developed. Recently elected right-wing president Sebastián Piñera had centred his campaign on issues such as government efficiency and reducing taxes, but ended up sponsoring a fiscal reform in order to increase fiscal revenue and a creating a national fund for reconstruction. A new national plan for disaster risk management was developed in line with the Sendai Framework for Disaster Risk Reduction, the ONEMI, the CSN and SHOA underwent important reforms, including the creation of a new Tsunami Early Warning Centre and a new seismographic network. Also, the government once more promoted scientific research related to disasters funding three major research centres in the areas of natural hazards and disaster risk. This shows that the mechanisms and dynamics that have linked earthquakes and state-building in Chile during the twentieth century remain operating in this century.

Overall, it is clear that Charles Darwin was not correct. Earthquakes alone are not sufficient to destroy the prosperity of a country. It can certainly happen, as we have seen in the case of Haiti, but in the case of Chile Gabriel García Marquéz has a better hypothesis. When we look at Chilean history taking earthquakes seriously as a historical actor, we see a dialogical process in which the Chilean state has learned to adapt to the telluric forces that visit the territory. As García Marquéz claims, this relationship has helped achieve a certain 'political maturity'. The state has had to adapt to enormous pressure generated by repeated catastrophes, and this has led to developments that are similar to what has been described to be the case of war in western Europe. In this case, however, the enemy is earthquakes. The basic role of the state is to control internal and external threats. Natural forces have always been part of this programme of control, but in the face of catastrophe this relationship is much more clearly perceived. It is not only that earthquakes are perceived as a powerful enemy but that they are also actually a challenge for state power, demanding a degree of organisation and protection that only strong political structures can provide. If non-existent, these structures have to be developed, becoming institutional legacies that are not only relevant for disaster management but offer important capacities for the everyday management of the state.

It is not at all clear that the Chilean state has learned as much from other hazards. As the climate crisis worsens the natural conditions of most of the Chilean territory, climate-related disasters have become the most salient problem for the disaster risk management system. The fire seasons of 2016–17 and 2022–3 have been particularly damaging for the country, but it seems that these challenges are unable to pressure a state response as strong as earthquakes have historically produced. There are certainly many explanatory factors for this, but I will argue that debris is an important actor in defining what happens in the aftermath of disaster. Rubble and debris demand decisions, prompting society into action. I have previously called this effect 'the imperative of debris', loosely defined as the need to deal with physical destruction or face the risk of collapse.[82] Other types of disasters with diffuse crises and different types of physical destruction may not have the same effect. Earthquakes create new needs in the areas of infrastructure, health and transportation, among others, forcing political actors to make difficult decisions. It may be the case that dust – especially dust that comes from the combustion of trees and not public infrastructure – cannot push institutions in the exact same way.

Finally, it is important to point out that as earthquakes made the Chilean state, this relationship also changed earthquakes. Of course, the hazard itself remains outside of human intervention, even in the context of the

Anthropocene. But earthquakes are today a different kind of threat to Chileans than when this story started. Mellafe himself, writing in the 1980s, uses the past tense to talk about the catastrophic mentality of Chileans 'because the man [sic] today does not suffer the negative telluric effects with the same force than a few decades ago', adding that 'the dialogue and contact [with earthquakes] is much shorter and carefree'.[83]

And certainly, most earthquakes today are fully normalised by Chilean society, barely giving the movement a second thought. Earthquakes have changed so much that the prominence of earthquakes is often presented as an opportunity for Chile's scientific leadership and technological development.[84] Still, it is important to always remember that the modern dream can work as an ideal worth striving for in order to save lives, but the liveliness of earth will continue to surprise us. Our best chance is to learn how to live with earthquakes in a coevolution that is not only resilient to the next event, but sustainable in the long term.

Notes

1. Gabriel García Márquez, *Chile, el golpe y los gringos*. Bogotá, Editorial Latina, Colección Cuadernos Alternativa, 1974, 15.

2. This research was partially funded by the Chilean National Research and Development Agency (ANID) under Fondecyt INICIO, Grant number #11220562.

3. Jenz Zinn, *Understanding risk-taking*. Switzerland, Palgrave Macmillan, 2020.

4. Max Weber, *The disenchantment of modern life* (2004 [1917]) quoted in Zinn, *Understanding risk-taking*, p. 20.

5. Centre for Research on the Epidemiology of Disasters (CRED), *Disasters in numbers*, UC Louvain, 2022.

6. Susan Neiman, *Evil in modern thought: an alternative history of philosophy*. Princeton, NJ-Oxford, Princeton University Press, 2002; Russel R. Dynes 'The Lisbon earthquake of 1755: the first modern disaster'. In: Theodore E. D. Braun & John B. Radner (eds.) *The Lisbon earthquake of 1755: representations and reactions*. Oxford, Voltaire Foundation, 2005, 34–49.

7. Neiman, 2012, p. 4.

8. An interesting exception is Gregory K. Clancey in his *Earthquake nation: the cultural politics of Japanese seismicity, 1868–1930* (Berkeley, University of California Press, 2006). See also, Jelle Zeilinga de Boer & Donald Theodore Sanders, *Earthquakes in human history: the far-reaching effects of seismic disruptions*. Princeton, NJ, Princeton University Press, 2005; Jürgen Buchenau & Lyman L. Johnson (eds.), *Aftershocks: earthquakes and popular politics in Latin America*. Albuquerque, University of New Mexico Press, 2009.

9. About a quarter of global energy is released in the Chilean territory. GFZ Centre Postdam, 'Seismic hazard in Chile', https://www.gfz-potsdam.de/en/section/seismic-hazard-and-risk-dynamics/projects/ shac-seismic-hazard-in-chile.

10. Moment magnitude scales are a measure of an earthquake's released energy, they are denoted explicitly with M_w (moment magnitude), M_L (local magnitude) or Ms

(superficial magnitude). The Chilean seismological center reports M_w for current earthquakes but Ms for older events, scales are very similar in the lower magnitudes, but M_w allows for a better understanding of major earthquakes. See USGS, 'Earthquake magnitude', https://www.usgs.gov/programs/earthquake-hazards/earthquake-magnitude-energy-release-and-shaking-intensity.

11. Linda Nash, 'The agency of nature or the nature of agency?', *Environmental History* 10 (2005), 67–9, p. 69.

12. For a historical development of this argument in disaster studies, see Ilan Kelman, *Disaster by choice: how our actions turn natural hazards into catastrophes* (Oxford: Oxford University Press, 2020); Kathleen J. Tierney, 'From the margins to the mainstream? Disaster research at the crossroads', *Annual Review of Sociology* 33, no. 1 (2007), 503–25; Enrico Quarantelli, 'A social science research agenda for the disasters of the 21st century'. In: Ronald W. Perry & Enrico L. Quarantelli (eds.) *What is a disaster? New answers to old questions*. Philadelphia, PA, Xlibris, 2005, 96–325.

13. See, for example, William Catton & Riley Dunlap, 'Environmental sociology: a new paradigm', *The American Sociologist* 13, no. 1 (1978), 41–9; Frederick H. Buttel, 'New directions in environmental sociology', *Annual Review of Sociology* 13, no. 1 (1987), 465–88; David N. Pellow & Hollie Nyseth Brehm, 'An environmental sociology for the twenty-first century', *Annual Review of Sociology* 39, no. 1 (2013), 229–50; Raymond Murphy, *Sociology and nature: social action in context*. Boulder, CO, Westview Press, 1997; Riley E. Dunlap (ed.) *Sociological theory and the environment: classical foundations, contemporary insights*. Lanham, MD, Rowman & Littlefield Publishers, 2002.

14. Besides environmental sociology and humanities, I recommend the work of philosopher Jane Bennet on this issue; Jane Bennett, *Vibrant matter: a political ecology of things*. Durham, NC, Duke University Press, 2010. See also, Gulshan Khan, 'Agency, nature and emergent properties: an interview with Jane Bennet', *Contemporary Political Theory* 8 (2009), 9–105.

15. Robert A. Stallings already argued this in 'Disasters and the theory of social order'. In: Enrico Quarantelli (ed.) *What is a disaster? Perspectives on the question*. London-New York, Routledge, 1998, 127–36.

16. Anthony Oliver-Smith & Susanna Hoffman, *The angry earth: disaster in anthropological perspective*. New York, Routledge, 1999, p. 1.

17. Here I paraphrase Philip Abrams's definition of an event in *Explaining events: a problem of method*. Bath, Cornell University Press, 1982.

18. William H. Sewell, Jr., 'Nature, agency and anthropocentrism', online discussion of Steinberg, 'Down to Earth', formerly available at http://www.historycooperative.org/phorum (7 September 2002) quoted in Richard C. Foltz, 'Does nature have historical agency? World history, environmental history, and how historians can help save the planet'. *History Teacher* 37, no. 1 (2003), 9.

19. Bennett, 2010, 69.

20. Emily O'Gorman & Andrea Gaynor, 'More-than-human histories', *Environmental History* 25, no. 4 (2020), 711–35.

21. Benjamin Subercaseaux, *Chile o una loca geografía*. Santiago, Chile, Editorial Universitaria, 1940.

22. Rolando Mellafe, 'El acontecer infausto en el carácter Chileno: una proposición de historia de las mentalidades', *Atenea* 442 (1980), 121–8. See also Rolando Mellafe, 'Historia de las mentalidades: una nueva alternativa', *Cuadernos de Historia* 2 (1982), 97–107.

23. Gabriela Mistral, 'Chile, suelo telúrico' [Manuscript], Biblioteca Nacional de Chile, http://www.bibliotecanacionaldigital.gob.cl/bnd/623/w3-article-141314.html.

24. Camus arrived in the middle of strong social protest; see Juan Rivas & Nibaldo Mosciatti, 'Apuntes sobre el viaje de Albert Camus a Chile'. In: Albert Camus, *Ni víctimas ni verdugos*. Buenos Aires, Godot, 2014, 81–101.

25. Eduardo Aguayo, 'Entre la ruina y el prodigio: narrativas del desastre en la literatura símica chilena', *Argos* 32 no. 63 (2015), 15–33.

26. Mauricio Onetto, *Temblores de tierra en el Jardín Del Edén: desastre, memoria e identidad: Chile, siglos XVI-XVIII*. Colección Sociedad y Cultura, LXII, Santiago, Chile, DIBAM-Centro de Investigaciones Diego Barros Arana, 2017.

27. Mauricio Onetto, *Discursos desde la catástrofe: prensa, solidaridad y urgencia en Chile, 1906–2010*. Santiago, Chile, Acto Editores, 2018.

28. Bárbara Silva & Alfredo Riquelme, *Una identidad terremoteada: comunidad y territorio en El Chile de 1960*. Santiago, Chile, Ediciones Universidad Alberto Hurtado, 2018.

29. Mellafe, 1980, 287.

30. Onetto, 2017, 301.

31. Patricio Manns, *Los terremotos chilenos*. Volume 1, Santiago, Chile, Editorial Quimantú, 1972, p. 6. He specifically compares earthquakes to Nicomedes Santa Cruz author of Maestro: '*Cada lección aprendida, te saca una nueva cana. Cada revisión de plana te marca una nueva arruga*'.

32. Paul Kovacs, 'Reducing the risk of earthquake damage in Canada: lessons from Haiti and Chile', Toronto, Institute of Catastrophic Loss Reduction, 2010; Richard A. Lovett, 'Why Chile fared better than Haiti', *Nature* (2010); Erin Wayman, 'Chile's quake larger but less destructive than Haiti', *Earth Magazine* (2012), https://www.earthmagazine.org.

33. Simon Collier & William F. Sater, *A history of Chile, 1808–2002*. Cambridge-New York, Cambridge University Press, 2004, 21–8.

34. Patricio Meller, *Un siglo de economía política Chilena (1890–1990)*. Santiago, Chile, Editorial Andrés Bello, 1996; Sofía Correa, Alfredo Jocelyn-Holt, Manuel Vicuña, Claudio Rolle & Consuelo Figueroa, *Historia del siglo XX Chileno*. Santiago, Chile, Sudamericana, 2001; see also, Alfredo Jocelyn-Holt, *Historia general de Chile*. Santiago, Chile, Sudamericana, 2004; Sofía Correa, *El proceso económico. Chile (1830–1880)*. Penguin Random House-Grupo Editorial España, 2015.

35. See, for example, Pablo Camus and Fabián Jaksic, *Clima y sociedad: el fenómeno El Niño y La Niña en la historia de Chile*. Santiago, Chile, Instituto de Geografía-UC, 2022.

36. Wide-ranging works like Sergio Villalobos's, *Historia de los Chilenos*. Santiago, Chile, Taurus, 2006; Rafael Sagredo, *Historia de la vida privada en Chile*. Santiago, Chile, Taurus, 2005. He uses some of these events as examples of social inequalities.

37. Joshua Savala, '"Let us bring it with love": violence, solidarity, and the making of a social disaster in the wake of the 1906 earthquake in Valparaíso, Chile', *Journal of Social History* 51, 4 (2018), 928–52; 'Contesting disasters: the 1906 Valparaíso earthquake, state violence, and working-class solidarity', Tufts University, Department of History, 2012.

38. Magdalena Gil, 'Disasters as critical junctures: state building and industrialization in Chile after the Chilean earthquake of 1939', *Latin American Research Review* 57, 4 (2023), 776; Magdalena Gil & Jorge Atria, 'Fiscal aftershocks: taxes and catastrophes in Chilean history', *Journal of Iberian and Latin American Economic History* (2021), 1–39; Magdalena Gil & Felipe Rivera, 'Strengthening the role of science in disaster risk reduction: the Chilean strategy', *Disasters* 47, no. 1 (2023), 136–62.

39. Gabriel Cid, '¿Castigo divino o fenómeno natural? Mentalidad religiosa y mentalidad científica en Chile en torno al terremoto de 1822', *Revista de Historia y Geografía* 30 (2014), 85–109; Magdalena Gil, 'God or nature? Catastrophes and modernity from Lisbon to Valparaíso', *International Journal of Mass Emergencies and Disasters* 35, no. 3 (2016), 115–36; Alfredo Palacios, *Entre ruinas y escombros: los terremotos en Chile durante los siglos XVI al XIX*. Valparaíso, Ediciones Universidad de Valparaíso, 2015.

40. 'Diario el mercurio de Chile, 19 de Noviembre and Vera y Pintado, B. 'Comunicado'. *El mercurio de Chile 16*' (2 December 1822), published in Guillermo Feliú (ed.), *El mercurio de Chile; 1820–1823*. Santiago, Chile, Editorial Nascimiento, 1960, 396.

41. Alfredo Palacios, 'Antecedentes históricos de la "abogacía telúrica" desarrollada en Chile entre los siglos XVI y XIX', *Historia Crítica* 54 (2014), 171–93.

42. Alexander Caldcleugh, 'An account of the great earthquake experienced in Chile on the 20th of February, 1835 with a map', *Philosophical Transactions of the Royal Society of London* 126 (1836), 21–6.

43. Charles Darwin, *Charles Darwin's Beagle diary*. Cambridge, Cambridge University Press, 2001, 323.

44. Carlos Eduardo, 'El terremoto y tsunami de 1835 en Concepción y la frontera del río Biobío: destrucción, relocalización, traslados y nuevas inversiones', *Diálogo andino* 67 (2022), 255–68.

45. Valentina Verbal, *La ruina. El gran terremoto y maremoto en Concepción de 20 de febrero de 1835. Sus consecuencias materiales y sociales*, Universidad Católica de Chile, Department of History, 2006.

46. 'Cartas', *El Mercurio* (Valparaíso), 9 October 1829, quoted in Fernando Montessus de Ballore, *Historia sísmica de los Andes Meridionales al sur del paralelo XVI*, Volume IV, Santaigo, Chile, Imprenta Cervantes, 1912, 129.

47. Earthquakes in 1847 (La Ligua, Copiapó and La Serena), in 1849 (Coquimbo), in 1850 (San José de Maipo), in 1851 (Huasco and Casablanca), in 1859 (Copiapó), in 1868 (Arica), in 1871 (Puerto Montt), in 1873 (La Ligua), in 1876 (Illapel), in 1877 (Iquique), in 1880 (Illapel).

48. Ari Ben-Menahem, 'A concise history of mainstream seismology: origins, legacy, and perspectives', *International Journal of Rock Mechanics and Mining Sciences & Geomechanics Abstracts* 33, no. 6 (1996), A243.

49. Andrés Bello, 'Discurso pronunciado en la instalación de la Universidad de Chile el día 17 de septiembre de 1843', *Anales de la Universidad de Chile* 49–52 (1943), 7–21. DOI:10.5354/0717-8883.1943.24033.

50. Paulino del Barrio, 'Memoria sobre los temblores de tierra i sus efectos en jeneral i en especial los de Chile', *Anales de la Universidad de Chile* (1855) Serie 1, 583–625; Luis Amunátegui, *Terremoto del 13 de Mayo de 1647*. Santiago, Chile, Jover, 1882.

51. Collier and Sater, 2004.

52. 'Nuevas y dolorosas informaciones de la catástrofe', *El Mercurio* (Valparaiso), 18 August 1906, p. 1.

53. Alfredo Rodríguez & Carlos Cruzat, *La catástrofe del 16 de agosto de 1906 en la República de Chile*. Santiago, Chile, Imprenta Barcelona, 1906. The total number of deaths was probably higher. We estimate about 7,000 using data from the Chilean Oficina Central de Estadística (1909).

54. *Ley de Comuna Autonoma* (Law of Autonomous Municipalities) of 1891; see Memoria Chilena. Biblioteca Nacional de Chile; 'Ley de Comuna Autónoma', http://www.memoriachilena.gob.cl/602/w3-article-93505.html.

55. Samuel Martland, 'Reconstructing the city. Constructing the state: government in Valparaiso after the earthquake of 1906', *Hispanic American Historical Review* 87, no. 2 (2007), 221–54; see also Pablo Paez, *La oportunidad de la destruccion en la urbanistica moderna. Planes y proyectos para la reconstruccion de Valparaíso tras el terremoto de 1906*. Santiago, Chile, Pontificia Universidad Católica de Chile, Instituto de Estudios Urbanos, 2008; Magdalena Gil, 'La reconstrucción del valor urbano de Valparaíso luego del terremoto de 1906', *ARQ (Santiago)* no. 97 (2017), 78–89.

56. The decree that creates this office clearly states that 'the need to start to produce statistics about workers became imperative after the catastrophe' (La Oficina de Estadística del Trabajo. Ministerio de Industria y Obras Pública, Imprenta Cervantes, 1907), p. 1. This office will acquire greater attributions in 1910 as the Bureau of Work (Oficina del Trabajo), later becoming the Ministry of Labour; see Óscar Mac-Clure, *En Los orígenes de las políticas sociales en Chile, 1850–1879*. Santiago, Chile, Ediciones Universidad Alberto Hurtado, 2012.

57. Francisco J. Ovalle, *Don Pedro Montt, ex Presidente de la República de Chile*. Santiago, Chile, Imprenta Universitaria, 1918.

58. Congreso Nacional de Chile, *Sesiones Extraordinarias* (1906), p. 167.

59. Charles Tilly, 'War making and state making as organized crime'. In: Peter Evans, Dietrich Rueschemeyer & Theda Skocpol (eds.) *Bringing the state back in*. Cambridge, Cambridge University Press, 1985, 169–87.

60. For more on this story, see José Luis Giordano, *La predicción del terremoto de 1906 ¿ciencia o fantasía?*, Editorial Académica Española, 2023.

61. Lorena B. Valderrama, 'Seismic forces and state power: the creation of the Chilean seismological service at the beginning of the twentieth century', *Historical Social Research* 40, no. 2 (2015), 81–104.

62. Valderrama, 2015, 94.

63. Felipe Rivera, Tiziana Rossetto & John Twigg, 'Understanding earthquake resilience in Chile: the pros and cons of safe buildings', *Proceedings of the SECED 2019 Conference*. Greenwich, London, SECED, 10 September 2019, https://www.seced.org.uk/index.php/proceedings; and 'An interdisciplinary study of the seismic exposure dynamics of Santiago de Chile', *International Journal of Disaster Risk Reduction* 48 (2020); Juan Carlos de la Llera, Felipe Rivera, Magdalena Gil, Hernán Santamaría & Rodrigo Cienfuegos, 'Infraestructura resiliente: lecciones del caso Chileno', *Integration & Trade Journal* 21, no. 41 (2017), 302–15.

64. José Fernandez Richard, 'Historia del derecho urbanístico Chileno', *Revista de Derecho Público* 77 (2012), 79–97.

65. Horacio Torrent, 'Historiografía y arquitectura moderna en Chile: notas sobre sus paradigmas y desafíos', *Anales del IAA* 42, no. 1 (2012); Humberto Eliash & Manuel Moreno, *Arquitectura y modernidad en Chile, 1925–1965: una realidad múltiple*. Santiago, Chile, Ediciones Universidad Católica de Chile, 1989.

66. Henry Frankel, 'The continental drift debate'. In: Hugo Tristam Engelhardt, Jr & Arthur Caplan (eds.) *Scientific controversies: case solutions in the resolution and closure of disputes in science and technology*. Cambridge, Cambridge University Press, 1987, 203–48.

67. *El Mercurio* (Santiago), 25 January 1939, p. 9.

68. Gil, 2023, 775–93.

69. Joaquín Edwards Bello, 'El terremoto', Diario *La Nación*, 27 January 1939, p. 3.

70. Gil & Atria, 2021, 9.

71. Monica Humeres & Magdalena Gil, 'Dreaming of a bright future: statistics, disaster, and the birth of energopolitics in Chile during the 1930s', *Technology and Culture* (forthcoming, 2024).

72. Gabriella Legrenzi, 'The displacement effect in the growth of governments', *Public Choice* 120 (2004), 191–204.

73. U.S Department of State, 'Chile: rebuilding for a better future', May 1961. Washington, DC.

74. Calculated with data from 'Defunciones' for years 1956–1961, Servicio Nacional de Salud. Sección Bioestadística y Control Médico Económico. Archivo Ministerio de Salud (Chile). The number of homeless people as reported in World Bank, 'Current Economic Position and Prospects of Chile', Washington, DC, The World Bank, 1961.

75. President Jorge Alessandri to Congress, 'Mensaje de S.E El Presidente de la Republica al Congreso al inagurar el periodo ordinario de sesiones'. Santiago, Chile, 1 May 1960.

76. José M. Navasal, 'Hace un año la tierra tembló', *El Mercurio* (Santiago), May 21, 1961, p. 9.

77. Moment magnitude scales are logarithmic; this means that for each whole number in the scale, the magnitude goes up ten times.

78. This time, there were not big discrepancies in numbers reported right after and those calculated later. I add missing to the tsunami casualties. For alternative but similar data tan the offitial report, see Erwin Nahuelpán & José Varas, 'El terremoto/ tsunami en Chile: una mirada a las estadísticas médico legales', *Investigación forense* 2 (2013), 1–16.

79. Stephanie Kane, Eden Medina & Daniel Michler, 'Infrastructural drift in seismic cities: Chile, Pacific Rim, 27 February 2010', *Social Text* 33 (2015), 71–9.

80. Felipe Rivera Jofre, Tiziana Rossetto & John Twigg, 'Understanding earthquake resilience in Chile: The pros and cons of safe buildings'. In: *Proceedings of the SECED 2019 Conference: Earthquake risk and engineering towards a resilient world*, SECED, Greenwich, London.

81. Anthony Oliver-Smith uses the same expression in *The Angry Earth*, arguing that the 1970s Peruvian earthquake of was in the making for 500 years.

82. Gil & Atria, 2021.

83. Mellafe, 1982, 285.

84. Gil & Rivera, 2023.

References

Abram, Philip, *Explaining events: a problem of method*. Ithaca, NY, Cornell University Press, 1982.

Aguayo, Eduardo, 'Entre la ruina y el prodigio: narrativas del desastre en la literatura símica chilena', *Argos* 32 no. 63 (2015), 15–33.

Amunátegui, Luis, *Terremoto del 13 de Mayo de 1647*. Santiago, Chile, Jover, 1882.

Ben-Menahem, Ari, 'A concise history of mainstream seismology: origins, legacy, and perspectives', *International Journal of Rock Mechanics and Mining Sciences and Geomechanics Abstracts* 33, no. 6 (1996), A243.

Bennett, Jane, *Vibrant matter: a political ecology of things*. Durham, NC, Duke University Press, 2010.

Boer, Jelle Zeilinga de & Donald Theodore Sanders, *Earthquakes in human history: the far-reaching effects of seismic disruptions*. Princeton, NJ, Princeton University Press, 2005.

Buchenau, Jürgen & Lyman L. Johnson (eds.), *Aftershocks: earthquakes and popular politics in Latin America*. Albuquerque, University of New Mexico Press, 2009.

Buttel, Frederick H., 'New directions in environmental sociology', *Annual Review of Sociology* 13, no. 1 (1987), 465–88.

Camus, Pablo & Fabián Jaksic, *Clima y sociedad: el fenómeno El Niño y La Niña en la historia de Chile*. Santiago, Chile, Instituto de Geografía-UC, 2022.

Catton, William & Riley Dunlap, 'Environmental sociology: a new paradigm', *The American Sociologist* 13, no. 1 (1978), 41–9.

Cid, Gabriel, '¿Castigo divino o fenómeno natural? Mentalidad religiosa y mentalidad científica en Chile en torno al terremoto de 1822', *Revista de Historia y Geografía* 30 (2014), 85–109.

Clancey, Gregory K., *Earthquake nation: the cultural politics of Japanese seismicity, 1868–1930*. Berkeley, University of California Press, 2006.

Collier, Simon & William F. Sater, *A history of Chile, 1808–2002*. Cambridge-New York, Cambridge University Press, 2004.

Correa, Sofia, *El proceso económico. Chile (1830–1880)*. Penguin Random House-Grupo Editorial España, 2015.

Correa, Sofía, Alfredo Jocelyn-Holt, Manuel Vicuña, Claudio Rolle & Consuelo Figueroa, *Historia del siglo XX Chileno*. Santiago, Chile, Sudamericana, 2001.

Dunlap, Riley E. (ed.), *Sociological theory and the environment: classical foundations, contemporary insights*. Lanham, MD, Rowman & Littlefield Publishers, 2002.

Dynes, Russel R., 'The Lisbon earthquake of 1755: the first modern disaster'. In: Braun, Theodore E. D. & John B. Radner (eds.) *The Lisbon earthquake of 1755: representations and reactions.* Oxford, Voltaire Foundation, 2005.

Eduardo, Carlos, 'El terremoto y tsunami de 1835 en Concepción y la frontera del río Biobío: destrucción, relocalización, traslados y nuevas inversiones', *Diálogo andino* 67 (2022), 255–68.

Eliash, Humberto & Manuel Moreno, *Arquitectura y modernidad en Chile, 1925–1965: una realidad múltiple.* Santiago, Chile, Ediciones Universidad Católica de Chile, 1989.

Foltz, Richard C., 'Does nature have historical agency? World history, environmental history, and how historians can help save the planet'. *History Teacher* 37, no. 1 (2003), 9–28.

Frankel, Henry, 'The continental drift debate'. In: Engelhardt Jr, Hugo Tristam & Arthur Caplan (eds.) *Scientific controversies: case solutions in the resolution and closure of disputes in science and technology.* Cambridge, Cambridge University Press, 1987.

GFZ Centre Postdam, 'Seismic hazard in Chile', https://www.gfz -potsdam.de/en/section/seismic-hazard-and-risk-dynamics/projects/ shac-seismic-hazard-in-chile

Gil, Magdalena, 'Disasters as critical junctures: state building and industrialization in Chile after the Chilean earthquake of 1939', *Latin American Research Review* 57, 4 (2023), 776.

Gil, Magdalena, 'God or nature? Catastrophes and modernity from Lisbon to Valparaíso', *International Journal of Mass Emergencies and Disasters* 35, no. 3 (2016), 115–36.

Gil, Magdalena, 'La reconstrucción del valor urbano de Valparaíso luego del terremoto de 1906', *ARQ (Santiago)* no. 97 (2017), 78–89.

Gil, Magdalena & Jorge Atria, 'Fiscal aftershocks: taxes and catastrophes in Chilean history', *Journal of Iberian and Latin American Economic History* (2021), 1–39.

Gil, Magdalena, & Felipe Rivera, 'Strengthening the role of science in disaster risk reduction: the Chilean strategy', *Disasters* 47, no. 1 (2023), 136–62.

Giordano, José Luis, *La predicción del terremoto de 1906 ¿ciencia o fantasía?* Editorial Académica Española, 2023.

Jocelyn-Holt, Alfredo, *Historia general de Chile.* Santiago, Chile, Sudamericana, 2004.

Humeres, Monica & Magdalena Gil, 'Dreaming of a bright future: statistics, disaster, and the birth of energopolitics in Chile during the 1930s', *Technology and Culture* (forthcoming, 2024).

Kane, Stephanie, Eden Medina & Daniel Michler, 'Infrastructural drift in seismic cities: Chile, Pacific Rim, 27 February 2010', *Social Text* 33 (2015), 71–9.

Kelman, Ilan, *Disaster by choice: how our actions turn natural hazards into catastrophes*. Oxford: Oxford University Press, 2020.

Khan, Gulshan, 'Agency, nature and emergent properties: an interview with Jane Bennet', *Contemporary Political Theory* 8 (2009), 9–105.

Kovacs, Paul, 'Reducing the risk of earthquake damage in Canada: lessons from Haiti and Chile', Toronto, Institute of Catastrophic Loss Reduction, 2010.

Legrenzi, Gabriella, 'The displacement effect in the growth of governments', *Public Choice* 120 (2004), 191–204.

Llera, Juan Carlos de la, Felipe Rivera, Magdalena Gil, Hernán Santamaría & Rodrigo Cienfuegos, 'Infraestructura resiliente: lecciones del caso Chileno', *Integration & Trade Journal* 21, no. 41 (2017), 302–15.

Lovett, Richard A., 'Why Chile fared better than Haiti', *Nature* (2010), https://doi.org/10.1038/news.2010.100

Mac-Clure, Óscar, *En Los orígenes de las políticas sociales en Chile, 1850–1879*. Santiago, Chile, Ediciones Universidad Alberto Hurtado, 2012.

Manns, Patricio, *Los terremotos chilenos*. Volume 1, Santiago, Chile, Editorial Quimantú, 1972.

Márquez, Gabriel García, *Chile, el golpe y los gringos*. Bogotá, Editorial Latina, Colección Cuadernos Alternativa, 1974.

Martland, Samuel, 'Reconstructing the city. Constructing the state: government in Valparaíso after the earthquake of 1906', *Hispanic American Historical Review* 87, no. 2 (2007), 221–54.

Mellafe, Rolando, 'El acontecer infausto en el carácter Chileno: una proposición de historia de las mentalidades', *Atenea* 442 (1980), 121–8.

Mellafe, Rolando, 'Historia de las mentalidades: una nueva alternativa', *Cuadernos de Historia* 2 (1982), 97–107.

Meller, Patricio, *Un siglo de economía política Chilena (1890–1990)*. Santiago, Chile, Editorial Andrés Bello, 1996.

Murphy, Raymond, *Sociology and nature: social action in context*. Boulder, CO, Westview Press, 1997.

Nahuelpán, Erwin & José Varas, 'El terremoto/tsunami en Chile: una mirada a las estadísticas médico legales', *Investigación forense* 2 (2013), 1–16.

Nash, Linda, 'The agency of nature or the nature of agency?',
  Environmental History 10 (2005), 67–9.
Neiman, Susan, *Evil in modern thought: an alternative history of philoso-
  phy*. Princeton, NJ-Oxford, Princeton University Press, 2002.
O'Gorman, Emily & Andrea Gaynor, 'More-than-human histories',
  Environmental History 25, no. 4 (2020), 711–35.
Oliver-Smith, Anthony & Susanna Hoffman, *The angry earth: disaster in
  anthropological perspective*. New York, Routledge, 1999.
Onetto, Maurício, *Discursos desde la catástrofe: prensa, solidaridad y
  urgencia en Chile, 1906–2010*. Santiago, Chile, Acto Editores, 2018.
Onetto, Maurício, *Temblores de tierra en el Jardín Del Edén: desastre,
  memoria e identidad: Chile, siglos XVI-XVIII*. Colección Sociedad y
  Cultura, LXII, Santiago, Chile, DIBAM-Centro de Investigaciones
  Diego Barros Arana, 2017.
Paez, Pablo, *La oportunidad de la destruccion en la urbanistica moderna.
  Planes y proyectos para la reconstruccion de Valparaíso tras el terre-
  moto de 1906*. Santiago, Chile, Pontificia Universidad Católica de
  Chile, Instituto de Estudios Urbanos, 2008.
Palacios, Alfredo, 'Antecedentes históricos de la 'abogacía telúrica'
  desarrollada en Chile entre los siglos XVI y XIX', *Historia Crítica* 54
  (2014), 171–93.
Palacios, Alfredo, *Entre ruinas y escombros: los terremotos en Chile
  durante los siglos XVI al XIX*. Valparaíso, Ediciones Universidad de
  Valparaíso, 2015.
Pellow, David N. & Hollie Nyseth Brehm, 'An environmental sociology
  for the twenty-first century', *Annual Review of Sociology* 39, no. 1
  (2013), 229–50.
Quarantelli, Enrico, 'A social science research agenda for the disasters of
  the 21st century'. In: Perry, Ronald W. & Enrico L. Quarantelli (eds.)
  What is a disaster? New answers to old questions. Philadelphia, PA,
  Xlibris, 2005.
Richard, José Fernandez, 'Historia del derecho urbanístico Chileno',
  Revista de Derecho Público 77 (2012), 79–97.
Rivas, Juan & Nibaldo Mosciatti, 'Apuntes sobre el viaje de Albert Camus
  a Chile'. In: Camus, Albert, *Ni víctimas ni verdugos*. Buenos Aires,
  Godot, 2014.
Rivera, Felipe, Tiziana Rossetto &, John Twigg, 'An interdisciplinary
  study of the seismic exposure dynamics of Santiago de Chile',
  International Journal of Disaster Risk Reduction 48 (2020), 1–12.
Rivera, Felipe, Tiziana Rossetto &, John Twigg, 'Understanding earth-
  quake resilience in Chile: the pros and cons of safe buildings',

Proceedings of the SECED 2019 Conference. Greenwich, London, SECED, September 10, 2019, https://www.seced.org.uk/index.php/proceedings.

Sagredo, Rafael, *Historia de la vida privada en Chile*. Santiago, Chile, Taurus, 2005.

Savala, Joshua, 'Contesting disasters: the 1906 Valparaíso earthquake, state violence, and working-class solidarity', Tufts University, Department of History, 2012.

Savala, Joshua, '"Let us bring it with love": violence, solidarity, and the making of a social disaster in the wake of the 1906 earthquake in Valparaíso, Chile', *Journal of Social History* 51, 4 (2018), 928–52.

Silva, Bárbara & Alfredo Riquelme, *Una identidad terremoteada: comunidad y territorio en El Chile de 1960*. Santiago, Chile, Ediciones Universidad Alberto Hurtado, 2018.

Stallings, Robert A., 'Disasters and the theory of social order'. In: Quarantelli, Enrico (ed.) *What is a disaster? Perspectives on the question*. London-New York, Routledge, 1998, 127–36.

Subercaseaux, Benjamin, *Chile o una loca geografía*. Santiago, Chile, Editorial Universitaria, 1940.

Tierney, Kathleen J., 'From the margins to the mainstream? Disaster research at the crossroads', *Annual Review of Sociology* 33, no. 1 (2007), 503–25.

Tilly, Charles, 'War making and state making as organized crime'. In: Evans, Peter, Dietrich Rueschemeyer & Theda Skocpol (eds.) *Bringing the state back in*. Cambridge, Cambridge University Press, 1985.

Torrent, Horacio, 'Historiografía y arquitectura moderna en Chile: notas sobre sus paradigmas y desafíos', *Anales del IAA* 42, no. 1 (2012), 55–75.

USGS, 'Earthquake magnitude', https://www.usgs.gov/programs /earthquake-hazards/earthquake-magnitude-energy-release-and -shaking-intensity.

Valderrama, Lorena B., 'Seismic forces and state power: the creation of the Chilean seismological service at the beginning of the twentieth century', *Historical Social Research* 40, no. 2 (2015), 81–104.

Verbal, Valentina, *La ruina. El gran terremoto y maremoto en Concepción de 20 de febrero de 1835. Sus consecuencias materiales y sociales*, Universidad Católica de Chile, Department of History, 2006.

Villalobos, Sergio, *Historia de los Chilenos*. Santiago, Chile, Taurus, 2006.

Wayman, Erin, 'Chile's quake larger but less destructive than Haiti', *Earth Magazine* (2012), https://www.earthmagazine.org.

Zinn, Jenz, *Understanding risk-taking*. Switzerland, Palgrave Macmillan, 2020.

Archival and primary sources

Barrio, Paulino, 'Memoria sobre los temblores de tierra i sus efectos en jeneral i en especial los de Chile', *Anales de la Universidad de Chile* (1855) Serie 1, 583–625.

Bello, Andrés, 'Discurso pronunciado en la instalación de la Universidad de Chile el día 17 de septiembre de 1843', *Anales de la Universidad de Chile 49–52* (1943), 7–21.

Bello, Edwards, 'El terremoto', Diario *La Nación*, January 27, 1939, p. 3.

Caldcleugh, Alexander, 'An account of the great earthquake experienced in Chile on the 20th of February, 1835 with a map', *Philosophical Transactions of the Royal Society of London* 126 (1836), 21–6.

'Cartas', *El Mercurio* (Valparaíso), 9 October 1829. In: Ballore, Fernando Montessus, *Historia sísmica de los Andes Meridionales al sur del paralelo XVI*, Volume IV, Santaigo, Chile, Imprenta Cervantes, 1912.

Congreso Nacional de Chile, *Sesiones Extraordinarias* (1906).

'Current Economic Position and Prospects of Chile', Washington, DC, The World Bank, 1961.

Darwin, Charles, *Charles Darwin's Beagle diary*. Cambridge, Cambridge University Press, 2001.

'Diario el mercurio de Chile, 19 de Noviembre and Vera y Pintado, B. 'Comunicado. '*El mercurio de Chile 16*' (2 December 1822). In: Feliú, Guillermo (ed.) *El mercurio de Chile; 1820–1823*. Santiago, Chile, Editorial Nascimiento, 1960.

Ley de Comuna Autonoma, (Law of Autonomous Municipalities) of 1891. In: Memoria Chilena. Biblioteca Nacional de Chile, http://www.memoriachilena.gob.cl/602/w3-article-93505.html.

'Mensaje de S.E El Presidente de la Republica al Congreso al inagurar el periodo ordinario de sesiones'. Santiago, Chile, 1 May 1960.

El Mercurio (Santiago), 25 January 1939, p. 9.

Mistral, Gabriela, 'Chile, suelo telúrico' [Manuscript], Biblioteca Nacional de Chile, http://www.bibliotecanacionaldigital.gob.cl/bnd/623/w3-article-141314.html.

Navasal, José M., 'Hace un año la tierra tembló', *El Mercurio* (Santiago), 21 May 1961, p. 9.

'Nuevas y dolorosas informaciones de la catástrofe', *El Mercurio* (Valparaíso), 18 August 1906, p. 1.

La Oficina de Estadística del Trabajo. Ministerio de Industria y Obras Pública, Imprenta Cervantes, 1907.

Ovalle, Francisco J., *Don Pedro Montt, ex Presidente de la República de Chile*. Santiago, Chile, Imprenta Universitaria, 1918.

Rodriguez, Alfredo & Carlos Cruzat, *La catástrofe del 16 de agosto de 1906 en la República de Chile*. Santiago, Chile, Imprenta Barcelona, 1906.

Servicio Nacional de Salud. Sección Bioestadística y Control Médico Económico. Archivo Ministerio de Salud (Chile).

U.S. Department of State, 'Chile: rebuilding for a better future', May 1961. Washington, DC.

Chapter 6

Human–insect relations in Northeast Brazil's twentieth-century sugar industry

José Marcelo Marques Ferreira Filho

Insects are everywhere, mostly populating the collective imagination as undesirable beings, precisely because most of us are unaware of their ecological function. Insects are fundamental as pollinators, ensuring the survival of numerous plant species. As decomposers, together with microorganisms such as bacteria and fungi, they extract the last bit of fixed energy from dead tissue and waste at every level in the food web, and in exchange return degraded nutrient chemicals to the plants.[1] In the field of ecology, they represent an important measure of the balance in a given natural environment, and only under specific circumstances can they play a threatening role as pests or vectors of disease.[2] Microbes, likewise, abound in nature: in the air we breathe, the soil, the water, our skin and hair, and even in the food we eat. They play a crucial role in maintaining the ecological balance by making the soil fertile, 'cleaning' the environment, and, in some cases, even protecting us from other undesirable microorganisms. However, most people (historians included) are barely aware of their existence, except when they become sick or must face a global pandemic.[3]

Even though plenty of insects, fungi, bacteria and viruses appear in the documentation regarding the history of sugar, Brazilian historiography has paid little attention to their agency.[4] Our goal here is to reveal the unconscious role (as pests or vectors of agricultural diseases) of various insect species (beetles, moths, termites, froghoppers and so on), alongside humans, in the history of sugar in Northeast Brazil in the late nineteenth and twentieth centuries. Here I argue that many human actions were mere responses, (re)actions to the agencies played by nonhuman beings in the context of what I call 'the spatial architecture of plantation'.[5] I contend that a very different history of sugar plantation was to unfold in Brazil had the economic elites (associated with the state and various scientists, especially plant pathologists, agronomists and entomologists) been able to prevail without inconveniences in the constant wars waged against insects. These armies of tiny undesirable beings were true enemies of the plantation productive logic that sought to submit, control and subdue *all* that was important to it (humans, vegetables, rivers, soils, climate, insects, fungi, bacteria, viruses and so on).[6]

For over a century, the sugar plantation system in Northeast Brazil has remained an important object of investigation in the most varied knowledge fields. It is one of those topics labelled as 'classic', about which one might argue everything has already been said. It is true that in the field of social history, recent theoretical and methodological advances have broadened the concept of plantation by considering the long and complex history of spatial relations, as well as by giving prominence to the workers' voice,[7] highlighting their original ways of reading their own history[8] and their protagonism through multiple forms of resistance,[9] even under a highly violent authoritarian regime.[10] Nonhuman beings, however, have never been the explicit centre of historical writing.

To claim that nonhuman beings were central players at certain moments in the history of sugar does not imply that humans were mere extras. Although animals and plants have assumed an increasingly prominent role in society and historiography, what I propose here is still based, almost involuntarily, on an anthropocentric perspective. For a long time, anthropoexclusivism (and not anthropocentrism, properly speaking) eclipsed the importance of the nonhuman world in constructing history.[11] Not only were plants and animals kept out of consideration about historical agency, but they were, in fact, almost wholly excluded from historiography. It was as if humans lived suspended in the air, adrift, disconnected from the material substratum that allows them to exist. It might be argued that until we find a way to perceive the world through the viewpoint of plants, insects and bacteria history will always remain somewhat anthropocentric, despite some attempts[12] to understand the intricacies of their thoughts, eloquence, ways of reasoning, classifying, dialoguing, interpreting, representing and deciding on the world.

Although, even now, we remain unable to understand the mechanisms of dialogue and negotiation between humans and most insect species, we can at least accept that they (as individuals or species) cannot live without interacting, in various ways, with each other. To be as explicit as possible, I am arguing that the spatial architecture of the sugar plantation resulted not only from the materialised relations between the dominant capitalist class of planters and the expropriated workers but also from the interactions between these two groups and various other species of non-human beings with whom they could not avoid sharing their businesses and lives. As Eduardo Gudynas suggests, we should think of history and its agents in terms of relationalities rather than rationalities.[13] In a certain way, therefore, this text intends to put sugarcane (the plant) and insects (the animal) in the history of sugar (the product). To that end, I divide my argument into two parts. First, I show that history is nothing but intra and interspecific ecological interactions projected in a space-time that humans perceive, signified and narrate. Then, in the second part, I show (focusing on various sugarcane pests and diseases) how insects helped to shape sugar history throughout the late nineteenth and twentieth centuries, arguing that we should rethink not only the place of humans in the history of sugar but the history of sugar in America itself.

On history, once more

The best way to unveil the importance, function and role of something is by asking: what would happen if this thing (anything) did not exist? For example, what would the history of America – or capitalism itself – have been like without sugar? One of my aims here is to try to answer one such kind of question: what would the history of sugar in Northeast Brazil have been like without insects? Before trying to answer it, though, I shall argue that we should take a step back and reflect on the foundations of the historical discipline. Running counter to the hegemonic monospecific paradigm[14] in Western academia, we currently witness a multispecies turn. Even anthropology, traditionally centred on humans, has tried to deanthropologize itself.[15] It has not been different in history, and several authors have recently demonstrated that animals (domestic or wild) and vegetables, 'supposedly voiceless and largely defenseless entities were in fact authentic actors in the historical drama'.[16] Even though Western historiography has only recently embraced the challenge of writing the world beyond the human,[17] animals have been considered agents and legally protectable individuals with collective rights since at least the twelfth century.[18] In some parts of medieval Europe, it was common to send a bailiff to the places where the animals being sued had settled to read to them, at least three times loud and clear, the summons to appear in person before the judicial authority. For example, in 1846, Charles Berriat-Saint-Prix wrote the *Rapport et recherches sur les jugements relatifs aux animaux*, highlighting numerous cases of excommunication of rats and caterpillars, as well as sentences against pigs, elephants, grasshoppers, beetles and even a rooster condemned to be burned for having 'laid an egg'.[19]

Although we have been experiencing, since at least the Industrial Revolution, what is conventionally called the Anthropocene,[20] humans never had complete control over the biosphere. From an environmental perspective, we are not creators *of* but mere participants *in* history. After all, 'societies' have never been solely adult, male, or rational.[21] It was precisely from such a perspective, for example, that in his classic *With Broadax and Firebrand: The Destruction of the Brazilian Atlantic Rainforest* (1995), Warren Dean questioned what Brazilian agriculture and history would have been like had no leaf-cutting ants appeared, 'capable of stripping a field of manioc in a night or two, invulnerable to any countermeasures?'[22] On the other hand, an ecology that closes its eyes to human social action is also incomplete, as 'both history and ecology are, as fields of knowledge go, supremely integrative'.[23] As William Cronon argued, 'human beings are not the only actors who make history. Other creatures do too, as do large natural processes, and any history that ignores their effects is likely to be woefully incomplete'.[24]

Indeed, all human actions occur within what we can call ecosystem dynamics. 'Human society coevolves with nature; human history unfolds within a broad natural context even as it helps shape that context', wrote the editors of the *Encyclopedia of World Environmental History*.[25] In this regard, Richard C. Foltz warns that 'we should remind ourselves that humans interact not only with each other, but in all times, places and contexts with the nonhuman world as well. All human actions take place within the context of ecosystems, and are affected by them in ways that differ enormously over time and space'.[26] As we distance ourselves from the planetary scale, human events seem to correspond to only a micro part of a much longer and broader story, which David Christian and Fred Spier call 'Big History'.[27]

In a way, environmental history is the attempt to de-banalise the banal and highlight the ecological complexity of what people take for granted. It proposes a story of the obvious, that is, we are not alone in the world. We cannot exist (any of the almost 8 billion inhabitants of the planet) without food (of animal or vegetable origin) or water, without excreting the waste that our organism metabolises daily, or dressing and building shelters to protect us from the sun, rain and animals; that is, without transforming what modernity calls 'nature'.[28] Once enunciated, such a statement (and all that is implied, even implicitly, in environmental terms) seems so obvious that perhaps this was the reason why historiography took so long to realise that all history is environmental history (to the same extent that all history is contemporary history, as Benedetto Croce claimed).

In fact, the obvious commonly blinds people, including historians, preventing them from questioning their origins, dynamics and effects. In this sense, as Enrique Leff stated, 'environmental history is the history of unspoken histories'.[29]

From this perspective, an immense group of nonhumans – which we could designate as biotic actants without anthropomorphising them – are not only passive recipients of human actions but active presences in the world.[30] Therefore, history always deals with an inseparable, solidary and contradictory (though not necessarily antagonistic) set of complex and dynamic social and environmental systems sharing their existences over time. In this sense, history is nothing but intra- and interspecific ecological interactions projected in a space-time that humans perceive, signify and narrate. Moreover, we are subject to the same evolutionary pressures as any other species, meaning we may become extinct anytime.

Therefore, analysing how elements (biotic and abiotic) interact in space is always more complex than simply investigating isolated, static forms and objects, as they involve relationships that are not always establishable directly or objectively.[31] In fact, the problem here is not to enlarge the number of actors, nor simply to describe their habitats, behaviours, forms of reproduction, and so on, but to capture them in their connection with the rest of the world.[32]

Back to sugar, humans and insects in Brazil

Caio Prado Júnior once wrote that 'Brazil is a gift of sugar'.[33] He is recognised as one of the greatest Brazilian historians, alongside Gilberto Freyre, whose celebrated *Nordeste* (1936) was translated into French as *Terres du Sucre*. Both expressions captured the essence of one of the most socially unequal regions in the world. It was ruled by a tiny economic elite that exploited forests, rivers, soils, and hundreds of thousands of human and nonhuman individuals (all perceived by the planter class as natural resources or *laboring landscapes*, in the expression coined by Thomas Rogers)[34] over five centuries. The introduction of the sweet *gramineae*, leading to the so-called 'sugar civilisation', caused profound transformations (a revolution, one might say) in the production model and landscapes in this part of the planet.[35]

The geography of the northeastern sugarcane area is confusing: the so-called Forest zone is essentially a coastal region whose name refers to its original biome, now almost extinct – the Atlantic Forest. Since these lands began to be colonised by Europeans, their exuberant arboreal vegetation has been devastated, opening the way to what geographers Gilberto Osório de Andrade and Raquel Caldas Lins Andrade designated as 'swollen lands': 'unmeasured latifundia' of sugarcane.[36] In an expression now common-place among regional inhabitants and academics, the 'forest zone' became the 'sugar zone'. Originating in Southeast Asia and brought to the West by the Arabs, 'sugar cane was first carried to the New World by Columbus on his second voyage, in 1493'.[37] The first cultivar introduced into Brazil was the so-called creole cane, or *da terra* (native), having been the longest cul-tivated (almost 270 years) until it was replaced by the cayenne variety in the early nineteenth century.

Although entomologists have reached no consensus, the newest meth-ods of evolutionary classification reveal that insects account for approximately 66 per cent of all animal species (over one million) in the world.[38] The entire colonial period holds no records of insects becoming pests in the Brazilian sugarcane fields. In 1648, physician and naturalist Willem Piso, together with cartographer and botanist Georg Markgraf, wrote *Historia Naturalis Brasiliae*, describing with no further details a spe-cies of winged black worms – called by the natives *guirapeacoca*, and by neo-Europeans *pão de galinha* (larvae of the beetle *Ligyrus fossator*) – which corroded roots and killed the sugarcane.[39] In 1711, missionary André João Antonil listed what he designated as the 'enemies of sugarcane': drought (lack of water and excessive heat); goats, oxen and pigs (some-times sacrificed by the planters, 'upon fair pain'); horses and thieves.[40] In his *Travels to the Northeast of Brazil* (1817), chronicler Henry Koster did not mention insects or the so-called blast, a bacterial disease that was devas-tating Caribbean sugarcane fields at the time. Instead, Koster stated that 'the cane is subject, naturally, to various diseases, but of a nature to be remedied. Rats destroy large quantities, and the fox is no less encountered'. Actually, in these accounts, humans are the ones described almost as 'pests', for 'they have no scruple, passing through the reeds, to cut a bun-dle of ten to twelve reeds and suck them, while they walk, or take them home. The damage committed [by thieves] is thus incalculable, especially in the cane fields situated along the edges of the roads frequented'.[41]

Such testimonies suggest that insects did not seriously threaten the sugar economy during the entire colonial period. But how come? How could we explain, for instance, that at that same time, sugarcane planta-tions in the Caribbean, as Matthew Mulcahy and Stuart Schwartz[42] demonstrated, were ravaged by armies of insects and various diseases caused by fungi and bacteria, while Brazil seemed free of such evils? As reported in the literature, references to creole plants are probably based on their genetic proximity to the wild species. In such cases, it tends to mean that it has greater genetic variability and therefore is less likely to be victimised by parasites and pathogens. A greater genetic variability implies fewer chances of a particular disease affecting all individuals of a species due to their genetic differences. This is why native or more adapted species (which evolve along with their possible pathogens) are more resistant and tolerant (or even immune), while exotic species tend to be more susceptible or to spread pathogens more easily and quickly.

Furthermore, crops closer to forests tend to take advantage of their ecological balance, as the cultivated species find a larger number of pollinators and a smaller number of pathogens due to increased competition.[43] The same occurs with pests. Agricultural activities cause several environmental impacts. For example, in the Caribbean, the monoculture system has rapidly replaced the native forest, where insects and plants benefit from co-evolutionary processes. Such events can cause numerous imbalances, like the proliferation of phytophagous agents that are now far from their natural predators.

Unlike the small islands in the Caribbean, where sugarcane and the forest competed for space, with an imposed need to create new cultivars to increase productivity, the continental Brazilian territory allowed sugarcane to expand without having to cut down all the forest. Since the 1970s, various studies in over fifty countries have led biologists to conclude that the larger number of insects listed as sugarcane pests is directly proportional to the increase in planted area.[44] Combining such findings with the data suggesting that 'until the middle of the nineteenth century, the neo-Brazilians converted no more than 8% of the Atlantic Forest biome to crops, pastures and urban areas',[45] one can infer two things: (i) creole cane benefited from its likely high genetic variability (for being closer to the wild plant), as well as from better-preserved forests until the mid-nineteenth century, and (ii) the occurrence of sugarcane diseases and pests in Brazil is directly linked to the lower genetic variability brought by the new cultivars in the nineteenth century, as well as intensified deforestation. The abundant forest fragments near monocultural fields during the colonial period seem to have favoured a small set of biologically different successional or pioneer species (such as creole cane). Such a mosaic composed of simplified and poor subsystems – such as monocultures – and dynamic and rich subsystems – like forests – seems to have ensured an 'alternative state of equilibrium',[46] thus generating a broader, more integrated steady system.

This hypothetical steady state probably collapsed in the late nineteenth century with the intense import of new cultivars, expansion of cultivated areas, intensified deforestation and the establishment of large mills (*usinas*). All these novelties drastically altered the sugar landscape and made the environment less able to recover from disturbances. These seem to have been the main factors that created the ideal conditions for the population of certain insect species – otherwise controlled by formerly abundant natural enemies (nonhuman enemies, to be more accurate) in the forest fragments – to become pests.

The introduction of the cayenne cane in the early nineteenth century was part of a major process of plantation renovation aimed at increasing production and competing more aggressively in the external market.[47] This new cultivar brought some advantages over creole cane due to its taller stem, thicker features, nodes further apart, and greater vegetative vigour. It also matured earlier (in only nine months), resisted better to poor weather and had more woody stalks and richer sucrose content, in addition to presenting greater purity. All these qualities turned cayenne into farmers' preferred cultivar, quickly spreading in various regions in Brazil.[48] However, it would not take long for the early effects of such interventions to emerge. In the mid-century, gummosis – the first plant disease in the world – appeared in Bahia. For the first time, Brazilian sugarcane fields were plagued by a large-scale disease for which no explanation or known solution existed. Coeval documentation reports 'cries of alarm' and 'panic' in the attempt to fight the terrible 'evil', the devastating 'disease' that caused so much damage and discouragement to the sugar industry. The *Revista Agrícola*, linked to the Imperial Fluminense Institute of Agriculture, was a major means of researching and disseminating agricultural practices in that period. It published eighteen articles on sugarcane culture only in its first seven issues (between 1869 and 1872), and even though coffee was the main Brazilian export at the time, sugarcane persisted in all its issues until 1876.[49] Scientists from all over Brazil were busy researching the causes and means to fight 'the plague', as it was known.[50] Meetings were called to deal with the matter, with documents showing the great interest of the authorities in Rio in managing the consequences of the sugarcane decadence, as well as providing the planters with new sugarcane cultivars, usually from selection or artificial crossbreeding. The neverending story of the search for new sugarcane cultivars starts at this point as an effort to save the plantation economy.

Even though gummosis was to be shown later to be a disease caused by a bacterium (*Pseudomonas vasculorum*), the early reports claimed that its pathogen was a caterpillar known as *fura canna* (*Procera sacchariphagus*). According to Ladislau de Sousa Mello Netto, editor of the *Revista Agrícola*, this was a moth of the Crambidae family, 'one of the most fearsome enemies that cane fields count on'.[51] In 1870, because of attempts to discover the actual causative agent of gummosis, Alois Krauss described large agglomerations of insects like the cochineal (genus *Dactylopius*) in Bahia's sugarcane fields. He even counted 200 insects in a single sugarcane node, with each individual cane often containing 3 or more nodes.

He concluded that those insects probably had some connection with the disease. He found four caterpillars per cane, and stated that they could become a pest if their natural predators were eliminated. Krauss also mentioned several other insects that used to attack sugarcane, such as beetles of the species *Noterus clavicornis*, lice and the rare cockroach.[52]

At the Cachoeirinha Plantation, in the municipality of Escada, state of Pernambuco, the use of natural hybrids in fortuitous pollination by wind or insects, a cultivar known as *manteiga* cane was the most accepted by planters and spread throughout the Northeast until the 1930s, when the mosaic virus devastated the sugarcane fields in the second great epidemic in the historical record. In the state of São Paulo, scientist Adrião Caminha Filho pointed out that in 1920 production fell from 800,000 sacks to 250,000 sacks of sugar, a drop of almost 70 per cent.[53] According to the newspaper *Diario de Pernambuco*, mosaic represented a great danger, a 'terrible pest', a 'disease of dire consequences' that was causing a 'great calamity'. Faced with the crisis, the Pernambuco state government created the Office against Mosaic, in August 1926, through an agreement with the Federal Government, mayors and business people. The Office stipulated a fine of 200,000 *réis* – doubled in recurrence cases – for those who would plant cane affected by mosaic. In cases of cane shipments from infected municipalities, the fine was 300,000 *réis*, also double in recurrence cases. In cases of a large extension of the disease, expropriation for public use was even more likely to occur through indemnification by the state. Besides the coercive nature, essential to ensure that the guidelines would be effective, according to health authorities, the Office against Mosaic also aimed to explain to those concerned 'the damage caused by the disease and the best way to mitigate or eradicate it, instructing, in this regard, farmers and people in general, through conferences, prints, posters, distribution of publications and teaching in schools in the region'. It was with this in mind that, in September 1926, the governor of Pernambuco ordered the reproduction and distribution of coloured prints of the sugarcane mosaic. The motto was that 'it will always be easier to convince a farmer not to plant a sick cane than to oblige him to uproot an already born plant'.[54] In February 1928, the Pernambuco Agriculture Auxiliary Society offered a prize of 100,000 *escudos* for whoever discovered the disease's aetiology.

The mosaic disease was already known on the island of Java as early as 1890. It appeared in Egypt in 1909 and the following year in Hawaii, spreading rapidly. It then spread to Puerto Rico, Argentina, Santo Domingo and the United States (Louisiana, Florida, Georgia, Alabama and Mississippi). Carrying a virus as the pathogen, mosaic is an infection that occurs within the living tissues of the plant and cannot be eliminated without destroying the cane itself – it is an 'incurable disease'. It spreads in two ways: through primary infection, when a sick stake produces sick canes, or through secondary infection, when insects spread the pathogen. Such a scenario created a kind of vicious circle: insects attacked the canes while transmitting the mosaic virus, which, in turn, weakened the plant making it more susceptible to attack by other insects. Referring to the state of São Paulo, renowned agronomist José Vizioli stated that 'the intensity with which pests and cryptogamic diseases have ravaged the state's sugarcane fields can be attributed to the weakened state of the plants, intensely attacked by "mosaic virus"'.[55]

Whether as pests or agents that transmit disease, insects helped shape the history of sugar production in Northeast Brazil throughout the twentieth century. Testimonies reveal that even before abolition, planters used to force 'more than a hundred unfortunate slaves' to spend 'the night wandering the extensive floodplains armed with *embira* [plant genus in the family Thymelaeaceae] flares to burn the beetles'.[56] In the 1910s, the beetle pest was already regarded as a 'matter of utmost importance to the northern states of Brazil', as Carlos Moreira claimed – head of the Agricultural Entomology Laboratory of the National Museum (linked to the Brazilian Ministry of Agriculture, Industry and Commerce). In a text entitled *Os besouros da canna de assucar*, Moreira proposed as a good measure to establish a modest prize, in money (100 *réis*), per kilo of beetle and *pão de galinha*, paid by the municipalities, or the state government, so that many children and women could have a small income catching these insects and larvae, killing them and keeping them until reaching one kilo or more, which the authority in charge would receive in exchange for the prize and then destroy by fire. He also points out that at that time, the damage caused by beetles was so recurrent that 'in the contracts for leasing land for planting sugarcane there was almost always a clause exempting the lessee from paying the lease of the land in the year in which the beetle appeared causing damage'.[57] The extensive area where the beetle pest prevailed has a sense of the challenges involved in combating the plague, something that the landowners had to live with for a long time. Studies from the 1950s recorded an average population of 700,000 insects per hectare regarding beetles and *pão de galinha* on infested land. In 1954, 100 per cent of the Pitangueira Plantation, for example, was lost.

Ligyrus fossator and *Podalgus humilis* were the two main species of coleoptera that plagued the sugarcane fields in the late nineteenth and early twentieth centuries. These insects are native to Brazil and live underground, digging galleries for food. Their biological cycle includes four stages: egg, larva, pupa (or chrysalis) and imago (adult stage). Before wholesale land clearing for sugar plantations, they lived on the roots and shoots of wild plants. Although nonhuman enemies generally limit their population, they eventually started to prefer cultivated plants. The simplified vegetation caused by monoculture modifies the humidity of the soil, making it more receptive. These beetles have nocturnal habits, flying from twilight and through the night. At dawn, they penetrate the soil. The females fertilise eggs in the soil (at a small depth) or under dry rotten cane straw. The larvae of the larger beetle (*Ligyrus fossator*), which live for an average of one year, are commonly named *pão de galinha* and are more harmful than adult insects as they attack the planted stalks even before they sprout. They destroy the buds and attack the body of the stalks, corroding them and, after penetrating, eroding their internal tissues and leaving the cane completely hollow. After devouring the plant's supporting roots, these larvae 'can promote the toppling of an already formed clump'.[58] These insects indiscriminately attack shoots, buds and young shoots as adults. In contrast, the larvae of the smaller beetle (*Podalgus humilis*) are less harmful and attack the stalks in two ways: gnawing and perforating new shoots a little below the soil surface, or perforating the stalk from end to end, ultimately bringing the need to replant them.

In addition to beetles, various other insects – such as caterpillars, cochineal, sugarcane borers and termites – plagued the sugarcane fields. The latter were 'among the most widespread pests of sugarcane in Pernambuco' in the 1950s, infesting almost all the hills and tableland areas, thus contributing to 'a sharp increase in the cost of production and a shortening of the crop's profit margin'.[59] Often associated with low germination of the stubbles, or their weakness and stunting, termites attacked canes at all ages, facilitating the ingress of 'rot microorganisms'. At that time, the average sugarcane yield in Pernambuco was one of the lowest in the world[60] – from 60 to 80 per cent of the buds rotted. The combination of low-quality seed cane, inadequate soil preparation and fertility, and getting the planting season wrong turned pests and diseases into one of the main reasons for this poor performance. According to Pimentel, the plant disease known as red rottenness was 'the main enemy of sugarcane',[61] as its pathogen, the fungus *Colletotrichum falcatum*, was spread by several pests such as *Castnia, Metamasius, Elasmopalpus, Xyleborus* and *Diatraea*, 'universally known as the insect that causes the most damage to the sugar industry'.[62] The attack of these invertebrates usually reduced or delayed cane germination by allowing certain microorganisms – present in its bark or in the soil itself – to penetrate through the wounds they opened. These fungi, bacteria and viruses destroyed the food reserves and tissues of the buds before they could grow.

Moreover, when in contact with constantly mutating microorganisms and enormous genetic plasticity, the resistance features of the cane cultivars – produced vegetatively and with a fixed genotype – tended to succumb, leading to degeneration. Such an issue was particularly visible when measuring ratoon production (harvests based on the annual regrowth of sugarcane in tonnes per hectare). According to agronomist Abdon Pereira da Silva, the low yield of ratoons was 'one of the most serious problems that have afflicted the country's sugar agroindustry'.[63] José Clóvis de Andrade – the first president of the Association of Agricultural Engineers of the Northeast (1947) and who represented the Sugar and Alcohol Institute at the Congress of Agricultural and Sugar Engineers, in Havana (Cuba), in 1948 – claimed that the diseases were 'the great problem, at all times, of the sugar industry'.[64]

The economic effects of the great diversity of pests and diseases became unbearable, and the problem started to be treated as a 'public calamity'. In this context, in 1953, the Commission to Combat Sugarcane Pests was created in the state of Pernambuco, a permanent body to study and control matters of such nature. The general objective of the commission was to investigate the consequences of diseases and pests on agricultural and industrial yields, in addition to proposing methods for combating them.[65] Initially planned to last only five years, supported by an annual budget of two million *cruzeiros*, the commission remained active until the late 1960s. The records published in the newspaper *Diario de Pernambuco*, the principal news outlet in the state at the time, show that the installation of the commission was considered 'a day of celebration for every farmer', as it was necessary 'to know the enemies, to know how many they are, to which family, the genus and species they belong. What evils they cause and the proportion thereof'.[66] Indeed, more was invested in science to combat pests than education and working-class welfare; the newspapers paid more attention to insects than the hundreds of thousands of tenants living isolated in sugar zone. The *Diario* enthusiastically applauded the initiative of allocating a plane, piloted by a war veteran, to combat pests, as in the excerpt below:

> The fight carried out using the spray plane targets not just one insect but several. The whole long series of predators affecting the sugarcane fields will be effectively hit by the insecticide [. . .]. The pilot, Bonifácio, executing the low flight, dumps a cloud of insecticide, which is slowly deposited on the ground [. . .]. The Amaragi Plantation's extremely rugged topography is a challenge to Bonifacio's skill as he climbs, descends, lowers, and shoves his way through tight canyons, leaving a trail of dust behind him. For the Amaragi planters, the test being performed is invaluable, and if the expected results emerge, then it will almost be a survival factor. According to our

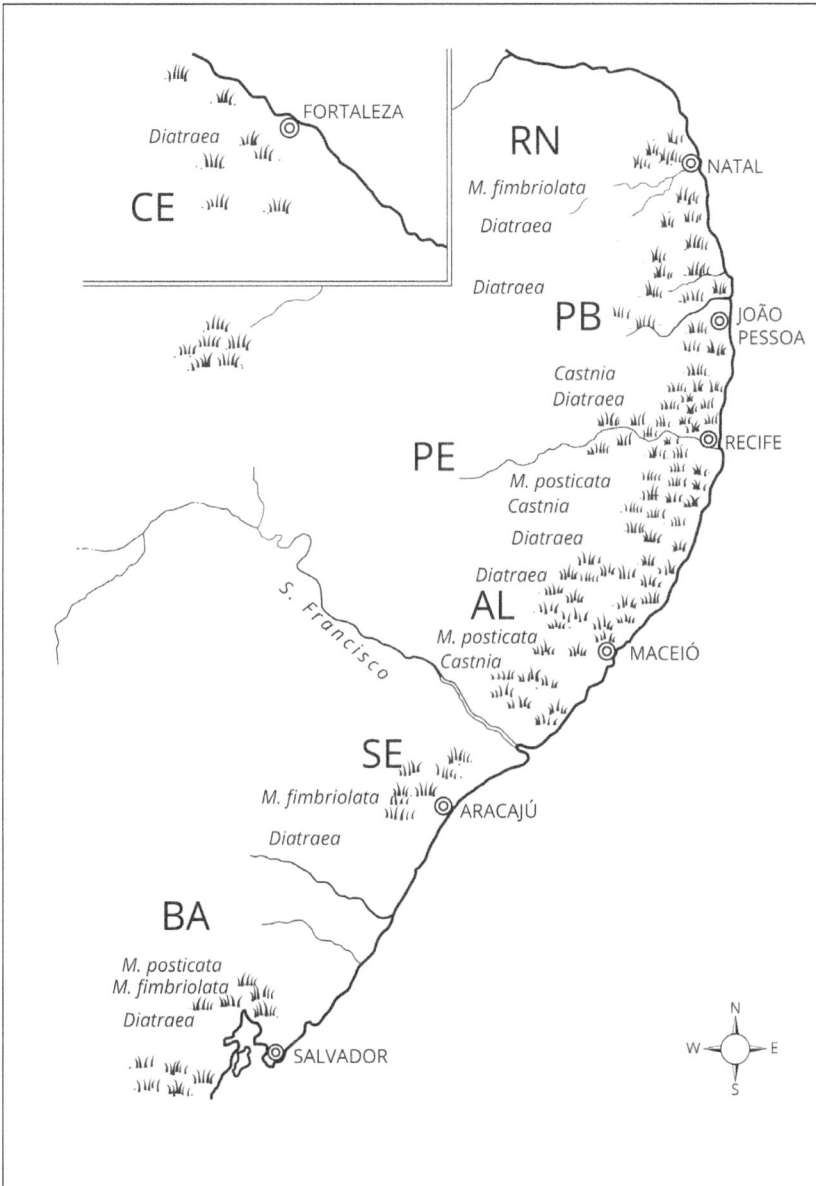

Map 6.1: Distribution of the most important pests (sugar zone in Northeast Brazil). Source: Pietro Guagliumi, *Pragas da cana-de-açúcar: Nordeste do Brasil*. Rio de Janeiro, IAA, 1972/1973, 13.

information, in 1951–52, Amaragi Plantation produced 5,700 tonnes of cane. In crop 52–53, on practically the same area, only 1,100 tons were harvested, in addition to the further loss that the cane field was planted four times. 'Beetles' accounted for almost all the damage and it is not without reason that the agronomists who visited the plantation at the time designated it 'beetles' headquarters'.[67]

In the 1960s, the sugarcane froghoppers (*Mahanarva posticata* and *Mahanarva fimbriolata*) were the main enemy of the sugar industry. This insect species destroyed everything, everywhere, attacking indiscriminately – all sugarcane cultivars, all ratoons, all ages and all topographies. The cornfields and hay fields adjacent to the cane fields were not spared either. In a single clump with 12 canes, at Pumatizinho Plantation, for example, researchers found 401 insects, among young and adults. Froghoppers soon became an 'economic scourge of considerable importance [. . .] a serious problem never before encountered',[68] with 'unpredictable consequences in the agricultural and industrial sectors. In a letter addressed to the Northeast Sugar Foundation, in 1965, the Commission to Combat Sugarcane Pests stated that the status of public calamity attributed to the froghopper forced public and private sectors to harmonise their interests in defence of the state's economy. After calling for an 'immediate control plan to safeguard sugarcane, the vanguard of Pernambuco's wealth', the document added: 'we cannot falter in the face of such a transcendental problem'.[69] Amid this 'unequal fight against a powerful enemy' a taskforce was then organised among various state, regional, federal and international agencies, in addition to the business class: (i) Commission to Combat Sugarcane Pests; (ii) Pernambuco Institute of Agronomic Research; (iii) Large Mill Cooperative of Pernambuco; (iv) Pernambuco Sugar Suppliers Association; (v) Sugar Study Group; (vi) Northeast Sugar Foundation; (vii) Special Group for the Rationalisation of the Northeastern Sugar Industry; (viii) Superintendency for the Development of the Northeast; (ix) Sugar and Alcohol Institute; (x) Ministry of Agriculture; (xi) Hawaiian Sugar Planters Association; (xii) U.S. Agency for International Development (USAID); and (xiii) Food and Agriculture Organisation of the United Nations (FAO). Most of these agencies met regularly to deliberate and create protocols to combat insects. In the extraordinary meeting held on 10 March 1967, Dr Mário Bezerra de Carvalho, from the Pernambuco Institute of Agronomic Research, stated that 'in the battle that was to be waged against the froghopper pest, all the specialised agencies should march together, thus pursuing a single interest, a single goal'.[70]

The difficulties in winning the war against insects led the Brazilian authorities to bring two internationally renowned entomologists to the Northeast sugar zone: Pietro Guagliumi, from FAO, and Roger Williams, from the International Research Institute, linked to USAID. Guagliumi spent five years in Brazil exploring sugarcane pests in several producing states of the country, including Pernambuco, Sergipe, Bahia, Rio de Janeiro, São Paulo and Paraná. His technical report, entitled *Combate à cigarrinha dos canaviais*, highlights that the insects had an 'extraordinary development' and were the 'most important sugarcane pests in Brazil'. Guagliumi identified two insect species: the so-called sugarcane root frog-hopper (*Sphenorhina liturata*) and the sugarcane leafhopper (*Mahanarva indicata*). To feed on the sap, the insects would inject an enzyme that acts as a toxin into the leaves and necrotises the tissues, initially *in situ* and then progressively around the affected area, forming elongated patches. Such burns reduce the capacity of the leaves to carry out photosynthesis, which, in turn, decreases sap circulation in the leaf lamina, drastically reducing sucrose content in the stalks. Moreover, by covering extensive areas, these spots can cause the leaves – and even the whole plant – to die.[71] Roger Williams, for his part, did not hesitate to state in his preliminary report that 'everyone will agree that the control of these insects is far more complicated than imagined'. Williams introduced the idea of 'economic threshold', that is, the density of a pest at which a control treatment would provide an economic return. He advocated this logic for two reasons: firstly, because 'we need to save money', and secondly, it allows 'delaying the time at which the leafhopper will acquire resistance to the insecticides' used to kill it.[72]

Several means were employed to eliminate the insects. Genetic control (that is, introducing new cultivars) was the most widely used and was always expected to generate excellent results. On the other hand, mechanical control was the most primitive way to fight pests since it required each insect to be manually collected from the sugarcane fields. Chemical control through insecticides was advised and encouraged, but it required specific equipment and trained labour; moreover, it did not work for pests in the larval stage because the insecticides hardly reached them. In such cases, stripping could considerably reduce the number of nymphs hiding under the leaf sheaths. However, the intense application of insecticides endangered the lives of many of the pests' nonhuman enemies, causing other pests to emerge (these were populations kept in check until then). This was also the reason why burning infested fields was not recommended. Despite having taken five to ten years to show the first results, biological combat was the most recommended method by scientists, even though it has not been adopted. Referring to the froghopper, Pietro Guagliumi argued that, to fight the insects and their larvae efficiently, 'there is no other resource but the use of their natural enemies (parasites, predators and fungi), that is, a well-studied and planned "biological control" that allows taking advantage of one or more limiting factors that for years or century have kept the pest in balance with other extrinsic and intrinsic factors, which constitutes the "habitat" of the same species'.[73]

Human–sugar–insect relations

One finds a new way of understanding and narrating the history of sugar in Northeast Brazil by paying attention to insects. This is a history of humans and nonhumans deeply connected with each other and the environment. Although microorganisms and insects are the main nonhuman protagonists in this story, people (a small group of humans comprising capitalists strongly supported by the state) are present throughout. After all, they were the ones who (i) brought sugarcane to Brazil; (ii) promoted intense deforestation altering the ecological balance of thousands of years; (iii) installed an unstable monoculture production model; (iv) created hundreds of sugarcane cultivars with little or almost no long-lasting immune response; and (v) created commissions, crisis committees, research institutes, machinery with state-of-the-art technology – all to propose solutions to the many diseases and pests that they (that is, this small group of humans) were primarily responsible for propagating. In contrast, rural workers – a group of humans whose interests were clearly distinct from those of the elite – concurred at least to: (i) subvert the capitalist monoculture logic, (ii) promote the maintenance of the sites and (iii) retrieve part of the forest balance in the degraded areas through crop diversification.[74] Moreover, these actors helped to promote an agroforestry system logic that precisely corresponded to an attempt to 'imitate' the forest ecological balance.

The theoretical implications of these interactions force us to rethink not only the place of humans in the history of sugar but the history of sugar in America as a whole. We must reassess the role of insects in all places where they became pests. Investigating the history of sugar only from a human point of view (whether that of planters or workers) is something like seeing and not seeing simultaneously. If interactions are all there is, with the entities influencing each other mutually, then their stories cannot be narrated in parallel, as if they did not touch each other. The human social history of sugar is inseparable from its botanical history, which, in turn, is inseparable from the history of the insects that affect both people and plants.

Notes

1. Edward O. Wilson, *The diversity of life*. Cambridge, MA, Harvard University Press, 1992.

2. Thomas Michael Lewinsohn, Leonardo Re Jorge & Paulo Inácio Prado, 'Biodiversidade e interações entre insetos herbívoros e plantas'. In: Kleber Del-Claro & Helena Torezan-Silingardi (eds.) *Ecologia das interações plantas-animais: uma abordagem ecológico-evolutiva*. Rio de Janeiro, 2012, 275–89. See also Mairla Santos Colins, 'Ecologia comportamental da interação inseto-planta', *Boletim PETBio-UFMA* 42 (2017), 5–11.

3. Arno Karlen, *Man and microbes: disease and plagues in history and modern times*. New York, G. P. Putnam's Sons, 1995; John Postgate, *Microbes and man*. Cambridge, MA, Cambridge University Press, 2000.

4. The only exception is perhaps Diogo de Carvalho Cabral (although sugar is not the only or even the biggest of his research subjects), who drew attention to the fact that the sugar economy 'was also made possible by the massape's unwillingness to host nests of leaf-cutting ants' since sugarcane is an 'Asian grass species that prefers waterlogged soils and coincidentally the ones that most hinder the development of leaf-cutting ant nest'; see Diogo de Carvalho Cabral, 'Into the bowels of tropical earth: leaf-cutting ants and the colonial making of agrarian Brazil', *Journal of Historical Geography* 50 (2015), 92–105.

5. José Marcelo M. Ferreira Filho, *Arquitetura espacial da plantation açucareira no Nordeste do Brasil (Pernambuco, século XX)*. Recife-PE, Editora UFPE, 2022.

6. Thomas D. Rogers, *The deepest wounds: a labor and environmental history of sugar in Northeast Brazil*. Chapel Hill, The University of North Carolina Press, 2010.

7. Marcela Heráclio Bezerra, 'Mulheres (des)cobertas, histórias reveladas: relações de trabalho, práticas cotidianas e lutas políticas das trabalhadoras canavieiras na Zona da Mata Sul de Pernambuco (1980–1988)', unpublished master's thesis, UFPE, 2012. See also Marcela Heráclio Bezerra, '"Se é pra ir pra luta, eu vou. Se é pra tá presente, eu tou": presença e atuação das trabalhadoras rurais da Zona da Mata de Pernambuco nos movimentos sociais (1979–1985)'. In: Marcília Gama da Silva & Thiago Nunes Soares (eds.) *Pernambuco na mira do Golpe: mundo do trabalho e dos trabalhadores*, volume 3, Porto Alegre, Editora Fi, 2021, 240–60.

8. Christine Rufino Dabat, *Moradores de engenho: estudo sobre as relações de trabalho e condições de vida dos trabalhadores rurais na zona canavieira de Pernambuco, segundo a literatura, a academia e os próprios atores sociais*, 2nd edn, Recife-PE, UFPE, 2012.

9. Pablo Francisco de Andrade Porfírio, 'O tal de Natal: reivindicação por direito trabalhista e assassinatos de camponeses (Pernambuco, 1963)', *Estudos Históricos* 29, no. 59 (2016), 745–66.

10. Antonio Montenegro, 'História política e cultura do medo', *Revista Esboços* 16, no. 21 (2009), 23–40.

11. Diogo de Carvalho Cabral, '"O Brasil é um grande formigueiro": território, ecologia e a história ambiental da América portuguesa parte 1', *Historia Ambiental Latinoamericana y Caribeña* (HALAC) 3, no. 2 (2014), 467–89.

12. For some attempts to understand the intricacies of nonhuman thought and their ways of reasoning, classifying, dialoguing, interpreting and representing, see for example Peter Wohlleben, *A vida secreta das árvores*. Rio de Janeiro, Sextante, 2017; Marc Bekoff, Colin Allen & Gordon M. Burghardt (eds.) *The cognitive animal: Empirical and theoretical perspectives on animal cognition*. Cambridge, MA, MIT Press, 2002; Robert W. Lurz (ed.), *The philosophy of animal minds*. Cambridge, MA, Cambridge University Press, 2009; Kristin Andrews & Ljiljana Radenovic, 'Animal

Cognition'. In: Hugh LaFollette, Sarah Stroud & John Deigh (eds.) *International Encyclopedia of Ethics*. Haboken, NJ, Wiley-Blackwell, 2013, entrance 050, PDF available at www.kristinandrews.org.

13. Eduardo Gudynas, *Derechos de la naturaleza: Ética biocéntrica y políticas ambientales*. Buenos Aires, Tinta Limón, 2015.

14. Felipe Süssekind, 'Sobre a vida multiespécie', *Revista do Instituto de Estudos Brasileiros* 69 (2018), 159–78.

15. Tobias Rees, *After ethnos*. Durham, NC-London, Duke University Press, 2018; Stelio Marras, 'Por uma antropologia do entre: reflexões sobre um novo e urgente descentramento do humano', *Revista do Instituto de Estudos Brasileiros* 69 (2018), 250–66.

16. Donald Hughes, 'What does environmental history teach?' In: Angela Mendonca, Ana Cunha & Ranjan Chakrabarti (eds.) *Natural resources, sustainability and humanity. A comprehensive view*. Dordrecht, Springer, 2012, 1–15.

17. Ewa Domanska, 'Posthumanist history'. In: Marek Tamm & Peter Burke (eds.) *Debating new approaches to history*. London, Bloomsbury, 2018, 327–52.

18. Luc Ferry, *A nova ordem ecológica: a árvore, o animal e o homem*. Rio de Janeiro, DIFEL, 2009.

19. Charles Berriat-Saint-Prix, 'Rapport et recherches sur les jugements relatifs aux animaux'. In: *Mémoiresde la Société des Antiquaires de France*, vol. VIII, Paris, 1829; Léon Menabrea, *De l'origine, de la forme et de l'esprit des jugements rendus au moyen âge contre les animaux*. Chambéry. Puthod, Imprimeur-Libraire, Éditeur, 1846.

20. Bruno Latour, *Diante de Gaia: oito conferências sobre a natureza no Antropoceno*. São Paulo-Rio de Janeiro, Ubu Editora, 2020.

21. Diogo de Carvalho Cabral, *Na presença da floresta: Mata Atlântica e história colonial*. Rio de Janeiro, Garamond-FAPERJ, 2014.

22. Warren Dean, *With broadax and frebrand: the destruction of the Brazilian Atlantic Rainforest*. Berkeley, University of California Press, 1995.

23. John McNeill, *Something new under the sun: an environmental history of the twentieth-century world*. New York, Norton, 2001, 362.

24. William Cronon, 'The uses of environmental history', *Environmental History Review* 17, no. 3 (1993), 1–22.

25. Shepard Krech III, John R. McNeill & Carolyn Merchant, *Encyclopedia of world environmental history*. New York, Routledge, 2004.

26. Richard C. Foltz, 'Does nature have historical agency? World history, environmental history, and how historians can help save the planet', *The History Teacher* 37, no. 1 – Special Feature Issue: Environmental History and National History Day 2003 Prize Essays (2003), 11.

27. David Christian, *Maps of time: an introduction to big history*. Berkeley, University of California Press, 2004; Fred Spier, *The structure of big history: from the Big Bang until today*. Amsterdam, University of Amsterdam Press, 1996.

28. On the concept of nature, see Clarence Glacken, *Traces on the Rhodian Shore: nature and culture in Western thought from ancient times to the end of the eighteenth century*. Berkeley, Berkeley University Press, 1967; Robert Lenoble, *História da idéia de natureza*. Rio de Janeiro, Edições 70, s/d.; Raymond Williams, *Keywords: a vocabulary of culture and society*. London, Famingo, 1983; Philippe Descola, *Outras naturezas, outras culturas*. São Paulo, Editora 34, 2016.

29. Enrique Leff, 'Construindo a história ambiental da América Latina', *Esboços* 13 (2005), 11–30.

30. Chris Philo & Chris Wilbert, 'Animal spaces, beastly places: an introduction'. In: Chris Philo & Chris Wilbert (eds.) *Animal spaces, beastly places: new geographies of human-animal relations*. London, Routledge, 2000, 1–32.

31. Milton Santos, *A natureza do espaço: técnica e tempo. Razão e emoção*. São Paulo, EdUSP, 2006.

32. Richard White, *The organic machine: the remaking of the Columbia River*. New York, Hill & Wang, 1995; Martha Few & Zeb Tortorici (eds.), *Centering animals in Latin American History*. Durham, NC-London, Duke University Press, 2013.

33. Caio Prado Júnior, *Formação do Brasil contemporâneo: colônia*. São Paulo, Brasiliense, 1922.

34. According to Thomas 'When they gazed at their plantations the planter class saw a laboring landscape – encompassing both human and non-human elements, it was a space to be commanded into material and symbolic productivity', Thomas D. Rogers, 'Laboring landscapes: the environmental, racial, and class worldview of the Brazilian Northeast's sugar elite, 1880s–1930s', *Luso-Brazilian Review* 46, no. 2 (2009), 22–53.

35. Christine Rufino Dabat, 'Sugar cane "plantations" in Pernambuco: from "natural vocation" to ethanol production', *Review (Fernand Braudel Center)* 34, no. 1/2 (2011), 115–38.

36. Gilberto Osório de Andrade & Raquel Caldas Lins Andrade, *Pirapama: um estudo geográfico e histórico*. Recife, Editora Massangana, 1984, 18.

37. Sidney W. Mintz, *Sweetness and power*. New York, Viking Penguin, 1985.

38. Zhi-Qiang Zhang, *Animal biodiversity: an outline of higher-level classification and survey of taxonomic richness*. Auckland, New Zealand, Magnolia Press, 2011; Nigel E. Stork, 'How many species of insects and other terrestrial arthropods are there on earth?', *Annual Review of Entomology* 63, no. 1 (2018), 31–45.

39. Wilhelm Piso & Georg Laet Marggraf, *Historia naturalis Brasiliae . . .* Lugdun. Batavorum; Amstelodami: Franciscum Hackium; Lud. Elzevirium, 1648. 2 v. em 1, Seção de Obras Raras | Biblioteca de Manguinhos, https://www.obrasraras .fiocruz.br.

40. André João Antonil, *Cultura e opulência do Brasil*. Rio de Janeiro, Casa de Souza e Comp., [1711] 1837, 50–51.

41. Henry Koster, *Viagens ao Nordeste do Brasil*. São Paulo-Rio de Janeiro-Recife-Porto Alegre, Companhia Editora Nacional, [1817] 1942, 427–8.

42. Matthew Mulcahy & Stuart Schwartz, 'Nature's battalions: insects as agricultural pests in the early modern Caribbean', *William and Mary Quarterly*, 3rd ser. 75, no. 3 (2018), 433–64.

43. Mike H. Bowie, 'Effects of distance from field edge on aphidophagous insects in a wheat crop and observations on trap design and placement', *International Journal of Pest Management* 45, no. 1 (1999), 69–73.

44. Donald R. Strong, Jr., Earl D. Mccoy & Jorge R. Rey, 'Time and the number of herbivore species: the pests of sugarcane', *Ecology* 58, no. 1 (1977), 167–75.

45. de Carvalho Cabral, 2014, 45.

46. Carlos A. Joly, Jean Paul Metzger & Marcelo Tabarelli, 'Experiences from the Brazilian Atlantic Forest: ecological findings and conservation initiatives', *New Phytologist* 204 (2014), 462–3.

47. Alice Canabrava, 'A grande lavoura'. In: Sérgio Buarque de Holanda (ed.) *História geral da civilização brasileira*, tomo I, volume 2, Rio de Janeiro, Difel, 1963, 198–206.

48. José Clóvis de Andrade, *Escorço histórico de antigas variedades de cana-de-açúcar*. Maceió, Associação dos Plantadores de Cana de Alagoas, 1985.

49. Begonha Bediaga, *Marcado pela própria natureza: o Imperial Instituto Fluminense de Agricultura (1860–1891)*. Rio de Janeiro, FGV, 2014.

50. Frederico Maurício Draenert, 'Moléstia da cana de açúcar na Bahia', *Jornal da Bahia*, 20 de janeiro de 1870.

51. Ladislau Netto, 'Investigações sobre a cultura e a moléstia da cana de açúcar', *Revista Agrícola* 1, no. 3 (1870), 5.

52. Alois Krauss, 'Relatório sobre a doença da cana-de-açúcar na província da Bahia', *Revista Agrícola* 1, no. 4 (1870), 22–7.

53. Adrião Caminha Filho, 'Doenças da canna de assucar no Brasil', *Rodriguésia*. Número especial: annaes da primeira reunião de phytopathologistas do Brasil (1936), 191–6.

54. *Diario de Pernambuco*, 12 de junho de 1926.

55. José Vizioli, 'O Mosaico e outras moléstias da canna em São Paulo'. In: *Relatório apresentado ao Dr. Gabriel Ribeiro dos Santos, Secretário da Agricultura*. São Paulo, Secretaria de Agricultura, Commercio e Obras Públicas do Estado de São Paulo, 1924.

56. Carta do senhor A. M. S. enviada ao *Diario de Pernambuco*, 15 de novembro de 1915.

57. Carlos Moreira, '*Os besouros da canna de assucar*'. Rio de Janeiro, Ministério da Agricultura, Indústria e Commercio, 1916, 17.

58. Geraldo F. de Queiroz, 'A praga dos besouros da cana-de-açúcar', Recife, Comissão de Combate às Pragas da Cana de Açúcar, Publicação no. 18 (1962).

59. Bento Dantas, 'O cupim dos rebolos da cana de açúcar', Recife, IAA, Comissão de Combate às Pragas da Cana de Açúcar, Publicação no. 3, 1957.

60. Bento Dantas, 'Melhore a germinação e aumente a produção com o tratamento fungicida dos rebolos', Recife, Comissão de Combate às Pragas da Cana de Açúcar, Publicação no. 4, 1957.

61. P. Pimentel, 'Levantamento fitossanitário da cana adulta da safra de 1954/5: relatório da parte estatística', Recife, Comissão de Combate às Pragas da Cana de Açúcar, 1956.

62. Carlos Antônio Albert, 'A posição atual da broca da cana de açúcar (Diatraea saccharalis, Fab) no estado de Pernambuco', Recife, Comissão de Combate às Pragas da Cana de Açúcar, Publicação no. 15 (1962). See also Adrião Caminha Filho, *A broca da cana de açúcar (Diatraea saccharalis, Fabricius)*. Rio de Janeiro, Ministério da Agricultura, 1940.

63. Abdon Pereira da Silva, 'Compensa o tratamento térmico em cana-de-açúcar', Recife, Comissão de Combate às Pragas da Cana de Açúcar, Publicação no. 17 (1962). See also, Rev. D. Bento Pickel, 'Lista das moléstias e dos fungos parasitários das plantas cultivadas em Pernambuco', *Rodriguésia*. Número especial: annaes da primeira reunião de phytopathologistas do Brasil (1936); Arsène Puttemans, 'Alguns dados para servir à História da Phytopathologia no Brasil e às primeiras notificações de doenças de vegetaes neste paiz', *Rodriguésia*. Número especial: annaes da primeira reunião de phytopathologistas do Brasil (1936), https://rodriguesia.jbrj.gov.br.

64. Clóvis de Andrade, 1985, 113.

65. Bento Dantas, 'Plano quadrienal para o estudo das principais doenças e pragas da cana e açúcar em Pernambuco', Recife, Instituto do Açúcar e do Álcool – Comissão de Combate às Pragas da Cana de açúcar no Estado de Pernambuco, 1956.

66. *Diario de Pernambuco*, 11 de outubro de 1953.

67. *Diario de Pernambuco*, 3 de outubro de 1954.

68. José Alexandre Ribemboim, Aluízio Ferreira Baltar Filho and Djalma Martins Santa Rosa, 'A cigarrilha da cana-de-açúcar ("Mahanarva indicata" Distant, 1909) em Pernambuco – Primeiros passos para seu controle'. Recife, Comissão de Combate às Pragas da Cana de Açúcar, Publicação no. 20, 1965.

69. Ofício 239/65 da Comissão de Combate às Pragas da Cana de Açúcar no Estado de Pernambuco à Fundação Açucareira de Pernambuco, 1965.

70. Ata da seção extraordinária da Comissão de combate às pestes da cana-de-açúcar no estado de Pernambuco de 10 de março de 1967.

71. Pietro Guagliumi, *Pragas da cana-de-açúcar: Nordeste do Brasil*. Rio de Janeiro, Instituto do Açúcar e do Álcool, 1972/3.

72. Rogers Williams, 'Relatório preliminar sôbre o contrôle da Cigarinha (Maranava indicata) da cana de açúcar'. Recife, 23 de fevereiro de 1967.

73. Pietro Guagliumi, 'Combate à cigarrinha dos canaviais'. Instituto do Açúcar e do Álcool, agosto de 1966.

74. Marcos A. B. Fiqueiredo, 'Prácticas campesinas agroforestales para incrementar la biodiversidad. El caso de Pernambuco, Brasil', *LEISA, Revista de Agroecologia* 35, no. 4 (2019), 5–8.

References

Andrade, Gilberto Osório de, & Raquel Caldas Lins Andrade, *Pirapama: um estudo geográfico e histórico*. Recife, Editora Massangana, 1984.

Andrews, Kristin & Ljiljana Radenovic, 'Animal Cognition'. In: LaFollette, Hugh, Sarah Stroud & John Deigh (eds.) *International Encyclopedia of Ethics*.

Bediaga, Begonha, *Marcado pela própria natureza: o Imperial Instituto Fluminense de Agricultura (1860–1891)*. Rio de Janeiro, FGV, 2014.

Bekoff, Marc, Colin Allen & Gordon M. Burghardt (eds.), *The cognitive animal: Empirical and theoretical perspectives on animal cognition*. Cambridge, MA, MIT Press, 2002.

Bezerra, Marcela Heráclio, 'Mulheres (des)cobertas, histórias reveladas: relações de trabalho, práticas cotidianas e lutas políticas das trabalhadoras canavieiras na Zona da Mata Sul de Pernambuco (1980–1988)', unpublished master's thesis, UFPE, 2012.

Bezerra, Marcela Heráclio, '"Se é pra ir pra luta, eu vou. Se é pra tá presente, eu tou": presença e atuação das trabalhadoras rurais da Zona da Mata de Pernambuco nos movimentos sociais (1979–1985)'. In: Silva, Marcília Gama da & Thiago Nunes Soares (eds.) *Pernambuco na mira do Golpe: mundo do trabalho e dos trabalhadores*, volume 3, Porto Alegre, Editora Fi, 2021.

Bowie, Mike H., 'Effects of distance from field edge on aphidophagous insects in a wheat crop and observations on trap design and placement', *International Journal of Pest Management* 45, no. 1 (1999), 69–73.

Canabrava, Alice, 'A grande lavoura'. In: Sérgio Buarque de Holanda (ed.) *História geral da civilização brasileira*, tomo I, volume 2, Rio de Janeiro, Difel, 1963, 198–206.

Christian, David, *Maps of time: an introduction to big history*. Berkeley, University of California Press, 2004.

Colins, Mairla Santos, 'Ecologia comportamental da interação inseto-planta', *Boletim PETBio-UFMA* 42 (2017), 5–11.

Cronon, William, 'The uses of environmental history', *Environmental History Review* 17, no. 3 (1993), 1–22.

Dabat, Christine Rufino, *Moradores de engenho: estudo sobre as relações de trabalho e condições de vida dos trabalhadores rurais na zona canavieira de Pernambuco, segundo a literatura, a academia e os próprios atores sociais*, 2nd edn, Recife-PE, UFPE, 2012.

Dabat, Christine Rufino, 'Sugar cane "plantations" in Pernambuco: from "natural vocation" to ethanol production', *Review (Fernand Braudel Center)* 34, no. 1/2 (2011), 115–38.

Dean, Warren, *With broadax and frebrand: the destruction of the Brazilian Atlantic Rainforest.* Berkeley, University of California Press, 1995.

de Carvalho Cabral, Diogo, 'Into the bowels of tropical earth: leaf-cutting ants and the colonial making of agrarian Brazil', *Journal of Historical Geography* 50 (2015), 92–105.

de Carvalho Cabral, Diogo, '"O Brasil é um grande formigueiro": território, ecologia e a história ambiental da América portuguesa parte 1', *Historia Ambiental Latinoamericana y Caribeña* (HALAC) 3, no. 2 (2014), 467–89.

de Carvalho Cabral, Diogo, *Na presença da floresta: Mata Atlântica e história colonial.* Rio de Janeiro, Garamond-FAPERJ, 2014.

Descola, Philippe, *Outras naturezas, outras culturas.* São Paulo, Editora 34, 2016.

Domanska, Ewa, 'Posthumanist history'. In: Tamm, Marek, & Peter Burke (eds.) *Debating new approaches to history.* London, Bloomsbury, 2018.

Ferry, Luc, *A nova ordem ecológica: a árvore, o animal e o homem.* Rio de Janeiro, DIFEL, 2009.

Few, Martha & Zeb Tortorici (eds.), *Centering animals in Latin American History.* Durham, NC-London, Duke University Press, 2013.

Figueiredo, Marcos A. B., 'Prácticas campesinas agroforestales para incrementar la biodiversidad. El caso de Pernambuco, Brasil', *LEISA, Revista de Agroecologia* 35, no. 4 (2019), 5–8.

Filho, José Marcelo M. Ferreira, *Arquitetura espacial da plantation açucareira no Nordeste do Brasil (Pernambuco, século XX).* Recife-PE, Editora UFPE, 2022.

Foltz, Richard C., 'Does nature have historical agency? World history, environmental history, and how historians can help save the planet', *The History Teacher* 37, no. 1 – Special Feature Issue: Environmental History and National History Day 2003 Prize Essays (2003), 11.

Glacken, Clarence, *Traces on the Rhodian Shore: nature and culture in Western thought from ancient times to the end of the eighteenth century.* Berkeley, Berkeley University Press, 1967.

Gudynas, Eduardo, *Derechos de la naturaleza: Ética biocéntrica y políticas ambientales.* Buenos Aires, Tinta Limón, 2015.

Hughes, Donald, 'What does environmental history teach?'. In: Mendonça, Angela, Ana Cunha & Ranjan Chakrabarti (eds.) *Natural resources, sustainability and humanity. A comprehensive view.* Dordrecht, Springer, 2012, 1–15.

Joly, Carlos A., Jean Paul Metzger & Marcelo Tabarelli, 'Experiences from the Brazilian Atlantic Forest: ecological findings and conservation initiatives', *New Phytologist* 204 (2014), 462–3.

Júnior, Caio Prado, *Formação do Brasil contemporâneo: colônia*. São Paulo, Brasiliense, 1922.

Karlen, Arno, *Man and microbes: disease and plagues in history and modern times*. New York, G. P. Putnam's Sons, 1995.

Krech III, Shepard, John R. McNeill & Carolyn Merchant, *Encyclopedia of world environmental history*. New York, Routledge, 2004.

Latour, Bruno, *Diante de Gaia: oito conferências sobre a natureza no Antropoceno*. São Paulo-Rio de Janeiro, Ubu Editora, 2020.

Leff, Enrique, 'Construindo a história ambiental da América Latina', *Esboços* 13 (2005), 11–30.

Lenoble, Robert, *História da idéia de natureza*. Rio de Janeiro, Edições 70, s/d.

Lewinsohn, Thomas Michael, Leonardo Re Jorge & Paulo Inácio Prado, 'Biodiversidade e interações entre insetos herbívoros e plantas'. In: Del-Claro, Kleber & Helena Torezan-Silingardi (eds.) *Ecologia das interações plantas-animais: uma abordagem ecológico-evolutiva*. Rio de Janeiro, 2012.

Lurz, Robert W. (ed.), *The philosophy of animal minds*. Cambridge, MA, Cambridge University Press, 2009.

Marras, Stelio, 'Por uma antropologia do entre: reflexões sobre um novo e urgente descentramento do humano', *Revista do Instituto de Estudos Brasileiros* 69 (2018), 250–66.

McNeill, John, *Something new under the sun: an environmental history of the twentieth-century world*. New York, Norton, 2001.

Mintz, Sidney W., *Sweetness and power*. New York, Viking Penguin, 1985.

Montenegro, Antônio, 'História política e cultura do medo', *Revista Esboços* 16, no. 21 (2009), 23–40.

Mulcahy, Matthew & Stuart Schwartz, 'Nature's battalions: insects as agricultural pests in the early modern Caribbean', *William and Mary Quarterly*, 3rd ser. 75, no. 3 (2018), 433–64.

Philo, Chris, & Chris Wilbert, 'Animal spaces, beastly places: an introduction'. In: Philo, Chris & Chris Wilbert (eds.) *Animal spaces, beastly places: new geographies of human-animal relations*. London, Routledge, 2000, 1–32.

Porfílio, Pablo Francisco de Andrade, 'O tal de Natal: reivindicação por direito trabalhista e assassinatos de camponeses (Pernambuco, 1963)', *Estudos Históricos* 29, no. 59 (2016), 745–66.

Postgate, John, *Microbes and man*. Cambridge, MA, Cambridge University Press, 2000.

Rees, Tobias, *After ethnos*. Durham, NC-London, Duke University Press, 2018.

Rogers, Thomas D., *The deepest wounds: a labor and environmental history of sugar in Northeast Brazil*. Chapel Hill, The University of North Carolina Press, 2010.

Rogers, Thomas D., 'Laboring landscapes: the environmental, racial, and class worldview of the Brazilian Northeast's sugar elite, 1880s–1930s', *Luso-Brazilian Review* 46, no. 2 (2009), 22–53.

Santos, Milton, *A natureza do espaço: técnica e tempo. Razão e emoção*. São Paulo, EdUSP, 2006.

Spier, Fred, *The structure of big history: from the Big Bang until today*. Amsterdam, University of Amsterdam Press, 1996.

Stork, Nigel E., 'How many species of insects and other terrestrial arthropods are there on earth?', *Annual Review of Entomology* 63, no. 1 (2018), 31–45.

Strong Jr., Donald R., Earl D. Mccoy & Jorge R. Rey, 'Time and the number of herbivore species: the pests of sugarcane', *Ecology* 58, no. 1 (1977), 167–75.

Süssekind, Felipe, 'Sobre a vida multiespécie', *Revista do Instituto de Estudos Brasileiros* 69 (2018), 159–78.

White, Richard, *The organic machine: the remaking of the Columbia River*. New York, Hill & Wang, 1995.

Williams, Raymond, *Keywords: a vocabulary of culture and society*. London, Famingo, 1983.

Wilson, Edward O., *The diversity of life*. Cambridge, MA, Harvard University Press, 1992.

Wohlleben, Peter, *A vida secreta das árvores*. Rio de Janeiro, Sextante, 2017.

Zhang, Zhi-Qiang, *Animal biodiversity: an outline of higher-level classification and survey of taxonomic richness*. Auckland, New Zealand, Magnolia Press, 2011.

Archival and primary sources

Albert, Carlos Antônio, 'A posição atual da broca da cana de açúcar (Diatraea saccharalis, Fab) no estado de Pernambuco', Recife, Comissão de Combate às Pragas da Cana de Açúcar, Publicação no. 15 (1962).

Andrade, José Clóvis de, *Escorço histórico de antigas variedades de cana-de-açúcar*. Maceió, Associação dos Plantadores de Cana de Alagoas, 1985.

Antonil, André João, *Cultura e opulência do Brasil*. Rio de Janeiro, Casa de Souza e Comp., [1711] 1837, 50–1.

Ata da seção extraordinária da Comissão de combate às pestes da cana-de-açúcar no estado de Pernambuco de 10 de março de 1967.

Berriat-Saint-Prix, Charles, 'Rapport et recherches sur les jugements relatifs aux animaux'. In: *Mémoiresde la Société des Antiquaires de France*, vol. VIII, Paris, 1829.

Carta do senhor A. M. S. enviada ao *Diario de Pernambuco*, 15 de novembro de 1915.

Dantas, Bento, 'O cupim dos rebolos da cana de açúcar', Recife, IAA, Comissão de Combate às Pragas da Cana de Açúcar, Publicação no. 3, 1957.

Dantas, Bento, 'Melhore a germinação e aumente a produção com o tratamento fungicida dos rebolos', Recife, Comissão de Combate às Pragas da Cana de Açúcar, Publicação no. 4, 1957.

Dantas, Bento, 'Plano quadrienal para o estudo das principais doenças e pragas da cana e açúcar em Pernambuco', Recife, Instituto do Açúcar e do Álcool – Comissão de Combate às Pragas da Cana de açúcar no Estado de Pernambuco, 1956.

Diario de Pernambuco, 12 de junho de 1926.

Diario de Pernambuco, 11 de outubro de 1953.

Diario de Pernambuco, 3 de outubro de 1954.

Draenert, Frederico Maurício, 'Moléstia da cana de açúcar na Bahia', *Jornal da Bahia*, 20 de janeiro de 1870.

Filho, Adrião Caminha, *A broca da cana de açúcar (Diatraea saccharalis, Fabricius)*. Rio de Janeiro, Ministério da Agricultura, 1940.

Filho, Adrião Caminha, 'Doenças da canna de assucar no Brasil', *Rodriguésia*. Número especial: annaes da primeira reunião de phytopathologistas do Brasil (1936), 191–6.

Guagliumi, Pietro, 'Combate à cigarrinha dos canaviais'. Instituto do Açúcar e do Álcool, agosto de 1966.

Guagliumi, Pietro, *Pragas da cana-de-açúcar: Nordeste do Brasil*. Rio de Janeiro, Instituto do Açúcar e do Álcool, 1972/3.

Koster, Henry, *Viagens ao Nordeste do Brasil*. São Paulo-Rio de Janeiro-Recife-Porto Alegre, Companhia Editora Nacional, [1817] 1942, 427–8.

Krauss, Alois, 'Relatório sobre a doença da cana-de-açúcar na província da Bahia', *Revista Agrícola* 1, no. 4 (1870), 22–7.

Menabrea, Léon, *De l'origine, de la forme et de l'esprit des jugements rendus au moyen âge contre les animaux*. Chambéry. Puthod, Imprimeur-Libraire, Éditeur, 1846.

Moreira, Carlos, '*Os besouros da canna de assucar*'. Rio de Janeiro, Ministério da Agricultura, Indústria e Commercio, 1916.

Netto, Ladislau, 'Investigações sobre a cultura e a moléstia da cana de açúcar', *Revista Agrícola* 1, no. 3 (1870), 5.

Ofício 239/65 da Comissão de Combate às Pragas da Cana de Açúcar no Estado de Pernambuco à Fundação Açucareira de Pernambuco, 1965.

Pickel, Rev. D. Bento, 'Lista das moléstias e dos fungos parasitários das plantas cultivadas em Pernambuco', *Rodriguésia*. Número especial: annaes da primeira reunião de phytopathologistas do Brasil (1936).

Pimentel, P., 'Levantamento fitossanitário da cana adulta da safra de 1954/5: relatório da parte estatística', Recife, Comissão de Combate às Pragas da Cana de Açúcar, 1956.

Piso, Wilhelm & Georg Laet Marggraf, *Historia naturalis Brasiliae* . . . Lugdun. Batavorum; Amstelodami: Franciscum Hackium; Lud. Elzevirium, 1648. 2 v. em 1, Seção de Obras Raras | Biblioteca de Manguinhos, https://www.obrasraras.fiocruz.br.

Puttemans, Arsène, 'Alguns dados para servir à História da Phytopathologia no Brasil e às primeiras notificações de doenças de vegetaes neste paiz', *Rodriguésia*. Número especial: annaes da primeira reunião de phytopathologistas do Brasil (1936), https:// rodriguesia.jbrj.gov.br.

Queiroz, Geraldo F. de, 'A praga dos besouros da cana-de-açúcar', Recife, Comissão de Combate às Pragas da Cana de Açúcar, Publicação no. 18 (1962).

Ribemboim, José Alexandre, Aluízio Ferreira Baltar Filho & Djalma Martins Santa Rosa, 'A cigarrilha da cana-de-açúcar ("Mahanarva indicata" Distant, 1909) em Pernambuco – Primeiros passos para seu controle'. Recife, Comissão de Combate às Pragas da Cana de Açúcar, Publicação no. 20, 1965.

Silva, Abdon Pereira da, 'Compensa o tratamento térmico em cana-de-açúcar', Recife, Comissão de Combate às Pragas da Cana de Açúcar, Publicação no. 17 (1962).

Vizioli, José, 'O Mosaico e outras moléstias da canna em São Paulo'. In: *Relatório apresentado ao Dr. Gabriel Ribeiro dos Santos, Secretário da Agricultura*. São Paulo, Secretaria de Agricultura, Commercio e Obras Públicas do Estado de São Paulo, 1924.

Williams, Rogers, 'Relatório preliminar sôbre o contrôle da Cigarinha (Maranava indicata) da cana de açúcar'. Recife, 23 de fevereiro de 1967.

Chapter 7

'We are the air, the land, the pampas . . .': *campesino* politics and the other-than-human in highland Bolivia 1970–90

Olivia Arigho-Stiles

We the Aymara, Qhechwa, Camba, Chapaco, Chiquitano, Moxo, Tupiguarani and other campesinos are the rightful owners of this land. We are the seed from which Bolivia was born and we are exiles in our own land. We want to regain our liberty of which we were deprived in 1492, to bring our culture back into favour and, with our own personality, be subjects and not objects of our history . . .

Declaration of the CSUTCB, 1979

This chapter outlines the ways in which the Bolivian peasant union confederation, the *Confederación Sindical Única de Trabajadores Campesinos de Bolivia* (Unified Syndical Confederation of Peasant Workers of Bolivia – CSUTCB), and its assorted *katarista*-influenced departmental and local unions articulated a politics of the other-than-human in the late twentieth century. In applying insights drawn from social anthropology and environmental history, I intend to unsettle distinctions between the 'political as human' and 'nature as nonhuman', opening a space to incorporate the other-than-human within social histories of left-Indigenous struggles. As Dipesh Chakrabarty argues, connecting human and nonhuman scales calls into question existing ways in which the political as a category has been understood.[1] It forces historians to contemplate how other forms of nonhuman life are part of historical processes unfolding at local, national and planetary scale.

In existing scholarship it has been widely documented that the CSUTCB's focus on ethnicity arose out of the *katarista* movement, which itself drew on a long tradition of Aymara ethnic consciousness. *Katarismo* emerged around La Paz in the late 1960s as a political expression of Aymara ethnic consciousness combined with class-based theories of exploitation.[2] It comprised an assortment of political, syndicalist and intellectual currents which in distinct ways denounced the racialised oppression of Indigenous peoples and the colonial character of the Bolivian nation state.[3] This chapter places emphasis on the environment and the nonhuman as an under-explored facet of syndicalist *katarismo*, with a focus on the CSUTCB.[4]

The organisational currents of *katarismo* coagulated in two parties; the MRTK (Movimiento Revolucionario Tupaj Katari) and MITKA (Movimiento Indio Tupaj Katari). The more pragmatic of these, the MRTK emerged under the leadership of Macabeo Chila and CSUTCB syndicalist Jenaro Flores.[5] The MRTK under the direction of Jenaro Flores would become enmeshed with the CSUTCB by the time the latter was founded in 1979.[6] In contrast, radical *katarismo*, sometimes elided with *Indianismo* which asserted an essential difference between Indian and non-Indian subjects, came to fruition under MITKA which was founded on 27 April 1978 in Pacajes, La Paz.[7] MITKA repudiated alliances with conventional left political parties, arguing that none adequately represented the interests of the Indian peasantry, and was far more visceral in its condemnation of the *q'aras* (foreigners) or the middle classes of predominantly Spanish descent in Bolivia.

Kataristas were acutely aware of the ecological dimensions of imperialist commodity extraction, and the importance of other-than human beings – mountains, glaciers, animals, plants – within Indigenous-*campesino* ontologies. The CSUTCB and the wider peasant movement articulated a role for these other-than-human beings, and implicitly contested the erasure of nonhumans from the political by other actors such as the miner-dominated trade union confederation, the *Central Obrera Boliviana* (COB) and national government. It is my objective here to show firstly how the CSUTCB constructed the natural world as a political actor with agency in itself, and secondly, that the new visibility of ecological ontologies in the highland *campesino* movement of the twentieth century must be understood as inextricably linked to the rise of a new anti-neoliberal and decolonial politics. I begin by outlining my methods, then I provide an overview of the rise of the CSUTCB and *katarismo* before assessing their perspective on the other-than-human.

The findings from this chapter derive from an interdisciplinary project employing historical methods that combine the analysis of audio and printed materials. I assess audio recordings of CSUTCB national and regional congresses between 1984 and 1989 housed in the Museo Nacional de Etnografía y Folklore (Museum of Folklore and Ethnography – MUSEF) in La Paz, Bolivia. The congresses were a forum in which internal proposals were debated, grievances aired and strategies adopted. They were central to the functioning of the union and to the dissemination of its political programs. The recordings of these meetings are invaluable in answering the questions posed in this article because they offer extensive insight into the CSUTCB's political and organisational priorities in the 1980s as well as a record of internal frustrations and viewpoints which do not always appear in the organisation's official publications. The meetings represent a space in which Indigenous peasants articulated a political programme linked to state transformation. They thus are a useful addition to the printed materials disseminated by the CSUTCB, which I also examine here.

I listened to sixteen separate recordings of CSUTCB congresses dated between 1984 and 1989 which total around 200 hours of audio time, and many of the meetings spanned several days. There were no available recordings of meetings prior to 1984. I compiled focused transcripts for eight of these recordings. The passages I quote in this chapter are drawn from these selected transcripts. The purpose of the transcripts is not to enable a detailed linguistic analysis but to capture key points arising from these meetings, and especially those that touch on questions of ecology, environment or ethnicity. The transcripts themselves can therefore be considered subjective and interpretive. The majority of the recorded meetings are conducted in Spanish, but the Quechua and Aymara languages occasionally feature, especially in the departmental meetings. I draw my findings from speeches made in the Spanish language only. In many of the recordings it is difficult to discern what is said due to poor audio quality, background noise and music or vocalisations such as whistles and shouts. In others, attendees begin to speak without introducing themselves or with their introductions cut off. Any errors in comprehension, transcription or translation are my own.

I argue that historians can understand these meetings as making partially visible peasant visions of the more-than-human. However, there are limitations to what can be precisely inferred from these audio recordings about these visions. In the twentieth century, many peasant communities were monolingual Quechua or Aymara speakers. The audio recordings of the national meetings are primarily in the Spanish language only, although in departmental meetings the Aymara and Quechua languages also appear to an extent. The views and political positions of Aymara and Quechua speaking union members may not show up explicitly in the national meetings which privileged the Spanish language. Secondly, the recordings do not reflect the entirety of the discursive output of the meetings; listeners are not privy to the conversations which took place outside of the official meeting space for example. Nor of course, do the national meetings capture the full variety of debates held at community, canton and provincial levels prior to the national meetings. Thirdly, the meetings were a place for the CSUTCB to discuss and debate political positions commensurate with a project of state transformation. Indigenous visions of the other-than-human did not always fit easily within these state-focused paradigms. In short, the recordings cannot tell us everything about how Indigenous peasants understood the other-than-human as a political actor beyond the official parameters of the national meeting spaces.

In addition to the recordings, I make extensive use of *katarista* pamphlets, periodicals and publications published in Spanish, principally, *El Katarismo*, Boletín *Chitakolla* and *Collasuyo*, published interviews and documents from the wider peasant movement throughout the 1970s and 1980s derived from archival research in the Archivo y Biblioteca Nacionales de Bolivia (National Archives and Library – ABNB) in Sucre as well as from public collections located in Senate House Library, London, and the Bodleian Library, Oxford (UK). These include documents published by the CSUTCB, as well as nongovernmental organisations such as the Centro de Información y Documentación de Bolivia (Bolivian Centre for Information and Documentation – CIDOB). For material related to agrarian reform I made use of papers in the Walter Guevara Arze archive at the ABNB as well as newspapers from the period. A large number of newspapers and magazines began to be published by *katarista* intellectuals from the 1970s and I argue that it would be an egregious error to see these as disconnected from the syndicalist and *campesino* currents of the movement. However, many recent studies of the CSUTCB and the peasant movement have overlooked the large body of written publications the movement produced, instead privileging ethnographic methods.[8]

The documents I work from in this chapter were produced by humans, and can be said therefore to reflect the human gaze on the natural world.[9] In this sense, to paraphrase Erica Fudge on animal histories, it is a history made by humans speaking about nonhumans.[10] In using written and audio primary sources, I draw inspiration from the work of Australian ethnohistorian Bronwen Douglas regarding the ways in which the presence and agency of Indigenous people infiltrated the writings of sailors, naturalists and artists during scientific voyages to Australia in the nineteenth century.[11] She argues they left 'countersigns', or metaphorical imprints in the representations by colonial actors. In this sense, I attempt to tease out the agencies of other-than-human entities through the dialogue of human actors. In a similar vein, I take inspiration from Diogo de Carvalho and André Vasques Vital's work addressing the role of animals as participants in human textual production.[12] They point out that nonhuman entities such as mosquitoes, ticks, fleas and wasps can be thought of as actively 'feeding in', or shaping the written work of historical actors whose bodies suffered from their bites and other irritating bodily interferences. They argue that nonhuman thinking can be made intelligible through written texts, in what they term 'human-animal emergent textualities'.

I build on this to suggest that we might also understand climatological phenomenon occurring in the past – catastrophes such as droughts, flooding, hail, as well as the everyday presence of nonhumans such as plants, lakes and mountains – to leave their mark in the CSUTCB's discursive claims around the environment articulated through recorded meetings and printed publications. How do we carve a place for these nonhuman entities within the written demands of the *campesino* movements, whose political worlds were intimately connected with them? How do we understand their role in the demands of the CSUTCB? Anglo-Eurocentric epistemes have constructed these other-than-human beings as existing outside 'politics', a realm understood to relate to the human alone. I argue that these documents reflect a vision of the nonhuman within a Indigenous-peasant world that saw the natural world as imbued with its own life-force, needs and agency. To echo Dipesh Chakrabarty, this offers the possibility to expand the political field beyond the secular limits imposed by European thought.[13]

Conceptualising the other-than-human in Latin America

Scholars have noted that unsettled boundaries – or 'leaky' distinctions to use Donna Harraway's term from *A Cyborg Manifesto*[14] – between the other-than-human and human in Latin America long preoccupied the colonial imaginary.[15] Interactions between humans and animals, and indeed other nonhuman beings have indeed been central to narratives of Latin American histories.[16] The sixteenth-century Spanish Jesuit missionary José de Acosta, for example, extensively chronicled relations between people and animals in South America, noting that the inhabitants of then-Peru 'worship bears, lions, tigers and snakes to prevent them from harming them'. Acosta was baffled by the ascribing of agency to nonhuman beings by the Indigenous peoples he encountered: 'They make another offering that is no less absurd, which is to pull out their eyelashes or eyebrows and offer them to the sun, or to the hills, and *apachitas* (piles of stones which mark sacred, liminal spaces in Andean mountains) to the winds or other things that they fear'.[17]

De Acosta's account reveals how the ritualised offerings practised by Indigenous peoples endowed the other-than-human beings – the hills and the sun – with sentience. It therefore raises the theoretical question of how to relate Indigenous ontologies with geographical conceptualisations of nonhuman agency. Hailstorms, floods and animal-beings perhaps offer a different exercise in conceptualising agency from that of intangible spiritual entities, or earth-beings, such as *achachilas* (Aymara ancestral mountain spirits). Mario Blaser argues that the tensions between notions of more-than-human agency and Indigeneity can be partially reconciled through a field of enquiry he terms 'political ontology', which entails a commitment to the pluriverse or 'the partially connected unfolding of worlds'.[18] He proposes that envisaging a political space defined by the interaction of multiple ontologies, other-than-human and human, goes some way to collapsing the tensions between geographical posthumanism and Indigenous perspectives on the nonhuman derived from ethnography. Through this chapter I address a connected question; building on Blaser, how do nonhuman beings emerge within an Indigenous-*campesino* 'pluriversal' politics in Latin America?

Spanish colonisation of Bolivia from the outset was bound up with a violent reordering and division of space and territory.[19] The existence of nonhuman agency and natural space is thus an important historical dimension to decolonial struggles in Latin America. I argue that the *katarista* peasant movement developed a politics of the environment which explicitly recognised the relationship between coloniality and the environment and acknowledged that colonialism had deprived both humans and other-than-humans of agency. In making this point, I engage closely with the rich body of research into animal-human histories, and particularly Philip Howell's work on 'ascribed agencies' in relation to animal history.[20] Howell makes the point that the question is not whether nonhuman animals have agency, because they certainly do, but what form this takes in historical scholarship. Ascribed agencies are characterised, for example, as narratives written by humans about named animals.[21] We might apply this to other-than-human beings more widely. Accordingly, this chapter is about human actors speaking about nonhuman beings in terms which explicitly recognise their agency as historical subjects.

An additional conceptual ballast for this chapter's arguments derives from the large body of anthropological literature on Indigenous cosmologies in Latin America. In recent decades, the Latin American ethnographic record has been clear on the far-reaching relations between humans and nonhuman beings and has problematised the nature-culture divide embedded in dominant Western epistemologies.[22] One focus of this literature has been on how environmental conflicts over extractive projects, which accelerated in the neoliberal era, have given new visibility to Indigenous perspectives on the natural world.[23] There is thus a close link posited between indigeneity and the natural world. These anthropological studies also share parallels with the theories of human–nonhuman relations based on 'relational' ontologies arising from a field known as Science and Technology Studies (STS), exemplified in Bruno Latour's actor-network theory, for example,[24] or Isabelle Stengers's 'cosmopolitics'.[25]

However, the perspectives outlined here have not been applied to the past specifically, nor in analysing the ways in which human–animal–landscape relations have changed over time (or not) and formed part of concurrent historical processes. In the Andean case, there has been little attempt by historians to grapple with the question of other-than-human beings and nature *as historical actors*. These anthropological approaches could allow historians to accommodate nonhumans within historical narratives as actors with agency. From a human-centred historical perspective, engaging with emergent multidisciplinary theories on the nonhuman serves to enrich the human stories under scrutiny by giving full scope to the plethora of relations with nonhumans that mark human life. A question I explore here is, then, the possibility to centre the nonhuman in the discourse and activity of the organised *campesino* movement in Bolivia. How could this enrich understanding of the trajectory of peasant-Indigenous politics in the region?

To address this, I apply the insights of the anthropological work by Marisol De la Cadena to an historical analysis of the peasant movement between 1970 and 1990 in highland Bolivia. Her work is particularly propitious for the purposes of this study because it is situated at the porous margins of organised peasant politics and highland Peruvian Indigenous worlds. She argues that in positioning nonhuman entities as political actors, ecological struggles waged by Indigenous peoples (such as in mining disputes concerning the sacred mountain Ausangate, Peru) hence have the potential to 'exceed the notion of politics as usual'.[26] 'In the story I am telling', De la Cadena explains,

> land was 'not only' the agricultural ground from where peasants earned a living – it was also the place that *tirakuna* [people of the *ayllu*] with *runakuna* [nonhuman people] were . . . As the convergence of both, land was the term that allowed the alliance between radically different and partially connected worlds. The world inhabited by leftist politicians was public; the world of the *ayllu*, composed of humans

and other-than-human beings, was not – not – or was only public in translation.[27]

In other words, terms such as 'land' can possess multiple meanings which are deployed in selective ways in the peasant movements' interactions with the state and other actors. The world of conventional politics is public; in other words, it is official, state-oriented and marked by colonial inheritances. In doing so, De la Cadena's work complicates approaches to peasant movements which, if seen through a Eurocentric gaze, may find them belonging to a solely material arena, or would find incommensurate the presence of nonhuman political actors such as mountains.

Bolivia's powerful social movements have commanded significant interest from anthropologists and political scientists in recent decades following to the highly successful 'Indigenous politics' of the ex-president Evo Morales and his social movement-backed party the *Movimiento al Socialismo*. Indeed, the rise of Indigenous political movements in Latin America in the 1990s has been closely linked with an environmental agenda.[28] In the Morales era (2006–19), *'buen vivir'* (*'suma qamaña'* in Aymara) or living well in harmony with nature was consolidated as a guiding principle of the decolonising Bolivian state, at least at the discursive level.[29] This is exemplified in the promulgation of a 2009 Plurinational Constitution and the 2010 'Law of the Rights of Mother Earth' which enshrined a defence of the rights of Mother Earth, or Pachamama.[30] This was achieved after sustained mobilisation by a coalition of Indigenous, *campesino* and assorted social movements in the cycle of anti-neoliberal protests of 2001–3.[31]

But what were the historical origins of this shift? What are the origins of the peasant movement's adoption of Indigenous cosmovisions within its political objectives? This chapter addresses this lacuna by tracing back the genealogy of the twenty-first-century 'Indigenous awakening' and its ecological dimensions to the 1970s.

Bolivia offers a particularly compelling case study for the emergence of organised left-*campesino* movements and their articulation of Indigenous ecological ontologies. Agriculture employed approximately 46 per cent of the country's labour force in 1987.[32] The landscapes and topography in which Bolivian peasants worked varied considerably, with the bulk of agricultural production taking place in the central valleys around Cochabamba which are warm and fertile. The Bolivian *altiplano* meanwhile reaches heights of 4,000 metres and is prone to the adverse effects of floods, droughts, avalanches, frost and hailstorms, which particularly affect the livelihoods of rural communities. The Altiplano and sub-Andean regions together comprise around 40 per cent of Bolivia's total territory.[33] Natural disasters made agriculture extremely challenging throughout the twentieth century; across the valleys and highlands, soil erosion was a persistent problem.[34] The later decades of the twentieth century in particular generated a number of acute challenges for *campesinos* and other workers in Bolivia.

Throughout this period, the Indigenous-*campesino* movement in Bolivia was keenly attentive to the natural indicators of climate change occurring in the Andes. This is reflected in the CSUTCB's debates around the environment in the 1980s which took place in the context of the 1982–4 El Niño, one of the greatest climatological catastrophes in recorded history. The term El Niño ('the Christ Child') was originally used by fishermen in northern Peru to refer to the warm ocean current that usually appears around December and lasts for several months, causing a number of changes to fish stocks.[35] In 1982 sea levels rose, precipitating a series of subtle but important ecological shifts which effected almost all parts of the world. It was especially devastating in the eastern Pacific and in Peru, Chile, Ecuador and Bolivia, where it caused torrential flooding in coastal areas coupled with severe drought in highland areas. Homes were destroyed and agricultural and fishing production was devastated. In the Bolivian highlands, it resulted in a severe and prolonged drought as well as the melting of glaciers. The loss to the world economy in 1982–3 amounted to over 8 billion dollars, with losses of 241 million dollars in Bolivia.[36] Analysing the CSUTCB's mobilisation around ecological concerns in the 1980s therefore also gives unique insight into how Indigenous-peasant movements in Bolivia reacted to extreme climate oscillations such as the 1982 El Niño before scientific studies had acknowledged its effects.

Origins of the *campesino* movement and the rise of the CSUTCB

The CSUTCB and related *katarista* syndicalist tendencies arose from a fractious history of peasant unions in Bolivia which were tied to state-led development initiatives.[37] Unions acquired considerable significance in the years following the 1953 agrarian reform, achieved as part of the 1952 National Revolution, steered by the political party *Movimiento Nacionalista Revolucionario* (National Revolutionary Movement – MNR) and a coalition of miners, peasants and reformist middle classes.[38] I will dwell here on agrarian reform because it emerges frequently in CSUTCB discourse, often as a conduit for wider grievances within the peasant movement. Indeed, the first conclusion passed at the Congress of Women *Campesinas* 'Bartolina

Sisas' (named after the anticolonial leader and partner of Tupaj Katari) was a condemnation of the minifundisation of land which had occurred as a result of agrarian reform.[39] The Aymara leader Tupaj Katari was executed by the Spanish on 15 November 1781 after leading a rebellion against Spanish rule in La Paz and his body was dismembered into four parts and scattered. Kataristas sought to recover histories that ran counter to the homogenising narratives of the Bolivian nation state.[40] In symbolic terms this was reflected in the recovery of Tupaj Katari as an anticolonial figurehead.

The abiding refrain of the *katarista* movement was 'we are not the peasants of 1952', which underscores *Katarismo*'s repudiation of what was perceived to be a deficient revolution.[41] The post-revolutionary state was able to install itself in peripheral rural areas (coded as Indigenous) through its control over official peasant unions which impeded the development of autonomous peasant organisations. In a dynamic of incorporation and co-optation, these unions were intended to replace traditional modes of Indigenous organisations such as *ayllus*, or communities. In areas where unions had existed prior, the dynamics of the post-revolutionary regime changed their structure and purpose and turned them into interlocutors between peasant and state via a rural bureaucracy loyal to the MNR leadership.[42] State appointed *dirigentes* controlled the votes of local *sindicatos*, and ultimately shored up the peasantry as a reliable constituency of the MNR. Peasants were thus freed from domination by *hacendados* but found themselves controlled by unions as the intermediaries of the post-revolutionary state. In this way, agrarian reform, according to Hurtado,[43] for more than twenty years served as the most important instrument of state domination.

There was also a racial logic driving the state's drive to transform rural space and modernise Indigenous peoples. Expanding the reach of the state into the countryside was a way of civilising both the landscape and the Indian populations who lived in it, thereby addressing the widely perceived problem of Indian 'backwardness' and rural under-development. Accordingly, the term peasant (*campesino*) was officially adopted by the architects of the 1952 revolution as part of a homogenising *mestizaje* vision of Bolivian society which sought to expunge the nation's Indian elements.[44] The terms *indígena* (Indigenous) and *indio* (Indian) were deemed feudal and pejorative, and so were replaced in state and popular discourse with the ostensibly modern, race-blind label *campesino* in a process of *campesinization*. An article published under the alias 'Huascar' on 26 July 1953 in national newspaper *La Nación* declared that 'agrarian reform is the policy of liquidating the indigenous as indigenous'. Agrarian reform would 'destroy and eliminate forever the condition of misery, hunger and the condition of a colonial country'. The article went on to claim that it would boost productivity in the countryside, 'elevating [the Indigenous] to the category of producer and consumer citizen'.[45] Agrarian reform was thus part of a racial project which aimed to establish a system of agrarian capitalism and transform Indians into rural proletarians within it.

Although the Indian communities of the highlands benefited from the redistribution of land, the devaluation of *ayllus* and the privileging of individual landownership (which eventually led to excessive smallholding) were perceived to be culturally and economically damaging by peasants. Publications and recordings from CSUTCB general meetings in the 1980s show that agrarian reform continued as a problem for the peasantry, and indeed to this day due to its unequal application.[46] Its 1983 Political and Syndicalist Thesis states that agrarian reform

> culminated a long process of fragmentation of our communitarian organisational forms . . . our oppressors have advocated by various means a systematic dispossession of our historical identity. They tried to make us forget our true origins and reduce ourselves only to peasants without personality, without history and without identity.[47]

Several speakers at the Third Congress of Peasant Unity in 1987 also raised agrarian reform in the historical context of peasant exploitation. An unnamed speaker criticised agrarian reform as both an attack against the livelihoods and value system of peasants. 'Agrarian reform legalised dispossession, abuse and discrimination, created more individualised agrarian labour, "minifundised" our plots', the speaker states. 'On the other hand, it strengthened new large landowners of the agro-industrial and rancher type in eastern Bolivia, who exploit a mass of sugar cane harvesters [*zafreros*], cotton pickers, farmers, etc., and are favoured with all kinds of advantages from the state. Agrarian reform has not even reached many areas'.

Agrarian reform was placed in a continuum of colonial exploitation against humans and other-than-humans. The same speaker states, 'large landowners have continued to exploit Chiquitania, Guarani [eastern lowland regions], etc under a colonial system and methods, *plundering and destroying the ecology of the tropical plains*' (emphasis added), undergirding how the expansion of agrarian capitalism was perceived to be environmentally destructive. Another unidentified speaker asked, 'What happened to agrarian reform? The redistribution of the land was limited, the fundamental problem of improving the living conditions of the peasant, *compañeros* . . . was forgotten'. He continues, 'It is a government in favour of big business, for the large businesses of this country and for the

transnationals [. . .] which have plundered this country's wealth'. He con-
cludes, 'The peasant problem is a national problem'.

In 1970, *katarista* Aymara leaders Jenaro Flores Santos and Macabeo
Chila were elected to the senior positions in the peasant unions in La Paz
and Oruro departments respectively.[48] Their arrival heralded a rupture
with the official status quo. In symbolic terms, they added 'TK' to the end of
the union name in honour of Tupac Katari.[49] In June 1979, the *Central Obrera
Boliviana* (Bolivian Workers Central – COB), the national trade union
federation, sponsored the First Congress for Peasant Unity in La Paz. The
CSUTCB was founded during this congress as the culmination of efforts by
katarista peasants to build an autonomous peasant movement. From its
founding, it was headed by Secretary General Jenaro Flores, who came from
Sicasica, La Paz, the birthplace of Tupaj Katari two centuries earlier. In 1980
he would also run unsuccessfully as presidential candidate with the MRTK.
With the COB leadership murdered, in hiding or imprisoned following the
coup by Garcia Meza between 17 July 1980 and 19 June 1981, Jenaro Flores
became de facto leader of the COB, the first time that an Indigenous-peasant
leader had ascended to the leadership.[50] It cemented the link between the
CSUTCB and the broader workers' movement. In an interview conducted
shortly after the coup in 1980, Flores declared, for example, 'they previously tried to alienate the workers from the peasants . . . But now there is a
close relationship between mining workers and peasants, because ultimately they are also from peasant extraction'.[51]

The CSUTCB and *campesino* ecological ontologies

I will here dwell closely on key passages from CSUTCB and peasant movement discourses on the natural world. Examining how and why the
CSUTCB articulated a discourse on the natural world is crucial in understanding the importance of the environment for the Indigenous-peasant
movement in Bolivia more widely. As I demonstrate, the CSUTCB's stance
on the environment points to the coalescence of environmental and
Indigenous politics within the organised peasant movement in Bolivia in
the late twentieth century. In the 1980s this emphasis on ethnic identity
became especially pronounced. At the Third Congress of Peasant Unity in
1987, interviews were conducted on tape recorder prior to the main meetings apparently for later dissemination on radio programmes. Javier
Condoreno, the executive secretary of the Sole Departamental Federation
of Peasant Workers Tupac Katari of La Paz states, 'we have to become aware
today more than ever *compañeros*, become aware of our own cultural
identity as a people, as a nation, as a culture'. He added, '[This congress]

marks a new historical milestone where nationalities, or oppressed nations, can consider a political thesis . . . and come together in this Third National Congress'.

Although it claimed to represent all Indigenous nations of Bolivia, the CSUTCB was dominated by Aymara-speaking peasants of the altiplano with lowland Indigenous groups having an especially negligible presence. This was despite the sustained focus on uniting all Indigenous peoples of Bolivia by emphasising a common experience of colonisation. The CSUTCB declared for example, 'The Aymara, Quechua, Cambas, Chapacos, Chiquitanos, Canichanas, Itonamas, Cayubabas, Ayoréodes, Guaranis, etc, peasants are the rightful owners of this land. We are the seed from where Bolivia was born but, even today, they treat us as exiles [*desterrados*] in our own land'.[52] It is perhaps interesting to note here the CSUTCB's use of '*desterrados*' rather than '*exiliados*' to convey exile. *Desterrar* has roots in the Latin for land (terra), and therefore conveys a more visceral sense of being separated from earth and land, rather than from the formal boundaries of the state. Ethnographic accounts of rituals practised by Quechua-speaking peasants stress the relations of reciprocity and mutual dependence between peasants and their physical environment. Ethnomusicologist Henry Stobart describes how peasants in Macha, Northern Potosí believe that their crops are sentient and will 'weep' (*waqay* in Quechua) if not cared for properly.[53] Meanwhile John McNeish observes how the physical environment acts as a repository of history for the highland Aymara community of Santuario de Quillacas, Oruro.[54] Mountains, hills and even the weather and seasons were understood to be intimately connected with local people's daily life and to provide a tangible connection with ancestors. Anthropologist and ex-*katarista* Simon Yampara characterises the Andean interaction between humans and their natural environment (*Jaqi-pachamama*) as one of reciprocity; 'nature' must receive offerings if it is to provide sustenance to humans. Moreover, humans must constantly be sensitive to their surroundings; forecasting weather, planting crops and harvests rely on the observations of stars, planets, flora and fauna as well as interpreting dreams, reading coca leaves and relations with *achachilas* (mountain spirits) and Pachamama.[55]

This belief in deep human-agricultural and natural environment interconnections is reflected in the political demands and criticism made by the CSUTCB in the 1980s. The report of the outgoing Executive Committee to the IV Ordinary National Congress 1988–9 contains a section on '*Tierra – territorio – libertad y poder*' (Land – territory – freedom and power) in which the CSUTCB demands, 'We want the preservation of the environment of the natural resources of flora and fauna, of the air we breathe, of the forests and jungle, because without them we cannot live'.[56] In addition, a proposal from the Red Offensive of Tupakatarista Ayllus, (*Ofensiva Roja de Ayllus Tupakataristas* – ORAT) to the IV Ordinary Congress of the CSUTCB in 1988 (passed by minority) exemplifies the belief in human–nature reciprocity as an integral part of the peasant's social world. Their proposals include a subsection entitled '*Pachamama o muerte*' (Pachamama or death) in which the group proclaim,

> since before Christ, we have been worshipping the hills, *Pukaras*, *Wak'as*, stones, *apachitas*, in the ceremonial and cosmic places, we are older than Western Christianity. Like our grandparents both in the time of Tiwanakinses [pre-Inca civilisation around Tiwanaku] and the Incas, they made sacrifices with gold and silver, with coloured wool, coca, etc. every year to our Tata Inti (Sun), moon, stars, and the Pachamama, which endure from generation to generation until this day.[57]

Grievances at the volume of food imports in Bolivia emerges as an equally germane issue in the group's proposals. In emotive rhetoric they lament, 'unfortunately it is terrible that instead of producing wheat, barley, quinoa, *kañawa*, beans, rice, maize, cassava, banana, potato, tubers, beans, etc, we are living off the foreigners and waiting for the *gringos* to send us their rotten leftovers from their rubbish dumps, [so] we are falling into food dependency'. The 1980s was a particularly fraught time for agricultural production in Bolivia. In 1983–4 severe droughts in the highlands and flooding in the lowlands caused so much damage that agricultural output was decimated, meaning substantial amounts of food had to be imported for many years afterwards. These natural disasters are explained by ORAT as symptoms of Pachamama's wilful anger and vengeance. The group states, 'the communities that we live in, "MACH'AS" [a communal unit comprising several *ayllus*], no longer produce crops, the animals die, it no longer rains and day by day we receive the punishments of our Mother Nature with hail, frost and drought. The once fertile Pachamama becomes sterile and no longer gives her produce to us native children as before'.[58]

The statement goes on to imbue acts of agrarian labour with cosmological importance expressed in visions of apocalypse:

> Another of the most important points that we must touch is to plough the earth with a cosmic consciousness, and to produce more and more, to accumulate and save that production in the *Pirwas* [storage barns], because for us, the discriminated and exploited, the most difficult days are coming, that is to say we are on the eve of the *awqa-pacha*

or the *pachakuti*, that is what the birds, the stones, the rivers, the hills, the rains and the lightning announce to us.

It continues by connecting transcendent social change with a politics of landscape: 'It is a necessity and an urgency that there must be the return of the last Inca tupak katari for a telluric transformation to our ancestral homeland'. *Pachakuti* is a well-documented concept in literature on Andean cosmovisions. *Pacha* refers to earth, time and space, and *kuti* refers to time or reversal but the concept can acquire different meanings and is often used to refer to a shift in time, revolution or profound upheaval in the cosmos.[59]

By 1985 CSUTCB unity was greatly weakened by a series of internecine struggles over political allegiances, as the frequently combative meetings from around this time attest. At the Third National Congress in 1985, the *katarista* faction headed by Jenaro Flores clashed with the *Movimiento Campesino de Base* (MCB) headed by Victor Morales which was more closely aligned to the traditional left and the COB.[60] At the 1987 Third Congress of Peasant Unity in the city of Cochabamba in 1987, a *compañero* named Victor Mercado stated optimistically, 'We believe that this Congress is going to come up with important solutions to lead the way, to seek the definitive liberation of our country. We consider this congress to be important, since it is in a difficult political moment'.[61]

From its founding, the CSUTCB was anxious to downplay the class stratification within the ranks of its membership by highlighting the overarching enemy of capitalism for both landless labourers and land-owning peasants. The CSUTCB's 1983 Political Thesis states defensively, 'We are far from petty bourgeois because we own plots of land. The land is for us primarily a condition of production and an inheritance from our ancestors, rather than a means of production'. Land is here conceptualised as a spatial and historical entity, rather than purely as an economic resource. In this we might read an attempt by CSUTCB protagonists to expand the parameters of what land signified in the conventional politics of the 1980s; as a resource subject to legally defined ownership and inhabited by human political actors. The CSUTCB statement instead invokes land as a dynamic and contingent space, articulated as representing a 'condition' of production, a phrase which makes possible alternative and multiple readings of 'land'.[62]

In July 1988, the First Extraordinary Congress of the CSUTCB had been held at the request of different departmental organisations and regional meetings of the peasant union movement. It was intended to revoke the mandate of the National Executive Committee of the CSUTCB elections the previous year, and it was in this congress that Genaro Flores was ousted as leader, heralding the zenith of the *katarista* domination within the organisation.[63] Nonetheless, the *katarista* emphasis on Indigenous cosmovisions and spiritualistic appeals to the natural world are widely present. As unnamed speaker at the meeting declares, 'We are aymaras, quechuas, amazónicos, guarani, we are from Bolivia, *we are the air, water, we are the land . . . the pampas*' (emphasis added). He continues, 'we are the communitarian civilisation, we aymaras, quechuas, amazónicos, guarani. We are *campesinos*'.[64] It underscores how grassroots members of the CSUTCB perceived a close connection between Indigenous-peasant identities and the natural world. However, more drastically, in asserting that *campesinos* do not only work the land for example, but embody it, the speaker's words suggest that a more profound ontological shift in the CSUTCB was going on. For the CSUTCB grassroots, imperialist exploitation is invoked not only as an economic assault on natural resources, but a historical process which conjures the suffering of the other-than-human. At the CSUTCB general meeting in the city of Potosi, in July 1988, an unnamed speaker urged his *compañeros* to defend their lands, stating,

> We, as natives of these lands of Kollasuyo, have been usurped by people who came to these lands. We are the ones who were born in these lands and these *k'aras* [foreigners] do not truly reflect this position. And those who came from another place, with another form of reflection, another way of life, impose their ways and customs.

He goes on to make the following remarks: 'there are two well defined interests; capitalism, although we should say colonialism. And feudalism – to exploit our riches, our lands, our Pachamama'. In his words, 'we have seen with our eyes them taking away the gold, silver, everything that exists in this country. This Andean country Bolivia, which was formerly Kollasuyo, was a rich country, as well as its inhabitants . . . [and now] we are beggars'.[65]

Conceptions of Pachamama as both victim and agent became a prevailing theme in the *katarista* movement more widely in the 1980s. The third issue (February 1986) of 'Boletín Chitakolla', a monthly *katarista* magazine published by the *Centro de Formacion e Investigacion sobre las Culturas Indias*, included an article entitled '*Dialectica de la Naturaleza*', which itself was taken from the 1979 book *Indianidad y Revolución (Raíz y vigencia de la indianidad)* by the Peruvian intellectual Virgilio Roel Pineda. It proclaims how 'the stars, the clouds, the hills, the seas, the lagoons, the ponds, the rivers, the valleys, the trees, the stones, the condors, the birds, the butterflies, the flowers, in short, everything that belongs to Pachamama maintains a constant and mutual reciprocal influence'.[66] The extract as a whole explicitly connects the preservation of human and nonhuman life with an anti-imperialist politics. It centres animals not so much as objects, but as agents and active allies in resistance to Western bellicosity. We can see here how categorical distinctions between species, between the natural world and humans, were rendered ambiguous:

> As a counterpart to Western aggressiveness, we Indians know that if we do not return what we have taken from the land, that if we do not treat Pachamama well, that if we attack the beautiful animals that are also her beloved children, it will happen that, in her anger, the farming areas will turn into deserts and the animals will disappear. To avoid this immense universal tragedy, today we must stop the criminal hand of the West which is destroying the fields, the llamas, the alpacas and the vicunas, and that in this way will destroy our families, up to the complete annihilation of the entire human race.[67]

Conclusion

This chapter has shown that from the 1980s, the CSUTCB and its *katarista* affiliates centred Indigenous concepts such as Pachamama, *achachilas*, *w'akas* and others within their critiques of colonial capitalism. This is important because it marks a new formulation of ecological ontologies within the peasant movement. It shows that the rise of the CSUTCB represents a crucial departure from the post-revolutionary erasure of Indigenous identities. A close reading of the organisation's documents reveals that they articulated an Indigenous vision of natural resource management within the parameters of organised labour (that is, the *sindicato*).

I conclude that the decolonial politics of the *katarista-campesino* movement in Bolivia dislodged dominant epistemologies to introduce new actors – animals, mountains, plants, glaciers – into the political arena. Further still, we can see these new actors can be thought of as shaping the CSUTCB's demands, of showing up within their words and political articulations. Embedded within the CSUTCB's critiques of imperialism and internal colonisation was a recognition that ecological destruction was connected with modes of domination, both epistemological and material. But by referring to the agency of nonhuman actors such as mountains, Pachamama for example, the CSUTCB went further in crafting pathways for the entry of the nonhuman into the realm of the political, paving the way for the later state-driven decolonisation attempts of the Morales era. This ultimately suggests that the rise of the 'other than human' as political actor formed the crux of a decolonial and anti-neoliberal politics of contestation in late twentieth-century Bolivia.

Notes

1. Dipesh Chaakrabarty, *The climate of history in a planetary age*. Chicago, University of Chicago Press, 2021, 8.

2. Xavier Albó, 'El retorno del indio', *Revista Andina* 9, no. 2 (1991), 299–366; James Malloy & Richard Thorn, *Beyond the revolution: Bolivia since 1952*. Pittsburgh, PA, University of Pittsburgh Press, 1971; Silvia Rivera Cusicanqui, *Oppressed but not defeated: peasant struggles among the Aymara and Quechua in Bolivia, 1900–1980*. Geneva, UNRISD, 1987; Javier Hurtado, *El katarismo*. La Paz, Hisbol, 1986; Rafael Archondo, 'Comunidad y divergencia de miradas en el katarismo', *Umbrales* 7 (2000), 120–32; Nicomedes Sejas Terrazas, *Katarismo y descolonizacion. La emergencia democratica del indio*. Bolivia, Imprenta Stigma, 2014; José Antonio Lucero, 'Fanon in the Andes: Fausto Reinaga, indianismo, and the black Atlantic', *International Journal of Critical Indigenous Studies* 1, no. 1 (2000); Donna Van Cott, *Radical democracy in the Andes*. Cambridge, Cambridge University Press; 2009; Susan Eckstein, 'Transformation of a "revolution from below". Bolivia and international capital', *Comparative Studies in Society and History* 25, no. 1 (1983), 105–35.

3. Carlos Macusaya Cruz, 'Indianismo y katarismo en el siglo XX: apuntes históri-cos'. In: Pedro Canales Tapia (ed.) *El pensamiento y la lucha: los pueblos indígenas en América Latina: organización y discusiones con trascendencia*. La Paz, Ariadna Ediciones, 2018; Fernando Calderon & Jorge Dandler (eds.), *Bolivia: la fuerza histórica del campesinado*. Cochabamba, CERES, 1984.

4. Primary sources include CSUTCB-1980: *Entrevista a Jenaro Flores*, órgano informativo en el exterior. Año1, no. 1 octubre. CSUTCB-1987: *III Congreso de Unidad Campesina, Confederación Sindical Única de Trabajadores Campesinos de Bolivia*, MUSEF, La Paz, Digital audio recording. CSUTCB-1988a: *I ampliado de la Confederación Sindical Única de Trabajadores Campesinos de Bolivia*, MUSEF, La Paz. Digital audio recording. SUTCB-1988b: *I Congreso Extraordinario de la Confederación Sindical Única de Trabajadores Campesinos de Bolivia*, MUSEF, La Paz, Digital audio recording. CSUTCB-1989a: *1er Ampliado nacional de la Confederación Sindical Única de Trabajadores Campesinos de Bolivia*. MUSEF, La Paz, Digital audio recording. CSUTCB-1989b: *Informe del Comite Ejecutivo saliente al IV Congreso Nacional Ordinario de la CSUTCB*, CEDOIN, Bolivia. CSUTCB-1992: *4to Congreso Confederación Sindical Única de Trabajadores Campesinos de Bolivia*, MUSEF, La Paz. Digital audio recording. El Diario de La Paz (January–May 1973) (British Library), *Katarismo* (after the first edition it is called El Katarismo) 1985–6. Archivo y Biblioteca Nacionales de Bolivia, Sucre. *La Nación*, 1953, Selected issues in Walter Guevara Arce Collection. *Los Tiempos* (Cochabamba) January–December 1968 (British Library), *Presencia* (La Paz) Selected editions 1978–January 1980 (Biblioteca Municipal de La Paz); Manifiesto de Tiahuanaco. La Paz. 30 de Julio de 1973 – retrieved from the James Dunkerley special collection at Institute of Latin American Studies (London).

5. Silvia Rivera Cusicanqui, 'Luchas campesinas contemporáneas en Bolivia: el movimiento "katarista": 1970–1980'. In: Rene Zavaleta (ed.) *Bolivia hoy*. Mexico, Siglo Veintiuno Editores, 1983, 136.

6. James Dunkerley, *Rebellion in the veins: political struggle in Bolivia, 1952–1982*. London, Verso, 1984, 215.

7. Jean-Pierre Lavaud, *Identité et politique : le courant Tupaj Katari en Bolivie*. Document de travail No. 24. France, CREDAL/ERSIPAL, 1982, 10.

8. Radoslaw Powęska, *Indigenous movements and building the plurinational state in Bolivia: organisation and identity in the trajectory of the CSUTCB and CONAMAQ*. Warsaw, Centre for Latin American Studies, 2013.

9. Rafi Youatt, 'Personhood and the rights of nature: the new subjects of con-temporary Earth politics', *International Political Sociology* 11, no. 1 (2017), 39–54.

10. Erica Fudge, 'A left-handed blow: writing the history of animals'. In: Nigel Rothfels (ed.) *Representing animals*. Bloomington, Indiana University Press, 2003, 3–18; Dorothee Brantz, *Beastly natures: animals, humans, and the study of history*. Charlottesville, University of Virginia Press, 2010.

11. Bronwen Douglas, 'In the event: indigenous countersigns and the ethnohistory of voyaging'. In: Margaret Jolly, Serge Tcherkézoff & Darrell Tryon (eds.) *Oceanic encounters; exchange, desire, violence*. Canberra, Australian National University Press, 2009, 175–98.

12. Diogo de Carvalho Cabral & André Vasques Vital, 'Multispecies emergent textualities: writing and reading in ecologies of selves', *ISLE: Interdisciplinary Studies in Literature and Environment* (2021), isab024.

13. Dipesh Chakrabarty, *Provincializing Europe: postcolonial thought and historical difference*. Princeton, NJ, Princeton University Press, 2000. See also, Felipe Quispe, *Tupaj Katari vive y vuelve, carajo*. La Paz, Aruwiyiri, 1990; Fabiola Escarzaga, 'Comunidad indígena y revolución en Bolivia: el pensamiento indianista-katarista de Fausto Reinaga & Felipe Quispe', *Politica y Cultura* 37 (2012), 185–210; Esteban Ticona, *Memoria, política y antropología en los Andes bolivianos. Historia oral y saberes locales*. Cochabamba, AGRUCO-UMSA, 2002; and 'Foreword' to Javier Hurtado, *El Katarismo*. 2nd edn, La Paz, CIS, 1986.

14. Donna Haraway, 'A cyborg manifesto: science, technology, and socialist feminism in the late twentieth century'. In: *Simians, cyborgs and women: the reinvention of nature*. New York, Routledge, 1991, 149–81.

15. Georgina Dopico Black, 'The ban and the bull: cultural studies, animal studies, and Spain', *Journal of Spanish Cultural Studies* 11, nos. 3–4 (2010), 235–49; see also Martha Few & Zeb Tortorici (eds.), *Centering animals in Latin American history*. Durham, NC, Duke University Press. 2013.

16. Germán Vergara,'Bestiario latinoamericano: los animales en la historiografía de América Latina', *História, Ciências, Saúde – Manguinhos* 28, supl. 1 (2021), 187–208.

17. José de Acosta, Jane E. Mangan & Frances Lopez-Morillas, *Natural and moral history of the Indies*. Durham, NC, Duke University Press, 2002, 262.

18. Mario Blaser, 'Ontology and indigeneity: on the political ontology of heterogeneous assemblages', *Cultural Geographies* 21, no. 1 (2014), 49–58.

19. Rossana Barragán & Florencia Durán, 'Tras las huellas de la historia'. In: *Collana. Conflicto por la tierra en el altiplano*. 1st edn. La Paz, Fundación Tierra, 2003, 26–36, pp. 26–8; see also Sinclair Thomson, *We alone will rule: native Andean politics in the age of insurgency*. Madison, University of Wisconsin Press, 2003; Forrest Hylton & Sinclair Thompson, *Revolutionary horizons: past and present in Bolivian politics*. New York, Verso, 2007.

20. Hilda Kean & Philip Howell (eds.), *The Routledge companion to animal–human history*. 1st edn. London, Routledge, 2019, 202.

21. Kean & Howell, 2019, 210.

22. Eduardo Viveiros De Castro, 'Cosmological deixis and Amerindian Perspectivism', *The Journal of the Royal Anthropological Institute* 4, no. 3 (1998), 469–88; Philippe Descola, *Beyond nature and culture*. Chicago, University of Chicago Press, 2005; Arturo Escobar, *Territories of difference: place, movements, life, redes*. Durham, NC, Duke University Press, 2008; Penelope Dransart (ed.), *Living beings: perspectives on interspecies engagements*. London, Bloomsbury, 2013; Marisol De la Cadena, 'Indigenous cosmopolitics in the Andes: conceptual reflexions beyond Politics as usual', *Cultural Anthropology* 25, no. 2 (2010), 334–70; and *Earth beings: ecologies of practice across Andean worlds*. Durham, NC, Duke University Press, 2015.

23. Escobar, 2008.

24. Bruno Latour, *Reassembling the social: an introduction to actor-network-theory.* ACLS Humanities E-Book. Oxford, Oxford University Press, 2005.

25. Isabelle Stengers, *Cosmopolitics.* Trans. Robert Bononno. Minneapolis, University of Minnesota Press, 2010.

26. De la Cadena, 2010, 334.

27. De La Cadena, 2010, 110–11.

28. Tania Murray Li, 'Environment, indigeneity and transnationalism'. In: Richard Peet & Michael Watts (eds.) *Liberation ecologies: environment, development, social movements.* 2nd edn. London, Routledge, 2004, 309–37; Joni Adamson, 'Environmental Justice, Cosmopolitics, and Climate Change'. In: Louise Wrestling (ed.) *The Cambridge companion to literature and the environment.* Cambridge, Cambridge University Press, 2013, 169–83.

29. Kepa Artaraz & Melania Calestani, 'Suma qamaña in Bolivia', *Latin American Perspectives* 42, no. 5 (2015), 216–33.

30. Nancy Postero, *The indigenous state: race, politics, and performance in plurinational Bolivia.* Berkeley, University of California Press, 2017.

31. Deborah Yashar, *Contesting citizenship in Latin America: the rise of indigenous movements and the post liberal challenge.* Cambridge, Cambridge University Press, 2007; *From movements to parties: the evolution of ethnic politics.* New York, Cambridge University Press, 2017; Jeffrey Webber, *From rebellion to reform in Bolivia: class struggle, indigenous liberation and the politics of Evo Morales.* Chicago, Haymarket Books, 2011.

32. Rex A. Hudson & Dennis M. Hanratty (eds.), *Bolivia: a country study.* Washington, GPO for the Library of Congress, 1989.

33. Estrategia Internacional para la Reducción de Desastres. Chapter 8, Fenómeno El Niño. Introducción general y descripción del fenómeno en Bolivia, no. 134, https://www.eird.org/estrategias/pdf/spa/ doc12863/ doc12863-9.pdf; Lorenzo Huertas Vallejos, *Diluvios andinos a través de las fuentes documentales.* Lima, Pontificia Universidad Católica del Perú, 2001.

34. For discussion of *katarista* discourses on soil erosion see Karl Zimmer, 'Soil erosion and social (dis)courses in Cochabamba, Bolivia: perceiving the nature of the environmental degradation', *Economic Geography* 69, no. 3, Environment and Development, Part I, 312–27.

35. Cesar Caviedes, 'El Nino 1982–83', *Geographical Review* 74, no. 3 (1984), 267–90.

36. National Oceanic and Atmospheric Administration (NOAA), *Reports to the nation on our changing planet. El Niño and climate prediction*, University Corporation for Atmospheric Research/National Oceanic and Atmospheric Administration, 1994, 145.

37. Pedro Mollinedo Portugal & Carlos Cruz Macusaya, *El indianismo katarista: un análisis crítico.* La Paz, Fundación Friedrich Ebert, 2016; Friedrich-Ebert-Stiftung, 'Pensamiento político indígena, II: "Indianismo y Katarismo"' [interview with katarista Constantino Lima], https://youtube.com/watch?v= 7bN1EwKTx3Q.

38. James Dunkerley, *Rebellion in the Veins: political struggle in Bolivia, 1952–1982.* London, Verso, 1984.

39. Collasuyo, 1978, 6; Uri Mendelberg, 'The impact of the Bolivian agrarian reform on class formation', *Latin American Perspectives* 12, no. 3 (1985), 45–58.

40. Javier Sajinés, 'Mestizaje upside down: subaltern knowledges and the known', *Nepantla: Views from South* 3, no. 1, 2002, 42.

41. Albó, 1991, 312; for the international context, Richard Patch, 'Bolivia US assistance in a revolutionary setting'. In: Richard Adams, Oscar Lewis & John Gillin (eds.) *Social change in Latin America today*. New York, Random House, 1960, 108–68.

42. James Kohl, 'The Cliza and Ucureña War: syndical violence and national revolution in Bolivia', *The Hispanic American Historical Review* 62, no. 4 (1982), 607–28; Yashar, 2005, 159.

43. Hurtado, 1986, 222.

44. Rivera Cusicanqui, 1987.

45. *La Nación*, 1953: n.p.

46. Willem Assies, 'Land tenure legislation in a pluri-cultural and multi-ethnic society: the case of Bolivia', *The Journal of Peasant Studies* 33, no. 4 (2006), 569–611.

47. CSUTCB, 1983. In: Carlos Toranzo Roca (ed.) *Crisis del sindicalismo en Bolivia*. La Paz, FLACSO- ILDIS, 1987, 226.

48. Cusicanqui Rivera, 1987, 112.

49. Xavier Albó, 'From MNRistas to Kataristas to Katari'. In: Steve Stern (ed.) *Resistance, rebellion, and consciousness in the Andean peasant world: eighteenth to twentieth centuries*. Madison, University of Wisconsin Press, 1987, 392; José Teijeiro. *La rebellion permanente; crisis de identidad y persistencia etnico-cultural aymara en Bolivia*. La Paz, PIEB, 2007 ; Fabiola Escárzaga & Raquel Gutiérrez (eds.), *Movimiento indígena en América Latina: resistencia y proyecto alternativo*. Mexico, Gobierno de la Ciudad de México-Casa Juan Pablos-BUAP-UNAM-UACM, 2005.

50. Silvia Rivera Cusicanqui, 'Luchas campesinas contemporáneas en Bolivia: el movimiento katarista: 1970–1980'. In: Rene Zavaleta Mercado (ed.) *Bolivia hoy*. México, Siglo Veintiuno Editores, 1983, 129–68, p.163.

51. CSUTCB-1980, 2.

52. CSUTCB-1983, 1.

53. Henry Stobart, *Music and the poetics of production in the Bolivian Andes*. Aldershot, Ashgate, 2006, 27. For other oral stories, see Waskar Ari, *Earth politics, religion, decolonization and Bolivia's indigenous intellectuals*. Durham, NC, Duke University Press, 2014.

54. John-Andrew McNeish, 'Globalisation and the reinvention of Andean tradition: the politics of community and ethnicity in highland Bolivia', *The Journal of Peasant Studies* 29, nos. 3–4 (2002), 228–69; Verushka Alvizuri, *La construcción de la aymaridad. Una historia de la etnicidad en Bolivia (1952–2006)*. Santa Cruz, Editorial El País, 2009.

55. Hans Van den Berg & Norbert Schiffers (eds.), *La cosmovision Aymara*. La Paz, Hisbol, 1992, 156–60.

56. CSUTB-1989b, 29.

57. CSUTCB-1989b, 31.

58. CSUTCB-1989b.

59. Rivera Cusicanqui, 'Pachakuti: the historical horizons of internal colonialism', which NACLA published as 'Aymara Past, Aymara Future', NACLA 25, no. 3, http://www.web.ca/~bthomson/ degrowth/pachakuti_cusicanqui_1991.pdf.

60. Albó, 'La búsqueda desde adentro. Caleidoscopio de auto-imágenes em el debate bolivano', *Boletín de Antropología Americana* 30, no. 51 (1994), 51–66, p.60.

61. CSUTCB-1987.

62. De la Cadena, 2015.

63. Ricardo Calla, José Enrique Pinelo & Miguel Urioste, *CSUTCB. Debate sobre documentos políticos y asamblea de nacionalidades*. La Paz, CEDLA, 1989.

64. CSUTCB-1988a.

65. CSUTCB-1988a.

66. Boletín Chitakolla, Selected editions, Archivo y Biblioteca Nacionales de Bolivia, Sucre; Senate House Special Collections, London (James Dunkerley Collection), 1986, 4.

67. Boletín Chitakolla, 1986, 4.

References

Acosta, José de, Jane E. Mangan & Frances Lopez-Morillas, *Natural and moral history of the Indies*. Durham, NC, Duke University Press, 2002.

Adamson, Joni, 'Environmental Justice, Cosmopolitics, and Climate Change'. In: Wrestling, Louise (ed.) *The Cambridge companion to literature and the environment*. Cambridge, Cambridge University Press, 2013.

Albó, Xavier, 'From MNRistas to Kataristas to Katari'. In: Stern, Steve (ed.) *Resistance, rebellion, and consciousness in the Andean peasant world: eighteenth to twentieth centuries*. Madison, University of Wisconsin Press, 1987.

Albó, Xavier, 'El retorno del indio', *Revista Andina* 9, no. 2 (1991), 299–366.

Albó, Xavier, 'La búsqueda desde adentro. Caleidoscopio de auto-imágenes em el debate bolivano', *Boletín de Antropología Americana* 30, no. 51 (1994), 51–66.

Alvizuri, Verushka, *La construcción de la aymaridad. Una historia de la etnicidad en Bolivia (1952–2006)*. Santa Cruz, Editorial El País, 2009.

Archondo, Rafael, 'Comunidad y divergencia de miradas en el katarismo', *Umbrales* 7 (2000), 120–132.

Ari, Waskar, *Earth politics, religion, decolonization and Bolivia's indigenous intellectuals*. Durham, NC, Duke University Press, 2014.

Artaraz, Kepa, & Melania Calestani, 'Suma qamaña in Bolivia', *Latin American Perspectives* 42, no. 5 (2015), 216–33.

Assies, Willem, 'Land tenure legislation in a pluri-cultural and multi-ethnic society: the case of Bolivia', *The Journal of Peasant Studies* 33, no. 4 (2006), 569–611.

Barragán, Rossana, & Florencia Durán, 'Tras las huellas de la historia'. In: *Collana. Conflicto por la tierra en el altiplano*. 1st edn. La Paz, Fundación Tierra, 2003.

Berg, Hans Van den & Norbert Schiffers (eds.), *La cosmovision Aymara*. La Paz, Hisbol, 1992.

Black, Georgina Dopico, 'The ban and the bull: cultural studies, animal studies, and Spain', *Journal of Spanish Cultural Studies* 11, nos. 3–4 (2010), 235–49.

Blaser, Mario, 'Ontology and indigeneity: on the political ontology of heterogeneous assemblages', *Cultural Geographies* 21, no. 1 (2014), 49–58.

Brantz, Dorothee, *Beastly natures: animals, humans, and the study of history*. Charlottesville, University of Virginia Press, 2010.

Calderon, Fernando & Jorge Dandler (eds.), *Bolivia: la fuerza histórica del campesinado*. Cochabamba, CERES, 1984.

Calla, Ricardo, José Enrique Pinelo & Miguel Urioste, *CSUTCB. Debate sobre documentos politicos y asamblea de nacionalidades*. La Paz, CEDLA, 1989.

Castro, Eduardo Viveiros De, 'Cosmological deixis and Amerindian Perspectivism', *The Journal of the Royal Anthropological Institute* 4, no. 3 (1998), 469–88.

Caviedes, Cesar, 'El Nino 1982–83', *Geographical Review* 74, no. 3 (1984), 267–90.

Chakrabarty, Dipesh, *Provincializing Europe: postcolonial thought and historical difference*. Princeton, NJ, Princeton University Press, 2000.

Chakrabarty, Dipesh, *The climate of history in a planetary age*. Chicago, University of Chicago Press, 2021.

Cott, Donna Van, *Radical democracy in the Andes*. Cambridge, Cambridge University Press, 2009.

Cusicanqui, Silvia Rivera, 'Luchas campesinas contemporáneas en Bolivia: el movimiento "katarista": 1970–1980'. In: Zavaleta, Rene (ed.) *Bolivia hoy*. Mexico, Siglo Veintiuno Editores, 1983.

Cusicanqui, Silvia Rivera, *Oppressed but not defeated: peasant struggles among the Aymara and Quechua in Bolivia, 1900–1980*. Geneva, UNRISD, 1987.

Cusicanqui, Silvia Rivera, 'Pachakuti: the historical horizons of internal colonialism', which NACLA published as 'Aymara Past, Aymara Future', *NACLA* 25, no. 3, 1991. http://www.web.ca/~bthomson/degrowth/pachakuti_cusicanqui_1991.pdf.

Cruz, Carlos Macusaya, 'Indianismo y katarismo en el siglo XX: apuntes históricos'. In: Tapia, Pedro Canales (ed.) *El pensamiento y la lucha: los pueblos indígenas en América Latina: organización y discusiones con trascendencia*. La Paz, Ariadna Ediciones, 2018.

de Carvalho Cabral, Diogo & André Vasques Vital, 'Multispecies emergent textualities: writing and reading in ecologies of selves', *ISLE: Interdisciplinary Studies in Literature and Environment* 30, no. 3 (2022), 705–27.

De la Cadena, Marisol, 'Indigenous cosmopolitics in the Andes: conceptual reflexions beyond Politics as usual', *Cultural Anthropology* 25, no. 2 (2010), 334–70.

De la Cadena, Marisol, *Earth beings: ecologies of practice across Andean worlds*. Durham, NC, Duke University Press, 2015.

Descola, Philippe, *Beyond nature and culture*. Chicago, University of Chicago Press, 2005.

Douglas, Bronwen, 'In the event: indigenous countersigns and the ethnohistory of voyaging'. In: Jolly, Margaret, Serge Tcherkézoff &

Darrell Tryon (eds.) *Oceanic encounters; exchange, desire, violence.* Canberra, Australian National University Press, 2009.

Dransart, Penelope, (ed.) *Living beings: perspectives on interspecies engagements.* London, Bloomsbury, 2013.

Dunkerley, James, *Rebellion in the veins: political struggle in Bolivia, 1952–1982.* London, Verso, 1984.

Eckstein, Susan, 'Transformation of a "revolution from below". Bolivia and international capital', *Comparative Studies in Society and History* 25, no. 1 (1983), 105–35.

Escárzaga, Fabiola, 'Comunidad indígena y revolución en Bolivia: el pensamiento indianista-katarista de Fausto Reinaga & Felipe Quispe', *Política y Cultura* 37 (2012), 185–210.

Escárzaga, Fabiola & Raquel Gutiérrez (eds.), *Movimiento indígena en América Latina: resistencia y proyecto alternativo.* Mexico, Gobierno de la Ciudad de México-Casa Juan Pablos- BUAP-UNAM-UACM, 2005.

Escobar, Arturo, *Territories of difference: place, movements, life, redes.* Durham, NC, Duke University Press, 2008.

Estrategia Internacional para la Reducción de Desastres. Chapter 8, Fenómeno El Niño. Introducción general y descripción del fenómeno en Bolivia, no. 134, https://www.eird.org/estrategias/pdf/spa/doc 12863/ doc12863-9.pdf

Few, Martha & Zeb Tortorici (eds.), *Centering animals in Latin American history.* Durham, NC, Duke University Press, 2013.

Fudge, Erica, 'A left-handed blow: writing the history of animals'. In: Nigel Rothfels, Nigel (ed.) *Representing animals.* Bloomington, Indiana University Press, 2003.

Haraway, Donna, 'A cyborg manifesto: science, technology, and social-ist- feminism in the late twentieth century'. In: *Simians, cyborgs and women: the reinvention of nature.* New York, Routledge, 1991.

Hudson, Rex A. & Dennis M. Hanratty (eds.), *Bolivia: a country study.* Washington, GPO for the Library of Congress, 1989.

Hurtado, Javier, *El katarismo.* La Paz, Hisbol, 1986

Hylton, Forrest & Sinclair Thompson, *Revolutionary horizons: past and present in Bolivian politics.* New York, Verso, 2007.

Kean, Hilda & Philip Howell (eds.), *The Routledge companion to animal–human history.* 1st edn. London, Routledge, 2019.

Kohl, James, 'The Cliza and Ucureña War: syndical violence and national revolution in Bolivia', *The Hispanic American Historical Review* 62, no. 4 (1982), 607–28.

Latour, Bruno, *Reassembling the social: an introduction to actor-network-theory.* ACLS Humanities E-Book. Oxford, Oxford University Press, 2005.

Li, Tania Murray, 'Environment, indigeneity and transnationalism'. In: Peet, Richard & Michael Watts (eds.) *Liberation ecologies: environment, development, social movements.* 2nd edn. London, Routledge, 2004.

Lucero, José Antonio, 'Fanon in the Andes: Fausto Reinaga, indianismo, and the black Atlantic', *International Journal of Critical Indigenous Studies* 1, no. 1 (2000).

Malloy, James & Richard Thorn, *Beyond the revolution: Bolivia since 1952.* Pittsburgh, PA, University of Pittsburgh Press, 1971.

McNeish, John-Andrew, 'Globalisation and the reinvention of Andean tradition: the politics of community and ethnicity in highland Bolivia', *The Journal of Peasant Studies* 29, nos. 3–4 (2002), 228–69.

Mendelberg, Uri, 'The impact of the Bolivian agrarian reform on class formation', *Latin American Perspectives* 12, no. 3 (1985), 45–58.

National Oceanic and Atmospheric Administration (NOAA), *Reports to the nation on our changing planet: El Niño and climate prediction.* University Corporation for Atmospheric Research/National Oceanic and Atmospheric Administration, 1994.

Patch, Richard, 'Bolivia US assistance in a revolutionary setting'. In: Adams, Richard, Oscar Lewis & John Gillin (eds.) *Social change in Latin America today.* New York, Random House, 1960.

Portugal, Pedro Mollinedo & Carlos Cruz Macusaya, *El indianismo katarista: un análisis crítico.* La Paz, Fundación Friedrich Ebert, 2016.

Postero, Nancy, *The indigenous state: race, politics, and performance in plurinational Bolivia.* Berkeley, University of California Press, 2017.

Poweska, Radoslaw, *Indigenous movements and building the plurinational state in Bolivia: organisation and identity in the trajectory of the CSUTCB and CONAMAQ.* Warsaw, Centre for Latin American Studies, 2013.

Quispe, Felipe, *Tupaj Katari vive y vuelve, carajo.* La Paz, Aruwiyiri, 1990.

Sajinés, Javier, 'Mestizaje upside down: subaltern knowledges and the known', *Nepantla: Views from South* 3, no. 1, 2002.

Stengers, Isabelle, *Cosmopolitics.* Trans. Robert Bononno. Minneapolis, University of Minnesota Press, 2010.

Stiftung, Friedrich-Ebert, 'Pensamiento político indígena, II: "Indianismo y Katarismo"' [interview with katarista Constantino Lima], https://youtube.com/watch?v= 7bN1EwKTx3Q.

Stobart, Henry, *Music and the poetics of production in the Bolivian Andes.* Aldershot, Ashgate, 2006.

Teijeiro, José, *La rebellion permanente; crisis de identidad y persistencia etnico-cultural aymara en Bolivia.* La Paz, PIEB2007.

Terrazas, Nicomedes Sejas, *Katarismo y descolonizacion. La emergencia democratica del indio*. Bolivia, Imprenta Stigma, 2014.

Thomson, Sinclair, *We alone will rule: native Andean politics in the age of insurgency*. Madison, University of Wisconsin Press, 2003.

Ticona, Esteban, *Memoria, política y antropología en los Andes bolivianos. Historia oral y saberes locales*. Cochabamba, AGRUCO-UMSA, 2002.

Vallejos, Lorenzo Huertas, *Diluvios andinos a través de las fuentes documentales*. Lima, Pontificia Universidad Católica del Perú, 2001.

Vergara, Germán,'Bestiario latinoamericano: los animales en la historiografía de América Latina', *História, Ciências, Saúde – Manguinhos* 28, supl. 1 (2021), 187–208.

Yashar, Deborah, *Contesting citizenship in Latin America: the rise of indigenous movements and the post liberal challenge*. Cambridge, Cambridge University Press, 2007.

Yashar, Deborah, *From movements to parties: The evolution of ethnic politics*. New York, Cambridge University Press, 2017.

Youatt, Rafi, 'Personhood and the rights of nature: the new subjects of contemporary Earth politics', *International Political Sociology* 11, no. 1 (2017), 39–54.

Webber, Jeffrey, *From rebellion to reform in Bolivia: Class struggle, indigenous liberation and the politics of Evo Morales*. Chicago, Haymarket Books, 2011.

Zimmer, Karl, 'Soil erosion and social (dis)courses in Cochabamba, Bolivia: perceiving the nature of the environmental degradation', *Economic Geography* 69, no. 3, Environment and Development, Part I, 312–27.

Archival and primary sources

Archivo y Biblioteca Nacionales de Bolivia, Sucre.

Boletín Chitakolla, Selected editions, Archivo y Biblioteca Nacionales de Bolivia, Sucre; Senate House Special Collections, London (James Dunkerley Collection) 1986, 4.

CSUTCB-1980, *Entrevista a Jenaro Flores*, órgano informativo en el exterior. Año1, no. 1 octubre.

CSUTCB-1987, *III Congreso de Unidad Campesina, Confederación Sindical Única de Trabajadores Campesinos de Bolivia*, MUSEF, La Paz, Digital audio recording.

CSUTCB-1983, In: Carlos Toranzo Roca (ed.) *Crisis del sindicalismo en Bolivia*. La Paz, FLACSO- ILDIS, 1987.

CSUTCB-1988a, *I ampliado de la Confederación Sindical Única de Trabajadores Campesinos de Bolivia*, MUSEF, La Paz. Digital audio recording.

CSUTCB-1988b, *I Congreso Extraordinario de la Confederación Sindical Única de Trabajadores Campesinos de Bolivia,* MUSEF, La Paz, Digital audio recording.

CSUTCB-1989a, *1er Ampliado nacional de la Confederación Sindical Única de Trabajadores Campesinos de Bolivia*. MUSEF, La Paz, Digital audio recording.

CSUTCB-1989b, *Informe del Comite Ejecutivo saliente al IV Congreso Nacional Ordinario de la CSUTCB*, CEDOIN, Bolivia.

CSUTCB-1992, *4to Congreso Confederación Sindical Única de Trabajadores Campesinos de Bolivia*, MUSEF, La Paz. Digital audio recording.

El Diario de La Paz (January–May 1973) (British Library), *Katarismo* (after the first edition it is called El Katarismo) 1985–6.

Lavaud, Jean-Pierre, *Identité et politique: le courant Tupaj Katari en Bolivie*. Document de travail No. 24. France, CREDAL/ERSIPAL, 1982.

Manifiesto de Tiahuanaco, La Paz. 30 de Julio de 1973 – retrieved from the James Dunkerley special collection at Institute of Latin American Studies (London).

La Nación, 1953, Selected issues in Walter Guevara Arce Collection.

Presencia (La Paz) Selected editions 1978–January 1980 (Biblioteca Municipal de La Paz).

Los Tiempos (Cochabamba) January–December 1968 (British Library).

Chapter 8

Tongues in trees and sermons in stones: Jason Allen-Paisant's ecopoetics in *Thinking with Trees*

Hannah Regis

Studies on the environment have historically been relegated to physical, chemical, meteorological and quantitative findings which are embedded in earth sciences and resource management. Landscapes and nature are therefore viewed as biomechanical matters to be controlled and used for economic gain. However, when one considers what cultural and creative workers in the Caribbean (and South America) have done with nature and the valences of explanations that move beyond the physical terrain, closer scrutiny is constrained. The specific historical backdrop of British imperialism in the West Indies encapsulates the deterministic cycles of degradation, extinction and extreme violence which maimed and slaughtered both human and ecosystems. A significant part of empire's outworkings comprised the rise of new global trade networks whose industrial practices generate other calamities such as the devastation of small economically fragile island societies, the objectification of agrarian-based communities, the intensification of forest destruction which exacerbate the islands' vulnerability to rising sea levels and higher land temperatures, and other embodied structures of supremacy that are linked to a capitalistic world-economy. The Caribbean natural world, despite its violent colonial history, continues to spread and proliferate in an entirety that exists outside of human control, thus providing us with proof of the resilience of Caribbean space. In his introduction to *The Womb of Space: The Cross-Cultural Imagination*, the Guyanese writer and philosopher Wilson

Harris asserts that the Caribbean landscape contains 'a live tapestry – of the universe . . . of black holes . . . of nameless entities [and] . . . gods'.[1] He specifically notes that 'the land is a spectral carcass'[2] in which legends are reborn and 'clothed in colour and music . . . of the forests, skies and earth'.[3] This is very much about the death of Indigenous culture and the remnants of races and cultural myths in the New World which seep into the landscape. Harris is conceptualising a medium and aesthetic expression that has come to convey the syncretic and vibratory nature of Caribbean space. He is concretely mapping the continuity of life that appears to have vanished in the New World through the intuitive imagination. His paradigm eschews the idea of the universe as flat. Rather, motion is seen in the context of stones that prate, woods that move, bubbles of the earth and pools of water that secrete with ancestral form. This provides a critical image of interconnection and enfolding relationships which is effectively spatialised in Allen-Paisant's first poetic collection, *Thinking with Trees*.[4] The poems touch on migration, genocide and unspeakable sufferings while finding a way to anchor the beauty that emerges through the enduring natural world.

Jason Allen-Paisant is a nature communicator and tree knower. He develops this sensibility while feeling the limits of being a black immigrant and living in Leeds. Europe is a type of mausoleum and there is a need to interpret the present in light of every fresh discovery of the meaning through a deep interaction with nature. More importantly, his work addresses the intersections of race, class and the environmental conditions that affect people groups in the Caribbean. He responds to the landscape (both Caribbean and English) as extensions of his sense of belonging, exile and ancestral connections. In Britain, the omniscient poet-narrator experiences a curtailed existence,[5] hardened by the fact that the Transatlantic slave trade has endured for over three centuries and was thorough in its methods, most of which are directed towards the restriction of human potential and the reduction of life forms to tools and objects. In this regard, Allen-Paisant gives voice to the black body in green spaces and brings into focus the kind of geographical and psychological binary of Britain and Jamaican, fixity and change. For example, he ruminates on who has the right to walk in the park and the performativity of it, and simultaneously raises the questions of who controls space and who has the right to be 'naturally' free. It is within this context of an estranging British milieu that he retreats into the cover of the forest and tunes into a profoundly meaningful Caribbean sensibility where the woodland exudes peace, agency and the right to be free.

This chapter therefore advocates for a greater reflexivity and a deeper understanding of human beings and their varied relationships with the natural world through discursive representations. Narrative should not be read as a neutral enterprise that is detached from life but should be engaged to produce new analytical insights and meanings of the world. Caribbean criticisms have long been engaged with the importance of temporality, the plural unity of life forms, mythic and Indigenous approaches to bodies, things, animality and trees, as well as their signifying functions in language. It constrains a viewing of the political agency of writer-activists such as Allen-Paisant and the communities he represents insofar that they been erased from official memory particularly on a planetary scale. Such an inquiry merges social analysis and critique with close attention to textual detail and social advocacy – a combination that, as Rob Nixon's book, *Slow Violence*, has demonstrated, opens up new avenues for interdisciplinary research which links with theories of environmental justice.[6]

For Allen-Paisant, this becomes the process of telling alternative versions of the Caribbean self, history and the Caribbean natural world. This alternative retelling is a core characteristic of postcolonial discourse which is significant in projects that challenge representations of the planet as singular – a trend that the poet deems to be deeply unsustainable. Elleke Boehmer's observation is useful in which she contends that 'postcolonial literature . . . is writing that sets out in one way or another to resist colonialist perspective' and to insist on 'symbolic overhaul, a reshaping of dominant meaning'.[7] Allen-Paisant conceives trees as a symbolic source of alternative power to contest economic and neoimperial machinations of power. The poet's interest in legend, old ceremonies, cosmic consciousness and ancestral worship marks a return to a lost kingdom of instinct. This in/quest expresses itself in terms of his interest in syncretic religious and Caribbean mythologies, which are undergirded by ideas of oneness of being and inner serenity. Nature becomes an ally that will regenerate, proliferate and move against new territorialisation and erasures. A deep analysis of the poems 'Cho-Cho Walks', 'Vein of Stone Amid the Branches', 'Twilight in Roundhay' and 'For Those Who Steal Away' will show that Allen-Paisant is indeed cultivating a praxis of radical listening – of tuning in to the sound, vibrations and rhythms of the earth. This encompasses a leaning on folk-based traditions to advance the point that his line of sight is contingent among many worldviews.

The poem 'Cho-Cho Walks' illustrates the sense in which the landscape tells a story of the way that cultural value and memory are attached to place. More specifically, Allen-Paisant articulates a framework to get at the meanings Caribbean people attribute to the environment that are based on ideologies, beliefs, myths and experiences. In 'Cho-Cho Walks', connection with nature in the Caribbean is ordinary, everyday, uncomplicated and matter-of-fact. The poet-persona avers: 'there is no doing here | [. . .] hearing is just walking | [. . .] becoming flesh of the flesh of the leaves | walking with caterpillars on all fours'.[8] As he ruminates on his boyhood, the persona remembers the core element of his Jamaican culture that rarely needs articulating as it is taught experientially and by rights. The associated images and references to 'hiding', 'silence' and 'walking with caterpillars on all fours' disclose his conceptualising of the land as an extension of Mother Earth that is further determined by his instinctive crawling activity. This intimate connection and childlike motion signify forms of initiation into self-knowledge and new awakening linked to an idea of place and community. Interestingly, an intergenerational responsibility and lesson are established in which the speaker's grandmother engages the methods of relational respect with the forest: 'Mammy carried a machete in her hand Spanish Bill | to part the succulent weeds to ask them to excuse us'.[9] This provides a clear visual anchor, which helps the speaker to access the deeply personal character of memory. As his grandmother decentres her human self, she tunes into the sensibilities of the vines. Her parting of leaves with reverence is not an act of payment; it is a way of acknowledging that a mutually respectful relationship exists and which affects processes in the material world. There is an additional patient and mindful practice of embodied and meditative interaction which is echoed in the lexical signifiers of 'walking', 'hearing', 'bending', 'hiding' and 'becoming'.[10] The theme is cosmic harmony that cannot be derived from destructive and material systems of dominance but is aligned with an elemental power. Since 'hearing' is equated with the activity of 'walking' and with the appearance of human 'shadow [that] bend with those of the vine'[11], one can plausibly discern that existence is determined as an environmentally saturated one. The poem itself becomes a meeting place – one that might support healing and unified ascent through the bedrock of these intersecting experiences.

This symbiotic ontological position resonates with Caribbean Indigenous worldviews that are based on a direct relationship with the Earth as a source of knowledge and meaning for human life and community rather than the hierarchal relationships of exploitation characteristic of Western cultures. For the Caribbean's First People, trees are considered persons and teachers. Marisol de la Cadena notes that several South American (Andes, Atacama, Aymara and others) and Caribbean Indigenous traditions (Macusi, Warrau, Taino and Kalinago) subsist on the deeply felt ideology that the land is both an ancestor and guide:

> Earth-practices enact the respect and affect necessary to maintain the relational condition between humans and other-than-human beings

that make life in (many parts of) the Andes.[12] Other-than-humans comprise animals, plants and the landscape. The latter [. . .] is composed
of a constellation of sentient entities.[13]

On similar detail, the distinguished Brazilian anthropologist, Eduardo
Viveros de Castro, having spent the last four decades of his life researching the ontologies of the South American and Caribbean First Peoples,
asserts a conception of 'ecosophic knowledge'[14] that comprises co-
evolution and reincarnation patterns between human communities and
the natural world. Like de la Cadena, de Castro contests epistemological
binaries that perpetuate segmentation between species within the context
of the Caribbean's First Peoples communities. These thinkers are signposting
an interactive awareness and responsibility between human communities
and nature. It provides an important complex knowledge-system wherein
plants, animals and ancestral energies operate seamlessly in everyday
human practices. This is ontological pluralism in practice. It offers a position that is essential for managing assumptions regarding nature and
the categories of being in the world that shape human action and eco-
ethical consequences.

Whether defined heuristically as 'Western', 'Eurocentred' or 'modern',
the ontology underpinning dominant environmentally based practices is
argued to rest on a longstanding hierarchical premise in which only
humans possess intelligence and mind, and everything nonhuman does
not. This premise which reflects the Cartesian mind-body dualism reifies
the subordination of other-than-human phenomena from viable, pre-
existing relational fields and reduces them from convivial subjects to
isolated objects. Whether found in policy mechanisms like payment for
ecosystems services or governing ideas like the green economy, such
approaches are anchored in the reduction and commodification of the
natural world and elide the rhizomatic, entangled cosmos of Indigenous
communities and societies that subsist on inter-species treatise and agree-
ments. A reckoning is thus performed in Allen-Paisant's discourse which
becomes apparent in the inherent relationships in and between all beings
and elements in the universe, across time and space. As the speaker
remembers 'becoming flesh of the flesh of the leaves',[15] he is documenting
a process whereby he moves towards self-identification with the landscape
he describes. Nature is internalised insofar that it becomes poetic currency
and the framing of the landscape is driven by tensions between present-
day experience and cultural memory. When he begins to think with the
help of trees, he enters into a different world from the one that is proposed
in Leeds. Such ontological framings constrain us to see nature as expansive and agential while enabling a recognition of how reality is continuously

enacted and transformed in practice. Withdrawing himself from this deep reflection of his boyhood, the poet returns to the present and crafts an extension of Jamaica's living heritage based in Coffee Grove with the trust that the trees in Leeds would be receptive to the intention motivating these gestures. As Allen-Paisant continues to seek out a grounding of the self in roots, sights and sounds that move away from the egotism and material-ism of the Western world, he methodically interrogates how nature oscillates between relative pastoral innocence and nuclear activity.

In the poem 'Vein of Stone Amid the Branches',[16] we encounter a mind which has known nature's cycle and one which looks at an age of high technology and longs for the opposite. Interestingly, the poem's epigraph references Giuseppe Penone – the Italian artist and sculptor whose work has long examined the interface between nature and culture. Penone's art takes to nature as the primary inspiration for new ideas, in which a care-ful elaboration of earthly shapes and forms reveal the essence of matter. Penone is known for his reconciliation of the organic earth with human touch. Allen-Paisant's allusion to the icon of the artist calls attention to the process of ethical creative activity within a milieu of high apocalyptic activity. Beneath the poem lies a fear of environmental erosion in which the tangled lianas of the thick rainforests have been replaced by the atomic power of civilisation. The line, 'tree makes nuclear reactors [and] shopping malls'[17] is a polemic at commercialism and the subjection of the natural world to market value. The poet seems to be asking – what happens when the semi-primal consciousness of the Caribbean migrant in exile is faced with the asphyxia of the contemporary concrete, metropolitan city? How does one, beginning as a colonial, break the circle of repression and repri-sal? What creative action brings the necessary release from this wheel? The poet grapples with the sense in which his most innermost being has been invaded by the city's iron. Hence, the paradoxical 'uranium trees mate in nuclear forests'[18] where the natural and organic world ('trees', 'for-ests) has been penetrated by the manufactured and inorganic ('nuclear'). Here, the speaker-poet witnesses the elevation of Western materialism into nuclear factories, and skyscraper – as evoked in the image of the 'trailer crane bulldozer'[19] and mushroom cloud. What precedes the first half of the poem is a remedy to facing the full stress of modern life. Allen-Paisant envisions a symbolic recovery through spirituality. The response, as enabled by his retreat into nature, is testimony, sermon, prophecy and an invocation of Afro-Caribbean cosmologies that value a symbiotic relation-ship with the natural world and its secretions of mythology. This is manifested with the first image of the tree as 'a rite of presence'[20] which provides us with a direct clue that the 'tree' which is being destroyed by bulldozers is an ancestor.

One way of thinking through the ecological ramifications of this notion is to consider Tim Ingold's idea of symbiosis, as outlined in 'The Temporality of the Landscape'.[21] In this essay, Ingold introduces what he calls a 'dwelling perspective, according to which the landscape is constituted as an enduring record of – and testimony to – the lives and works of past generations who have dwelt within in'.[22] The landscape is, in Ingold's view, a constructed and enduring record of history. The true nature of the landscape, described by Ingold as 'heterogenous . . . a contoured and textured surface'[23] replete with diverse energies, resonates throughout Allen-Paisant's poem. Such an appreciation of nature will place it beyond its physicality and convert the trees to an enduring energy or talisman, endued with memory and power to protect its community against future evil. Such is Allen-Paisant's enduring dream and commitment in the face of a grim-capitalist-intensive reality. The question that 'Vein of Sone Amid the Branches' poses is how does one extract a sense of the sacred out of an ongoing history of evil? How does such a history nuclearise when the very word 'nuclear' (repeated thrice by the persona) implies that the process of fission and reaction will involve a physical and spiritual torture that is emphasised historically in the Caribbean experience? Allen-Paisant turns to a transhistorical and transcendent vision to locate a sense of continuity and reverence amidst a reality of destruction. He declares: 'but since this is conjuring tree/but since this is a vodou tree | but since this is a hoodoo tree | but since this is a medium | psychic science tree | magic spirit tree | it will not harm'.[24]

The word 'but' is ambiguous. It serves as a pointer to and intensifier of the statement which succeeds it. Initially, the poet begins his polemic with a victimising image of nature and high capitalist activity when he asserts: 'think of a factory | and it appears | let the word *nuclear* press you | with its weight | uranium trees mate in nuclear forests | make trailer crane bulldozer fission'.[25] It is a process which he cannot control but imagines an alternative voice of resistance which challenges this reality. The voice is enveloped in a magico-religious sensibility that can only be released via chant[26] and memory. The staccato lineation and unpunctuated phrases (common to all of the poems) weigh both attention and strain. More overtly, the poet is setting out to identify the exact texture of a mood and of moments of history which contained both the supernatural fervour and desperate hope of the exploding folk. The principles of Vodou and Hoodoo denominations are recast as complex and curative. Vodou broadly encompasses a worldview that is adept in its search for higher grounds and purpose in life. As an ancestral religion that has its roots in continental African Dahomey cults, it is a key element of Haitian consciousness, which provides moral coherence through common cosmological understandings.

Patrick Bellegarde-Smith's encompassing definition of Vodou sheds light on the manner in which Allen-Paisant deploys it as an epistemological device to express the syncretic nature of Caribbean identity and realities:

> Vodun is a coherent and comprehensive system and worldview in which every person and everything is sacred and must be treated accordingly. In Vodun, everything in the world – be it plant, animal or mineral – share similar chemical, physical, and/or genetic properties. This unity of all things translates into an overarching belief in the sanctity of life, not so much for the thing as for the spirit of the thing.[27]

Creating dissonance in nature's polyrhythms, disturbing the harmonious flow of things, and bringing about division in the community, are all acts which represent moral transgression in the Vodou world. 'Vein of Stone Amid the Branches' embodies this complex interconnection between the sacred and the secular while also illuminating the organic functional aspect of the religion that regulates chaotic actions. Harold Courlander's commentary further exemplifies Vodou's functions and pervasiveness:

> Vodou permeates the land, and, in a sense, it springs from the land. It is not a system imposed from above, but one which pushes out from below . . . Vodou is strong and it cannot die easily . . . You cannot destroy something with such deep genuine roots. You may warp it, twist it, make it crawl along the ground instead of growing upright, but you cannot kill it . . . [especially] in light of the inner history of the [African] race.[28]

According to Courlander, this inter-connectedness with nonhuman life signposts a deep Afro-Caribbean sensibility that values a symbiotic relationship with nature and its secretions of mythology. Allen-Paisant is thus concluding that the African bloodline can never be severed since a process of reversal takes place through the ancestor tree that nurtures his creative spirit. Channelled through form, spiritual energy becomes art – hence, there is a dramatic reenactment of memory that is cathartic. These are the ichor and incense of the survival moment traditional in the Afro-Caribbean and in this poem. The poet extracts from rituals (still very much alive in the Caribbean) various motifs, symbols and images relevant to his act of possession. One of the fundamental characteristics of Vodou and Hoodoo[29] is the control of energy. This is epitomised during ritual occasions in which the priest or *houngan* in Vodun ceremonies controls the powers which ascend from the underground up the lightning conductor of the central pole in the *hounfort* (temple). Comparatively, Allen-Paisant exercises the same control in the process of creating his poem. For example, beneath the poet's use of repetition with its conventional enthusiasm and gusto, lies a ritual intelligence. An incantatory, rhythmic voice is evident in the lines: 'but since this is a conjuring tree | but since this is a vodou tree | but since this is a hoodoo tree | but since this is a medium | psychic science tree | magic spirit tree'[30] which stress the endurance of nature that pivots itself on a spirit-perception.

By turning to ideas of the numinous, the speaker embodies a desperate commitment to revolutionary reprisal for all that the long history of colonisation mutilates. The spirit of revolution ignites the landscape, wind, wave, creek and forest. The importance of repetition as an aesthetic expression is that it tightens the bond between individual and group and affirms an acknowledgement of an enduring ancestral presence that is rooted in the environment. Under pressure, the natural world begins to prophesy, to evoke legend, myth and dread omen out of the materials of everyday horror. The trees are not inert. They secrete a potential life which may be restored by invocation, meditation and the artistic imagination. The poet performs a leap in the imagination where ruins are recognised as totems. In this sense, vision is never just vision, but a part of a larger kaleidoscope of intention, sensation and relationships.

The poem draws to a close in celebrating the spiritual characteristics of trees which will not harm but heal and nourish the senses. He states 'you will stand underneath it | and close your eyes | and when you open them | you will be in the world again'.[31] Trees bring internal awakenings, and despite their ecological rape, their instrumentality prevails. By finding value in the spiritual and numinous, the poet reorients our critical gaze. It is a redirecting of our conceptual lenses from imperialist framing of the landscape as inert. The postcolonial ecocritic Elizabeth DeLoughrey states that among other things, imperialism led to the conceptual erasure of first knowledge systems and the 'erection of a hierarchy of species' that is evident in race, class and gender.[32] This hegemonic schema is again rehearsed and visualised in the 'uranium trees [that] mate in nuclear forests' and the 'trees [that] make shopping malls'.[33] Metaphors of specie objectification characterise empire's imagination and its self-proclaimed legitimising authority for specific ideological conceptions of territory. However, Allen-Paisant rejects this reading of nature as finite and limiting. He concludes with questions posed outside the anthropocentric view and advances the endurance of natural systems beyond the human. Trees are conceived of their temporal dimension in relation to the questions of memory and spiritual knowledge of the past. In this articulation of rehabilitating the landscape, Allen-Paisant gestures to a different knowledge system, as linked to African and Caribbean magico-spiritual traditions that envision a democratic and nonexploitative relationship between human communities and the land. An understanding of how contemporary Caribbean poets in the metropole are using rhythm as image to conjure up, as effectively as any word picture, the energies and real presences that are latent in the environment, can enable us to explore our own spaces in fresh ways by expanding our notion of technique and form.

The idea of continuity is also evident stylistically and rhetorically in the poem 'Twilight in Roundhay' and is a nod to the St Lucian laureate, Derek Walcott. Allen-Paisant asserts:

> I dream the red sun of Coffee Grove
> in this sky crisscrossed [. . .]
> to see a bird gliding in the milky wave
> of the yam vines [. . .]
> while the goats' hooves prance on rough asphalt [. . .]
> kerosene oil makes dark burnings in the air.[34]

Several interesting ideas emerge but what is most apparent is the poet's evocation of Walcott's 1990 epic poem *Omeros*. The resonances with the laureate's notion of in-betweenness as a lived process are undeniable. Characteristically, the twilight (as in the title of the piece), the bird that glides and makes criss-crosses in the sky, the smoke that encircles the asphalt road, the yam vines that curl and the goats that make tracks on the road are major images in Walcott's *Omeros*.[35] This sort of discovery is the most tangible proof of the existence of a continuum. The network of allusions indicates that art has become for Allen-Paisant, the expression of private tensions. His task has become one of rescuing experience from the turbulence within and investing it with verbal shape. It is a movement that heralds an intersection of the private with the communal and is a marriage of the surreal with the concrete. More specifically, the vast themes of history and politics of identity which Walcott had long grappled with, on the one hand, and the private turmoil in which he wrestled with belonging to both European and Caribbean traditions seem to overtake Paisant. The 'wave'[36] that is referenced in the fourth stanza is symbolically the Atlantic and it connects with the idea of the poet's own middle passage to the metropole. To contend with the sense of alienation which pervades the collection (since Leeds ceases to provide constant spiritual sustenance that is necessary for the Caribbean poet), Paisant looks to his predecessors for hope and inspiration. The poet is therefore relying on the graces of inheritance. In this articulation, the observation of the esteemed Barbadian poet Kamau Brathwaite is useful in which he argues that art becomes 'a very learned and conscious procedure'.[37] Like Walcott at the start of his epic, *Omeros*, Allen-Paisant is preoccupied with the journey from the secret forest of the heartland's unconsciousness[38] to the rhythms of Caribbean waking life and society.

There is an obvious wrestle between dream and reality in this poem. The 'dream' in the third stanza suggests a journey through the deep waters of the unconscious and there is a shift from the aloneness of exile in Britain to the exuberant rhythm of the Caribbean. Furthermore, Leeds is measured, judged and rejected by the tropical eye which recognises England as a symbol of cold Western rationalism. The juxtaposition of the 'silence [of] the light above | the cold lines from aeroplanes' in the West Yorkshire sky with the warmth and soft glow of the Caribbean 'kerosene oil'[39] lamps convey a sense of the being buried under a burden of time which is often overwhelming in the metropolitan city. Allen-Paisant, much like Walcott, is engaged in recalling an amber landscape of another life and shares in the bleakness and bitterness of exilic living. His instinct is to recognise a need to re-enter a ceremonious and folk-based past. Consequently, he attempts a descent into memory to unearth a rich ancestral identity. It is a journey back from the deadly void of modern Europe toward an old-time innocence of pastoral celebration. For example, the visual images of the 'red sun of Coffee Grove', the 'roads of smoke', the 'bird gliding in the milky wave | of the yam vines', the auditory stimulus of the 'goats' hooves [that] prance on rough asphalt' and the olfactory image of the fragrant 'kerosene oil' can be associated with a paradise of primal innocence.[40] The search for an Adamic renewal finds support in the poetic methods he employs. Interestingly, there is semi-autobiographical first-person narration which provides the skein of a chronological narrative around which the entire collection is constructed. There is a personal voice whose function is partly to name a distant home-based society by constantly describing the village ('the people ribboned in darkness'), its people and customs ('the shepherd's machete scrapes the ground') or analysing the social structure of rural Jamaica. Every word is loaded. There are anecdotes (also evident in the poem 'Cho-Cho Walks'), which reveal an understanding of the oral tradition that undergirds the Caribbean. The poem is thusly a lyrical meditative passage, whose major themes are memory and history, while the tonal effect is one of transition and motion within a context of timelessness. A lack of punctuation adds to the theme of fluidity and like the communication of trees, necessitates an idiosyncratic grammar in which a personal journey is accommodated via memory.

Most significantly, 'Twilight in Roundhay' describes a search through the landscape for a sense of rootedness. The desperate need to belong is echoed in the line: 'The bird is comfort | a conversation going on | between me and all I see | I will learn to name this me'.[41] There is a thrice reference to the bird which invokes its function as guide (a spirit of the air) and is a space where the poetic imagination dwells. It is an image that connects with the creative process. Moreover, the lines reflect an effort to confront the inner self that can only be summoned in the warmth and energy of the Caribbean. The poem itself thus becomes a kind of cryptic shorthand, hieroglyph and riddle of an ambiguous process hence the fluid association of ideas, images, allusions and word echoes. Here is a version of the poet who talks about a return to the tropics, a descent into the first, Adamic man which marks a movement back to the green beginnings of the world. It allows him a way out of his trapped vision of a deformed world. There is hope in the poet's grounded grasp of both a great heritage of Caribbean craftsmanship and a rooted, earthly and essential spirituality that surrounds him, albeit via memory. That the entire poetic collection is entitled *Thinking* [and not *Walking*] *with Trees* is significant to the discussion at hand as the poet reconsiders and re-roots the black body in an alternative space – whether through memories of a pastoral childhood, nature, ecology, the woods in Leeds or the Anglophone Caribbean poetic tradition. There is an obligation that turns into an imprecation in 'learn[ing] to name this me'.[42] The negotiation between sensitivity and force is apparent throughout the collection, as the poet skilfully navigates the boundary between relief and tension. As with 'Vein of Stone Amid the Branches' in which he foregrounds the material consequences of history and in 'Cho-Cho Walks' where he reclaims the memory of lived freedom in the Caribbean landscape, Allen-Paisant in 'Twilight in Roundhay' is uncompromising when digging down through the undergrowth of imperial forces. He certainly succeeds in replanting new narratives on the same soil where old colonial and toxic ideologies used to, and still, reside.

This residual characteristic of nature is further embodied in the poem 'For Those Who Steal Away'. It begins with a salutation to the African Methodist Episcopal (AME) Church, which has its origins in the clandestine gathering of a congregation in Charleston, South Carolina, until the end of the American Civil War. In this poem, Allen-Paisant connects the roots of the Saint Mary Parish AME Church in Jamaica with its American counterpart. Anita Scott Coleman's mapping of space and its interface with the movement of the black body is useful in this regard. Coleman in her essay, 'Arizona and New Mexico – the Land of Esperanza' charts the contradictions of the free African's experience onto the 'boundless space' of the American West.[43] While the vastness of western geography indeed signifies freedom, possibility and ease of movement, Coleman opines that black migrants still struggled against discriminatory odds. She observes, 'here and there goes negroes, likes straggly but tenacious plant growing, nevertheless, though always in the larger towns. Becoming fewer and fewer in all of the remoter hamlets and towns they are as sparse as rouse bushes upon the prairies'.[44] Interestingly, Coleman's botanical image casts African bodies as transplanted specimens whose patterns of migration both empower and imperil black survival. As Coleman's 'tenacious plants' – embodied as the African subject – contend for a claiming of Western soil as their own, they receive only limited access to the 'life-giving ozone and revivifying sunlight' that, she argues, shines liberally upon the region's white seekers.[45] Nevertheless, the transplanted African American community managed to survive in isolated and vibrant patches. By contextualising the black migrant experience against that of white migrants who travelled westward in search of land and a space to call home, Coleman probes at deeper cultural anxieties regarding black survivability during the period of the Great Migration. Interestingly, Coleman's critical formulations dovetail with Allen-Paisant's argumentation of the African subject's search for a home in 'For Those Who Steal Away'. Like Coleman, Allen-Paisant's devotion to different botanic motifs ('my guide in roots', 'underland of spirits | running through slavery and | ports of blood | connecting roots of AME | Philadelphia Baltimore New Orleans | [. . .] running through these Saint Mary hills'),[46] metaphors of transplantation and wilderness imagery untangle the historical nuances of black migration that proliferate both within and beyond the context of enslavement.

Moreover, the poet's meditation on the relationship between landscape and narratives of belonging or displacement enables a reading of black identity not just in terms of politics, but also in terms of spatial relations and questions of environment. His spatial turn to the formation and proliferation of black spiritual communities in Philadelphia and South Carolina in the 1800s, for example, signposts the point that space is endemic to the black body whose entanglement with processes of migration fundamentally resists fixity. This unfolding, transgeographical and intergenerational narrative of social and cultural relationships that are preserved across space and time is illuminated when the poet declares in his epigraph:

The African Methodist Episcopal Church (AME) was founded in Philadelphia in 1816. Emmanuel AME Church (Mother Emmanuel) was established when the congregation in Charleston, South Carolina, met in secret until the end of the American Civil War. In Saint Mary, Jamaica, the ruined building of an AME church can be found at the site of a former sugar plantation, in the dense forest near Kwame Falls. As stated on the plaque on its front wall, its leader was one Mrs. F. Aicheson. On the plaque is inscribed the date '3rd June '20'.[47]

Here, Allen-Paisant debunks assumptions that Afro-communities in the diaspora are devoid of kinship ties. The epigraph demonstrates that the relational vision of survival was steeped in bodies, personalities and black revolutionary leaders whose interdependence was grounded on a spiritual network enabled through an interconnection with the landscape. There is also an unmistakable gendered inflection that the poet imbibes in the imagistic descriptions of black women's bodies enmeshed in their surroundings: 'women are born from rock [. . .]. | Mrs F Aicheson | is covered by ruins [. . .] a guango rises from the body | of praying mothers'.[48] In these images, the black female body is indistinguishable from the unbounded landscape and it confirms the force and spiritual ecology that constitute Allen-Paisant's crafting of an enchanted universe. This harkens to Vodoun cosmology (as previously argued) where emphasis is placed on an intergenerational nexus that exists in the material world. Since a history of migration and movement is rehearsed, the poem requires an alternative mode of hearing – a reverent one – as the poet begins his pronouncements. In the restaging of these active maternal presences in nature, he is presenting the Jamaican landscape as a metabolic entity. Thus, Caribbean space turns on the axis of cosmic integrity and is moving into a wider syncretic spiritual continent. The language of 'wind and leaves' that 'keep memory' and the 'guango sapling: that pieces "through the belly"'[49] affirms the text's circular logic. Allen-Piasant is also signposting an imaginative ethics of interaction. Here, vines and wind become nearly synonymous with the black body in transition and evoke a broader nascent transition toward social and cultural belonging vis-à-vis the material world. Furthermore, metaphors of transplantation recall the logic of rootwork inherent in the plantation context in which ideas of maroonage and socio-territorial movements took shape. Historical mobility and agency are therefore repurposed to suit a new context of migration and social mobility in Allen-Paisant's discourse.

Midway through *The Souls of Black Folk*, W. E. B. Du Bois offers a striking vision of emergent Afro-diasporic communities across the globe. He notes: 'Now a rising group of people are not lifted bodily from the ground like an inert solid mass, but rather stretch upward like a living plant with its roots still clinging in the mould'.[50] Spatialised in Du Bois's botanical image of rootedness and upward growth is the poet's reference to Mrs Aicheson's act of successfully transposing the fierce ethos of the Philadelphian church into a Caribbean context. The stanza's language of an 'understory'[51] establishes this deep interconnection and belongingness to a broader ecology. The aim is, in part, to engage the landscape as a vessel of communal, cross-cultural and historical negotiation. As part of his contemplation of home and mobile geographies, Allen-Paisant routinely tropes on roots and the sense of being uprooted from one plot of soil and replanted in another. Despite the inherent violence found in processes of transplantation and migratory patterns, the poem climaxes with an image that completes the text's vision of a matrix enlivened by permanent interpersonal and spiritual bonds. This is embodied in the image of the ancestral 'souls' that reside 'inside trees'.[52] Undeterred by the terror of chattel slavery and its violent aftermath, the speaker feels enveloped by a cosmogram-like circle in which he accepts a profound generational connection that can only be reawakened through a psychic relationality with the landscape.

To participate with nature, as Allen-Paisant has done, is to participate in the sacred. Himself a pilgrim, the poet learns of place on its own terms and provides multiple epistemologies to encapsulate a broader range of perception. Through innovations in poetry, he expresses a reparatory vision of the cosmos in which the divine, the human and the vegetal interlock and provide prophetic contours with liberatory focus and theoretical rigour. *Thinking with Trees* undoubtedly moves into an expansive terrain of sacred traditions, ancestral pools of reflections and spiritual portals to subvert the stigma and perceptions of soul sickness and cultural impotence. As a fluid and complex collection, Allen-Paisant's poems advocate for moving away from the limitations and fragmentations of modern, anthropocentric perspectives steeped in Western paradigms, and call for increased environmental empathy and holistic interactions with nature. In this mindfulness, one may begin to move in empathetic relations with the planetary environment we live in and by extension, with our human selves, for we, too, as the poems in the collection demonstrate, are nature.

Notes

1. Wilson Harris, *The Womb of Space: The Cross-Cultural Imagination*. California, Greenwood, 1983, xvi.

2. Wilson Harris, 'Reflections on intruder in the dust'. In: *The Womb of Space: The Cross-Cultural Imagination*. California, Greenwood, 1983, 11.

3. Wilson Harris, 'The schizophrenic sea'. In: *The Womb of Space: The Cross-Cultural Imagination*. California, Greenwood, 1983, 25.

4. See Jason Allen-Paisant, *Thinking with Trees*. Manchester, UK, Carcanet, 2021.

5. In the poem, 'Going Still', for example, the poet states, 'I even think a handicapped dog | is a person in ways I cannot be' (26). The distinction between walking for leisure and going (title of the piece) purposefully anchors the book's preoccupation with the privilege of having access to nature (or not) as determined by one's embodied, racialised identity. Similarly, in 'All of a Sudden' the poet-narrator laments, 'I never allowed my body | to occupy space | the way these people do' (34), while in 'Finding Space (III)' he declares, 'This is not home' (37). The trope of the black body that suffers intense isolation and internalised subjection marks the context of a racially marked metropole, which the larger neocolonial context of the

aforementioned poems reveal. The speaker's displacement that is turned inward, folded and guarded is a reminder that he is too black to be considered a full citizen. The legacy of the Middle Passage looms. Racial segregation has manifested itself in many ways, including in the form of an affective and social residue that hinder the pursuit of healthy human–environment relationships. See Jason Allen-Paisant, 'Going still'. In: *Thinking with trees*, 2021, 25–6; Jason Allen-Paisant, 'All of a sudden'. In: *Thinking with Trees*, 2021, 34–5; and Jason Allen-Paisant, 'Finding space III'. In: *Thinking with trees*, 2021, 36–7.

6. Rob Nixon, *Slow Violence and the Environmentalism of the Poor*. Cambridge, MA, Harvard University Press, 2011.

7. Elleke Boehmer, *Colonial and Postcolonial Literature: Migrant Metaphors*. Oxford, Oxford University Press, 1995, 3.

8. Jason Allen-Paisant, 'Cho-Cho walks'. In: *Thinking with Trees*, 2021, 105.

9. Allen-Paisant, 2021, 105.

10. Allen-Paisant, 2021, 105.

11. Allen-Paisant, 2021, 105.

12. The topography of the Andes also encompasses Venezuela, the Guiana Highlands and the Caribbean Sea. Eduardo Gomez Molina and Adrienne V. Little contend that 'a complete understanding of [Andes] ecology would be impossible without also considering certain contiguous lowland areas. These areas include the coastal plains of the Caribbean Sea and the South Pacific Ocean, large valleys and basins connected with these plains, and those parts of the Orinoco, Amazon, and Parana-La Planta rivers which originate in the foothills of the Andes' (116). Moreover, they note that the 'zoogeographic divisions of the Andes are known as (1) the Patagonia-Chilea subregion, from northern Peru to Tierra del Fuego (Central and Southern Andes), and (2) the Guiana-Brazilia subregion which includes highland Venezuela, Colombia, and Ecuador (Northern Andes)' (128); see Eduardo Gomez Molina & Adrienne V. Little, 'Geoecology of the Andes: the natural science basis for research planning', *Mountain Research and Development* (1981), 115–44.

13. See Marisol de la Cadena, 'Indigenous cosmopolitics in the Andes: conceptual reflections beyond "politics"', *Cultural Anthropology* 25, no. 2 (2010), 341–2.

14. Eduardo Viveiros De Castro, 'Cosmological perspectivism in Amazonia and elsewhere', *HAU Journal of Ethnographic Theory* 1 (2012), 83–117.

15. Allen-Paisant, 'Cho-Cho walks', 105.

16. Jason Allen-Paisant, 'Vein of stone amid the branches'. In: *Thinking with Trees* (2021), 64–5.

17. Allen-Paisant, 'Vein of stone amid the branches', 64.

18. Allen-Paisant, 'Vein of stone amid the branches', 64.

19. Allen-Paisant, 'Vein of stone amid the branches', 64.

20. Allen-Paisant, 'Vein of stone amid the branches', 64.

21. Tim Ingold, 'The temporality of the landscape', *World Archaeology* 25, no. 2 (1993), 152–74.

22. Ingold, 'The temporality of the landscape',1993, 152.

23. Ingold, `The temporality of the landscape',1993, 174.

24. Allen-Paisant, 'Vein of stone amid the branches', 64–5.

25. Allen-Paisant, 'Vein of stone amid the branches', 64, emphasis Allen-Paisant's.

26. From this perspective, it is significant that Allen-Paisant imbricates African-Caribbean spirituality into various forms of matter: in leaves, trees, stems, stones.

One implication of this formulation is that spirituality is also geographically relative.

27. Patrick Bellegarde-Smith, *The Breached Citadel*. Boulder, CO, Westview Press, 1990, 13.

28. Harold Courlander, *The Drum and the Hoe*. Berkeley, University of California Press, 1973, 7.

29. In Hoodoo tradition, root working entails the use of natural and organic remnants of nature in the performance of actions to make things happen, whether healings, poisonings or supernatural prediction. Yvonne P. Chireau calls this divination, which is central to African diasporic traditions. This formation of reclamation from the inside of ritual is recognised in Allen-Paisant's vision that pivots on renewal, endurance and longevity. The tree is a repository of venerated traditions that have lodged itself into the earth. It is a sentient, agentic and conscious entity with a unique ontology and lifeway that is alive in an ongoing relation within Afro-diasporic communities; see Yvonne P. Chireau, *Black Magic: Religion and the African American Conjuring Tradition*. Berkeley, University of California Press, 2003.

30. Allen-Paisant, 'Vein of stone amid the branches', 64.

31. Allen-Paisant, 'Vein of stone amid the branches', 65.

32. Elizabeth M. Deloughrey, 'Ecocriticism: the politics of place'. In: Michael A. Bucknor & Alison Donnell (eds.) *The Routledge Companion to Anglophone Caribbean Literature*. London, Routledge, 2011, 265.

33. Allen-Paisant, 'Vein of stone amid the branches', 64.

34. Jason Allen-Paisant, 'Twilight in Roundhay'. In: *Thinking with Trees*, 2021, 107.

35. Evidence of creative overlapping is found through a reflection on the images that are frequent in Walcott's 1990 epic. This is evident in Walcott's description of the big 'yam leaves [which are] like maps of Africa' (20); the sea-swift which signifies the unweaving and reweaving of the poet's journeys and Peneolopean needlework (319), the goat track that leads to La Soufrière along which Ma Kilman has also travelled (238) and the 'Aruacs' smoke' (5) that rise out of the forest which signals the death of the first peoples. Allen-Paisant's use of 'twilight' in the poem's title similarly overlaps with the personal dividedness that Walcott feels in relation to New and Old Worlds. He opens the fifth book of *Omeros* by saying, 'I crossed my meridian' (189). The meridian is an in-between state, a horizon that is ahead in which an individual's position can change with the new view; see Derek Walcott, *Omeros*. New York, Farrar, Straus and Giroux, [1990] 2014.

36. Allen-Paisant, 'Twilight in Roundhay', 107.

37. Edward Brathwaite, 'The new West Indian novelists: part II,' *BIM* 8, no. 32 (1961), 273.

38. The forest for Walcott is a receptacle of Indigenous spirit presences. St Lucia is an island that vibrates with Indigenous genocidal memory – a crisis felt to varying degrees in all the islands of the region. Genocide and ecocide were complementary projects in the Caribbean. Walcott notes in *Omeros*: 'Seven Seas would talk | bewilderingly that man was an endangered | species now, a spectre, just like the Aruac | or the egret, or parrots screaming in terror | when men approached, and that once men were satisfied | with destroying men they would move on to Nature' (300). Spirits are therefore not eradicated from the landscape; rather they have become part of the region's ecology. They are undead witnesses that endure every apocalyptic turn in Caribbean history.

39. Allen-Paisant, 'Twilight in Roundhay', 107.

40. Allen-Paisant, 'Twilight in Roundhay', 107.

41. Allen-Paisant, 'Twilight in Roundhay', 107.

42. Allen-Paisant, 'Twilight in Roundhay', 107.

43. Anita Scott Coleman, 'Arizona and New Mexico: the land of esperanza'. In: Laurie Champion & Bruce A. Glasrud (eds.) *Unfinished Masterpiece: The Harlem Renaissance Fiction of Anita Scott Coleman*, Texas, Tech University Press, 2008, 182.

44. Scott Coleman, 'Arizona and New Mexico: the land of esperanza', 182.

45. Scott Coleman, 'Arizona and New Mexico: the land of esperanza', 179.

46. Allen-Paisant, 'For those who steal away'. In: *Thinking with Trees*, 2021, 75.

47. Allen-Paisant, 'For those who steal away', 75.

48. Allen-Paisant, 'For those who steal away', 77–9.

49. Allen-Paisant, 'For those who steal away', 76.

50. William Edward Burghard Du Bois, *The Souls of Black Folk*, with an introduction by Brent Hayes Edwards. Oxford, Oxford University Press, 2007, 121.

51. Allen-Paisant, 'For those who steal away', 77.

52. Allen-Paisant, 'For those who steal away', 76.

References

Allen-Paisant, Jason, *Thinking with Trees*. Manchester, UK, Carcanet, 2021.

Bellegarde-Smith, Patrick, *The Breached Citadel*. Boulder, CO, Westview Press, 1990.

Boehmer, Elleke, *Colonial and Postcolonial Literature: Migrant Metaphors*. Oxford, Oxford University Press, 1995.

Brathwaite, Edward, 'The new West Indian novelists: part II,' *BIM* 8, no. 32 (1961), 273.

Chireau, Yvonne P., *Black Magic: Religion and the African American Conjuring Tradition*. Berkeley, University of California Press, 2003.

Coleman, Anita Scott, 'Arizona and New Mexico: the land of esperanza'. In: Laurie Champion & Bruce A. Glasrud (eds.) *Unfinished Masterpiece: the Harlem Renaissance Fiction of Anita Scott Coleman*, Texas, Tech University Press, 2008.

Courlander, Harold, *The Drum and the Hoe*. Berkeley, University of California Press, 1973.

De la Cadena, Marisol, 'Indigenous cosmopolitics in the Andes: conceptual reflections beyond "politics"', *Cultural Anthropology* 25, no. 2 (2010), 341–2.

Deloughrey, Elizabeth M., 'Ecocriticism: the politics of place'. In: Michael A. Bucknor & Alison Donnell (eds.) *The Routledge Companion to Anglophone Caribbean Literature*. London, Routledge, 2011.

Du Bois, William Edward Burghard, The *Souls of Black Folk*, with an introduction by Brent Hayes Edwards. Oxford, Oxford University Press, 2007.

Harris, Wilson, *The Womb of Space: The Cross-Cultural Imagination*. California, Greenwood, 1983.

Ingold, Tim, 'The temporality of the landscape', *World Archaeology* 25, no. 2 (1993), 152–74.

Molina, Eduardo Gomez & Adrienne V. Little, 'Geoecology of the Andes: the natural science basis for research planning', *Mountain Research and Development* 1 (1981), 115–44.

Nixon, Rob, *Slow Violence and the Environmentalism of the Poor*. Cambridge, MA, Harvard University Press, 2011.

Viveiros De Castro, Eduardo, 'Cosmological perspectivism in Amazonia and elsewhere', *HAU Journal of Ethnographic Theory* 1 (2012), 83–117.

Walcott, Derek, *Omeros*. New York, Farrar, Straus and Giroux, [1990] 2014.

Primary sources

Allen-Paisant, Jason, 'All of a sudden'. In: *Thinking with Trees*. Manchester, UK, Carcanet, 2021.

Allen-Paisant, Jason, 'Cho-Cho walks'. In: *Thinking with Trees*. Manchester, UK, Carcanet, 2021.

Allen-Paisant, Jason, 'Finding space III'. In: *Thinking with Trees*. Manchester, UK, Carcanet, 2021.

Allen-Paisant, Jason, 'For those who steal away'. In: *Thinking with Trees*. Manchester, UK, Carcanet, 2021.

Allen-Paisant, Jason, 'Going still'. In: *Thinking with Trees*. Manchester, UK, Carcanet, 2021.

Allen-Paisant, Jason, 'Twilight in Roundhay'. In: *Thinking with Trees*. Manchester, UK, Carcanet, 2021.

Allen-Paisant, Jason, 'Vein of stone amid the branches'. In: *Thinking with Trees*. Manchester, UK, Carcanet, 2021.

Harris, Wilson, 'Reflections on intruder in the dust'. In: *The Womb of Space: The Cross-Cultural Imagination*. California, Greenwood, 1983.

Harris, Wilson, 'The schizophrenic sea'. In: *The Womb of Space: The Cross-Cultural Imagination*. California, Greenwood, 1983.

Chapter 9

Animating the waters, hydrating history: control and contingency in Latin American animations

André Vasques Vital
Translated by Diogo de Carvalho Cabral

The word 'animation' has different meanings. One refers to an impulse, a primary desire to perform irrational, repetitive or even obsessive acts, making what is imagined come true.[1] It is in this sense that animations have the potential to help one understand political and intellectual climates, revealing the feelings of an era. They can also serve as a source of inspiration for new ways of thinking and acting. After all, fiction is a way to reflect on reality and to create new meanings, relationships and possibilities of being in the world.[2] By radically subverting reality, animations of the fantasy genre produce several comments on contemporary themes, including the relations between humans and nonhumans. These animations are anchored in political, social, cultural, economic and environmental contexts where their producers are immersed. Thus, the anxieties and fears that emerge during the period in which an animation is produced translate into various suggestions to viewers, children or not, impacting their worldviews.[3]

Several historians have pointed to the importance of analysing different genres (including fantasy and science fiction), whether in cinema or TV series, to understand the feelings of a given epoch on issues such as race, gender, politics, environment and even the very constitution of time and history.[4] Some philosophers understand the potential of science fiction and fantasy in proposing new ontologies. Donna Haraway, for example, through the figure of the cyborg and her definition of speculative fabulation, explores the potential of science fiction and fantasy works in the formation of new ways of understanding and acting on themes related to gender, technology and environment – which Haraway sees as interwoven.[5] Less common, but no less important, are the historians for whom the fantasy genre is an important field of controversy about human and nonhuman agency in history. Few environmental historians are venturing to analyse animations, either as evidence of a period's feelings and intellectual climate (especially about the environment) or as potential sources of inspiration for new ways of thinking about the role of nonhumans and humans in history. Drawing on philosopher Theodor Adorno, Adam O'Brien argued that nonhumans, even if they appear mutely in artworks, are eloquent in their silence. As for moving images, like films, there are different ways in which this silence is eloquent. A film does not need to have nonhumans as protagonists for them to play a role in the story and to send messages or give clues about issues involving the environment. For example, the film *Titanic* (1997) does not have nonhumans as the narrative centre, but the ship's collision with an iceberg is eloquent about the relationship between technology and the environment.[6]

However, the subversion of reality operated by the fantasy genre, especially in animations, can literally make nonhumans speak. This can be advantageous for the analyst. The animated series *Steven Universe*, featured by the pay-TV channel Cartoon Network between 2013 and 2020, has gender relations as its central theme, mainly because it uses genderless aliens as protagonists.[7] However, the character Lapis Lazuli, an elemental or anthropomorphic incarnation of water, with all its history of suffering, ambivalent behaviour and drama, also offers clues to understanding the relationships between different human groups, institutions and water. A queer character par excellence, Lapis Lazuli touches on various issues beyond the relationship between humans and water, shedding light on the ultimate existential mismatch between the physical manifestations of water and those human desires and representations anchored in a modern ideal of ordering and controlling that which is framed as 'nature'.[8] Thus, in addition to being an indication of current anxieties related to the environmental crisis and its relationships with colonialism and gender, Lapis Lazuli also inspires new ways of thinking historically about the relationships between water, humans and the planet as a whole. Above all, it raises questions about the human capacity to control and manage water within the framework of modernity.

In the case of the animation *Steven Universe*, this questioning of the role of nonhumans goes beyond the character Lapis Lazuli. Like Lapis Lazuli, the bodies of Homeworld aliens – protagonists of the plot along with the main character Steven (a human-alien hybrid child) – are formed by gems. As the environmental historian Evelyn Ramiel pointed out, an ecological and geological stratum permeates the entire plot. It expands the notion of an ethic of care to encompass queer populations, including an ethic of coexistence towards the whole planet and its different inhabitants.[9] On the one hand, Ramiel's analysis aligns with O'Brien's previously cited position on the presence of nonhumans in moving images. On the other hand, it confirms the potential of animation films and series to propose new ways of thinking about the environment through the subversion of reality.

In the case of animations that touch on environmental themes, issues related to the role of nonhumans become particularly evident in the fantasy and science fiction genres. It is the nature of environmental animations to produce knowledge, subjectivities and speculations about the planet's future and humanity, problematisations that typically emerge from the centrality of nonhumans as subjects in the narrative.[10] There are several examples. In the Brazilian short animation *Entrevista com o Morcego* (Interview with the bat), released in 2000 by Dustan Oeven and Moisés Cabral, the main character is a bat that reveals some of the intricacies of the destruction of its former habitat (a cave) and its consequent migration and adaptation in a new habitat: cities.[11] In *O Diário da Terra* (The earth's journal, 2011), by Diogo Viegas, the main character is a child who tells how climate change affects their daily life.[12] The shadow of extinction hangs over them and the other beings in the story, producing a sense of a 'common future' where everyone is both producer and victim of unprecedented transformations. Thus, environmental animations are prolific sources for the work of environmental historians, with the potential to produce new ways of thinking about nonhumans and their role in people's lives.

Drawing on these analyses, here I interpret the short films *Abuela Grillo* (2009), by Denis Chapon, and *Nimbus, o Caçador de Nuvens* (2016), by Marco Nick and Matheus Antunes. The former is a Danish-Bolivian co-production, and the latter is a Brazilian production. Both works address social attempts to control and manage water through technical and economic apparatuses. On the one hand, both animations outline anxieties and highlight historical tensions related to the crisis of what geographer Jamie Linton calls 'modern water' (an element subject to privatisation, exploitation and management),[13] associated with social conflicts around water in Latin America. On the other hand, these animations inspire alternative ways of thinking about water and its agency, especially due to its dissolution powers and as a producer of contingencies. The agency of water itself turns attempts at managing and controlling it into a perpetual dice rolling with unpredictable outcomes.

As short films, these works share some general characteristics. Walt Disney Studios produced the first animated short films, and usually the stories revolved around a character with a specific goal that was never achieved. These characters' struggles to achieve their goals generate dramatic and conflicting situations, causing the spectators to laugh. Currently, however, the structure of screenplays is freer, contemplating events that affect a well-defined protagonist. It is their experiences that move a story with a reduced number of secondary characters.[14] In the case of *Abuela Grillo*, the main character is the incarnation of water, who is affected by different attempts to control it, either to produce its scarcity or abundance. In *Nimbus*, the protagonist is a boy who lives in a small village. He tries to control the water for distribution and use in his small community but is faced with an unexpected event. Both productions outline anxieties related to water distribution in Latin America, rejecting the notions of water resource and representation and forging new meanings that recognise the active role of water in the constitution of the planet – active not in the sense of conscious action but in the sense of producer of historical realities through meetings and events.

Abuela Grillo: privatisation and the Water War in Cochabamba

Abuela Grillo is an animated short film produced by the Animation Workshop, with the participation of Nicobis Escorzo, from the Comunidad de Animadores Bolivianos and with the support of the Embassy of Denmark. The animation was directed by French filmmaker Denis Chapon, with the participation of the important Bolivian animation director Alfredo Ovando and Luzmila Carpio, an internationally recognised Quechua singer and songwriter.[15] The narrative consists of two intertwined stories, one mythological and the other based on recent events. The former is the myth of the Ayoreo Indigenous people living in Bolivia and Paraguay about Abuela Direjná (or Abuela Grillo), the mistress of water. According to stories told by these Indigenous people and described in a children's work by the Bolivian writer Liliana de la Quintana, one day, Abuela Grillo produced catastrophic rainfall, forcing the Ayoreo to expel her from the community. After Abuela Grillo's departure, a great drought hit the region, causing the grandchildren of the inhabitants who expelled Direjná to set out on a journey to bring her back.[16] The second story is about the popular uprising in Cochabamba in 2000 against the privatisation of water led by a conglomerate of multinational companies.

Thus, *Abuela Grillo* focuses on Direjná's errant trajectory. At first, she settles in a village, producing welcome rains for local subsistence agriculture. The problem is that these rains become torrential and even catastrophic, so the community decides to expel her. Later, business agents find Abuela Grillo in the city, imprisoning her. They start to charge for the water she produces while singing, while the poorest populations and those in the interior begin to suffer both from the lack of rain and the abusive prices for water, now privatised. During the peak of conflicts between Indigenous populations and security forces defending corporate interests, Abuela Grillo produces a great cataclysm that ends the war.

In part, this animation dialogues with a movement of reaction to the expansion and intensification of the capitalist/extractivist model in South America. In peasant and Indigenous communities in the Andes, this reaction has as a striking feature the environmentalisation of struggles in the ontology of *buen vivir*.[17] Buen vivir (*sumak kawsay and sumaq qamaña*) is a complex set of knowledge and practices based on the remnants of the historic livelihoods of Andean Indigenous peoples. It has been recognised as an alternative to European notions of progress, development and consumption-based well-being.[18] It is a broad and diverse concept that develops in particular ways through the practices of different Indigenous populations, Andean social movements and state policies, as in Bolivia and Ecuador. Common to all these versions is the criticism of the notion of development, anthropocentrism and patriarchy, proposing multicultural forms of existence, consensual participation in the political sphere and a non-hierarchical relationship with nonhumans, who can be understood as subjects of rights just like humans.[19] The biocentric and even animist dimension – related to the notion of Pachamama – is identified as fundamental in the formulations of buen vivir. *Abuela Grillo* is somehow part of this movement of ontological contestation of Cartesian realism that is the basis of the capitalist economic model and of the modern State, suggesting alternatives for the relationship between humans and nonhumans.

On the other hand, the animation addresses the historical episode of the reaction to the privatisation of water in Cochabamba led by international organisations and which became known as the Water War. Cochabamba has been the scene of conflicts related to water, both because of its semi-arid condition and the great inequality in urban supply, producing a chronic problem of scarcity.[20] In the 1990s, the World Bank recommended and supported a broad structural reform in Bolivia, which included water distribution services, which should be privatised and water taxed according to market criteria. At the end of 1999, without popular consultation and in breach of due legal process, the municipal water distribution company was granted to the multinational company Águas Del Tunari. In addition to the concession having provoked tension with several Indigenous communities, peasants and irrigators who controlled water management in their territories, in January 2000, the company

implemented a 35 per cent increase in tariffs, which provoked the rebellion. As a result of massive protests with tens of thousands of people taking
to the streets, violent repressions and negotiations, the concession was
cancelled in April of the same year. This was an important victory for
social movements against a neoliberal and globalising logic of water
management.[21]

Despite the animation portraying the episode of the Water War in
Cochabamba, there is no explicit sign of praise or exaltation to the event.
It appears more as a backdrop to water itself, embodied in Abuela Grillo
and her powers. This is perhaps due to the controversial circumstances following the rebellion. Water scarcity continued in Cochabamba, as well as
uneven distribution in the urban area, especially as city dwellers remained
on the sidelines of the protests.[22] Despite the solidarity at the time of the
rebellion, the maintenance of peasant and Indigenous autonomy turned
into a dispute over water. Finally, the idea of democratising decision-
making processes, very much in vogue in the movement's slogans,
resulted in limits and tensions involving the state and local groups that
controlled irrigation infrastructure and were also at the forefront of the
protests.[23] Given this scenario, most of the participants in the Cochabamba
rebellion supported the mega-project for water transposition and the construction of the Misicuni hydroelectric power plant, which caused several
impacts on the environment and the livelihoods of the Indigenous and
peasant communities of the Misicuni valley.[24]

On the other hand, as much as Abuela Grillo is somehow inserted in
the movement that values Andean Indigenous ontologies as ways of contesting the philosophical bases of capitalism, she also keeps an implicit
distance in relation to the ideas and activities framed as buen vivir. Some
studies describe buen vivir (or *vivir bien*) as a concept encompassing cul-
turalist, contradictory, hybrid and idealised discourses constructed by
extracting practices and knowledge in specific Indigenous and peasant
contexts.[25] According to some authors, these notions are often unknown to
most Indigenous and Andean populations. However, they are generalised
in formulating public policies to raise funds for international organisations
that support environmental conservation while disguising alternative
and conventional capitalist development projects.[26] Far from focusing
on transcendental dimensions or on the Ayoreo myth itself, the animation uses the idea of buen vivir as a support for a narrative anchored much
more in the immanence of water – which is visible in Abuela Grillo's
behaviour – thus avoiding these controversies.

The animation *Abuela Grillo* starts from some implicit anxieties about
the various contradictions, conflicts and debates around water. The rejec-
tion of green capitalism – which calls for increased management and

efficiency in water use through technical, scientific and economic control – is explicitly portrayed as negative and even perverse, expressed in the most varied ways that capitalist agents violate Abuela Grillo. On the other hand, the peasants who expelled Abuela Grillo go to the city to rescue her from her capitalist prison, even though she does not return to the peasant community after the end of the conflict, as in the Ayoreo myth. The hypothesis to be developed later in this text is that, far from siding with either contesting force, this animation uses them to reject the modern idea of water as a resource, contradicting the perspective of a fragile or passive element awaiting preservation or conservation.

Nimbus, o Caçador de Nuvens: water and developmentalism in Brazil

While in *Abuela Grillo* water is amid social conflicts over different forms of economy, ways of life and material needs, in *Nimbus, the Cloud Hunter* the dilemmas are much more implicit and existential. This is a Brazilian short animation released in 2016 by Marco Nick in partnership with Factorio Studio and Leben 108 Filmes, participating in several national and international festivals. The story is centred in a small village in the midst of a dense forest, whose population has clothes and customs that resemble traditional peoples. The protagonist of their traditions is Nimbus, a boy who spends his days hunting and trapping clouds and stars. The stars are used as bait to capture the clouds, which are placed in a machine that forces them to precipitate water and emit electricity, both used to generate the drinking water that supplies the village. However, a mysterious spirit of the forest appears in the village and causes a small event that distracts Nimbus during the functioning of the rain-generating machine. This minor distraction is enough for the clouds to break free, causing a massive storm that devastates the village. After the catastrophe, Nimbus continues his journey to imprison more clouds and restart its work.

Although he is a dreamy and innocent boy, Nimbus manages the water distribution in the village, which justifies the imprisonment of clouds and stars to generate well-being for the community. But this practice proves to be perverse, constituting a sort of torture of nature (in this case, clouds and stars) along the lines of what was widely defended in the works of Scientific Revolution philosophers in the seventeenth century. According to Carolyn Merchant, philosophers such as Francis Bacon used torture and rape as metaphors for the scientific method. Just as the inquisitors imprisoned, interrogated and tortured witches to obtain their secrets and confessions, scientists should imprison, interrogate and torture nature to unveil its secrets with a view to the progress of humanity.[27] The indirect reference to the imprisonment and torture of nature using characters that embody water is not exactly new in animations, as seen in the case of the character Lapis Lazuli in the first season of *Steven Universe*, which ran between 2013 and 2015.

The animation was produced in the final moments of the new developmentalist model implemented by leftist governments in Latin America, especially in Brazil, between 2003 and 2016 (the Lula da Silva and Dilma Rousseff administrations). This model was initially highly praised for having as its motto the reduction of social inequality with income redistribution policies, wage increases and GDP growth. However, in reality, what was seen was macroeconomic stability sustained by the explosion of exports of primary goods (commodities) with the intensification of the exploration of land, minerals, forests and water, construction of large hydroelectric projects and increased consumption, with limited results in terms of reducing social inequality.[28] Also, this development was linked to a green capitalist model, which tried to combine accelerated economic growth with the transformation of biodiversity, forests, and water into environmental services under the tutelage of the global financial market.[29] The relative success of this model and its emphasis on strengthening the national bourgeoisie was also fundamental for Brazil's sub-imperialist expansion in Latin America via the financing of the construction of infrastructure megaprojects such as the Cachuela Esperanza hydroelectric plant in Bolivia.[30]

With all its contradictions, the political, geopolitical, economic and environmental circumstances in South America, especially in Bolivia and Brazil, are the background that unites *Abuela Grillo* and *Nimbus*, in the seven years that separate the release of the two animations. However, in *Nimbus*, there is a clear tendency to exempt the protagonist from any malevolent intention regarding the clouds and stars. Nimbus is portrayed as a boy who, innocently, does not understand that there may be other ways to generate water in the village other than using technocratic measures. In *Abuela Grillo*, contradictions exist both in the way peasants deal with water and in the perverse treatment given to Direjná by businessmen for profit. On the other hand, in *Nimbus*, there is a softer connotation of the intentions behind the attempt to dominate the waters. This stems from the emphasis that the animation gives to the moral lesson and the proposition of an alternative ethics in the relationship with water and other nonhumans. This ethic has a much more cooperative than antagonistic connotation, which perhaps has impacted the structure of the narrative.

However, even though there is an emphasis on moral teaching and ethical principles at the end of *Nimbus*, both animations are linked much more to the immanence of phenomena than to ideas. The encounters, events and affections are fundamental in Nimbus's repentance and in forming an ethical alternative that mysteriously expands in the village. As in *Abuela Grillo*, the notion of water as a resource is rejected through an alternative and immanent perspective of water. On the other hand, in his relationships with the rest of the world, water somehow forces the protagonist to produce new meanings and representations in the face of what manifests itself as wonderful, surprising and even terrifying. These concrete aspects, which will be analysed later, are fundamental to the story's ending.

Indifference, dissolution and contingency

As a character, Abuela Grillo is not openly portrayed as water but as an anthropomorphised cricket. This has to do with the very core of the Ayoreo myth, where the mistress of the water is shaped like a cricket. Despite this appearance, Abuela Grillo is considered to be water, regardless of what can be seen directly on the character's surface. In the case of Abuela Grillo, water works as something very close to a last-instance identity in a Laruellian sense: it is a real essence apparently 'removed', but which is neither a backdrop nor an attribute, but a transunary manifestation of the world.[31] 'Transunary' means that, as a trope, the real manifests itself as a limit, traumatising the production of meanings and languages, and determining thought while remaining indifferent to concepts, theories and representations.[32] Thus, water determines Abuela Grillo's behaviour, regardless of her thoughts, conscious desires and body appearance, similar to what happens to Elsa of Arendelle in the animation *Frozen*.[33] But unlike Elsa, who experiences the drama of being water herself throughout *Frozen* and its sequel, *Abuela Grillo* does not resist this indifferent determination imposed by reality.

Perhaps because *Abuela Grillo* does not show any resistance to this determination, the indifference of the waters is manifested in the character's behaviour throughout the nearly thirteen minutes of animation. Arriving in a subsistence farming village, Abuela Grillo makes it rain and stays there after a child invites her to stay. After she decides to stay, she delivers an ear of corn to the child's father, symbolising the possibility of abundant harvests. But this is just a possibility. By making it rain day and night and producing a catastrophe, Abuela Grillo provokes in that man the desire to throw the corn she had given him in her face, making her stop singing and leave. Abuela Grillo's irritation is momentary. She leaves in the same calm way she had arrived, thus continuing her journey through cities, fields and high mountains, producing rain, snow and winds with varying intensities, being well received and treating everyone politely. For the population that expelled it, what was left was a devastating drought, killing rivers, animals and agriculture. Abuela Grillo doesn't need anyone, but all living beings need her and her singing.

While they understand that human society depends on water, business-men do not understand that substance's uncontrollability. They believe they can control, conceptualise and value matter, something that is at the heart of capitalism, as argued by Katerina Kolozova.[34] In the city, Abuela Grillo is imprisoned and forced to sing so that she produces ever-growing amounts of water. Then the businessmen that imprisoned her start to pro-duce and manage an artificial scarcity, limiting the quantity of water to be consumed by each inhabitant. The man that threw corn on Abuela Grillo's face is the one who finds her imprisoned and tortured, instigating the rural population to rise in rebellion in the city. Even though tortured, humiliated and imprisoned, Abuela Grillo reacts violently only when she sees her face on the surface of a bar-coded plastic bottle. The devastating storm she creates destroys the entire city and frees her. However, after this, she continues her journey. She does not care much about the rural folk that tried to free her; there is no sign of gratitude. On the contrary, those same people start to follow her, singing with her. Thus, the most evident situa-tion in *Abuela Grillo* is how much the water affects different human social groups in different ways due to an unavoidable physical dependence. On the other hand, water's most fundamental attributes prove little affected by human actions, as Abuela Grillo's imprisonment and torture do not change her behaviour and power over the planet.

In *Nimbus*, indifference is much less evident. In reality, the universe seems more collaborative and stable, being disturbed by human attempts at technological domination. Thus, animals, humans, clouds, liquid water and stars are all inserted and participate in the constitution of the same world, which is disturbed by an erroneous notion of a relation-ship with the Other. Unlike what happens in *Abuela Grillo*, the main character is a human, and the anthropomorphic clouds (clusters of water and ice particles with eyes and mouths) are secondary characters, though of paramount importance to the story. These clouds are tortured and oppressed by a machine that makes them produce precipitation to supply the village with water. Not only do humans benefit from the water plucked from the clouds, but the demand for domestic animals and livestock, treated empathetically by humans in the village, is also met. This fictional society has a clear hierarchical differentiation between organic and inor-ganic, even if wild animals rarely appear in the story. Thus, *Nimbus* is less centred on the nature of water and more on how water constitutes a universe that is one and plural at the same time. Here, indifference makes sense when one observes how water manifests itself in certain moments of the plot.

Even though it is less centred on the identity of water, it manifests itself in *Nimbus* as strikingly as it does in *Abuela Grillo*. This identity is linked to dissolution in a broad sense. There are several studies that emphasise the dissolutive manifestation of water, and how much this has been approached in different forms of art today.[35] In these works, dissolution is generally described as catastrophic: creative death, or the formation of new scenarios, things and lives through the dissipation of what existed previously. This is usually more evident in hydrometeorological phenomena, although it also occurs at the molecular level. In *Nimbus*, upon destroying and freeing themselves from the machine responsible for their torture, the imprisoned clouds unite and form a great storm, destroying the village, dreams, work and the boy's reputation. The water supply in the village also becomes subject to the risk of shortages, with the destruction of the technical apparatus responsible for its management. Despite the main character's apparent determination to return to the village to resolve the situation, he proves unable to do anything in the face of the event's grandeur. Everything he had conquered dissolved, and a new beginning was needed.

In *Abuela Grillo*, the dissolutive aspect manifests at the story's beginning and end. Fearing the consequences of the heavy rains brought by Abuela Grillo, the peasant populations expelled her. Later, this dissolutive condition manifests more dramatically, mixing with the urban struggles for water and eventually destroying the latter and the privatisation ambitions. Although it suggests destruction resulting from the battle between people, the sequence is ambivalent because water is abundantly present on all sides, indicating previous flooding at a catastrophic level. As a dissolution agent, the water cannot be understood within the parameters of modern law – that is, as a public and private good (which is at the heart of the debate about the Water War in Cochabamba) – but as a phenomenon and event that escape the production of meanings and means of control, whether collective or individual. And it is through this immanence that the story provokes the audience to think about the idea of water as a good, whether public or not.

Indifference (markedly intense in *Abuela Grillo* and less evident in *Nimbus*) and dissolution (as something that belongs to an identity of waters) lead to a contingency principle in both animations. In the first scene of the animation, the appearance of Abuela Grillo in the small farming community bringing a welcome rain in the sowing period was not expected. Likewise, no one imagined that her staying would bring the spectre of famine upon the occurrence of torrential rains. The expulsion of Abuela Grillo generated a much more dramatic and unexpected effect: the drought, which turned the possibility of famine into a concrete event. Imprisoning her in the city would have other effects, such as privatising water and producing a shortage leading to mass protests and clashes in the city. Though at this point in the plot, everyone acted as if Abuela Grillo were a fragile, manipulable entity, liable to be imprisoned or whose liberation required humans, she surprises again by creating a great storm that induces the resolution of the social struggle.

A parenthesis is in order about the apparent fragility and sadness of Abuela Grillo in prison, which contaminates the perception and attitude of practically all the characters in the story. If indifference and dissolutive power characterise Abuela Grillo, why does she submit to torture and jail in the city? This ambivalence is associated with the power and the resigned and sad attitude of water elemental characters, which is related to the element's identity. Gaston Bachelard observes this fundamental ambivalence through contradictions and a fluidity typical of water, which operates simultaneously with fragility and strength, femininity and masculinity, death and life, calm and devastation.[36] Water is contradictory and extreme, which applies to Abuela Grillo's behaviour. This behaviour is very similar to that of Lapis Lazuli, who was also imprisoned and tortured in the animation *Steven Universe*. Despite being the most powerful character in this animated series, Lapis Lazuli is the one who suffers the most throughout the story and also the one who demonstrates the most ambivalence in her behaviour. She varies between a melancholy passivity and the manifestation of immense powers that victimise and subjugate both those who consider themselves capable of oppressing her and those who consider themselves capable of protecting her. Like water, both Abuela Grillo and Lapis Lazuli 'withdraw' from total intelligibility by manifesting self-contradictory and non-linear behaviours consistent with a water identity. This condition intensifies the contingent character of the agency of water in the world.

In *Nimbus*, the ambivalent character of water is also evident in the performance of clouds. Faced with the collapsing machine, the clouds break through the cages' bars that imprison them. Why didn't they do it before? This is an unanswered question but one that the non-linear and self-contradictory identity of the waters can explain. On the other hand, although the clouds formed a great storm and devastated the small village, Nimbus's change at the end of the story engenders a peaceful and collaborative attitude on his part towards human affairs, as they relinquish their posture of control and dominion over water. This surprising ending is very different from what happens in *Abuela Grillo*. Still, it also highlights the contingent character that always leaves the viewer and the characters themselves in doubt about the possibilities, future events and consequences of relationships with water. The very turn in Nimbus's thinking and attitudes is the result of a contingency: guided by a kind of forest spirit to the top of a mountain where an intense storm was raging, Nimbus does not find death and destruction, but the collaborative creation of a sublime universe that delights him.

Thus, in both animations, contingency is very close to the definition proposed by the philosopher Quentin Meillassoux, which is a pure possibility without causality or reason for being. It is not related to the inevitable precariousness and destructibility of things at some point in the future but only to a possibility that may or may not materialise.[37] Dissolution is an important part of water's identity, but this power may or may not manifest itself in historical processes. In both *Abuela Grillo* and *Nimbus*, water is not manageable and controllable. Still, at some point, it was under apparent human control and dominion (justifying its significance as a 'resource') without any reason for this submission. Likewise, the disruptions that dissolved scenarios, plans, meanings and intentions also occurred without apparent causality. The exception is the big storm produced by Abuela Grillo in the city, hinting at a rebellion against its commodification. In *Nimbus*, there is no reason for the storm that devastates the village, although the machine's collapse that trapped the clouds can be understood as a facilitator of the process. Thus, three aspects that summarise water in both animations are indifference, dissolution and contingency.

In historical terms, these alternative ways of thinking about water can inspire the analysis of its agency, which affects all aspects of human life. Both animations analysed here show frustrated attempts to control and dominate water for human consumption, to maintain an economic system or ways of life marked by dichotomies that produce an idealised and hierarchical world. Even under apparent human control, water acts through its indifference to desires and meanings, dissolving and traumatising various aspects of human social life in a contingent way. Thus, success or failure in managing water or manipulating it as a resource has a logic that can be compared to the randomness of a dice roll. The dice-rolling metaphor is used by Louis Althusser when analysing the randomness of the effects of encounters: nothing can guarantee their success or failure, their consequences, or even their effectiveness.[38] Both animations suggest that the historian should understand human interventions on the water as encounters, going beyond the representations of human actors who understand – and often describe in the sources they produce – they are dominating and controlling natural elements. In this way, one must primarily observe the unexpected and undesirable effects of/in these processes, understanding the successes not as triumphs of human reason but as possibilities that could (not have) come true.

Final remarks

Abuela Grillo and *Nimbus, o Caçador de Nuvens* are animations of the environmental genre anchored in different historical, political and social circumstances, reflecting anxieties about the water problem in Latin America. On the one hand, *Abuela Grillo* reflects the debates on buen vivir in the Andean countries and, on the other hand, the reactions and movements to contest the neoliberal water regime implemented in the late 1990s and early 2000s. Rather than an exaltation of these movements, the animation indirectly draws attention to the controversies surrounding these processes, highlighting the contradictions in the behaviour of different social groups in the face of the erratic flow of water embodied in the character Abuela Grillo. These controversies are related to the moment after the historical events portrayed in the animation, when leftist governments appropriated specific ideas of traditional populations, continuing management practices and capitalist development in new ways. *Nimbus* is immersed in this developmentalist context. Despite speeches and propaganda about social well-being and the reduction of inequality, developmentalism retained the logic of management by intensifying water exploitation.

In addition to being important sources of a historical analysis of conflicts related to water in Latin America, these animations can inspire the historian to go beyond the classic notion of water as a resource, representation or scenario of human actions. Rejecting the idea of water as a resource to be managed or protected/conserved by humans, both animations suggest an identity of water linked to the notions of indifference, dissolution and contingency, which are central to analysing its active dimension in the constitution of the past. Thus, these animations tease the viewer about something that environmental historians usually ignore: that water movement is a real phenomenon that often escapes human narratives, meanings and control. A story that prioritises human narratives, ideas and intentions as its engines – retaining the notion of water as a resource or representation of human agents – is nothing more than a social story that unduly appropriates the 'environmental' label. Here 'environmental' is more an adjective than an alternative possibility of thinking, being and living on the planet and with the other entities that form it. In this sense, more than serving as historical sources, environmental animations can be powerful instruments of social, theoretical and methodological change for history and other humanities disciplines.

Notes

1. Philip Kelly Denslow, 'What is animation and who needs to know? An essay on definitions'. In: Jayne Pilling (ed.) *A reader in animation studies*. London, Jon Libbey, 1997, 1–4.

2. Jelisaveta Blagojević, 'Thinking WithOut'. In: Katerina Kolozova & Eileen A. Joy (eds.) *After the speculative turn: realism, philosophy, and feminism*. Santa Barbara, CA, Punctum Books, 2016, 95–106.

3. Lincoln Geraghty, 'Introduction: future visions'. In: Lincoln Geraghty (ed.) *Channelling the future: essays on science fiction and fantasy television*. Lanham, MD, Toronto and Plymouth, UK, The Scarecrow Press Inc., 2009, vii–xviii; David Whitley, *The idea of nature in Disney animation*. Hampshire, Ashgate, 2008; Peter Hunt, 'Introduction: fantasy and alternative worlds'. In: Peter Hunt & Millicent Lenz (eds.) *Alternative worlds in fantasy fiction*. London, Continuum, 2001; Paul Wells, *Understanding animation*. London and New York, Routledge, 1998.

4. David C. Wright, Jr., 'Constructing a grand historical narrative: struggles through time on highlander: the series'. In: David C. Wright, Jr. & Allan W. Austin (eds.) *Space and time: essays on visions of history in science fiction and fantasy television*. Jefferson, NC, McFarland & Company, 2010, 116–30; Judith Lancioni, 'The future as past perfect: appropriation of history in the Star Trek series'. In: *Space and Time*, 2010, 131–55.

5. Haraway, Donna, *Simians, cyborgs and woman: the reinvention of nature*. New York, Routledge, 1991; *Staying with the trouble: making kin in the Chthulucene*. Durham, NC, Duke University Press, 2016.

6. Adam O'Brien, *Film and the natural environment: elements and atmosphere*. London-New York, Wallflower Press, 2018.

7. Eli Dunn, 'Steven Universe, fusion magic, and the queer cartoon carnivalesque', *Gender Forum. An Internet Journal for Gender Studies* 56 (2016), 44–57.

8. André Vasques Vital, 'Lapis Lazuli: politics and aqueous contingency in the animation Steven Universe', *Series – International Journal of TV Serial Narratives* 4, no. 1 (2018), 51–62; Vasques Vital, 'Water, gender, and modern science in the Steven Universe animation', *Feminist Media Studies* 20, no. 8 (2019), 1144–58.

9. Evelyn Ramiel, 'Growing up in the Crystallocene: how Steven Universe teaches compassion for broken worlds'. In: John R. Ziegler & Leah Richards (eds.) *Representation in Steven Universe*. London, UK, Palgrave Macmillan, 2020, 171–96.

10. Nicole Starosielski, '"Movements that are drawn": a history of environmental animation from The Lorax to FernGully to Avatar', *The International Communication Gazette* 73, nos. 1–2 (2011), 145–63.

11. Dustan Oeven & Moisés Cabral, *Entrevista com o morcego* [Animated Short Film]. Etnia Produções e Cinematografia, 2000.

12. Diogo Viegas, *O diário da Terra / Earth Diary* [Animated Short Film]. Viegas Estúdio, 2011.

13. Jamie Linton, *What is water? The history of a modern abstraction*. Vancouver, UBS Press, 2010.

14. Pat Cooper & Ken Dancyger, *Writing the short film*. Third Edition, Amsterdam, Elsevier Focal Press, 2005, 1–5.

15. Giannalberto Bendazzi, *Animation: a world history. Volume 3: contemporary times*. Boca Raton, FL, CRC Press, 2017, 323.

16. Liliana de la Quintana, Abuela Grillo, *ComKids*, August 14, 2013, https://comkids.com.br/abuela-grilo.

17. Adriana Michéle Campos Johnson, 'An expanse of water: how to know water through film'. In: Lisa Blackmore & Liliana Gómez (eds.) *Liquid ecologies in Latin American and Caribbean art*. New York and London, Routledge, 2020, 54–70.

18. Nicolás Cuvi, 'Indigenous imprint and remnants in the tropical Andes'. In: John Soluri, Claudia Leal & José Augusto Pádua (eds.) *A living past: environmental histories of modern Latin America*. New York, Berghahn, 2018, 67–90.

19. Eduardo Gudynas & Alberto Acosta, 'La renovación de la crítica al desarrollo y el buen vivir como alternativa', *Utopía y Praxis Latinoamericana* 16, no. 53 (2011), 71–83.

20. Nicola Neso, 'De la guerra del agua hasta la guerra del gas – los movimientos sociales de Bolivia y la elección de Evo Morales', *Iberóforum. Revista de Ciencias Sociales de la Universidad Iberomaericana* 8, no. 15 (2013), 207–32.

21. Carlos Crespo Flores, 'La "Guerra del Agua" en Cochabamba: movimientos sociales y crisis de dispositivos del poder', *Ecología Política* 20 (2000), 59–70.

22. Thomas Perreault, 'From the "Guerra Del Agua" to the "Guerra Del Gas": resource governance, neoliberalism and popular protest in Bolivia', *Antipode* 38, no. 1 (2006), 150–72.

23. Nina Laurie, Robert Andolina & Sarah Radcliffe, 'The excluded "indigenous"? The implications of multi-ethnic policies for water reform in Bolivia'. In: Rachel Sieder (ed.) *Multiculturalism in Latin America: indigenous rights, diversity and democracy*. New York, Palgrave, 2002, 252–76; Maisa Soledad Bascuas & Irene Provenzano, 'El agua en Bolivia después de la crisis neoliberal: entre la apertura democratizadora y los límites del andamiaje estatal', *La Revista del CCC* 19, no. 7 (2013), https://www.centrocultural.coop/revista.

24. Paul Hoogendam & Rutgerd Boelens, 'Dams and damages: conflicting epistemo-logical frameworks and interests concerning "compensation" for the Misicuni Project's socio-environmental impacts in Cochabamba, Bolívia', *Water* 11, no. 3 (2019).

25. Víctor Bretón Solo de Záldivar, 'Etnicidad, desarrollo y "buen vivir": reflexiones críticas en perspectiva histórica', *Revista europea de estudios latinoamericanos y del Caribe – European Review of Latin American and Caribbean Studies* 95 (2013), 71–95; Andreu Viola Recasens, 'Discursos "pachamamistas" versus políticas desarrollistas: el debate sobre el sumak kawsay en los Andes', *Íconos: Revista de Ciencias Sociales* 48 (2014), 55–72; Pablo Alonso González & Alfredo Macías Vázquez, 'An ontological turn in the debate on buen vivir – sumak kawsay in Ecuador: ideology, knowledge, and the common', *Latin American and Caribbean Ethnic Studies* 10 (2015), 315–34.

26. Alison Spedding Pallet, '"Suma qamaña" ¿Kamsañ muni? (¿Qué quiere decir "vivir bien"?)', *Fe y Pueblo* 17 (2010), 4–39; Sandro Mezzadra, 'América Latina: entre impasse y nuevo conflicto social. Notas para reabrir la discusión'. In: Mauro Cerbino & Isabella Giunta (eds.) *Biocapitalismo, procesos de gobierno y movimientos sociales*. Quito, FLACSO, 2012, 97–108; Denise Arnold, María Clara Zeballos & Juan Fabbri, El "vivir bien" (suma qamaña / sumaq kawsay) en Bolívia: un paraíso ìdealizado no tan "andino"', *Etcétera. Revista del Área de Ciencias Sociales Del CIFyH* 4 (2019), 1–29.

27. Carolyn Merchant, *The death of nature: women, ecology, and the scientific revolution*. San Francisco, CA, Harper & Row, 1980.

28. Lauro Mattei, 'Brazilian development at the beginning of the 21st century: economic growth, income distribution, and environmental destruction'. In: Heinrich Böll Foundation (ed.) *Inside a champion: an analysis of the Brazilian development model*. Berlin, Heinrich Böll Stiftung, 2012, 31–44.

29. Camila Moreno, 'Green economy and development(alism) in Brazil: resources, climate and energy politics'. In: Heinrich Böll Foundation, 2012, 45–59; Larissa

Packer, 'From nature to natural capital: how new legal and financial mechanisms create a market for the green economy'. In: Heinrich Böll Foundation, 2012, 114–28.

30. Armando Boito, Jr. & Tatiana Berringer, 'Brasil: classes sociais, neodesenvolvimentismo e política externa nos governos Lula e Dilma', *Revista de Sociologia e Política* 21, no. 47 (2013), 31–8; Rafael Teixeira Lima, 'Entre o imperialismo e o subimperialismo: a projeção brasileira à Bolívia e ao Peru nos governos Lula da Silva (2003–2010)', *Rebela* 6, no. 3 (2016), 530–45.

31. François Laruelle, *Theory of identities*. Translated by Alyosha Edlebi. New York, Columbia University Press, 2016, 45.

32. Katerina Kolozova, *Capitalism's holocaust of animals: a non-Marxist critique of capital, philosophy and patriarchy*. New York, Bloomsbury, 2019, 21–2.

33. André Vasques Vital, 'Water spells: new materialist theoretical insights from animated fantasy and science fiction', *HALAC-Historia Ambiental Latinoamericana y Caribeña* 12, no. 1 (2022), 246–69.

34. Kolozova, 2019.

35. Astrida Neimanis, 'Feminist subjectivity, watered', *Feminist Review* 103 (2013), 23–41; Vasques Vital, 2018; Vasques Vital, 2019; Edwige Tamalet Talbayev, 'Seawater', *Contemporary French and Francophone Studies* 21, no. 2 (2021), 207–17.

36. Gaston Bachelard, *A Água e os sonhos: ensaio sobre a imaginação da matéria*, Translated by Antônio de Pádua Danesi. São Paulo, Martins Fontes, 1997.

37. Quentin Meillassoux, *After finitude: an essay on the necessity of contingency*. London, UK, Bloomsbury Academic, 2008.

38. Louis Althusser, 'The underground current of the materialism of the encounter'. In: Olivier Corpet & François Matheron (eds.) *Philosophy of the encounter: later writings, 1978–1987*. London, Verso, 2006, 163–207, p. 174.

References

Althusser, Louis, 'The underground current of the materialism of the encounter'. In: Olivier Corpet & François Matheron (eds.) *Philosophy of the encounter: later writings, 1978–1987*. London, Verso, 2006.

Arnold, Denise, María Clara Zeballos & Juan Fabbri, 'El "vivir bien" (suma qamaña / sumaq kawsay) en Bolívia: un paraíso idealizado no tan "andino"', *Etcétera. Revista del Área de Ciencias Sociales Del CIFyH* 4 (2019), 1–29.

Bachelard, Gaston, *A Água e os sonhos: ensaio sobre a imaginação da matéria*, Translated by Antônio de Pádua Danesi. São Paulo, Martins Fontes, 1997.

Bascuas, Maisa Soledad & Irene Provenzano, 'El agua en Bolivia después de la crisis neoliberal: entre la apertura democratizadora y los límites del andamiaje estatal', *La Revista del CCC* 19, no. 7 (2013), https://www.centrocultural.coop/revista.

Bendazzi, Giannalberto, *Animation: a world history. Volume 3: contemporary times*. Boca Raton, FL, CRC Press, 2017.

Blagojević, Jelisaveta, 'Thinking WithOut'. In: Kolozova, Katerina & Eileen A. Joy (eds.) *After the speculative turn: realism, philosophy, and feminism*. Santa Barbara, CA, Punctum Books, 2016.

Boito, Jr., Armando & Tatiana Berringer, 'Brasil: classes sociais, neodesenvolvimentismo e política externa nos governos Lula e Dilma', *Revista de Sociologia e Política* 21, no. 47 (2013), 31–8.

Cooper, Pat & Ken Dancyger, *Writing the short film*. Third Edition, Amsterdam, Elsevier Focal Press, 2005.

Cuvi, Nicolás, 'Indigenous imprint and remnants in the tropical Andes'. In: Soluri, John, Claudia Leal & José Augusto Pádua (eds.) *A living past: environmental histories of modern Latin America*. New York, Berghahn, 2018.

De la Quintana, Liliana, Abuela Grillo, *ComKids*, August 14, 2013, https://comkids.com.br/abuela-grilo.

Denslow, Philip Kelly, 'What is animation and who needs to know? An essay on definitions'. In: Jayne Pilling (ed.) *A reader in animation studies*. London, Jon Libbey, 1997.

Dunn, Eli, 'Steven Universe, fusion magic, and the queer cartoon carnivalesque', *Gender Forum. An Internet Journal for Gender Studies* 56 (2016), 44–57.

Flores, Carlos Crespo, 'La "Guerra del Agua" en Cochabamba: movimientos sociales y crisis de dispositivos del poder', *Ecología Política* 20 (2000), 59–70.

Geraghty, Lincoln, 'Introduction: future visions'. In: Lincoln Geraghty (ed.) *Channelling the future: essays on science fiction and fantasy television*. Lanham, MD, Toronto and Plymouth, UK, The Scarecrow Press Inc., 2009.

González, Pablo Alonso & Alfredo Macías Vázquez, 'An ontological turn in the debate on buen vivir – sumak kawsay in Ecuardor: ideology, knowledge, and the common', *Latin American and Caribbean Ethnic Studies* 10 (2015), 315–34.

Gudynas, Eduardo & Alberto Acosta, 'La renovación de la crítica al desarrollo y el buen vivir como alternativa', *Utopía y Praxis Latinoamericana* 16, no. 53 (2011), 71–83.

Haraway, Donna, *Simians, cyborgs and woman: the reinvention of nature*. New York, Routledge, 1991.

Haraway, Donna, *Staying with the trouble: making kin in the Chthulucene*. Durham, NC, Duke University Press, 2016.

Hoogendam, Paul & Rutgerd Boelens, 'Dams and damages: conflicting epistemological frameworks and interests concerning "compensation" for the Misicuni Project's socio-environmental impacts in Cochabamba, Bolívia', *Water* 11, no. 3 (2019), 408–28.

Hunt, Peter, 'Introduction: fantasy and alternative worlds'. In: Hunt, Peter & Millicent Lenz (eds.) *Alternative worlds in fantasy fiction*. London, Continuum, 2001.

Johnson, Adriana Michéle Campos, 'An expanse of water: how to know water through film'. In: Blackmore, Lisa & Liliana Gómez (eds.) *Liquid ecologies in Latin American and Caribbean art*. New York and London, Routledge, 2020.

Kolozova, Katerina, *Capitalism's holocaust of animals: a non-Marxist critique of capital, philosophy and patriarchy*. New York, Bloomsbury, 2019.

Lancioni, Judith, 'The future as past perfect: appropriation of history in the Star Trek series'. In: Wright, Jr., David C. & Allan W. Austin (eds.) *Space and time: essays on visions of history in science fiction and fantasy television*. Jefferson, NC, McFarland & Company, 2010.

Laruelle, François, *Theory of identities*. Translated by Alyosha Edlebi. New York, Columbia University Press, 2016.

Laurie, Nina, Robert Andolina & Sarah Radcliffe, 'The excluded "indigenous"? The implications of multi-ethnic policies for water reform in Bolivia'. In: Sieder, Rachel (ed.) *Multiculturalism in Latin America: indigenous rights, diversity and democracy*. New York, Palgrave, 2002, 252–76.

Lima, Rafael Teixeira, 'Entre o imperialismo e o subimperialismo: a projeção brasileira à Bolívia e ao Peru nos governos Lula da Silva (2003–2010)', *Rebela* 6, no. 3 (2016), 530–45.

Linton, Jamie, *What is water? The history of a modern abstraction*. Vancouver, UBS Press, 2010.

Mattei, Lauro, 'Brazilian development at the beginning of the 21st century: economic growth, income distribution, and environmental destruction'. In: Heinrich Böll Foundation (ed.) *Inside a champion: an analysis of the Brazilian development model*. Berlin, Heinrich Böll Stiftung, 2012.

Meillassoux, Quentin, *After finitude: an essay on the necessity of contingency*. London, UK, Bloomsbury Academic, 2008.

Merchant, Carolyn, *The death of nature: women, ecology, and the scientific revolution*. San Francisco, CA, Harper & Row, 1980.

Mezzadra, Sandro, 'América Latina: entre impasse y nuevo conflicto social. Notas para reabrir la discusión'. In: Cerbino, Mauro & Isabella Giunta (eds.) *Biocapitalismo, procesos de gobierno y movimientos sociales*. Quito, FLACSO, 2012.

Moreno, Camila, 'Green economy and development(alism) in Brazil: resources, climate and energy politics'. In: Heinrich Böll Foundation (ed.) *Inside a champion: an analysis of the Brazilian development model*. Berlin, Heinrich Böll Stiftung, 2012.

Neimanis, Astrida, 'Feminist subjectivity, watered', *Feminist Review* 103 (2013), 23–41.

Neso, Nicola, 'De la guerra del agua hasta la guerra del gas – los movimientos sociales de Bolivia y la elección de Evo Morales', *Iberóforum. Revista de Ciencias Sociales de la Universidad Iberomaericana* 8, no. 15 (2013), 207–32.

O'Brien, Adam, *Film and the natural environment: elements and atmosphere*. London-New York, Wallflower Press, 2018.

Oeven, Dustan & Moisés Cabral, *Entrevista com o morcego* [Animated Short Film]. Etnia Produções e Cinematografia, 2000.

Packer, Larissa, 'From nature to natural capital: how new legal and financial mechanisms create a market for the green economy'. In: Heinrich Böll Foundation (ed.) *Inside a champion: an analysis of the Brazilian development model*. Berlin, Heinrich Böll Stiftung, 2012.

Pallet, Alison Spedding, '"Suma qamaña" ¿Kamsañ muni? (¿Qué quiere decir "vivir bien"?)', *Fe y Pueblo* 17 (2010), 4–39.

Perreault, Thomas, 'From the "Guerra Del Agua" to the "Guerra Del Gas": resource governance, neoliberalism and popular protest in Bolivia', *Antipode* 38, no. 1 (2006), 150–72.

Ramiel, Evelyn, 'Growing up in the Crystallocene: how Steven Universe teaches compassion for broken worlds'. In: Ziegler, John R. & Leah Richards (eds.) *Representation in Steven Universe*. London, UK, Palgrave Macmillan, 2020.

Recasens, Andreu Viola, 'Discursos "pachamamistas" versus políticas desarrollistas: el debate sobre el sumak kawsay en los Andes', *Íconos: Revista de Ciencias Sociales* 48 (2014), 55–72.

Starosielski, Nicole, '"Movements that are drawn": a history of environmental animation from The Lorax to FernGully to Avatar', *The International Communication Gazette* 73, nos. 1–2 (2011), 145–63.

Talbayev, Edwige Tamalet, 'Seawater', *Contemporary French and Francophone Studies* 21, no. 2 (2021), 207–17.

Viegas, Diogo, *O diário da Terra / Earth Diary* [Animated Short Film]. Viegas Estúdio, 2011.

Vital, André Vasques, 'Lapis Lazuli: politics and aqueous contingency in the animation Steven Universe', *Series – International Journal of TV Serial Narratives* 4, no. 1 (2018), 51–62.

Vital, André Vasques, 'Water, gender, and modern science in the Steven Universe animation', *Feminist Media Studies* 20, no. 8 (2019), 1144–58.

Vital, André Vasques, 'Water spells: new materialist theoretical insights from animated fantasy and science fiction', *HALAC-Historia Ambiental Latinoamericana y Caribeña* 12, no. 1 (2022), 246–69.

Wells, Paul, *Understanding animation*. London and New York, Routledge, 1998.

Whitley, David, *The idea of nature in Disney animation*. Hampshire, Ashgate, 2008.

Wright, Jr., David C., 'Constructing a grand historical narrative: struggles through time on highlander: the series'. In: Wright, Jr., David C. & Allan W. Austin (eds.) *Space and time: essays on visions of history in science fiction and fantasy television*. Jefferson, NC, McFarland & Company, 2010.

Záldivar, Víctor Bretón Solo de, 'Etnicidad, desarrollo y "buen vivir": reflexiones críticas en perspectiva histórica', *Revista Europea de Estudios Latinoamericanos y del Caribe – European Review of Latin American and Caribbean Studies* 95 (2013), 71–95.

Primary sources

Chapon. Denis, Abuela Grillo [Animated Short Film]. The Animation Workshop, Nicobis, Escorzo, and the Community of Bolivians Animators, 2009.

Nick, Marco, *Nimbus: o caçador de núvens* [Animated Short Film]. Cento e Oito Filmes, 2016.

Afterword: more complete stories and better explanations for a renewed worldview

Claudia Leal

The past is mostly nonhuman: we humans came into the picture really late, and even later to the Americas. But *more-than*-human includes the human, so, in the case of what recently came to be called Latin America and the Caribbean, we are talking about roughly 15,000 years, a fraction of the history of humankind, mammals or life on earth. Yet, usually, when we refer to the *history* of this region we narrow it down quite considerably to the last 500 years, for history is defined by a methodology that privileges written documents. Thus, history departments like the one I work in in Bogotá have specialists in the twentieth and nineteenth centuries, and in the colonial past, which spanned 300 years. The millennia before are reserved, for very understandable methodological reasons, to archaeologists. The disinclination historians in general feel towards studying bones or pieces of ceramic has led most to confuse the reach of their expertise with *the past*, producing the odd outcome on shrinking time, at least in their minds. Those studying Latin America and the Caribbean became the champions of this dubious form of magic.

The lack of acknowledgement of deep time (and even of not-so-deep time) is closely related to another form of blindness that makes it difficult for social scientists and humanists to see the interconnections between nonhuman elements and the kind of topics that we study. If besides seeing social classes and identities we remember that we are a species that has a very long evolutionary history, it becomes harder to set ourselves apart from everything that surrounds us and co-constitutes the world. This issue is again related to methods: since we cannot master the expertise of geologists or biologists, we assume that their objects of study – mountains, animals and trees – simply do not exist. Well, to be more precise, they are mostly erased from the universe of elements to be seriously considered within our disciplines, because – of course – those of us who have dogs not only acknowledge their presence but somehow organise our lives partly around it, or, in the case of those of us who live in Bogotá, we are totally aware of the mountains that that allow us to distinguish north from south.

This book calls our attention to the potential of recognising that human pasts are more-than-human. But we may well ask if that is not precisely what environmental history set out to do half a century ago. This subdiscipline has been telling all sorts of stories that involve what we call the environment or nature, thus taking history explicitly beyond the human. During these decades, it has grown and gained recognition, more so in the United States than elsewhere. While this approach is much more recent in Latin American and Caribbean history, where it still needs to carve a more secure place for itself through further contributions, it has made significant inroads. This book does not solely seek to expand those inroads with good case studies; it wishes to make environmental history more significant for understanding Latin American pasts by pointing out and analysing various ways in which nature has affected human trajectories. In other words, the editors and authors of this volume propose to expand the array of actors and actresses that played in the dramas that have made our history, to include drought, earthquakes, mules and water, to name a few examples. For our region, such an approach is not entirely novel, and has behind it the weight of what has come to be called post-humanism and multi-species studies, among other relatively new scholarly trends, but it is certainly a way of doing history that has been rarely explored and holds the promise of helping us compose more complete historical narratives and devise better explanations.

That this proposal is to a large extent a novelty has to do with the history of environmental history and the conundrums of our time. This area of research emerged tied to the concerns of the environmental movement and thus emphasised how people and the social institutions within which they operate have degraded nature. It has since moved in many directions, among them more nuanced ways of assessing transformations that include but go beyond mere harm. We came to understand places as complex 'organic machines', to borrow the expression Richard White used in 1996 to refer to the highly transformed Columbia River, inextricable amalgamations of nature and society. In this manner, environmental history has played a key role in questioning and overcoming the nature–culture divide that so profoundly defines how we think. Despite its variegated expressions, some core elements have remained throughout, recently reinforced by the pressing challenges that geoscientists have made us aware of. As climate change became a serious concern throughout the globe, reinforced by the notion that we are in a geological era – the Anthropocene – defined by the human imprint on the planet, environmental history has had to continue reconstructing and explaining how human actions have so profoundly shaped every corner of the globe. Thus, just as in any other branch of history, human actions have remained usually unchallenged and alone at the centre of the stories.

More-Than-Human Histories of Latin America and the Caribbean is a call to accept that nature has not only been a part of human history but that it has helped make that history. For such a proposition to be considered, it was necessary to scare away the ghosts of environmental determinism, a mindset that prevailed long before the emergence of the social sciences in the late nineteenth century, and from which these needed to break away in order to carve a place of their own. One influential way in which environmental determinism operated was considering that climate defined the character of different peoples and ultimately their fate. Within this tendency to subsume the social into the natural, social thought had to find social causes for social affairs – a move that allowed for the development of the valuable analytical tools that we have for examining the convoluted world we live in. But every advance has its costs, and this one led to separating the social from its connections to the natural world. Environmental history could emerge and blossom by revealing human ways of shaping the environment; moving into natural causation meant treading into discredited terrain. Geography opened a similar path many decades before history did, in a successful effort to shake off the entrenched influence of environmental determinism.

The risk of reducing the social to just a part of the natural created – and still creates – resistance, more so in a context in which the social sciences and the humanities have to continually prove their worth. But for several decades now, factoring in any kind of environmental causation raised a red flag in many corners; the idea that everything is socially constructed reinforced this tendency. Saying that nature has agency, which is what ultimately the call for more-than-human history entails, may sound just like environmental determinism striking back in a new guise. The word agency generates apprehension, for we associate it with deliberate action. How can one exercise power or influence, or accomplish anything (to follow the dictionary's definition of agency), without doing something purposefully to that effect? And, well, it is problematic, to say the least, to affirm that rivers flow with an intent or that cows eat to provide juicy meat for *Homo sapiens*. However, as Gary Shaw has argued, not all human actions that have consequences are deliberate or were meant to produce the outcomes they ultimately had.[1] Therefore, if unintended human actions can play a historical role, so, too, can the behaviour of mules, viruses and storms. Plus, in fact, animals, diseases and disasters caused by extreme climate conditions are mentioned in many historical accounts as doing something, even though authors often do not stop to think what that means in terms of historical agency.

Ascribing agency to non-acting elements of nature (or to those that in human temporalities seem inert) is a harder step to take. However, if we put aside the word agency and focus on the ability of nonhuman elements to affect the course of events, more-than-human history can have quite an extensive reach and encompass minerals, trees and soils. But that reach has limits, for not every meadow, every butterfly or every element in the periodical table can demand historians' attention. For parts of nature to acquire historical visibility they need not merely to exist but to cross paths with social realities in a meaningful way.

Take the case of so-called natural disasters. If a storm destroys houses and infrastructure, bringing death, sorrow and mighty challenges, it enters history. But if it crosses an uninhabited island, it does not, even if the resulting landscape looks ruinous to us. Similarly, if infrastructure has been built to withstand storms, a new one might not make it into history; for the storm to have historical importance it needs a favourable social setting. However, to continue with the previous example, the predecessors of a non-devastating storm would have gained their place in history books, because they set in motion a major change, such as that recounted in Magdalena Gil's excellent chapter about Chile's earthquakes. This assertion is certainly far from implying that disasters only have human causes; it means that nature can only act in conjunction with society to have an impact on human lives and historical trajectories.

Elements of nature much less conspicuous than storms and earthquakes have always intersected history. Take the case of precious metals, which have been embedded in Latin American geology for millions of years and became major protagonists of history when a people obsessed with them organised a society around their extraction. The locations and kinds of deposits contributed to shape the colonial world. That Cerro Rico had the richest silver mines in the world is the ultimate reason that Potosí, one of the largest cities that existed in the sixteenth century, was built in a most inauspicious location: at 4,000 meters above sea level, where everything had to be brought in from afar. Furthermore, the attraction that gold and silver exert over so many people, and their wide use as means of exchange, is possible due to the very particular traits these metals have, which include their durability, lack of toxicity, and melting temperature. This is just one example, mentioned rather than thoroughly developed. Reading Timothy LeCain's *The Matter of History* helped me understand the meaning and reach of this kind of thinking, so, for non-believers or those who are simply puzzled, I would recommend the brilliant explanations that this book offers on how cows, caterpillars and copper have made our world.[2]

Explicitly accepting that elements of nature can be historical players leads to the question of how Latin American and Caribbean histories have been shaped by these often-unacknowledged forces. This book gives us some good examples, from which I want to highlight three kind of potential contributions. I will start, first, with the two chapters on colonial climate, one on extreme cold and rains in Chile and Argentina and a second one on droughts in Guatemala and Mexico. Being aware of the Little Ice Age and the Maunder Minimum (of solar activity), leads Margarita Gascón – in detective mode – to uncover a variety of events caused by climatic anomalies in the early decades of colonisation in the Southern Cone. Rather than connecting different kinds of incidents with climate, Luis Alberto Arrioja Díaz Viruell and María Dolores Ramírez Veja shed light on drought, which caused more noticeable and thus better-known episodes of hunger in the eighteenth century. In the end, these researchers help insert climate, in particular its extremes, as a factor that needs to be considered to understand a period, as well as agriculture and hunger, and other less obvious topics such as war. The basis for these contributions relies on leaving our comfort zone by looking into climate and trying to understand and reconstruct it. Their work can encourage others who examine the same period and localities to make connections that have escaped them, for not everyone is willing to tread into unknown territory. Putting into focus questions that are not in the radar of many should ultimately help compose a better understanding of bygone eras. Brad Skopyk and Katherine Mora Pacheco have published books that illustrate the possibilities that this path brings.[3]

A second kind of contribution is exemplified by Lise Sedrez and Bruno Capilé's chapter, which nicely reconstructs the many entanglements nineteenth-century Rio de Janeiro had with water. To do this thoroughly, the authors, among other things, travel upstream along the creeks that made Rio possible, and downstream to the Guanabara Bay, to follow the labour of the waters that drained into the capital and of those that provided a much-needed sanitary service. Through their careful reconstruction the authors make the reader realise that the geomorphology of the creeks and the tides were crucial to the way the city functioned. In their story, waters are not only subjected to people's labour and designs, but they in themselves play a key role in bringing to life that beautiful and unequal city. This second kind of contribution is not centered on causation but in entanglements, of which nature as an agent is a part.

The third and last contribution I would like to highlight is that in which understanding the agency of nature can dramatically alter historical narratives, such as in the case of Magdalena Gil's chapter. While earthquakes have long been recognised as a defining feature of Chile, historians have not tended to take them seriously. Gil proposes that since the beginning, the formation of the Chilean republican state, which has long been held up as a regional example, was to an important degree crafted in response to the threat of earthquakes. The movements of the earth led to the development of state responsibilities and institutions, and to citizens demanding and accepting these new powers. Furthermore, she mentions that tsunamis were often deadlier than the earthquakes themselves, something that makes Chilean geography an actor, for it is the existence of that long coast and narrow territory that made tsunamis possible.

Such potent re-readings of major historical processes based on taking nature's agency seriously are hard to come by, but they are not entirely novel. John McNeill provided a superb case in *Mosquito Empires*, where he explains how the sugar industry set the scene for yellow fever and its vector, *Aedes aegypti*, to together become a major player in siege war, altering the fate of a region in which European powers fought one another.[4]

With these various contributions, this book suggests new avenues of enquiry. The reader may well ask themself what defines Latin American nature and physical geography, as earthquakes define Chile, to examine how these have helped shape history in large and modest ways. Forests, for instance, that covered over three-thirds of the region's territorial expanse, appeared abundantly in early Latin American environmental history as vanishing nature, victims of broadaxes and chain saws, government policies, and market dynamics. Conversely, they figure prominently in conservation areas, contributing to another form of state building. Additionally, they probably played a part in the extension of the organic energy regime, which was replaced by oil, sidestepping a coal phase. Similarly, the region's water abundance is fundamental to explain why hydraulic infrastructure serves as a major source of electricity in contrast to most of the rest of the world. Forests are the most salient of native ecosystems, which partly because of their tropical location are very diverse, and largely due to low population density had – and still have – a prominent presence. Their existence, exuberance and power helped shape ideas of bountiful nature as well as related practices, while they also provided rural folk with food, medicine and construction materials, contributing to livelihoods, and associated social relations such as labour regimes.

Animals are another a case in point, and a growing and promising area of research. Animal history does not necessarily include nonhuman animals as historical actors in their own right; it can revolve around what happens to them or to the institutions, people and landscapes associated with them, as my own efforts attests.[5] However, these creatures who fascinate us for being similar to us, yet so impossible to fully decipher, and who cross our paths throughout history in so many different ways, are a powerful source of stories. Cows and mules, for instance, have been absolutely key in forging Latin America into what it is. Mules' resolve, physical resistance and shrewdness were fundamental to transportation for several centuries, just as cows' innate ability to turn grass into muscle (meat), skin (hides), dung (fertiliser) and meat, as well as to walk to market, made them invaluable assets behind the development of private property and landscape transformation. Susanna Hecht, decades ago, and Shawn Van Ausdal and Robert Wilcox, more recently, have pointed at how the characteristics of cows are fundamental to understand their historical role.[6] What these geographers have done in relation to cows serves as an example of what still needs to be done with mules, following the steps taken by Sedrez and Capilé in their article about Rio.

This book is therefore an invitation to alter the way we do history. It is an ambitious project, reflected in the wide time-frame and in the varied geographies examined, which show that there is a very broad scope for implementation. Further evidence is found in its inclusion of anthropologists, a geographer, a sociologist and a literary scholar among the authors and editors, which brings me to my last point.

Recognising the agency of the natural world ultimately implies a deep change, epistemological, but also ontological; it encourages examining our way of being in the world, something that goes well beyond history and knowledge production. It is ultimately a stance for living in the Anthropocene that implies recognising thoroughly that we are part of a wider natural world, that we have affected it deeply and perilously, but that it also shapes us, that there is just one world co-constituted by everything it holds. That is why André Vital is fascinated with animations, and why the book closes with Hannah Regis's study of Jason Allen Paisant's poetry. Fiction and art are forms of expression where we more easily recognise the agency of the natural world, or some sort of fusion with it. Scholarly works are not fiction; while they can be highly imaginative, they are bounded by sources and reality.

However, our work as scholars can and should find inspiration in films and poems, and also in Indigenous ontologies, which have a place in this book, for these do not draw a stark line separating the realms of nature and of human culture and society. However, as Marisol de la Cadena brilliantly conveys in *Earth Beings*, we can only have partial understandings with those for whom mountains are, in a non-metaphorical sense, beings who – as such – contributed, for instance, to Peru's agrarian reform.[7]

Most historians and social scientists working on Latin America might find it easier to relate to novels than to shamans transforming into jaguars, just as it is more likely that their imprecise concern about climate change opens a window to affect their mental exclusion of what we tend to consider nature, rather than reading Bruno Latour, no matter how masterful his work is. My eighty-six-year-old father, who is an accomplished sociologist, is very concerned about the planetary environmental crisis, and he got there through his personal experience, plus the media and other readings, not through scholarly considerations. Well-crafted and convincing historical narratives can present an alternative way of thinking with the potential to mould both life and scholarship. That is why it is worthwhile engaging with the stories and histories that this book brings together.

Notes

1. David Gary Shaw, 'The torturer's horse: agency and animals in history', *History and Theory* 52, no. 4 (2013), 146–67.

2. Timothy LeCain, *The matter of history: how things create the past*. Cambridge, Cambridge University Press, 2017.

3. Bradley Skopyk, *Colonial cataclysms: climate, landscape, and memory in Mexico's little ice age*. Tucson, AZ, The University of Arizona Press, 2020; Katherine Mora Pacheco, *Entre sequías, heladas e inundaciones: clima y sociedad en la sabana de Bogotá, 1690–1870*. Bogotá, Universidad Nacional de Colombia, 2019.

4. John McNeill, *Mosquito empires: ecology and war in the greater Caribbean, 1620–1914*. Cambridge, Cambridge University Press, 2012.

5. Claudia Leal, 'Wild and trapped: a history of Colombian zoos and its revelations of animal fortunes and state entanglements, 1930s–1990s', *História, Ciência, Saúde – Maguinhos* 28, suppl. 1 (2021), 81–101.

6. Susanna Hecht, 'The sacred cow in the green hell: livestock and forest conversion in the Brazilian Amazon', *The Ecologist* 19, no. 6 (1989): 229–34; Shawn Van Ausdal & Robert Wilcox, 'Hoofprints: cattle ranching and landscape transformation'. In: John Soluri, Claudia Leal & José Augusto Pádua, *A living past: environmental histories of modern Latin America*. Oxford, UK-New York, Bergham Books, 2018, 184–204.

7. Marisol de la Cadena, *Earth beings: ecologies of practice across Andean worlds*. Durham, NC, Duke University Press, 2015.

References

De la Cadena, Marisol. *Earth beings: ecologies of practice across Andean worlds*. Durham, NC, Duke University Press, 2015.

Hecht, Susanna. 'The sacred cow in the green hell: livestock and forest conversion in the Brazilian Amazon', *The Ecologist* 19, no. 6 (1989), 229–34.

Leal, Claudia. 'Wild and trapped: a history of Colombian zoos and its revelations of animal fortunes and state entanglements, 1930s–1990s', *História, Ciência, Saúde – Maguinhos* 28, suppl. 1 (2021), 81–101.

LeCain, Timothy. *The matter of history: how things create the past*. Cambridge, Cambridge University Press, 2017.

McNeill, John. *Mosquito empires: ecology and war in the greater Caribbean, 1620–1914*. Cambridge, Cambridge University Press, 2012.

Mora Pacheco, Katherine. *Entre sequías, heladas e inundaciones: clima y sociedad en la sabana de Bogotá, 1690–1870*. Bogotá, Universidad Nacional de Colombia, 2019.

Shaw, David Gary. 'The torturer's horse: agency and animals in history', *History and Theory* 52, no. 4 (2013), 146–67.

Skopyk, Bradley. *Colonial cataclysms: climate, landscape, and memory in Mexico's Little Ice Age*. Tucson, AZ, The University of Arizona Press, 2020.

Van Ausdal, Shawn, & Wilcox, Robert. 'Hoofprints: cattle ranching and landscape transformation'. In: John Soluri, Claudia Leal & José Augusto Pádua, *A living past: environmental histories of modern Latin America*. Oxford, UK and New York, Berghahn Books, 2018, 184–204.

Index